UNDERSTANDING
ANTHONY POWELL

Understanding Contemporary British Literature
Matthew J. Bruccoli, Series Editor

Volumes on

Understanding Kingsley Amis • Merritt Moseley
Understanding Martin Amis • James Diedrick
Understanding Julian Barnes • Merritt Moseley
Understanding Alan Bennett • Peter Wolfe
Understanding Anthony Powell • Nicholas Birns
Understanding Anita Brookner • Cheryl Alexander Malcolm
Understanding John Fowles • Thomas C. Foster
Understanding Graham Greene • R. H. Miller
Understanding Kazuo Ishiguro • Brian W. Shaffer
Understanding John le Carré • John L. Cobbs
Understanding Doris Lessing • Jean Pickering
Understanding Ian McEwan • David Malcolm
Understanding Iris Murdoch • Cheryl K. Bove
Understanding Tim Parks • Gillian Fenwick
Understanding Harold Pinter • Ronald Knowles
Understanding Alan Sillitoe • Gillian Mary Hanson
Understanding Graham Swift • David Malcolm
Understanding Arnold Wesker • Robert Wilcher
Understanding Paul West • David W. Madden

UNDERSTANDING
ANTHONY POWELL

Nicholas Birns

University of South Carolina Press

Published in Columbia, South Carolina, by the
University of South Carolina Press

Manufactured in the United States of America

08   07   06   05   04   5   4   3   2   1

Library of Congress Cataloging-in-Publication Data

Birns, Nicholas.
Understanding Anthony Powell / Nicholas Birns.
    p. cm. — (Understanding contemporary British literature)
  Includes bibliographical references and index.
  ISBN 1-57003-549-0 (alk. paper)
 1. Powell, Anthony, 1905– —Criticism and interpretation.
  2. Autobiographical fiction, English—History and criticism.
  3. England—In literature. I. Title. II. Series.
  PR6031.O74Z625 2004
  823'.912—dc22   2004004430

Contents

Editor's Preface

The volumes of *Understanding Contemporary British Literature* have been planned as guides or companions for students as well as good nonacademic readers. The editor and publisher perceive a need for these volumes because much of the influential contemporary literature makes special demands. Uninitiated readers encounter difficulty in approaching works that depart from the traditional forms and techniques of prose and poetry. Literature relies on conventions, but the conventions keep evolving; new writers form their own conventions—which in time may become familiar. Put simply, *UCBL* provides instruction in how to read certain contemporary writers—identifying and explicating their material, themes, use of language, point of view, structures, symbolism, and responses to experience.

The word *understanding* in the titles was deliberately chosen. Many willing readers lack an adequate understanding of how contemporary literature works; that is, what the author is attempting to express and the means by which it is conveyed. Although the criticism and analysis in the series have been aimed at a level of general accessibility, these introductory volumes are meant to be applied in conjunction with the works they cover. They do not provide a substitute for the works and authors they introduce, but rather prepare the reader for more profitable literary experiences.

M. J. B.

Preface

This book is directed to anybody who has enjoyed the works of Anthony Powell and is interested in learning more about them. The viewpoint is from the United States in 2004, though this should not prove restrictive with respect to either place or time. The book builds on the distinguished academic work that has already been done on Powell, in both book and article form, largely though not exclusively in the United States. It also takes a particular interest in Powell's place in the overall course of the novel in the twentieth century as well as the historical background to his achievement. Part of a basic comprehension of Powell's work must be a firm sense of his relationship to his immediate novelistic predecessors as well as to literary history in general. Comparisons to Proust have been made so well elsewhere that they are not necessary here. Of the multitudinous references and allusions to earlier literary texts in Powell's novels, I have focused only on those pivotal to explaining the structure and meaning of his works. I have especially explored cross-references within Powell's work.

The reliance on the idea of "the reader" throughout the volume has in mind the first- or second-time reader of Powell, even though the past generation of reader-response theory has shown us that the process of reading is at once more subjective and more systematic than this implies.

My mother introduced me to this author, as well as to literature in general, and encouraged my early interest in Powell as well as contributing substantially to the field of critical work on him with her 1981 article in the *Literary Review*. My mother has, in general, had to go through a lot on my behalf, and I really appreciate it.

Special thanks are owed to Keith Marshall not only for starting, and steadfastly maintaining, the Anthony Powell web site, the Anthony Powell Internet mailing list (APlist), and eventually the Anthony Powell Society, but also for encouraging me to submit papers for the 2001 and 2003 Anthony Powell conferences in England and for proofreading and commenting on several portions of my manuscript. I thank George Lilley for publishing an enormously helpful bibliography covering Powell's entire career. The Lilley bibliography and Powell's own *Journals* have been the two works that have most occasioned this one.

Barry Blose encouraged this project from the beginning. The two anonymous readers for the University of South Carolina Press provided rigorous and stimulating feedback without which this book would be much the poorer. Irving Malin's extensive knowledge of not only modern literature but also the criticism on that literature provided constant and informative anecdotal reassurance. Hugh Massingberd saved me from embarrassing mistakes and was generous and supportive in a way that mattered. Richard Maxwell helped me attain an academic perspective on the subject. Peter Kislinger generously shared aspects of his own significant work on Powell. Stephen Holden encouraged me to contribute short pieces to the *Anthony Powell Newsletter* that helped jump-start the writing process. Informal meetings provided the opportunity to air out ideas with, in New York, Leatrice Fountain, William Warren, John Gould, Edwin Bock, Keeley C. Schell, and Jonathan Kooperstein, in Britain, Keith Marshall, Noreen Marshall, Stephen Holden, Simon Culley, Maggie Noach, Tony Robinson, Peter Haley Dunne, David Bryant, and Michael Skaife d'Ingerthorpe, and, in Australia, Andrew Clarke, whose drive through the Hunter

Valley to Newcastle I will never forget. The Anthony Powell Internet mailing list has been a wonderfully diverse forum, a constant source of stimulating discussion and of always expert advice; John Gilks, John Horton, and Michael Skaife d'Ingerthorpe are to be particularly thanked.

Michael C. Meredith of the Eton College Library very helpfully shared some details of Powell's manuscripts on deposit there. With similar congeniality, Nicholas Scheetz provided me with access to the Powell-Monagan correspondence and the other riches in the Special Collections Room at the Georgetown University Library. A memorable lunch with John Monagan at the Cosmos Club gave a needed injection of energy into the entire project. The Rev. Canon J. Robert Wright, Hugh Nissenson, and Annette Sloane provided helpful general counsel throughout. The valued assistance of Harold Bloom, Perry Meisel, Richard S. Kim, Peter Wolfe, the late Geoffrey Summerfield, and Riecelle Dubitsky Schecter on previous projects continued to bear fruit in this book.

I also wish to thank friends and family who have not been directly involved with this project but whose persistent support I deeply appreciate.

Chronology

Begins to write regularly for the *Spectator* and the *Daily Telegraph*.

1939 Commissioned as second lieutenant into the Welch Regiment (in which his father had also served) at start of Second World War. Later serves in the Intelligence Corps as a liaison officer to various London-based governments in exile and rises to the rank of major.

1940 First son, Tristram, born.

1945 Leaves the army in December.

1946 Second son, John, born.

1947 Awarded Czechoslovakian Order of the White Lion and the Belgian Order of Leopold II. Becomes fiction editor of the *Times Literary Supplement*.

1948 Awarded Luxembourg Croix de Guerre and Order of the Oaken Crown. *John Aubrey and His Friends* published by Eyre and Spottiswoode.

1951 Publishes *A Question of Upbringing*, first novel in *A Dance to the Music of Time* sequence.

1952 Moves to the Chantry, near Frome in Somerset.

1953 Appointed literary editor of *Punch*.

1954 Mother, Maud Powell, dies.

1956 Awarded Commander of the British Empire (CBE) by Queen Elizabeth II.

1958 *At Lady Molly's*, fourth volume of *A Dance to the Music of Time* (published 1957), awarded the James Tait Black Memorial Prize.

1959 Resumes contributing biweekly reviews to the *Daily Telegraph* after leaving *Punch* at end of 1958.

Father, Philip Lionel Powell, dies.

1961   *Venusberg* published by Penguin, the first of
        Powell's novels to be published by that firm.
        Visits United States.

1964   Travels to Japan, South Vietnam, the Philippines,
        and Thailand, and revisits United States.

1968   Travels to India. Son Tristram marries Virginia
        Lucas, a painter.

1971   Travels to Guatemala and Mexico; Awarded
        honorary D.Litt. by University of Sussex.

1973   Declines offer of a knighthood by the govern-
        ment of Edward Heath.

1974   *Temporary Kings,* eleventh novel in *A Dance to
        the Music of Time* (published 1973), awarded the
        W. H. Smith Prize.
        Made an honorary fellow of Balliol College,
        Oxford.

1975   *Hearing Secret Harmonies,* final book of *A
        Dance to the Music of Time,* published by Heine-
        mann; appears in the United States from Little,
        Brown in 1976.

1976   First volume of memoirs, *Infants of the Spring,*
        published; subsequent volumes appear in 1978,
        1980, and 1982.
        Awarded honorary D.Litt. by University of
        Leicester and by University of Kent.

1977   Elected an honorary fellow of American Acad-
        emy of Arts and Letters.

1979 to *Dance* dramatized on BBC Radio 4, adapted by
  1982   Frederick Bradnum. The adaptation was rebroad-
        cast on BBC Radio 7 in late spring 2003.

1980   Awarded honorary D.Litt. by University of
        Oxford.

1981   Named honorary fellow of Modern Language
        Association of America.

1982   Awarded honorary D.Litt. by University of
        Bristol.

1983   *O, How the Wheel Becomes It!* published by
        Heinemann; appears in United States from
        Holt in 1984.

1984   Receives the Bennett Award, conferred by the
        Hudson Review, and the T. S. Eliot Prize for
        Creative Literature, conferred by the Ingersoll
        Foundation.

1986   *The Fisher King* published in U.K. by Heinemann
        and the United States by Norton.

1988   Named Companion of Honour by Queen
        Elizabeth II in New Year Honors List.

1990   Resigns as regular reviewer for the *Daily
        Telegraph.*
        Miscellaneous Verdicts, collected criticism,
        published by Heinemann; appears in United
        States from Chicago University Press in 1992.

1992   *Under Review* published by Heinemann; appears
        in the United States in 1994.
        Awarded honorary D.Litt. by University of
        Wales.

1995   *Journals, 1982–1986,* first volume of diaries,
        published by Heinemann; subsequent volumes
        published in 1996 and 1997.
        Suffers a fall, damaging health.

1997   Elected vice president of the Society of
        Genealogists.

CHAPTER 1

Understanding Anthony Powell

The life of Anthony Powell figures in his writing. It might be said that he goes over the same autobiographical experience three times: in the novel sequence *Dance to the Music of Time,* at least in its premises if not in its precise content; in the four volumes of his memoirs, *To Keep the Ball Rolling;* and in the three volumes of his *Journals,* which though ostensibly documenting only the years 1982 to 1992, reflect widely over the previous years.

Anthony Dymoke Powell (pronounced AN-to-ny DIMM-ok PO-ell) was born on 21 December 1905. His father was Philip Lionel Powell, a regular army infantry officer who rose to the rank of Colonel, was a company commander in the First World War, and received the honors of Commander of the British Empire and Distinguished Service Officer, and his mother was Maud Wells-Dymoke. Anthony Powell was extraordinarily interested in genealogy, and not just in his own. The reason was not snobbery, as many people presume, but lies in the way a genealogical concern embodies, as Hugh Massingberd has put it, "an expression of interest in other people" and "a punctilious attention to detail," both of which were in the marrow of Powell's novelistic practice.[1] Genealogy, in Powell's writing, provides a context for human life, one far more flexible than other constructs imported from outside immediate circumstances. The Powell family originated in Radnorshire some miles west of the traditional Anglo-Welsh border. They were distantly descended from the Lord Rhys, who effectively controlled all Wales in the late twelfth century; more immediate forebears were prominent local Radnorshire landowners, successful tanners, and starting in the eighteenth century, soldiers and sailors.

The Wells-Dymokes originated in Lincolnshire. The Wellses and the Dymokes were members of the same extended family who frequently intermarried. In the fifteenth century, the Dymokes, headquartered at Scrivelsby in Lincolnshire, became hereditary King's Champions, succeeding the Marmion family, fictively portrayed in Sir Walter Scott's poem of that name. Powell's immediate ancestors were not the main line of the Dymokes. At one point they seemed poised to inherit the Championship. But the honor devolved upon another cousin, and a counterclaim put in by Powell's great-grandfather did not succeed. Against the presumption that Powell was born into the upper reaches of society, one may quote Robert Selig: "On Anthony Powell's maternal side, the Wells-Dymokes of Lincolnshire had no exalted kings or princes in their history, but instead had parsons and squires. Although, generally speaking, young Powell might qualify by birth as one of the privileged classes, he began life pretty much on the fringes."[2] Selig may underrate the class level of the Wells-Dymoke family, which even if the claim to the Championship was never won was still reasonably well pedigreed and affluent, but he is right in that Powell's path through life was by no means assured merely by the station of his parents. The parents' decision to send the young Anthony to Eton, the well-known boarding school, was based less on their wealth and on Eton's traditional place in the schooling of men in their family, which was slight apart from Powell's depressive grand-uncle, D. R. Jefferson, than on their wish that their son have the best available academic education.

When Powell was born, he was "expected to survive at most two days" (*Infants,* 1), little prefiguring a life of ninety-four years. After spending his earliest years in London, he moved around as his father was posted to various stations. One of the family's longer residencies produced the model for Stonehurst in *Kindly Ones* and evidently had similar ghosts. Powell went to preparatory school in Kent during the First World War. In the midst of this generally ghastly experience, he met the first of his friends to become part of the literary world, Henry Yorke, who wrote his novels as Henry Green (1905–74), and came to know another Henry, Lord Henry Thynne, Viscount Weymouth, later the sixth Marquess of Bath.

At Eton, Powell met future belletrists such as Cyril Connolly and Harold Acton. Powell joined the Eton Society of Arts, filled with the budding aesthetes of that generation, and according to Michael Meredith, "was fascinated by them, listened to their opinions and prejudices, and enjoyed their company before retiring to Walpole House and his less assertive companions there."[3] During breaks from school spent with his parents at home in St. John's Wood, he met the bookstore proprietor, 1890s relic, and noted eccentric Christopher Millard.

Powell always spoke positively, although this side of sentimentality, about his time at Eton. His impressions of the years between 1923 and 1926 at Balliol College, Oxford, seem more mixed. Though he liked his tutor, Kenneth Bell, he did not particularly distinguish himself academically, taking only a Third in history, "without the satisfying conviction that I had never done a stroke of work" (*Infants,* 160). But this is not to say that his exposure to the academic study of history left his writing untouched. As Lynette Felber points out, Powell's study of history may have contributed to the extraordinary way his work illuminates "the potential of narrative, when attended by insight and aesthetic judgment, to render history with as much accuracy as is humanly possible."[4] This engagement with the nuts and bolts of history not only deepened Powell's sense of former times and his ability to spark anecdotal life out of archival remnants but also gave him insight into narrative structure and the power of consequent perceptions to alter our sense of what has happened in the past. He became a member of the salon held by the young academic C. M. Bowra, only to offend Bowra by pointing out limitations in the milieu of Oxford of which Bowra was utterly uncognizant. Powell's too-candid admission that he did not like Oxford alienated Bowra for a while, although the two eventually renewed their friendship. The atmosphere of the Hypocrites Club attracted a gallery of eccentrics among Powell's own generation. Other people he encountered at Oxford were Robert Byron, Peter Quennell, Graham Greene, and, of an older age group, Lady Ottoline Morrell.

Powell traveled to several European capitals, combining undergraduate adventure and visits to his father, who was posted abroad as a military attaché. He went to Paris, Berlin, and then to several cities just recently become capitals of independent states: Belgrade, Budapest, Tallinn (then called Reval in the West), and Helsinki (just emerged from being called by its Swedish name, Helsingfors). These travels bore early fruit in *Venusberg*. As suggested by a family friend, Thomas Balston, Powell took a job at a London publishing house, Duckworth, a name well known to literary historians of twentieth-century Britain because of the Duckworths' family connection to Virginia Woolf and the accusations of abuse Woolf raised against her Duckworth half-brothers. Among the writers Powell brought to Duckworth was Evelyn Waugh; he also worked with

talents as diverse as those of Sacheverell Sitwell and Cecil
Beaton. Among Powell's London friends were the bohemian
painter Adrian Daintrey and the modernist composer Constant
Lambert (popularly conceded to be the models for the painter
Barnby and the composer Moreland in *Dance*), and on a far
more restricted level, the novelist Graham Greene. One may
assume that Duckworth, headed by three brothers of that name,
was the model for Judkins and Judkins in Powell's novel *What's
Become of Waring*. ("Which Judkins do you prefer?" "Judkins,
emphatically"; *Waring*, 9.) *Waring* was, coincidentally or not,
the only one of Powell's five prewar novels not published by
Duckworth. Powell's early novels are short and comic, each con-
centrating on a certain physical and social setting. They contain
much terse, gnomic, and taut dialogue and only rarely have the
kind of discursive, ambling quality characteristic of Powell's later,
more analytic work. But the prewar novels' continuity with others produced by people of the same generation is less striking
then their discontinuity with most previous British fiction.

The prewar novels, at first glance, look flimsy and trivial
when compared with the great modernist master works produced just a few years earlier: James Joyce's *Ulysses* (1922), Virginia Woolf's *Mrs. Dalloway* (1925) and *To the Lighthouse*
(1927), E. M. Forster's *Passage to India* (1924), and D. H.
Lawrence's *Women in Love* (1920). What we might call, for
shorthand's sake, the Powell-Waugh generation, was the first
such generation born in the twentieth century. It was also the
first to have no choice but to inherit a twentieth-century aesthetic. The slow odyssey from Victorian complacency and optimism was not for them a perilous quest but a point given. Not
for the generation born in the twentieth century was the deliberate "case" against Victorian serenity made by Virginia Woolf

in *To the Lighthouse,* in which the Victorian synthesis personified by Mr. Ramsay yields, in time and resonance, to the
momentary epiphanies of the artist Lily Briscoe. Its maturity
expedited by the trauma of the First World War, and in any
event totally severed from anything Victorian, Powell's generation came to adulthood after that indefinable moment, whether
or not in December 1910, when "human nature changed." As
Robert Morris comments, "Most of Powell's early novels [are]
indebted to the films for much of [their] terminology, technique,
and design."[5] Certainly this engagement with the quintessentially twentieth-century narrative form could not be said of
Virginia Woolf or E. M. Forster. In part this is because Powell
wrote for the movies in both England and Hollywood, but a
good ingredient of this ease with filmic technique is simply generational. People Powell's age grew up with the cinema as much
as any later generation.

Powell's novels attracted good reviews, but he did not blaze
like a supernova in the literary firmament, especially compared
with other writers of his generation, such as Greene and Waugh.
Some critics, though, perceptively responded to his genius;
among these was G. U. Ellis, whose treatment of Powell in *Twilight on Parnassus* is appreciative and discerning.[6] Powell also
produced a poem in this period, *Caledonia,* an eighteenth-
century-style satire on Scottish cultural self-assertion (its animus
proceeding as much from Powell's Welshness as his Englishness,
though in a letter to Julian Symons of 12 March 1982, Powell
states that he does not "really bear any animus against the Cale-
donians"). Although hardly poetic in any traditional sense of
the word, *Caledonia* does show that Powell could write in fixed,
metric verse forms, something by no means every novelist can
do. This metric sensibility mirrors a regular, rhythmic, almost

reassuring pattern in his far more ornate and idiosyncratic prose. Studded with obscure references to Scotsmen, Englishmen, and even Africans, *Caledonia,* in its original, privately printed form, is now worth several thousand dollars on rare book markets.

Caledonia was published to celebrate the September 1934 engagement of Powell to Lady Violet Pakenham, the third daughter of Brigadier General the 5th Earl of Longford, who had been killed in the Gallipoli campaign of 1915. Powell and Lady Violet were married in December 1934. The Powells had two sons, Tristram, born in 1940, and John, born in 1946. In the early years of their marriage, they lived in London and, briefly, in Hollywood, where Powell sought work as a scriptwriter (he had previously worked for Warner Brothers in London as a writer of "quota quickies" to provide local content to complement the imported Hollywood product). In the course of his California sojourn, he encountered F. Scott Fitzgerald, a crucial influence on his major work.

Lady Violet Powell (1912–2002) was a member of a large family, many of whom produced literary and/or biographical works, such as her sister-in-law Elizabeth Longford and her nieces Antonia Fraser and Rachel Billington, or were notable public figures, such as her older brother, the 7th Earl of Longford (1905–2001), the noted antipornography and prisoners' rights advocate. Violet Powell was in her own right a memoirist and biographer of distinction with a signature, often sardonic style. Her book on E. M. Delafield, *The Life of a Provincial Lady* (1988), is one of the best literary biographies of a British writer in the twentieth century. She is also judged by most who knew the Powells personally to have contributed significantly to the richness, depth, and polish of Powell's work. American poet and novelist Jay Parini, in an appreciative obituary of Powell in the *Sewanee Review*, describes Lady Violet as "the daughter of an English Lord." Although the Pakenham family is of English descent and holds English peerages, the Longford peerage itself is Irish, and for centuries the family seat was in Ireland (not in County Longford, but in County Westmeath). Similarly, Parini describes the Chantry, the house near Frome in Somerset where the Powells moved in 1952, as "a house that had not changed for many centuries," when in fact the Chantry, as Powell makes clear in his memoirs, was a Regency-era house, built in 1826.[7] Elements of "the invention of tradition" always occur when one country looks at another's social forms and heritage. That these transatlantic misunderstandings flow both ways can be seen in the entry on the American novelist James Fenimore Cooper in the *Cambridge Guide to English Literature*, edited by the late Ian Ousby. Here it is said that Cooper married "Susan Delancy, who was descended from the early governors of New York colony." The entry not only spells the lady's name incorrectly but also erroneously implies that the DeLanceys were at one point hereditary governors of New York colony.[8] It is admittedly nitpicking to point out these errors, but from such misunderstandings a misleading picture of the author can proceed. This is especially so in the case of Powell, whose work has long been mischaracterized as being of interest only to aristocrats.

Powell, who had been in Officers' Training Corps at Oxford and served in the 1920s in a South London Territorial (analogous to the U.S. National Guard) battery as a gunner, tried to join the army as soon as war broke out in 1939. He soon obtained a commission in the Welch Regiment, in which his father had served during the First World War. After service with the regiment, primarily in Northern Ireland, Powell was transferred to the military Intelligence Corps. He worked here for the balance of the war effort.

By war's end, Powell had reached the rank of major. He worked primarily as a liaison with the governments-in-exile of Belgium, Czechoslovakia, and Luxembourg, and was decorated with awards from all three countries. He even wrote articles after the war for a Luxembourgeois periodical, although he seems never to have visited Luxembourg. His sometime-superior, Denis Capel-Dunn, is occasionally described as the inspiration for Powell's villain and greatest comic character, Widmerpool. Capel-Dunn was killed in an airplane crash on his way to the opening United Nations meeting in San Francisco. Far more than this happenstance, the war had a substantial effect on Powell's writing, deepening and ramifying it. This was due in part to the transformative pressure of the events themselves, about whose effects on society Powell was prescient even before war began. The world about which Powell's first five novels was written was no longer there, and Powell, unlike some of his contemporaries, realized this and knew that his life's work had to record not the world that had vanished but the transformation occurring in its wake. But Powell's specific wartime experiences also changed his writing. His service in the Welch Regiment brought him into contact with a group of officers and enlisted men, largely English-speaking but Welsh in their middle- to working-class background and nonconformist Protestant religion. This was a group far from the drawing rooms and pubs of London. His subsequent work in military intelligence, dealing with Britain's many and diverse allies during the great conflict, exposed him to different facets of foreign cultures. So did the political-military course he took during wartime at Cambridge, which centered on Russian and Eastern European history. And even though Powell found he was not capable of writing fiction during the war, his other literary activities crucially affected his future career as a novelist. In researching a biography of the seventeenth-century antiquarian, biographer, scholar, and gossip John Aubrey, for example, Powell learned to emulate some of Aubrey's surface techniques.

The Aubrey book prepared the way for *Dance* in sundry ways. The historical research Powell did in order to insightfully portray a time three centuries different redounded in the unusually deep portrait of his own time in his postwar fiction. In other words, it helped him look at his own age from outside, as a historian would. Nomenclature uncovered during the course of the Aubrey research proved crucial. ("Widmerpool" was the name of a Roundhead Captain of Horse, from the *Memoirs* of Lady Lucy Hutchinson, a work now well respected in feminist and new historicist circles, and of which Powell took note long before its recent admirers.)[9] Indeed, the Aubrey book, along with Powell's own genealogical researches, can be credited with the matchless onomastic skill that characterizes his use of personal names. It appears that Powell derived his character names from two historical clusters: the Hundred Years' War era in the fourteenth and fifteenth centuries and the seventeenth century. These, plus a few place names (e.g., Leintwardine, Warminster) and names inspired by their appearance in the works of other writers (e.g., Stringham may well owe something to Susan Stringham in Henry James's *Wings of the Dove* and Farebrother to Camden Farebrother in George Eliot's *Middlemarch*), constitute Powell's onomasticon, of which it may be said, as Edith Wharton said of her own, that "sometimes these names seem to be affected, sometimes almost ridiculous; but I am obliged to own they are never fundamentally unsuitable."[10] The Aubrey researches thus cannot come near to bearing the honor of producing all of Powell's character names, but they yielded a good many, and the method by which these researches were conducted is exemplary of Powell's ability to gain texture from his knowledge of history, geography, and English and world literature.

Aubrey was the model of a writer whose work brought him into political spheres. Obviously Royalist in sympathy, he nevertheless studiously avoided taking sides explicitly in England's most divisive historical period, the time of the struggle between King and Parliament, Cavalier and Roundhead. Powell too had clear political convictions in his own day, which saw democracy's struggle after successive struggle with fascism and communism. But he emulated Aubrey's tact and lack of ideological carapace. *John Aubrey and His Friends* (1948) is a surprisingly academic book, far more so than most nonfiction books by famous novelists. It shows that Powell could have become, if he had wished, a successful academic. In fact, it is more scholarly than many academic books published in its day, before the emigration of Continental intellectuals and the buildup of the American university system along German lines, which ratcheted up the degree of rigor with which Anglophone academic scholarship was pursued and evicted sherry-drinking amateurs from their Edenic bower. Powell's genealogical interests no doubt enabled him to tolerate a certain necessary dryness of approach that most people who can write creatively would find hard to take. But some of the secrets of the brilliance of *Dance* are to be found here. When in the late 1940s Powell was free to pursue his magnum opus, the intellectual foundation had already been laid.

Powell published a volume of *A Dance to the Music of Time* every two or three years concluding in 1975. At first the sequence was called *The Music of Time;* the full title began to appear on book covers in the early 1960s. The title is taken from a painting by seventeenth-century French painter Nicolas Poussin, which is most commonly supposed an allegorical painting of the seasons. In the sequence's opening pages, the narrator meditates on this painting and how it represents the weird alternation of pattern and contingency in which it seems his life has been cast. The sequence includes over four hundred characters and covers a time frame stretching from 1914 (in flashback; chronologically, the action begins in 1921) to 1971. *Dance* is a mammoth novel, and arguments have even been made for it being the world's longest, even though realistic estimates dictate otherwise. The sequence creates a substantially peopled world, one in which readers steep themselves for its own sake. The reader gets a full view of the changes that, for good or ill, defined the twentieth century in England and the West in general.

The sequence features a narrator, Nicholas Jenkins, whose career is similar to Powell's but who is not simply an authorial surrogate. Jenkins is an onlooker and a recorder. He is not a traditional protagonist. The most visible events in the sequence are those that happen not to Jenkins but to other people. The initial focus is on Jenkins's relationship with three contemporaries at a school much like Eton. Charles Stringham is charming but troubled by family problems, Peter Templer is not a man of high learning but is filled with a no-nonsense, appealing vitality, and Kenneth Widmerpool is an ambitious boy of dubious social origins. Widmerpool initially inspires derision with his ungainly appearance, nerdy eyeglasses, and inappropriate overcoat. Jenkins soon finds that his life is mysteriously intertwined with Widmerpool's. For a time they are interested in the same women. In the Second World War, Jenkins is stunned to find that Widmerpool is his immediate superior in the army. In the 1920s, Widmerpool exudes an unblinking trust in corporate success; in the 1930s, briefly, he becomes a potential courtier of King Edward VIII's intended consort, Wallis Simpson; in the 1940s, he becomes a Stalinist fellow traveler; and in the late 1960s, he becomes a camp follower of hippie culture and joins an authoritarian mystical cult. Widmerpool is so complacent in his oily narcissism, so opportunistic in manifesting what is merely a symptomatic relationship to the age in which he lives, that he has become a memorable character. But *Dance* is not simply "the Widmerpool show." The interplay of the raffish bohemians and high-society notables is figured in the depiction of the painter Ralph Barnby and the composer Hugh Moreland, both of whom, through their romantic relationships and their career ambitions, end up being connected with the unforgettable tycoon Sir Magnus Donners.

The onset of war in 1939 causes a fundamental change in the world of the sequence. In fact, without the war there would be no *Dance*. Powell first got the idea for the sequence in 1938, when he sensed not only the inevitability of war but also how it would irrecoverably change British society, a change recorded in the sequence, though not in the simple "decline of the aristocracy" scenario, as so many critics have alleged. This change is conveyed by the deaths of Stringham, who has struggled with alcoholism only to die as a member of the Mobile Laundry in captured Singapore, and Templer, who dies aiding the resistance in occupied Yugoslavia. The war years see the emergence of Pamela Flitton, Stringham's niece and Templer's sometime romantic interest, who later marries Widmerpool as the latter achieves his social ambition and becomes a member of Parliament and, later, life peer and chancellor of a "plate-glass" university, that is, one founded in the 1960s and embracing innovative educational policies. Jenkins lives to see Widmerpool's eventual downfall. His survival is a kind of triumph, yet the sequence closes on a melancholy, contemplative note.

The conclusion of many readers that *Dance* is simply about putting unseemly interlopers in their place is off by a wide margin. The sequence is filled with allusions to history, politics, art, music, and architecture. A reader could get a university-level education simply by looking up all the references Powell makes. Jenkins is interested in everything; his ability to notice, register, and analyze is almost uncanny. Although written in a ruminative, Latinate, polished but often eccentric style, *Dance* is curiously unpretentious, and this lack of pomposity was most likely a product of the substantial American influences on Powell's writing. Powell was often accused of only writing about the upper classes. This is untrue; in fact, many of the characters in *Dance,* especially in the war volumes, are not upper class. In addition, one of the themes of the sequence is class mobility, both upward and downward.

The following excerpt, which concerns St. John Clarke, an older, middlebrow novelist generally conceded to be based on John Galsworthy, author of *The Forsyte Saga* (Galsworthy wrote for a time under the pseudonym "John Sinjohn"), gives the flavor of the prose style in *Dance:*

> No other journal took sufficient interest in the later stages of St. John Clarke's career to keep up to date about these conflicting aspects of his final decade. They spoke only of his deep love for the Peter Pan statue in Kensington Gardens and his contributions to Queen Mary's Gift Book. Appraisal of his work unhesitatingly placed *Fields of Amaranth* as the

peak of his achievement, with *E'en the Longest River* or *The Heart Is Highland*—opinion varied—as a poor second. *The Times Literary Supplement* found "the romances of Renaissance Italy and the French Revolution smacked of Wardour Street, the scenes from fashionable life in the other novels tempered with artificiality, the delineations of poverty less realistic than Gissing's."

I was surprised by an odd feeling of regret that St. John Clarke had gone. Even if an indifferent writer, his removal from the literary scene was like the final crumbling of a well-known landmark; unpleasing perhaps, at the same time possessed of a deserved renown for having withstood demolition for so long. (*Casanova*, 192)

The acidic if reserved detail, as Clarke is portrayed as a pompous, second-rate writer, suddenly turns to a classical poise as Jenkins realizes that Clarke was, no less, a human being. The literariness, complexity of sentence structure, directness of address, and compassionate irony of *Dance* are all abundantly in evidence.

Powell is an unusual novelist in that, though not an overt stylistic innovator, he is clearly not content to reside in the formulaic contrivances of the genre. As he says in his memoirs, "I have never felt particularly at ease in the eighty-thousand-word framework myself" (*Faces*, 212). This unwillingness to stay within the formal bounds of the conventional-length novel is quite a radical move on his part (witness the standard length of novels that tend to win the Pulitzer or Booker Prizes). Powell's suspicion of the usual lineaments of the novel form also leads to innovation in plot. The sheer length, the historical embeddedness, and the allusive stretch of *Dance* undoes the sort of contrived plotting that has beset the novel more and more as it ages past its peak of vitality in the nineteenth century. The recurring characters, though a feature found in nineteenth-century French novel cycles such as *La Comédie Humaine* of Honoré de Balzac, manages to "break and dispose of an old convention, the convention that insists on a novel beginning at one fixed point and ending at another."[11] Following in the wake of innovators such as Virginia Woolf and James Joyce, Powell expands the novel beyond the expected plots and machinations that a reader used to the form can easily anticipate. In the midst of a century of experimentation, *Dance* questions the inherited form of the novel as much as any avowedly modernist or post-modernist work.

Much of *Dance* seems quintessentially English (or, given Powell's Welshness and his and his protagonist's deliberate serv-ice with the Welch Regiment in the Second World War, British). Its plot is concerned with specifically English aspects of univer-sity, army, and aristocratic life. But in fact the kind of beefy, hearty Englishness to be found in novelists one or two genera-tions older than Powell is not in his work. Nor does he indulge in the sort of furnished panoply endemic to the BBC programs aired on the Public Broadcasting System's *Masterpiece Theatre* (such as the aforementioned *Forsyte Saga*) or the literary film adaptations of Ismail Merchant and James Ivory. This is no doubt why the 1997 television version of *Dance,* for all its cov-erage of what Americans would see as quintessentially British idiosyncrasies and class and status gradations, was not televised by *Masterpiece Theatre.* Powell, British, or Anglo-Welsh, to the core, was not immured in self-conscious Britishness. As we shall see, the most pivotal influence on his narrative approach in *Dance* is not Anthony Trollope or E. M. Forster but F. Scott Fitzgerald.

Powell learned a lot from Fitzgerald's combination of high rhetoric and casual ease, as well as his ability to convey a lot of information within a brief compass. Powell's relatively large American audience responded not only to his unmistakably English social milieu (and place and character names) but also to a certain Americanness in his style and presentation, an up-to-date quality, a comfort with a twentieth-century world in which America had become more prominent. Waugh and Greene, from political positions to the right and left of Powell respectively, lacked this kind of American sensibility in their work. Powell was also extremely receptive to Continental influences. Despite his opposition to closer British integration into the European Union (see *Journals,* 4 June 1992), he was not a "Little Englander." Far from being parochial or isolationist, throughout his career he traveled widely in Europe and was familiar with European history and culture, not only in Western Europe but also in Eastern Europe, in an era when that region was thought to be under perpetual Soviet domination not therefore not of particular interest. French writers such as Stendhal and Marcel Proust, or Russian writers such as Fyodor Dostoevsky and Mikhail Lermontov, seemed to have mattered far more to Powell than the standard writers on the English syllabus (always excepting Shakespeare, with whom he achieved not only a general but also a personal literary relationship, a rare achievement for a modern writer). Although Powell's work refers to a much broader range of cultural precedents than the works of most British writers, in a way this liberates the non-British reader, as he or she does not have to have taken "Brit. Lit. 101" to appreciate his work. Long before the self-conscious wave of cosmopolitanism that reanimated British literature in the 1980s and after in the work of Julian Barnes, Ian McEwan, and Kazuo Ishiguro, Powell's work was never parochially

British. It was always unquestionably part of world literature. Readers, British or not, generally become addicted to the books or are totally indifferent to them. This remains true today, in that, if people have heard of Powell, they tend to either love or hate his work. There is not the dutiful normative respect coupled with limited concrete enthusiasm garnered by so many canonical modern writers.

Powell's ability to regularly produce volumes of his *Dance* sequence was helped immeasurably by a congenial publisher. Freed from the clutches of Eyre and Spottiswode after a dispute involving Graham Greene (at that time a literary decision maker for the publisher) about the publication of *John Aubrey and His Friends,* Powell began his long and productive association with Heinemann. Working with editor Roland Gant, Powell produced volumes of *Dance* at a regular pace. Meanwhile, he energetically participated in the life and work of the London literary world. As fiction reviews editor of the *Times Literary Supplement,* he worked with editor Alan Pryce-Jones to reconstruct a sense of European literature after the cataclysm of the war by reviewing translations of distinguished work from the Continent. As literary editor of *Punch* from 1953 to 1959, Powell made the magazine less constrained by its own traditions of "humor" and more of a literary forum. At *Punch,* he worked under Malcolm Muggeridge, the television personality and (eventual) Catholic convert with whom Powell had a dramatic falling-out after Muggeridge wrote a strangely hostile review of the seventh volume of *Dance, The Valley of Bones* (1964).[12]

From 1959, Powell became a regular reviewer for the *Daily Telegraph.* Writing reviews that appeared every other Thursday, he concentrated mainly on biography and literary criticism. But he also covered an astonishing range of material, giving proportionate space to American, English, and European literature. Powell became friends with a younger generation of writers, including such eventual luminaries as Kingsley Amis and V. S. Naipaul. During the 1950s and 1960s, the Powells traveled widely, driving around England and taking extensive foreign trips to destinations as exotic as Iran, Japan, and Guatemala, as well as to the culturally more familiar climes of the United States and Western Europe. In 1956, he received the honor of Commander of the British Empire (CBE) from Queen Elizabeth II, the award having been suggested by the government of Prime Minister Anthony Eden. In 1973, Powell declined the offer of a knighthood; to the end of his days he remained Mr. Powell.

Despite some caviling from politically hostile reviewers miffed by Powell's allegiance to the Conservative Party and, no doubt, his vigilant and principled opposition to Soviet totalitarianism, *Dance* was recognized as a major work from the start. Its fourth volume, *At Lady Molly's,* won the James Tait Black Prize in 1958, and the eleventh volume, *Temporary Kings,* won the W. H. Smith Prize in 1974. *Dance* was never a bestseller, but it quickly developed an intense and widespread following. Though a portion of this fan base was anchored in the British upper and upper middle classes, sales of the sequence were virtually the same in the United States as in England (George Lilley's bibliography of Powell gives average sales figures of about six thousand per book). *Dance's* American followers were from all walks of life. (For example, when my mother wrote Anthony Powell, the postal clerk who handled the letter looked at it quizzically and asked, "Is this *the* Anthony Powell?")

Powell made a number of close American friends, among them the novelist Alison Lurie (who refers obliquely to Powell's genealogical interests in her novel *Foreign Affairs*), onetime U.S.

ambassador to Great Britain David Bruce and his wife Evangeline, and the academic and F. Scott Fitzgerald scholar Arthur Mizener. A crucial American friend was John S. Monagan, U.S. congressman (D-Connecticut) from 1959 to 1973, with whom he maintained a decades-long correspondence.

Dance also attracted proportionately sized followings in Canada and Australia. The fact that one of Powell's most prominent current Australian admirers is New South Wales premier Bob Carr alerts us to the fact that Powell has as strong a following among politicians (especially, against what might be expected, among politicians of the center-Left such as Carr and, in Britain, Roy Jenkins and Denis Healey), historians, sociologists, journalists, and other professionals as he does among academics.[13] In fact, the last formal paper presented on Powell at a Modern Language Association convention was by Daniel Traister of the University of Pennsylvania in 1977, even though the MLA made Powell an honorary fellow in 1981. Among practicing writers, Powell is much more popular. This is particularly true among detective story or thriller writers: Donald Westlake, Alan Furst, Robert Harris, Ian Rankin, and "Bill James" (pseudonym for James Tucker, who is also the author of a critical study of Powell) are all admirers. This may be because Powell's plots, though not mysteries, emphasize reversals and revelations and have casts of characters who turn out to reveal different aspects of themselves than at first noticed—as do suspects in a mystery story.

Dance's reception in Continental Europe (the sequence has been at least partially translated into all major European languages, even Catalan) seems slightly different in that it is more centered among literary people, particularly highbrow novelists. This surprising tandem of audiences in different parts of the world clearly testifies against any sense of *Dance* being restricted to an insular set of snobbish devotees.

In the late 1960s, Powell wrote two plays, *The Rest I'll Whistle,* set in the Welsh border country, and *The Garden God,* set on a Greek archaeological expedition. In addition, he adapted *Afternoon Men* into a play. As with most writers skilled in narrative fiction, these excursions into drama were not Powell's best work, despite the dramatic talents he so often showcased in his fiction. More happily, from 1976 to 1982, he published four volumes of memoirs. Though inevitably covering some of the same territory as his fiction, the memoirs are less patterned, more anecdotal, and less comic in tone. They are still the least appreciated aspect of Powell's work but gain immeasurably when read in conjunction with either *Dance* or the author's later *Journals.* Writing memoirs usually connotes the idea of serene retirement, but for Powell this was not the case. He continued as regular reviewer for the *Telegraph* and, going frequently to London, maintained an active role on the cultural scene. The election of Margaret Thatcher as prime minister in 1979 marked a new era in British political history. Powell, a traditional Tory when such a posture was very unfashionable among the intellectual classes, supported the Thatcher government and met Thatcher herself several times at both official and unofficial gatherings. Powell also served on the boards of various organizations, including the National Portrait Gallery, and wrote introductions to a number of reissued literary works. Contributing still more to his cultural influence was the dramatization of *Dance* from 1979 to 1982 on BBC Radio 4 in a scrupulously faithful adaptation by Frederick Bradnum.

Awards began to pile up for Powell during this era. In 1984, he received two awards from the United States, one from the

prestigious *Hudson Review* and another, the T. S. Eliot Prize for
Creative Literature, from the politically conservative Ingersoll
Foundation. Powell was unable to make the trip to the cere-
mony in Chicago to receive the latter award, but the *Hudson
Review* sponsored a lavish lunch in London that Powell at-
tended.

When Powell produced a novella, *O, How the Wheel Becomes It!* (1983), many reviewers were surprised a writer Powell's age would produce another work of fiction, especially after
writing such a long masterpiece and an apparently autumnal
set of memoirs. But *Wheel,* a wry account of jealousy and publicity in the literary world, though indifferently comprehended,
received good reviews, especially in America. The reception of
the full-length *The Fisher King* (1986) was universally positive.
Fisher is a novel about a domineering photographer on a cruise
around Britain and, allegorically, about the way everyone's life
has the potential to be made into myth. Both these books are
now somewhat neglected. They show that Powell was still capable of wryly observing the contemporary scene, even into the
1980s. They also emphasize some of his continuing preoccupations, such as memory and voyeurism. His late work reveals him
as something of a novelistic philosopher of the technique of the
observer.

In his later years, Powell received a number of honorary
degrees from British universities, the most pertinent being from
the University of Wales in 1992, underscoring Powell's connections to Wales in spite of not being a Welsh speaker or a propo-
nent of politicized Welsh nationalism. Powell continued to write
for the *Daily Telegraph* until 1990. Somebody might well suppose that Powell, nearing eighty-five, stepped down because of
age, but in fact it was because his book of collected reviews and

critical pieces, *Miscellaneous Verdicts* (1990), was given a savagely negative review by Auberon Waugh. Whether Waugh's
review was motivated by a sort of Oedipal antagonism against
his own father, Evelyn, a friend and colleague of Powell's, or
conversely, to prosecute a lingering grievance of his father's
remains a mystery.[14] Both *Miscellaneous Verdicts* and its companion volume, *Under Review* (1992), received wide praise and
were published in the United States by the University of Chicago
Press. As unpretentious as the critical books are in their individual components, in bulk they are tantamount to a refracted cultural history of the modern West. In 1988, Powell received the
culminating public recognition of his career when Queen Elizabeth II appointed him a Companion of Honour (CH).

Shortly after his seventy-sixth birthday, Powell began keeping a regular journal. After publication of the two critical books,
when it became clear there was still substantial interest in Powell's work despite his withdrawal from writing fiction, Heinemann issued the journals in three volumes from 1995 to 1997.
The journals, as yet not published in the United States, garnered
overwhelming acclaim and reignited interest in Powell's career.
They are freewheeling, exuberant, intellectual, and, in their depiction of the personalities and scenarios Powell encounters,
uncannily accurate. They rank with the diaries of Virginia Woolf
among journals produced by creative writers of the first order in
the twentieth century. In 1997, Powell's long wait for a television
dramatization of *Dance,* whetted by the acclaim given to television adaptations of similar but less meritorious works and by the
bad luck that attended previous attempts to adapt his own work,
was gratified by a lavish, eight-hour Channel 4 production.

The project starred many prominent and talented British
actors, including Simon Russell Beale (as Widmerpool), Zoë

Wanamaker (as Mrs. Maclintick), Miranda Richardson (as Pamela Flitton), and in one of his last roles, Sir John Gielgud (as St. John Clarke). Yet it received only mixed reviews. Its accidentally mistimed release in October 1997, when cultural currents were for various superficial reasons not favorable to it, was partly to blame.[15] Powell himself, somewhat to his own surprise, approved of the programs. But the adaptation frustrated hardcore Powell fans with its quick pace and elimination of some minor characters. The dissemination of the program, shown in every major world market other than the United States, helped keep Powell's name in view, as did his rightful appearance in a number of Best of the Century lists.[16] The availability of the lavishly designed University of Chicago paperback editions of the sequence, released in 1995, raised Powell's American visibility once again. And the new medium of the Internet proved a viable avenue for the dissemination of Powell's work. A Powell admirer, Keith Marshall, developed a popular web site that soon became a locus for enthusiasm about Powell's work.[17] In 2000, the Anthony Powell Society was formed on the basis of this enthusiasm. Headquartered in Britain with members from all over the world—a good 40 percent of its membership lives outside the United Kingdom—it publishes a quarterly newsletter and holds a biennial conference.

By the mid-1990s, Powell's health had deteriorated. His steady and redoubtable productivity was finally diminished. As late as 1998, though, he contributed an article on his favorite American writer, F. Scott Fitzgerald, to the *Daily Telegraph* Book of the Century series. His introduction to the posthumously published *A Writer's Notebook,* probably written in 1999, uses the adverb "coincidentally" with a Latinate precision any other writer would covet.

If one accepts the guidelines of the late Martin Seymour-Smith, in his *Guide to Modern World Literature,* that a twentieth-century writer is someone who "survived 31 December 1899," then Anthony Powell, who lived through all the significant events of the twentieth century and died on 28 March 2000, is a twenty-first-century writer.[18] His fiction certainly will live on in the twenty-first century; indeed, freed from the twentieth century's preoccupations and political illusions, it shines brighter than ever. The lavish and demonstrative obituaries that appeared in many newspapers and magazines around the world augur a substantial growth in Powell's reputation.[19] Whether this will actually happen is an open question. So is whether Powell, who so loved in his own reading to muse over the quirky, the eccentric, and the undervalued, would even have found this development desirable.[20] What cannot be doubted is that Powell richly deserves continued, and renewed, attention.

CHAPTER 2

A Company of Giddy-Heads
Understanding Powell's Fiction of the 1930s

Afternoon Men (1931)

It is inevitable that the five novels Powell published in the 1930s should be overshadowed by *Dance,* an imposing edifice beside which those five slim novels seem but antechambers. The point-of-view characters (or, with regard to *What's Become of Waring,* the narrator) in the 1930s novels are in many ways imperfect versions of Nicholas Jenkins, the sequence's narrator. Powell himself points this out when he notes that Lushington in *Venusberg* is said to have Anglo-Catholic leanings, Atwater in *Afternoon Men* to have failed at the Foreign Office, descriptions "not applicable to myself" (*Faces,* 213), whereas the general outline of the Jenkins character, however fictive its execution in detail, is in broad terms applicable to Powell. Neil Brennan has aptly termed the early protagonists as exemplifying a type, which "may be called the parody-*raisonneur,*" that only incompletely represents any point of view that can be wholeheartedly endorsed by the reader.[1] This is opposed to *Dance,* in which, to readers who like the book, Jenkins's narrative comes to represent the point of view of the reader, at least the nonresisting reader.

So the relationship between the early novels and *Dance* is not just negative or implied. The early books have the droll

humor and taste for unexpected resolution that are hallmarks of
Dance. However, the early books consist largely of dialogue and
short, almost affectless sentences, whereas *Dance* is highly allusive, discursive, and even digressive. (There are of course exceptions even in *Afternoon Men;* not only the "Heath Robinson"
description of Atwater's sex with Lola but also Fotheringham's
disquisition on friendship.) But what is most disconcerting
about the early books is not their relationship to what comes
after them, but to what comes before them. In many ways, they
seem to come out of nowhere. They eschew the comic or quasi-
providential reassurance and the luxuriant sense of emotional
education to which readers of the traditional novel have become
used. And this newness is not imbued with a sense of freshness
but with a kind of resigned and mordant, yet not pessimistic,
exhaustion.

Martin Seymour-Smith calls Powell, on the basis of his
prewar work, the "best comic novelist of his generation" and
differentiates him from Evelyn Waugh, Powell's rival for that
laurel, by noting that "the hypomanic and cruel element in
Waugh is absent. Powell is thoughtful as if he were trying to
define what social sanity might consist of."[2] Certainly Powell's
early fiction has thematic traits—disillusionment, skepticism,
diminution of affect, and a portrayal of hedonistic scenes at
which the narrative itself stays to one side—that can be ascribed
to a postwar generational malaise.

A crucial influence here, one masked by the fact that he and
Powell have totally different public images as authors, is Ernest
Hemingway. Powell has spoken of the effect that *The Sun Also
Rises* (1926; published in England as *Fiesta*) had on him, and
the first five novels are full of reverberations from Hemingway's
book: the jaded cast of only intermittently aristocratic young

people, the clipped and nonredemptive sense of "Europe," the terse dialogue that hides or evades as much as it communicates, the deliberately anticlimactic endings in which neither joy nor pathos is allowed to be indulged. This last is perhaps the most important. Before and after his visit to Hollywood, Powell avoided "Hollywood endings"—and the traditional resolution patterns of nineteenth-century English fiction from which Hollywood endings are derived.[3] Unlike in Hemingway, though, the conclusion drawn is not negative or despairing. It is characterized by a kind of extreme skepticism, a noncommitted quality in which very little conclusively tallies and sadness is no more legitimate an option than happiness.

Novelists who overplay their hand nonetheless show that they know how to be ambitious in their writing, whereas novelists who underplay their hand—such as Powell in *Afternoon Men*—face pressure to show that they can write ambitiously. Actually, once the reader focuses, there are a fair amount of discursive scenes: the description of Susan near the beginning of chapter 3 certainly is Hemingwayesque in its minimal elaboration but is a lot more romantic than Hemingway would permit himself. The balance between the world of the characters and anything outside it is a subtle one. It is too much to say, as does Christopher Ames, that Powell reveals "the shallowness of the characters and their limitations from the narrator's consistent and unflinching point of view."[4] A consistent and unflinching point of view is, in its magisterial, Victorian quality, a costly impediment this twentieth-century book cannot afford.

As Sir John Gielgud put it, "The angry young man of the twenties was . . . somewhat more decadent than his counterpart of the fifties and sixties, but the rebellion against convention . . . has always been the same in every generation."[5] It is, in

Powell's early books, more a rebellion of manners than one of intellect. The references to Bertrand Russell and Nietzsche are not meant to be taken seriously, not meant to inform the texture of the novel, unlike many of the intellectual references in *Dance*. With their incongruity—the pretension of these references and the banality of the characters who are making them—they are meant to cause laughter. There is also a sense that the characters suppose intellectual references are a kind of solution to their personal problems, whereas the narrative perspective, appreciably more intellectual, knows enough to know this is not so. Nosworth, as translator, actually does some intellectual work, but it does not place him on a higher precipice of wisdom.

A comparison of Powell's early work with that of Waugh is inevitable. Despite myths of the *Brideshead* generation, the heterogeneity of Powell's generation should be assumed, not argued, and its study should become academically canonical in a way that it currently is not, should be studied as amply as have the generations of Wordsworth and Coleridge, Keats and Shelley, Hemingway and Fitzgerald. Both Powell and Waugh are key figures in the second generation of British modernism (compare the relationship of the Shelley/Keats generation of romanticism with the Wordsworth/Coleridge one), which is the proper term for this group, more fairly treated without reference to *Brideshead* and its aura of social climbing. Powell's generation came after the initial, utopian and/or catastrophic wave of modernism (witness the fact that it is Pringle's parents who purchased a Cézanne painting as more or less a growth stock). Both the early Powell and Waugh in his books of the same period use comedy as a way of negotiating this complicated position in the modern century. Waugh, in novels such as *Decline and Fall* or *Vile Bodies,* is, joke for joke, word for word, more straightforwardly funny than Powell in his early novels. In fact, *Dance* more closely matches Waugh's early work in terms of laugh-out-loud jokes. But Powell's early work, though perhaps no deeper, does consistently yield more on further readings and relates to the reader on a level of intellectual pattern, not just sequential funniness. Also, its tone is much more neutral. Powell's work rarely either celebrates or, as Waugh was later to do in *Brideshead,* elegizes. Powell is matter-of-fact and observant, even when, as often occurs in the early work, he is observing covert or overt craziness.

Waugh himself commented on the difference between Powell's prewar novels and *Dance* in his review of *Casanova:* "[The prewar novels] were brilliant studies in the grotesque; in the later books the characters behave as anarchically but they are seen as cohesive. They have not merely the adventitious connection of crossing the path of a single character; they all hang together apart from him."[6] Waugh's generalization is more applicable to *Afternoon Men* than to any of the other works, as, especially in *Agents and Patients* and *What's Become of Waring,* there are scattered hints of the coordinating sensibility whose presence in *Dance* (and in Waugh's early satires, which have the obverse confidence of a traditional satiric viewpoint) Waugh astutely discerns. Powell's first five novels are works of the 1930s, a decade whose personification in British literature is tied almost exclusively to proletarian literature and the political ups and downs of the Auden generation. Our image of either 1930s literature or Powell has to give a bit in reading these works. Certainly Powell's early work should be valued for its own sake and put in its 1930s context.[7] As some older critics of Shakespeare valued *Titus Andronicus* only for its anticipation of *Hamlet* in the revenge motif, so most critical readers have looked to the prewar novels as but trumpets of a prophecy, the fulfillment being the appearance of *Dance*. Yet it might do well to canvass "the *Titus Andronicus* problem" by asking, What is Powell doing in these books? Why did he write them the way he did?

The plot of *Afternoon Men* is Powell's most intricate. The first section is titled "Montage," a filmic title that clarifies the work's modernist affiliation, the idea of the literary adaptation of the patterned slicing together of images being a far less clichéd one when Powell wrote the book than it is today. As Robert Morris points out, Powell's early work is "indebted to the films for its terminology, technique, and design."[8] Powell establishes our protagonist, what Brennan terms our parody-*raisonneur,* Atwater. Atwater is a promising if unrealized young man who is in love with the beauteous Susan Nunnery. His friend, the painter Pringle, an Ulsterman of a go-getting, eccentric, middle-class family background, warns Atwater off Susan. Atwater, Pringle, and their social confreres Nosworth and Fotheringham occasionally speculate on Undershaft, one of their number, who is living with an Annamite (Vietnamese) woman in New York (many years before New York could boast a large quantity of Vietnamese women). A bit of bizarre comic exercise is provided by the intrusion of Dr. Crutch, who presses a treatise—half manic self-help pamphlet, half visionary artistic manifesto—on a staggered Atwater.

In the novel's second section, "Perihelion" (the nearest approach of the orbiting body to the sun, signifying both the intense heat of the London summer and Atwater's misinformed sense that he is nearer to winning Susan's love than ever before), Atwater, who has begun a desultory affair with a slightly too-available woman named Lola, hopes to make his relationship with Susan more intimate, only to be foiled by the sudden

entrance of Susan's father, George Nunnery. Nunnery is described (106) as a "retired failure" (cf. *Writer's Notebook,* 169,
the entry on "retired social climber," a category likely to swell
some decades hence). Susan is listed in the phone directory
under "George Nunnery" (111), a comic foreshadowing of
Susan's father precluding any sexual culmination to Atwater's
evening with Susan and delivering the "news" about Verelst at
the end. Atwater and Susan float together through a randomly
arranged social world that includes Verelst, a man described as
"hardly looking like a Jew at all," as well as Harriet, a woman
Raymond Pringle decides to court. During a surreal boxing
match (one of the fights on the undercard being between an
inner-city Londoner and a Welshman), it seems as if Susan is
breaking off relations with Atwater, but the dialogue is so arch
and elliptical, the reader expects nothing.

In the third section of the book, "Palindrome" (a palindrome is a word that is the same both backward and forward),
the two customary means of closure in the traditional novel,
marriage and death, are deflected. While walking on the beach,
Pringle discloses to Atwater that he is going to marry Harriet.
He then walks in on Harriet having sex with another man. Harriet later reveals to Atwater, while they are walking in the
woods, that she his actually in love with a third party, living
in Spain. Atwater and Harriet, in a manner very elliptically
described, kiss, in a foretaste of the equally delphic scene between Nicholas Jenkins and Gypsy Jones in *A Buyer's Market.*
Pringle meanwhile does not return from bathing. After an
apprehensive wait, the house party finds a suicide note. Shocked
by Pringle's death, all manner of guilt, regret, recrimination,
moral self-assessment, and personal revaluations occur. Pringle
then nonchalantly returns, brought in by a fisherman. He has,

on a whim rather than a renewed sense of life's desirability, decided not to kill himself. Without obvious embarrassment, Atwater returns to London, where he finds Lola has broken up with him. He calls up Susan, only to have the phone answered by George Nunnery, who invites him over. Nunnery reveals his daughter has gone off to America with none other than Verelst. After an unexpectedly emotional reaction to this news, Atwater reencounters Nosworth and Fotheringham and is told that Undershaft has left the Annamite woman in New York and ended up with Lola. Atwater has received a double amatory comeuppance, but at the end of the novel he seems unaffected, going to a new round of parties as if all the previous events had never occurred. The disappointment of his loss of Susan—recorded in unbelievably delicate language—coexists with a sense of arbitrariness, as if his losing her or even his knowing her in the first place was a kind of cosmic, or comic, accident.

There is a sense not only of there being nothing serious in this world but also of any aspirations toward seriousness preveniently cut down. For instance, when Fotheringham says, "I should like to find something that brought me in touch with people who really mattered. Authors and so on" (68), he is diagnosing the malaise of the book's world, but his aspiration is seen as fatuous and offering no solution.[9]

The Annamite woman, given structural prominence by her appearance, or citation, near the beginning and end, is a kind of structural complement to Verelst. She is a foreigner who mixes amorously with these privileged English people. As Susan goes to New York, where the Annamite woman had been, she also in some sense mimics her Asian counterpart. The neatness of these acts of musical chairs, along with the novel's heavy reliance on immediate dialogue, made it a natural to be adapted into a play.

Powell comments in his memoirs on the 1963 production of *Afternoon Men* that critics, of both the original book and the drama produced from it thirty years later, condemned it as having to do with "drifting purposeless promiscuous young bohemians" (*Strangers,* 113). This puts *Afternoon Men* in the category of a "these young people today" book, and it stands up pretty well in this company, considering the entire category labors under the doom of any given generation of young people always growing old. The critics seem to have come to this evaluation independent of their undoubted knowledge of Powell's later work, which if anything has been accused of having too many "positive" values. However much *Afternoon Men* might be most valued as a plausible germ of *Dance,* it also contains its own fictional world, and one still capable of disconcerting readers many decades after its first publication.

Powell, in *Strangers* (112), also comments upon the pervasive air of futility in the book, which is expressed in both "happy" and "unhappy" events. Verelst, an older, Jewish man, functions as a comic comeuppance to Atwater, who loses his girlfriend to someone *collectively* underestimated. The loss of Susan to Verelst, though depressing, is not tragic, especially as Atwater has already had a memorably described affair with the more raffish Lola (a prototype of Gypsy Jones in *A Buyer's Market,* with Susan as Barbara Goring). Pringle's reappearance, on the other hand, is a "happy" event, but it is a jolt to novelistic convention; usually, when characters are announced as dead, they stay dead, and even when they reappear, they do so in a far more melodramatic way than the affectless, offhand way in which Pringle remanifests himself.

In having Pringle reappear, Powell is exercising the freedom of the novelist to do whatever he or she wants with the characters or action of a novel. Unlike in historical or journalistic writing, there are no restraints on what can happen in a work of fiction. Pringle can die, live, be turned into a mushroom, become military leader of a small Baltic country. His reappearance is hardly a violation of the laws of imaginative fiction, as fantastic, though not inconceivable, as it would be in real life. It is a violation of certain genre expectations of the "mainstream novel," but Powell, though not explicitly interested in destroying those conventions, is not all that interested in conforming to them either. Yet Powell's triumph is in how unspectacular Pringle's reappearance is within the context of the plot. Atwater seems stoic in his response to it. He lets himself have a brief moment of emotion, then is immediately composed and formulaic. The attention clearly shifts from the miracle of Pringle's reappearance to the odd specifics of it. The narrative does not pause to admire its own legerdemain. It does not miss a beat as the characters continue to interact and cross-pollinate as if Pringle's "death" had never happened.

Those reading *Afternoon Men* for the first time may, unconsciously, find themselves drawn to the nomenclature. Powell is extraordinarily deft in avoiding both naturalistic realism and Dickensian caricature in his names; there is not a "Clyde Griffiths" to be found in his books, or a "Pecksniff." He will use a name such as Nunnery, not a typical English surname (no doubt alluding to Hamlet's bawd imprecation to Ophelia, "Get thee to a nunnery"), and make us feel that it is not totally comic or arbitrary. Conversely, he will take a known surname such as "Atwater" and, in his comic deployment of it, tease out its linguistically constructed aspect ("at" as preposition plus "water" as common noun) or concoct a name like "Nosworth," which is close to existing names but has a clear deformative element.

Atwater and Nosworth are compounds of nouns and preposi-
tions, prefixes, and suffixes—prototypes of the segmental mixing and matching that Powell, as onomastic wizard, will make
his own.

As far as the *Titus Andronicus* problem is concerned, the
continuity between *Afternoon Men* and Powell's masterpiece is
remarkable. The narrative refers to "two Shakespearean murderers, minor thugs from one of the doubtfully ascribed plays"
(22), which is just the kind of shifting between registers, view-
ing observed data in the light of learned analogies, that *Dance*
will make its hallmark. The title itself comes from Burton's
Anatomy of Melancholy, the masterwork of seventeenth-
century prose later to play such a major allusive and structural
role in *Dance,* an excerpt of which is used as the epigraph for
Afternoon Men and contains not only the phrase "afternoon
men" but also "a company of giddy-heads," which can neatly
characterize all the characters of Powell's five prewar novels.

Afternoon Men is so tightly written it is hard often to find
concrete referents in it. Yet there has been some controversy
about the book's references to Jews. When Verelst is first mentioned, there is this dialogue:

> "I suppose he's a Jew."
> "I suppose so." (128)

This exchange clearly does designate Jews as a "marked"
category, but no more than that, and any negative expectations
it arouses are to lull the reader into dismissing Verelst as a character of no seriousness. ("Jew" was originally uncapitalized, as
were all the proper adjectives, as a kind of e. e. cummingsesque
orthographic experiment that found its happier outlet in the

cogent characterization of "*old bitch wartstone*" in *The Military Philosophers*.) Verelst emerging out of the novel's soft-pedaled farcical fray in a privileged status garners a laugh from the reader not because of his inherent inferiority but because Atwater, our point-of-view character, had underestimated him or not reckoned with him sufficiently. The lesson here is about the unpredictability of circumstances and the limited ability of our expectations to predict reality, not the inappositeness of Verelst's ending up with Susan. In addition, the older Verelst has served in the First World War and thus could be seen as possessing a gravity, a sense of purpose lacking in the rather vapidly hedonistic Atwater and potentially attractive to Susan, despite Verelst's own rather sallow physical appearance. (The First World War veterans in *Dance* who do not end up being career officers—Jeavons, Umfraville—are in many ways less conventional as people than Verelst seems to be.) Powell cannot be accused of stacking the decks against certain characters because, in his early books, he is at pains not to stack the decks in favor of the men who are his nominal protagonists.

There is admittedly a sense here that Jews are in a different category, not fully integrated into the "imagined community" of the upper-class gilded youth in England. This was, of course, largely true, and the book cannot be blamed for reflecting a social situation it did not create. As Powell says (*Journals*, 1 December 1988), "People too young to have grown up before the war simply write as if they would never dream of making a Jewish joke." Those who have caviled against Powell on this point are being oversensitive. The barbarism of the Holocaust made the kind of genteel anti-Semitism that had flourished in "civilized" spheres in all Western countries no longer morally acceptable. But even in the 1931 of *Afternoon Men*, Jewish characters such as Miriam and Verelst are seen as potential romantic candidates (for that matter, so is the far more, in 1930s terms, racially exotic Annamite woman in New York). The book, in its interpersonal weft, implies that in actual if not de jure terms, Jewish people are part of this social world.[10] Verelst's ending up with Susan at the end makes him, in traditional comic terms, the underrated character who wins out in the end. It is not Verelst, but those who have underrated him, who are mocked by the narrative of *Afternoon Men.*

As difficult as it is to read as a result of its crowded cast of characters and acerbic tone, *Afternoon Men* sets the essential premises of Powell's fiction. The reader comes to expect the unexpected and even the uncanny. We realize that situations can reverse themselves in rapid order and sense that the characters in the fiction have aspirations, both idealistic and self-serving, as well as the mechanisms to cope, through irony and understatement, with the disappointment of these aspirations.

Venusberg (1932)

Venusberg is one of Powell's rare excursions to a setting outside England. Only the Berlin scenes of *Agents and Patients,* the Provence scenes of *What's Become of Waring,* and the France (*Question of Upbringing*) and Venice (*Temporary Kings*) scenes in *Dance* are equivalent in their length of situation in Continental Europe. Lushington, a young journalist, has had a bad breakup with his girlfriend Lucy, whom he has lost to an, in his view, inferior man named Da Costa, with whom he had been at school. A further complication is that Da Costa has no real feelings for Lucy. When Lushington's newspaper sends him as a political correspondent to a small Baltic country, where, coincidentally, Da Costa is already posted is a diplomat, he accepts the position phlegmatically. On board the ship, Lushington meets the comic Count Scherbateff and the sultry Austrian Ortrud Mavrin, with whom he quickly begins an affair. Lushington settles in to an aimless round of party-going and intermittent political reportage, disrupted slightly by Count Scherbateff's domestic troubles with his grandmother and, then, his unexpected and somewhat absurd death. Ortrud's husband, the garrulous Professor Mavrin, is suspicious that his wife is having an affair, but he is convinced the culprit is not Lushington but da Costa. At this point, we might expect Professor Mavrin to kill da Costa in a duel. But instead da Costa is killed, mistakenly, by an assassination attempt on the country's potential military strongman. This incident also takes the life of Ortrud. Lushington stumbles back to London, where, only half-buoyantly, he recommences his relationship with Lucy.

Venusberg is superficially classifiable as a takeoff on the "Ruritanian novel" concerning hijinks in backward Eastern European countries on the model of Anthony Hope's *Prisoner of Zenda* (1894), after whose heroine Flavia Wisebite, Stringham's sister in *Dance,* may well have been named. But it is less a parody of Ruritania, like Agatha Christie's hilarious *The Secret of Chimneys* (1925), than a wry if serious example of "the literature of new countries."[11] The independence of the Baltic states was big news in the 1920s, as it was in the 1990s, and Powell's exploration of a country that, whatever the author's asseverations, is clearly modeled on Estonia is comparable to the controversial Lithuanian section of Jonathan Franzen's *Corrections* (2001) in its mixture of satire on the preposterousness of the new country with serious reportage on its importance. Powell's contemporary, Graham Greene, and his good friend V. S. Naipaul, wrote several books of this sort on the "emergent" Asian and African states of the 1960s and 1970s. *Venusberg,* for all its lightness of touch, is little different. Witness this dialogue between Lucy and Lushington:

> "It's a new country, isn't it?"
> "Yes."
> "Who used to own it?"
> "Russia. I think Germany had some of it too. I'm not sure." (12)

Unlike the other books mentioned, though, the new country is not treated in a quasi-documentary fashion. The background is lightly sketched, and there is little travelogue, although Powell's depiction of Lushington's destination is enough to have landed *Venusberg's* High Town and Low Town a reference in Alberto Manguel's *Dictionary of Imaginary Places.* Perhaps this is the point of the sketchiness, to render the place as an imaginary setting without plunging into overt fantasy. There is also little exoticism about the descriptions in the novel; they have a mundane, even humdrum quality about them, as in this unromantic description of the North Sea: "The North Sea, an ingrained tract of sheet-iron, heaved a little. All the sky was grey" (15). There is no boyish excitement at setting out on a foreign voyage. Nor are the culture and manners of the new country romanticized, as the harsh treatment of minorities, presumably Russians, is given full ventilation by the remarks of Count Scherbateff in chapter 3.

The title of *Venusberg* comes from the sensual mountainous enclosure where the hero takes sanctuary in Richard Wagner's opera *Tannhauser.* As one would not on the face of it expect

Powell to be an admirer of Wagner, there is an irony, a deflation
to the title. In general, the action in the prewar novels tends to
be less consequential than the works' titles would suggest,
whereas the novels in the *Dance* sequence possess more inherently consequential plot developments than their often low-key
and offbeat titles would suggest. The philosophy of *nitchevo,* or
"it means nothing," with which the bogus Count Bobel tries to
console Lushington after Ortrud's death militates against any
Wagnerian grandeur, although for Powell even Count Bobel's
philosophy is treated with a firm, comic lack of commitment.
The novel, in essence, says *nitchevo* to any possible sustained
philosophy of *nitchevo.*

As with *Afternoon Men,* the reader of *Venusberg* who is
coming from *Dance* will feel a bit disconcerted by Powell's
reliance on dialogue and understated, minimal descriptions.
Other than in the somewhat overdone rhetoric of Professor
Mavrin—and it is his penchant for rhetoric, not his intellect,
which is being made fun of—there is little of the rich and complex exposition that is one of the chief comforts of Powell's
masterwork. Individual motifs, though, do anticipate the later
sequence. The jibe at the middlebrow novelist and playwright
John Galsworthy, when the Female Deputy asks Madame The-
vioy, "*Vous en avez vu, Madame? Le* Loyalties *de Galsworthy
au Théâtre National*" (77), foreshadows a constant theme in
Dance, found also in the prewar novels: writers thought noteworthy in the previous generation are now profoundly irrele-
vant. It also pokes fun at the tendency of foreigners to be
interested in just the writers in their own country, whatever it is,
who are at the moment hideously out of style. In addition, Lushington and Da Costa's romantic rivalry over Lucy and, incipiently, Ortrud is reminiscent, for example, of Jenkins's rivalry

with Tompsitt (and Widmerpool) over Barbara Goring in *A Buyer's Market*. Da Costa is at school with Lushington much like Widmerpool was with Jenkins, and like Tompsitt, he is a (presumably mediocre) diplomat. After da Costa's demise, there is no obstacle to Lushington's once again pursuing his relationship with Lucy, so he is actually one of the more fortunate of the early protagonists. The book thus has a happy ending, if a very muffled one.

The weak-kneed rationalizations of the literary editor in chapter 36 about the impossibility of punishing the murderer of Ortrud and da Costa foreshadows the paradigm, so prominent in Powell's later work, of those willing to accept evil in the world. *Venusberg* also anticipates *Dance* in its subsidiary attention to world politics, especially in Eastern Europe. Politics are not prominent in the novel, and when they are they are not treated ponderously or as if they were of central importance. But the backdrop of political awareness is there, like a hum in the distance.

Venusberg once seemed a quaint curiosity, a chronicle of a long-eclipsed era, but it gained new currency with the renewed independence of the Baltic states after 1991, which Powell lived to see. While the rest of the world wrote off the Baltic countries and even half-cheered their integration into the Soviet colossus, Powell's novel kept the flame of their envisioned independence burning until the light dawned.

From a View to a Death (1935)

James Henle, the American publisher of this book (earlier noted for working with Theodore Dreiser), retitled it *Mr. Zouch, Superman*. This title alludes to Zouch's self-concept as a Nietzschean superman, an agent who needs no authorization other than his own, a modern and, were he to be revived today, possibly postmodern buccaneer, a man on the make in every way imaginable. As Zouch embarks on his courtship of the aristocratic Mary Passenger amid the background of hunting and country life, though, we as readers do not necessarily despise him. As a highbrow entering a den of middlebrows, Zouch's plight elicits sympathy from most people who read *From a View to a Death,* who are more likely to be Zouch types than bluff rural sportsmen such as Mary's father, Vernon Passenger. In a way, we feel *nous sommes tous* Zouch. Zouch is a Young Man from the Metropole trying to make his career in the provinces. He appears to have resolved life on his own terms, when he suffers a surprise death, which makes the novel end on what Neil McEwan calls a "sour, uncomfortable note."[12] Zouch, as a character, thinks he has it made, simply because it is such a conventional novelistic situation, up-and-coming middle-class man marrying aristocratic woman—the stuff of every bourgeois comedy. He has forgotten he is a character in an Anthony Powell novel, and anything can happen to him. If Pringle can return, so can Zouch die.

Mary, bored with the limited, Philistine horizons of her aristocratic world, looks to Zouch for some stimulation; she wants him to provide a breath of fresh air. She is interested in Zouch *because* he is an artist, even though she herself, like Zouch, does not have a deep interest in art. Zouch is using art merely as a passport into the enclaves of the wealthy, much like a character from Stendhal—a writer of particular interest to the early Powell—becoming a priest exclusively for purposes of self-advancement. He has no interest in being an artist for art's sake. Zouch does not even have, as an analogous character in Victorian fiction might, a desire to enlighten the aristocracy or at least make it more alive to beauty. Similarly, he seems to find the attractions of Mary less in her physical beauty than in her social status, this insensitivity to a woman's appearance being particularly notable for a painter. Even so, when Zouch, in his own terms, gets the girl, the reader is likelier than not to say, "Oh, Zouch has gotten the girl, who would have thought it? A victory for art!" But whether through the impassivity of fate, the arbitrariness of malice, the muteness of chance, or, least likely, the premeditation of design, Zouch is foiled. In a Victorian novel, this would have been seen as a punishment for Zouch's overreaching aspirations, but here it is more of a grotesque accident.

Zouch gets his comeuppance. His attempt to parlay his artistic talent into social status (perhaps an anticipation of Charles Ryder in Waugh's *Brideshead Revisited*) is viewed with a withering contempt that is all the sharper as in many ways Zouch has been the reader's point-of-view character, the outsider to the hunting world of the Fosdicks and Passengers. *From a View to a Death* sets forth a key difference between a pleasure that the gentry like one's art (pleasure that in theory will accrue when any interested audience comprising something of a critical mass does so) and the wielding of the art exclusively as a tool for social climbing. Zouch, though, is not punished in the melodramatic sense. He is merely upended by a kind of low-key, almost random sequence; thus the quotation from the folk song "John Peel" that gives us the title: "From a find to a check, from a check to a view, from a view to a death in the morning." Death is the next step in the progression. It just happens, with a sense of random or analytic propinquity rather than destiny, and life goes on for others in a kind of level way after death, just as it would have in the case of Pringle in *Afternoon Men* had Pringle actually died. There is a grim inevitability to Zouch's fate, but it is an ironic, not pathetic, inevitability. Vernon Passenger, after all, did not intend Zouch's death. When he mounted Zouch on the mischief-prone horse Creditor, he intended some humiliation, perhaps he had even conceived a stratagem that would foil the engagement, but nothing more.

So Zouch, and his opportunistic, self-promoting values, do not prevail. He does not become a new cog in the old order. This is all to the satisfaction of Passenger, his prospective father-in-law, and we may half suspect that the novel shares this satisfaction. This is only partly true, but even to the extent that it is true, it must be recognized that this is not a prototype for how Powell will portray aristocrat-opportunist interaction. There is no character in *Dance* who is the good squire, the gallant aristocrat righteously defending his domain, as Passenger can be said to be. The closest might be someone such as Chips Lovell's (second) Sleaford uncle (*At Lady Molly's,* 213). But he is a totally offstage character and given no attributes other than owning a great house, Dogdene, which Widmerpool as opportunist attempts to use for his sexual and social coup turned fiasco. James Tucker's assumption that in "all important matters caste will decide behavior" may be true of Passenger. It certainly is not true of Erridge in *Dance.*[13]

Fosdick seems the stereotypical, two-dimensional retired officer. His sequined dress is funny because nothing has prepared us for it. His transvestism is as shocking as Pringle's return from presumed death. Powell—to use a fishing rather than hunting analogy—lured the reader with one convention, the reader then bites, and the narrative quickly switches in an unexpected direction. Fosdick's transvestitism completely explodes the book;

it stops being a novel about hunting in the country and becomes a novel of the preposterousness of life. Fosdick is at first a stock character, and his liking "to repair to his dressing room in the afternoon in order to read *Through the Western Highlands with Rod and Gun* attired in a large picture hat and a black sequinned evening dress" shakes up our expectations (and note that Fosdick's unconventional behavior is accompanied by conventional reading matter).[14] As in an Agatha Christie mystery, such as *After the Funeral,* where the benign old maid is revealed to be a psychotic poisoner, Fosdick's incarnation of the bluff, intransigent squire as secret transvestite blows the cover off the conventions by which the innocent might suppose the novel to be operating.

What *From a View to a Death* contributes to *Dance* is not only the country-house atmosphere and idea of rising in society through the shrewd deployment of artistic talent. The novel exemplifies Powell's habit of not treating sadistically even those characters who are the object of the often acidic irony of his fictional perspective. On one level, Passenger cannot fully comprehend the precise nature of his triumph over Fosdick and assimilates it to a more conventional model. Passenger, in his almost reassuring cloak of narcissism, behaves with an odd mixture of reserve and banality that excludes any excessive or sadistic gloating. He does not enforce a victor's peace on Fosdick. He attains his immediate objective, the end of shooting on the North Copse, and leaves it at that. Passenger will not seek to derive a permanent sense of entitlement from his neighbor/rival's ruin. Fosdick's relatives put him away, but this is not because Passenger has bruited about Fosdick's eccentricities. Nor does the novel end with the old values safely reinstated. The Restoration pageant is more a farce than a recuperative celebration of the continuity of English life. Indeed, it is less this than is the village pageant at Poyntz Hall in Virginia Woolf's later novel, *Between the Acts*. If *From a View to a Death* is an update of the hunting novels of R. S. Surtees, much admired by Powell, the updater has brought his own century to the task. The unjust and the foolish have fallen. But that does not mean that the just or those who are not fools declaratively triumph. The "John Peel" lyrics express the inevitable, mute sequence that, in relentless algorithm, as if chance is running a relay race, grinds down Zouch's outsized aspirations. The reader derives a sardonic enlightenment from this, even a sense of dissipating tension as the process plays itself out. But there is precious little reassurance at the end of the novel.

Agents and Patients (1937)

Powell found his fourth novel's technique "deviating a little from the bare naturalism that had once seemed the only literary goal" (*Faces*, 2). Powell is a perceptive critic of his own work, and notwithstanding ways in which all the books share common traits and yet are in some way on their own imaginatively, his observation is worth pondering. (He also, in *Journals*, 8 July 1988, provides a nimble run-through of the characters in *Agents and Patients* and the models for them.) Certainly, for all the colorful background of the hunt in *From a View to a Death*, there is not the sense of a "world" being deliberately fashioned as there is in *Agents and Patients*, especially in the Berlin and film scenes. The characters also seem more real. This is true even of Blore-Smith, our rather pitiful protagonist, as it is of such very broad comic characters as Mrs. Mendoza and the Marquis de la Tour d'Espagne.

Agents and Patients is the most interesting of Powell's early book titles. The "X and Y" format owes something to the work of Ivy Compton-Burnett, but the way it operates is more conceptual. The title contrasts, in a philosophical sense, agents, the originators of action, and patients, those who receive or even suffer that action. In terms of the book's plot, the agents are the filmmakers-cum-con men Maltravers and Chipchase, the patient the ingenu Blore-Smith. Usually we are taught to think that to act is better than not to act, but the narrative does not privilege the agents over the patients. In a dichotomy that is anticipatory of the one between men of will and men of imagination in *Dance*, Powell leads us to sympathize more with the preyed-upon Blore-Smith, as foolish and feckless as he is, than with cool operators Maltravers and Chipchase—even though Blore-Smith, unlike Moreland and Trapnel in *Dance*, has no imagination. His main goal in life is "opportunities for friendship with the opposite sex" (8), opportunities he pursues ineptly. The age-old theme of the exploitation of the hapless and innocent by the cunning and experienced is given a different twist in this era. Twentieth-century people, at least as depicted in twentieth-century novels, cannot rely on existing social codes. Thus they are vulnerable to being preyed upon by cultural "advances" such as psychoanalysis.

Chipchase and Maltravers are "post-war types, already perhaps a little dated" (*Agents and Patients*, 1), a label perhaps attesting to Powell's slight worry, mentioned in *Faces* (1), that his style was not changing with the climate caused by the 1930s "trade depression" (2). Chipchase and Maltravers are making a "psychoanalytical film" (*Agents and Patients*, 75). The idea of the film-within-a-book is surreal and reflexive, reminiscent of the cinematic and apocalyptic *The Day of the Locust* by Powell's American near-contemporary Nathanael West. As a kind of palliative for his feeling that his life "showed every sign of being a disappointment" (9), Blore-Smith agrees to be the subject of the psychoanalysis to be filmed by the two con men. But his status as a "patient" in the literal, medical sense (or patient and film star in the scheme of the "two knaves" [248]) is only symptomatic of the way he is, on a fundamental level, someone who is acted upon, not himself an agent. This is analogous to the way we speak of the "passion" of Jesus Christ because his suffering was something he underwent, or how a medical patient is someone who, in terms of role, undergoes a procedure. Psychoanalysis, as a discourse that aspired to operate on both soul and body, in many ways blends the empirical and philosophical senses of "patient." Powell is registering psychoanalysis as a social phenomenon of the time, but he is also making fun of the way it is seen as a cure-all when it in fact can as readily be a con game. As far as film goes, the book implies that film gives no greater access to reality than fiction ever did. It may be a new medium, but it is unlikely it can deliver a new message.

Blore-Smith's sexual liaison with Mrs. Mendoza (the time in the book when he thinks he is the most "cured") is misdirected. It is sexuality unhinged from cognition, and as such is meant to be funny. Chipchase and Maltravers stage the affair with the sadism of a director deliberately casting an unattractive actress as Beatrice in *Much Ado about Nothing* or someone intentionally introducing two people he knows will not get along. Although Blore-Smith, who cannot even decide at which restaurant he should eat, seems to find Sarah Maltravers and Mrs. Mendoza equally attractive, the reader knows that only Sarah, with her "irresistible" (40) manner, is genuinely so, and that Mrs. Mendoza, though possessing an inexplicable erotic appeal, is also palpably androgynous, "tall and fair-haired" and wearing an "overcoat of military cut" (19). Blore-Smith, in fact, imagines that his sexual fulfillment via Mendoza is more legitimate in the eyes of the world than it really is. Commander Venables, Mendoza's longtime standing love interest (perhaps a precursor, as navy man, of Buster Foxe in *Dance*), goes to Berlin to pursue Mendoza, but Chipchase and Maltravers maneuver it so that she and Blore-Smith leave before a rapprochement can be effected. Blore-Smith's subsequent humiliation at the hands, or through the medium, of Mrs. Mendoza, his submersion below the Mendoza line, places him in the role of utter sap. Blore-Smith is not "sadder, but wiser" at the end, as in a traditional morality tale. He does not gain any wisdom. But experience itself is enough, as it has changed him in some way, even though his situation might seem "palindromic," the same at the end as at the beginning. Experience counts for something, even if our protagonist has, to quote T. S. Eliot in "The Dry Salvages," "had the experience and missed the meaning."[15]

The Paris and Berlin scenes are notable for, without specific political reference, representing the nervousness and frenzy of the Continent during the rise of totalitarianism. The film scene in *Mittelafrika,* with the English, French, and German soldier quarreling over a woman but otherwise manifesting national stereotypes, is astonishingly perceptive, as it foreshadows the war to come yet, in its foregrounding of colonial rivalry, is more like the First World War, or even more like people thought that war would be at its beginning. The questions of Fraulein Grundt about traffic and the youth movement in London, which "could not always be answered on the spot" (97), also embody inevitable cross-cultural miscommunication but, as with the Africa scene, endow it with a ludicrous foreboding. The scenes at the film canteen and the Berlin zoos, with their confusion between the sexes and the species, almost unhinge the novel from a realistic frame. The reentry of Commander Venables is, in this context, a counterstroke on behalf of realism, an anchor to prevent the book from ascending into the surrealist empyrean.

The narrative achieves the difficult balance of taking psychoanalysis seriously while satirizing it for its all-knowing pretensions. The book posits psychoanalysis as a con game and film as not a transparent medium for real life but a forum for deception just as much as any mode of storytelling can be. *Agents and Patients* is very modern in not seeing modern media and modes of thought as ipso facto liberating, unlike, say, St. John Clarke is portrayed in *Dance,* a Victorian convert to modern enthusiasms who takes them on full bore.

The names in *Agents and Patients* resemble the names in *Dance* more than those in *Afternoon Men, Venusberg,* and *From a View to a Death.* Maltravers, for instance, is one of the subsidiary titles of the Duke of Norfolk. *Agents and Patients* would not have a name like Zouch, for all the comic tone of, say, Chipchase. The emotions are also less monochromatic. The attraction between Blore-Smith and Sarah Maltravers, never realized, is one of the most winning aspects of the book; Maltravers, unlike Susan Nunnery in *Afternoon Men,* is seen as a woman whose beauty is worthy of respect, not just desire. Mrs. Mendoza, a flower-shop proprietor (the "cattleya" is a reference to the prominence of that flower in Proust, as translated by Scott Moncrieff) who has been married and tacitly done many other things "more than once" (34), is a farcical figure. Blore-Smith's entire involvement with her is farcical—and not just farcical in the sense of being funny, but in its portrayal of what happens when ideals are unrealized, when disorder replaces conceived order or rational hope. Mrs. Mendoza ends up abandoning Blore-Smith first for Commander Venables (the name Venables was probably taken from the mid-Victorian cleric Francis

Kilvert's *Diary,* depicting the border country of some of Powell's Welsh ancestors) and then for the Marquis de Tour d'Espagne. This latter name is an explicit homage to T. S. Eliot's quotation of the Gérard de Nerval line "Le prince d'Aquitaine dans la tour abolie" in "The Waste Land." As a name, it is at once comedically pleasing, in a preposterous way, and a complicated philological joke—as funny to the several hundred souls who understood it on the book's publication as, for example, the more broadly comic Barbara Goring sugar-pouring incident in *A Buyer's Market* was to its far larger audience.

What *Agents and Patients* contributes to *Dance* is its sense of the mute pathos of the victim, of the person who is the object of power rather than the wielder of it, even though Blore-Smith does not have the tragic dimensions of, say, Stringham or Trapnel. As disappointed as he is on the surface, Blore-Smith's clear inner realization that he is better off having got rid of Mrs. Mendoza is one of the first moments of insight that this bland, self-effacing, and self-loathing figure has allowed himself. *Agents and Patients* contains a moral lesson: experience is worthwhile even if nothing of substance is gained from it. Blore-Smith has achieved no more at the end of his unproductive odyssey than at the beginning, but he has experienced more. Thus his embarrassment is not fruitless. His ordeal has not, after all, been a mere palindrome. Similarly, readers who during the course of the novel feel they have been on an amoral romp, emerge from the book with expanded horizons, if not necessarily enlightenment.

What's Become of Waring (1939)

The view that *What's Become of Waring* is the key forerunner of *Dance* because of its first-person narrator and its being the last of the five prewar books is no longer as popular as it once was. For one thing, it is based on developmental assumptions that, as will be detailed in chapter 5, are not greatly applicable to Powell's career. Robert Morris, for instance, notes that the character of Captain "Tiger" Hudson has aspects of Rowland Gwatkin in *Dance;* in his bluff amiability, he also anticipates Peter Templer.[16] But Hudson, Waring, *and* the narrator have certain traits in common. They are all seekers after a pattern that will provide them with more than they have in their daily lives. The rogue Pimley/Waring goes so far as to counterfeit that pattern. Though we know even less about the narrator of *What's Become of Waring* than we do about Jenkins, he is "in play" more as a character, on a level with the others, than is Jenkins.

T. T. Waring is a successful young writer of travel books. He stands for "the glorious extramundane idea of Youth" (47), though most of his readers are the kind who find "author's names hard to remember" (32). He flourishes in a literary environment in which people such as Roberta Payne dream of writing their memoirs at twenty-five—"I've had an adventurous life" (13)—in the awareness that, if published, they will be largely read by consumers of much older vintage. (In fairness, there is also the motive, adduced in Henry Green's real-life memoir *Pack My Bag,* of the need to take stock of one's life due to the menace of the impending war.) This is a hyperinflated cultural milieu, one where "making a literary reputation . . . had never been so easy" (32). (Hugh Judkins eventually dissents from this milieu, only to suffer a nervous breakdown, in a way punishment for violating the laws of his own universe.) The unnamed narrator is also a writer who works in the publishing firm of Judkins and Judkins. He is working on a book, *Stendhal; or, Some Thoughts on Violence,* a far cry from the more glibly commercial books being produced by his own firm. There is more than a hint that the narrator, though characteristically self-effacing, is a better writer than most of the people he shepherds through the publication process. Perhaps one day, it is suggested, the tortoise will outpace the hare.

But immediately the narrator is faced with a crisis in the firm when it is announced that Waring is dead. It soon becomes evident that Waring, whom nobody in the firm had ever met in the flesh, was a pseudonym, or at least a heteronym, and in an implied detective-story convention, we assume the solution to this identity riddle is one of the characters already present in the book's world. There is in fact a double solution: Alec Pimley, brother of Captain Hudson's beloved Beryl, turns out to be Waring (so Hudson is in a way displacing his love for Beryl and his admiration for "Waring" in a fraternal to and fro). Moreover, at least one of the Waring books has been plagiarized from the most unlikely source—Pimley's own grandfather, a drooling old Victorian remnant.

There are the usual Powellian turns and surprises. The fortune-telling practices of Mr. Ram Lal, unexpected fiancé of one of the minor characters (whose Indian origins are not simply categorized as "black" but defended with the analogy that "the Chinese were at the height of their civilization before the Greeks and Romans were ever heard of" [130]), foreshadows the presence of the eldritch figures of Mrs. Erdleigh and Dr. Trelawney in *Dance*. In both cases, the occult functions as a way to heighten the suspense and tell the reader that, though transpiring on a realistic plane, the fictional narrative is not subject to the logical boundaries of reality. We are reminded of this as all sorts of originally unlikely events happen. The seemingly Olympian Hugh Judkins leaps into the romantic fray by having an affair with Roberta. And there is the almost preposterous, yet intuitively plausible, revelation that the hopelessly senile Captain Pimley, Alec and Beryl's grandfather, a stage Victorian relic (the equivalent today would be a burned-out old beatnik), in fact wrote the book on Ceylon that, after it had sunk into oblivion, his grandson republished an epoch later as his own—only to be hailed as the fresh young voice of a new generation.

Browning's poem "Waring" concerns a friend who has mysteriously disappeared from his social circle and vanished into obscurity. The model for Waring, Alfred Domett, in fact became prime minister of New Zealand, later writing what at the time was considered *the* great poem of New Zealand, "Ranulf and Amohia"—an interesting instance of "obscurity." The Waring parallel, however, was evidently not intended as the keystone of the book throughout its composition. As Michael C. Meredith of the Eton College Library (where Powell's manuscripts are now housed) has commented, the name of the Waring character was originally Stokes and was amended at a comparatively late stage, so the premise of the story, its seed or Jamesian *donnée,* was presumably not the Browning poem. Yet like the original Waring, *What's Become of Waring*'s T. T. Waring similarly gave all those involved in publishing him "the slip," though Powell's Waring is a less noble and, upon unmasking, less enigmatic figure than was Domett. The latter-day Waring, ostensibly the energetic young voice of the modern century, is in fact subsisting on his grandfather's Victorian-era work. He represents a residual, not an emergent paradigm. There is an object lesson here: what seems most new may actually be a reiteration of the old, and the truly new may not be nearly as flashy as imitation versions, such as the travelogues of T. T. Waring, proffered for ready consumers. Powell's work in the publishing industry lent him an ideal background for making the point that original work gets lost in the shuffle of literary promotion, and that publishers are happy to pass off familiar ideas as new and exciting ones.

Captain Hudson, at first the most eager to find out the "truth" about Waring, is a nonpareil example of the disillusioned biographer/follower (somewhat like Marlow to Kurtz in Conrad's *Heart of Darkness,* though, crucially, Hudson is not the narrator here, being in this way more like Gwinnett in *Temporary Kings*). Hudson has taken Waring as his ideal, filled him with all sorts of romantic expectations, then found his idol to have had feet of clay all along. The reader certainly feels more pathos for him, in this regard at least, than for anyone else in the book. But Hudson inevitably has overtones of a well-meaning buffoon. His tour of Provence, in finding emptiness instead of exoticism, is much like the tour around the Bay of Biscay in *The Sun Also Rises;* but the bluff, winsome Hudson is without a Hemingwayesque stoic poise. Yet no one else represents unequivocally positive values: there is no Jenkins, no Moreland, no General Conyers, none of the moral and temperamental lodestones of *Dance.* In this way, *What's Become of Waring,* like all Powell's novels of the 1930s, refuses or does not attempt a sort of comic transcendence. It eschews the magisterial and enabling confidence in perspective that the narrative of *Dance* has from the beginning.

Waring is notable for the striking matter-of-factness of Powell's portrait of the world of writing and publishing. He regards it with the same measured distance he does the world of hunting, even though, by his own admission, he was one of the world's worst hunters and, in the opinion of many, one of its best writers. Powell was involved, at one point or another, with every stage of publishing, from production to dissemination, from contracting for publication to reviewing the final product in the press. That he became world famous for the allegedly most crucial stage in the process, actually writing the book, did not mean he considered the act of writing the sine qua non of the world of books. In Powell there is none of the egoism of "the great writer," none of the guru-like authority with respect to his own vision, none of the sense of the writer as a being qualitatively distinct from his peers endemic to so many writers' self-presentation. It is easy to fob this lack of egoism off on Powell being an antiromantic, either in classicist or modernist mode. Despite the romantic nature of the ideology of "the great writer," though, classicists, modernists, and postmodernists have just as eagerly manifested this egoistic state of mind. Powell's tacit deflation of the "great writer" ideology is far more attributable to his workaday immersion in the world of publishing and, later, reviewing.

The setting in the world of publishing means that titles such as the American middlebrow epic *Lot's Hometown* (198; cf., for instance, Steinbeck's *East of Eden*) or Minhinnick's *Aristogeiton: A Harmony* (77), a play on the names of the ancient Athenian tyrannicides, are mentioned in the manner of the book titles in *Books Do Furnish a Room,* one of Powell's later novels (tenth volume of *Dance*). The revelation that the senile Captain Pimley is in fact the author of the Waring books is a reversal out of a folktale or fable. The unlikely candidate is in fact "the great writer," and that teaches two moral points: we can never underestimate anyone and the outward and inward correlates of human achievement can in fact be quite different. And our narrator, more self-effacing even than Nicholas Jenkins in *Dance* as he is unnamed, unmarried, unsituated, and given no particular

attribute except a phantasmal book on Stendhal that is still
unfinished at the end of the book, remains standing, unbowed if
not particularly glorified, as he has never given anyone reason to
overestimate him. He has never proffered himself as the center
of a myth to which believers such as Hudson can adhere. And
yet he is alive at the end of the book, whereas "Waring," in all
senses, is dead (the fullest answer, perhaps, to the question
"What's become of Waring?").

What *What's Become of Waring* contributes to *Dance* most
crucially is its sense that the world of culture and the arts is full
of the same practicality and even maniacal power seeking as
characterizes the world of politics and public affairs. Thus the
light and often zany surface of the novel conceals a serious sub-
current. This is no more evident than in the narrator's meditation on power at the end: "It was power Hugh wanted too.
Everybody wanted power. Bernard wanted power, Lipfield
wanted power. Roberta wanted power. T. T. Waring wanted
power. Did Eustace want power? It was an interesting question"
(252). What is gratifying here is the willingness to call things
as they are, without any fudging or imputation of humanistic
motives not corresponding to the characters as actually portrayed. We are not meant to pessimistically conclude that *everyone* wants power or to equate the motives of *all* who want
power—as Powell would have been well equipped to reflect in
1939, both Churchill and Hitler wanted power, but different
sorts of power for different purposes. But the book squarely
faces people's power needs instead of sentimentally pretending
they are not there. Any redress to this power pandemic is to be
found only through further and more rigorous thought. The
narrator's work on the book *Stendhal: or Some Thoughts on
Violence* is by far the most serious intellectual citation in any of

the prewar books. (The title of the book also refers to Georges Sorel, author of *Reflexions sur la violence,* and to what Powell has termed "the racking international atmosphere" [*Faces,* 75] of late 1938, when *What's Become of Waring* was being written.) Stendhal stands for a skeptical and unpremeditated ideal, lived at a higher level of self-scrutiny, than a commodifier of literature such as T. T. Waring, who only publishes his books for acclaim, status in the eyes of other people, and "the need to earn a living" (189), not honest self-worth. The narrator thus reaches a greater sense of self-awareness than does Blore-Smith at the end of *Agents and Patients,* though it cannot be said that he derives any more positive wisdom from experience. Like the social-climbing Zouch with regard to his painting, "Waring" sees his travel books as only a tool, not an end in themselves. But when Alec Pimley is exposed, his name, like Major Fosdick's, is not unduly—publicly—humiliated. And this turns out splendidly for Beryl and Captain Hudson, whose personal happiness the narrator regards benignly. But T. T. Waring's giddy-headed, power-minded dream of literary fame is forever ended.

CHAPTER 3

Widmerpool and Theocritus
Understanding *A Dance to the Music of Time*

Steps of the *Dance*

Discussing a twelve-volume sequence in a short space obviously has its pitfalls. A broad overview might easily become a fictive version of an "Outline of History," overlooking the reality that much detail valuable to the novel itself in its composition is superfluous to a critical exposition. A look at the shape of *Dance* may help situate the reader. Although these surface "steps of the dance" are less intrinsically meaningful than the specific content, understanding them will put the reader well toward understanding Powell's central work.

Powell always referred to *Dance* as a unified novel, although it comes more naturally to the critic to refer to it as a sequence. If it is a novel, though, it is a novel in twelve parts, and each of those parts was published separately and marketed and reviewed as a separate novel, even if always discussed as being part of the overall grand design. Readers certainly read the books as individual novels, and even Little, Brown, their original American publisher, issued the sequence in four volumes of three novels each (a procedure continued in the 1995 University of Chicago Press paperbacks), the trilogy obviously being a more digestible unit than a twelve-book series. In a sense, the books behave as trilogies. Books two, five, eight, and eleven are all unusually dark, for instance, and all involve at least one death. Whereas books one, four, seven, and ten are all about introducing new milieus and have some of the exuberance of such an occasion, although in book seven the action is distinctly downbeat.

But what of the relationship of individual book to the entire design? The matter of titles might prove useful here. *A Dance to the Music of Time,* as a title, is certainly a grand, elevated one. But the titles of the individual novels are less so. In fact, if Powell, like Vergil in the Fourth Eclogue, is singing a "higher song" with *Dance* than with his self-effacing prewar novels, the titles of the individual novels are reminiscent of those given to the prewar novels. They are quirky, ironic, and pithy, not revealing much of what is inside. *A Question of Upbringing* or *At Lady Molly's* could have easily fallen into the prewar world. Even titles that sound a bit weightier, such as *The Valley of Bones* or *Hearing Secret Harmonies,* not to mention *The Soldier's Art* or *The Military Philosophers,* do so because there is a tacit reference to death in them, and in the prewar novels we have *From a View to a Death.*

Yet the titles of the twelve *Dance* novels are not to be read individually but as part of a sequence. And that sequence constitutes a narrative of sorts that we superficially comprehend before we have even read the books, and understand rather thoroughly before we have got very far in them. To illustrate: to a Greek-speaking reader of the translated Old Testament, the first three books of the Bible, Genesis, Exodus, and Leviticus, would constitute a narrative sequence—beginning, going out of, the laws—from which one could discern the general contents of the books and the general flow of the narrative therein. Winston Churchill's World War II memoirs are similar. If one knows anything about the Second World War, and sees six books in a row on a bookshelf titled *The Gathering Storm, Their Finest Hour, The Hinge of Fate, The Grand Alliance, Closing the Ring,* and *Triumph—and Tragedy,* one gets the general idea of how things turn out, even if one thinks *Their Finest Hour* refers to the other side's finest hour. There is an ominous beginning, a brush with danger, a moment of decision, and then steady progress toward a positive, though not unequivocally happy, outcome.

Now, consider the titles of the individual volumes of *Dance. A Question of Upbringing* clearly connotes starting out in life; *A Buyer's Market* seems to have to do with money, although the resonance in the actual book is as much social as financial. Conversely, *The Acceptance World,* in many ways part of a diptych with its immediate predecessor, seems to refer to social acceptance, although the empirical derivation of the title comes from the financial world.

The reader does not know who precisely is the Lady Molly of *At Lady Molly's*—she is a figure not conveniently predicted by any anterior expectations—and the expectations of conventional "aristocracy" are jettisoned immediately upon reading, but the impression of some sort of social venue or gathering place is conveyed, as indeed happens with the next volume, *Casanova's Chinese Restaurant.* Unlike many of the other titles, the obvious contradiction in terms here conveys a kind of surface resonance to the reader. Even if the reader does not know that *The Kindly Ones* is a euphemism for the Eumenides, the Furies—even, in other words, if it is not sensed that the title is ironic—there is still a suggestion of a break in the action, of being catapulted to a different sphere. This expectation is fulfilled not only by the onset of wartime but also by *The Kindly*

Ones being the only novel of the twelve set in two completely different time periods (1914 and 1939). *The Kindly Ones* is also the first of a pair of titles inspired by religion, the next being *The Valley of Bones*. The first comes from ancient Greek religion, the second from the Old Testament Book of Ezekiel, but the solicitation of a spiritual plane does connote the greater depth and sense of urgency of these "hinge" works in the sequence. *The Soldier's Art* and *The Military Philosophers* are similar not just in their obvious wartime reference but also in the counter-balancing of belligerence and reflection in a kind of happy conjunction, *discordia concors*. Like *The Kindly Ones, Books Do Furnish a Room,* as a title, suggests a pause, a respite, and when the previous war titles are factored in, the reference becomes to a respite from war. The word "temporary" in *Temporary Kings* is all the more fortified by the temporariness being embedded in a sequence of novels. In addition, any writer whose prose style is so steeped in Latinity as is Powell's carries the overtones of "temporality," of time passing. And *Hearing Secret Harmonies* carries a connotation of conclusion, especially harmonious in a sequence that is using music as a structural metaphor. This is again a case in which the precise referent is only graspable upon reading the book—"hearing secret harmonies" refers to death—but the reader on looking at a list of titles does get a sense of how the twelfth and closing novel fits into the overall sequence.

Each of the twelve novels introduces new characters—not just one or two new characters, but a whole set, a set coherent in its relation to the trajectory of the narrator, even if, in literal terms, the characters do not all know one another from the beginning. Indeed, it is the function of each of the twelve novels to introduce new characters and then gradually reintegrate the old ones. That is part of the fun of reading the sequence. It is a process of discovery and rediscovery. In *A Question of Upbringing,* we not only meet the friends who, with the exception of Moreland, will mean the most to Jenkins throughout his life, but also figures such as Quiggin, Members, and Short, who will set his social and professional milieu for the remainder of the series. In *A Buyer's Market,* we meet largely bohemians for the first time (Mr. Deacon, Gypsy Jones, Barnby, Milly Andriadis), but they are counterbalanced to some extent by more stuffed-shirt figures such as Sir Gavin Walpole-Wilson and Tompsitt. We meet older eccentrics such as St. John Clarke, Horace Isbister, and Mrs. Erdleigh in *The Acceptance World,* even though the main narrative thrust of the book does not concern them. In *At Lady Molly's,* new characters, aside from the voluminous Tolland family, are connected with the aristocracy, whether by birth (Chips Lovell) or marriage (Ted Jeavons). Of course, there is the singular figure of General Conyers. In *Casanova's Chinese Restaurant,* we have more bohemians, with the emphasis this time on music, not the visual arts: Moreland, Maclintick, Gossage, and Carolo. In *The Kindly Ones,* most of the new characters—Albert, Bracey, Billson, and Dr. Trelawney—are in the flashback, in the 1914 section; there are very few new characters in the present-day section, as if the onset of war precludes such innovation. *The Valley of Bones,* the volume in which the discovery and rediscovery process is probably the most intense, introduces scores of Welsh soldiers, along with the anomalous figure of Flavia Wisebite, Stringham's sister. In *The Soldier's Art,* we see a whole gallimaufry of personages associated with Divisional Headquarters, including Biggs, Soper, Diplock, Deanery, and Hogbourne-Johnson. The emphasis in *Military Philosophers* is on the foreign military attachés. Most of the characters introduced in the war novels never reappear—probably a reflection of the realistic social principle that, unless one is a career army officer like Jenkins's father, one meets people in wartime whom one does not meet otherwise. The side effect of this is to make the "recurring characters" idea less mechanical than it could have been, similar to Honoré de Balzac's feat of creating a fictional world that appears to be continuous on its own terms, as a heterocosm or "second world," not simply as a patent facsimile of our own world concocted by an author. Balzac is surely the inspiration for Powell, however abhorrent General Liddament might find the principles of his very operation as a character underwritten by the Balzac whose citation by Jenkins as model novelist so unnerves him.

The new characters in *Books* are from the literary world (the alliterative intelligentsia of Shernmaker, Salvidge, and Shuckerley); in *Temporary Kings*, we have figures relating, very unconventionally, to the arts and culture (Glober, Gwinnett, and Tokenhouse), although the dominant focus of the book is more political; and in *Hearing Secret Harmonies*, there are figures related to the occult and the otherworld (the cult leader Scorpio Murtlock, the semiwayward prelate Canon Fenneau, and even the poet-publicist Delavacquerie, who though consummately above board in his public life, is nonetheless spooky) as well as far more modestly sketched figures in the Jenkinses' country life such as Mr. Gauntlett and Ernie Dunch.

Rather than being braided into the narrative from the beginning, these new milieus are deliberately presented, often at the beginning of the individual book. This is both to give background and to mark the book out as occupying a different terrain than its predecessor and therefore bringing its own flavor to the overall sequence. Evelyn Waugh, Powell's contemporary and fellow novelist, presciently discerns that Powell "is not content to manipulate a single already numerous and diverse cast; more and more characters appear in each book, all intricately but tenuously connected with their predecessors."[1] This is a technique most understandable by reference to classical precedent. Herodotus (a source cited by Powell in his deployment of the Gyges and Candaules motif in *Temporary Kings,* and implicitly, by Mr. Deacon in his painting *Boyhood of Cyrus*) at the beginning of different books in his *Histories* digresses to bring in background on particular peoples, interrupting the main flow of the narrative in order to do so. For instance, at the beginning of Book Four of Herodotus, there is an excursus on the Scythians, taking several pages to give background on this and providing three possible different versions of the Scythians' origins, taking only a circumspect position on which one of them is correct.[2] In the previous books, there were similar briefing reports on the Lydians, Egyptians, and Persians. But the Scythian example is particularly notable because Herodotus goes on to say, when going into a particular anecdote about mules being unable to be bred in Elis, "I need not apologize for the digression—it has been my plan throughout this work." This is similar to Powell's technique; Jenkins very deliberately stops the onward narrative to go into pages about how his family came to know General Conyers or Deacon or Trelawney. The discursive passages on Conyers and the Tolland family in *At Lady Molly's,* Moreland's musical milieu in *Casanova's Chinese Restaurant,* and the book reviewers Shernmaker and Salvidge in *Books* are the Powellian equivalent of Herodotus stepping out of the stream of his *histoire* to give a digressive background on the Persian Empire's barbaric northern neighbors. The introduced milieus of Tollands, musicians, and books constitute what Robert Morris calls "a new swatch" in *Dance*'s fictive frame.[3] They give each book its own tone, its own mental landscape.

The chapters within the *Dance* novels are also salient. There are no fewer than three (in *Soldier's Art,* making convenient army-London-army triptych) and no more than seven (in *Hearing Secret Harmonies,* the extra seventh chapter indicates the special status of the last book, in which extra tableaux are needed to close out the presentation). The chapters lend the sequence and underlying shape, a backbeat, a "formal measure" (*Harmonies,* 272). The divisions between individual novels are governed by the particular stretch of time and are of life that they emphasize, the subdivisions are designed to display plot turns. The subdivisions and the individual books are units in the compositional syntax of *Dance,* regulating what is inside them as rhythmically as do the more routine sentences and paragraphs. Each subdivision is comparable to an act in a five-act drama, at least in the amount of plot development contained within it. Yet the subdivisions often conclude anticlimactically, with an anecdote that has nothing to do with the main line of the plot; its effect is ironic and deflating, not satisfying primitive readerly needs for consummation or pathos.

For instance, Dicky Umfraville, at the end of *Books,* chapter 2, mentions to Pamela's stepfather, Harrison Wisebite, his invention of a "refreshing cocktail" (62) appropriate for a man of the American West called "Death Comes for the Archbishop." Similarly, Widmerpool, in *Casanova's Chinese Restaurant,* at the end of chapter 2, commends then-French premier Léon Blum, saying, "A shrewd man, Monsieur Blum" (128). In a wry, gentle way, these anticlimactic endings let the air out of the chapters so their cumulative effect is not too pompous. At other times, though, the endings build to a crescendo. This is true of the endings of *A Buyer's Market* ("careering un-controllably down the slippery avenues of eternity," 274) and *Casanova's Chinese Restaurant* ("A Ghost Railway . . . moving at last with dreadful, ever increasing momentum towards a shape that lay across the line," 229). It is also true, for instance, of the memorable ending to chapter 1 of *The Kindly Ones,* which in its litany of the exactions of the Furies in the First World War is, as Christopher Hitchens and others have noted, one of the most forceful passages of the sequence. Individual books also vary in whether their endings are climactic or anticli-mactic. *A Buyer's Market, Casanova's Chinese Restaurant,* and *Hearing Secret Harmonies,* for instance, end climactically, lyri-cally, eloquently; *At Lady Molly's, Books Do Furnish a Room,* and *The Military Philosophers,* anticlimactically, ironically, in a minor key; *A Question of Upbringing, The Acceptance World, The Kindly Ones,* and *Temporary Kings* end in a measured, equivocal manner ("I crossed Whitehall swiftly. Another burst of vintage cars was advancing towards the bridge"; *Temporary Kings,* 280). *Valley of Bones* and *Soldier's Art* are in classes of their own as they respectively end with a major political event (the fall of France) and a personal tragedy (the loss of Barnby on an air raid), both conveyed in a low-key, almost inconclusive manner. This is probably because they are really the first two installments of a so-called war trilogy that has a greater internal unity. Just as Shakespeare's two *Henry IV* plays are linked to each other beyond their membership in the historical tetralogy, so the very mordant "Except the underclothes" (242) ending of *Military Philosophers* is really the ending for all three books. In other words, sometimes the effect of anecdotal anticlimax that tails off the subdivisions ("A shrewd man, Monsieur Blum") is applied to the end of the entire novel ("Except the underclothes") in a way that perhaps facilitates the integration of a drama in the individual book into the overall sequence but, in the context of an individual novel, is strikingly, refreshingly, understated.

The title of the sequence, *Dance to the Music of Time,* is potentially confusing in that it does not describe what the book is about. There are certainly musicians (Hugh Moreland, Maclintick) and even dancers (Norman Chandler) in the sequence's cast of characters. But these are far outnumbered by visual artists, and there are many more references to the visual arts in the sequence than to either music or dance. The title itself, from a 1638–40 Nicolas Poussin painting at the Wallace Collection in London, comes from the visual arts, and the stylization, classicism, and partially suppressed emotion of the painting provides a closer sense of what the experience of reading the novel is like than any assumptions about music or dance. Is the title simply ornamental or frivolous? One way to answer this question is to speculate that the title does not refer to the sequence's subject or its characters' preoccupations but to its *organization.* Time, especially in its inwardly experienced sense, is certainly part of the subject of the novel. Yet it is also a key to its organization, which encompasses nearly sixty years and several pronouncedly different historical eras, as well as, allusively, stretching back into the deep past. There are clearly questions here about the static versus the dynamic, the spatial versus the temporal, but the key to the sequence's procedures are in how categorical questions are managed by the organizational structure. Just as music can be fast or slow, emotional or cerebral, strain to a crescendo or dwindle into a diminuendo, the narrative of *Dance* sometimes eddies, sometimes escalates. And structural questions having to do with tempo are particularly prominent in the last three books. The pace is varied as the pre-war equilibrium is irretrievably disturbed. The musical element in the sequence, seemingly just a structural premise, becomes activated as the tempo becomes modal and variant.

It is during the second half of the sequence, between *Soldier's Art* and *Military Philosophers,* that Powell produced his two plays, *The Garden God* and *The Rest I'll Whistle.* Though his plays achieved the same genteel lack of success afforded those of Henry James, fortunately minus the public humiliation, it cannot be said that their dramatic principles inspired the later fiction, as is alleged in the case of James. But if the plays are of any relevance in the overall corpus, it is that they might have affected this variation of pace. They probably helped Powell manage the interaction of the sheer volume of characters, incarnate and remembered, on the canvas, or more aptly on stage, in the last three novels, if it is agreed that handling the interaction of three or four characters in drama is equivalent to handling sixty or seventy in prose fiction. The last three novels, separated by longer intervals (ten years each) in their temporal setting, and all containing at least five subdivisions, six in the case of *Temporary Kings,* seven in the case of *Hearing Secret Harmonies,* are less tightly knit. Their expansiveness is not just attributable to the need to recapitulate, but of going, at least in an organizational and technical way, where the other books have not gone —and of revealing more.

The music conceit is not just a superficial adornment but a way of talking about how the narrative itself handles time. Thus it is vital, even though the work, on the surface, refers much more to visual art than to music. Art constitutes the foreground, music the back beat, so what is often seen as a trait of Powell's fiction, reflecting his own particular interest in the visual arts, may, however adventitiously, be a structural feature of much if not all narrative fiction.

Dance is often termed a roman-fleuve, or "river-novel," meaning a novel as long and meandering as a river, one that courses through several volumes and eras of history or consciousness. (Famous examples are Marcel Proust's *À La Recherche du Temps Perdu* or Dorothy Richardson's *Pilgrimage*.) It is as roman-fleuve, and subjective rendering of the consciousness of the narrator, that *Dance* has been most analyzed. It might be said, however, that the concept of the sequence as a block of twelve individually entitled books that function in relationship to one another as a kind of argumentative outline does as much as the idea of roman-fleuve to guarantee the work's unity.

The other French term tossed around with respect to *Dance* is roman à clef. The roman à clef, or "key novel," in which every fictional character has a close real-world equivalent, has never been highly regarded. Even in the seventeenth century, when John Aubrey praised Shakespeare's comedies over those of his own contemporaries as the latter "reflect so much upon particular persons . . . that twenty years hence, they will not be understood," there was a sense that the more specific the references, the more superficial the work.[4] The function of the roman à clef is usually reduced to gossip, coterie intrigue, or necessarily time-bound polemical specificity. Part of the force of Powell's continual insistence that Dance was not a roman à clef was probably to separate his work from vastly inferior instances of that genre. As Edith Wharton, a writer much admired by Powell (*Journals,* 26 April 1990), put it,

All novelists who describe (whether from without or within) what is called "society life," are pursued by the exasperating

accusation of putting flesh-and-blood people in their works.
Any one gifted with the least creative faculty knows the
absurdity of such a charge. "Real people" transported into a
work of the imagination would instantly cease to be real;
only ones born of the creator's brain can give the least illusion of reality. . . . The low order, in fiction, of the genuine
roman à clef (which is never written by a born novelist) naturally makes any serious writer of fiction indignant at being
suspected of such methods.[5]

Thus *Dance* cannot fit securely into this category. How fictional
are the characters in *Dance?* A cursory reading of a paragraph-
long biography or an encyclopedia article on Anthony Powell
reveals substantial similarities between his life and that of
Nicholas Jenkins. Attempts have also been made to identify
"character models" for personages mentioned in Powell's fiction. Indeed, this is often the principal interpretive operation
applied to the book—something very different, say, from criticism of Virginia Woolf, even though most people assume that
her characters, also, are modeled on personages Woolf knew in
her own milieu. Powell bridled at overexplicit identification of
characters with real-life figures. He seemed to feel that, even if
the characters are real in inspiration ("I try never to use a character or incident of which I do not have some personal knowledge"; letter to a Mr. Jenkins, 7 October 1966), the design and
overall purpose in which they are embedded can be exclusively
expressed in imaginative literature. He also felt that characters
particularly memorable in real life are "likely to be unsuitable as
characters in novels" (*Infants,* 14). It would be self-defeating,
however, to pretend that there are not resemblances or echoes
between art and life, and that Nicholas Jenkins is, say, as unlike

Anthony Powell in circumstance as if *Dance* was a historical or science fiction novel. Powell went over his life experience three different times, in novels, memoirs, and journals. This is not so much a testimony to Powell's sense of his life's inherent interest —there have been many lives more outwardly exciting—but to his keen sense that expressing similar material in different genres yields substantially different effects. As a classicist, Powell was well equipped to understand that genre is constitutive to imaginative meaning, and that the genre of fiction requires fictional procedures.

Despite its dependence on reality as source, *Dance* has a self-enclosed air, almost like that of a fantasy novel. In this way, it is similar to the works of Jane Austen, which, notwithstanding their scrupulous social observation, correspondent to the felt reality of their own day, create their own world in the same way that a good fantasy novel does. Signaling this self-enclosure, the world of *Dance* is almost completely immured from Powell's nonsequence novels. The only exception is the reference to Isbister at the end of *Fisher*, when, on the Orkney Islands, the characters encounter the surname of the great portraitist and Royal Academy member, subject of a book published by the firm for which Jenkins worked in *The Acceptance World*. This, at the end of not only the book itself but also Powell's entire fictional oeuvre, is a kind of closure-providing in-joke, a playful capping of the novelist's fictional world. But it is almost as much an acknowledgment of source (Isbister is in fact an Orkney place name, and Powell had found it during his researches into genealogy and local history) as a self-referential gesture. None of the rest of *Fisher* contains a cross-reference to *Dance*, although certainly a novelist like Valentine Beals would have had ample opportunity to meet fellow best-seller producers such as Evadne

Clapham or Ada Leintwardine. And there is no reference to *Dance* in *Wheel*, despite clear opportunity for overlap with characters from the sequence, especially those introduced in the last three books (or for that matter, Shadbold and Winterwade could have easily known Members or Quiggin in the early stages of their literary careers).

Moreover, *Dance* does not employ a single reference to the prewar books, even though there is not only an inevitable similarity of setting but also several characters who, if anything, have too short an appearance on the stage in the earlier books and merit further use. There is no reference to Judkins in the publishing chronicles of *Books*, no reference to Geoffrey Sleaford or Dicky Umfraville hearing the odd tale of a man called Zouch, no rumor in the discussion of Barbara Goring of another beautiful debutante named Susan Nunnery. This is largely true of the relation of *Dance* and the two postsequence novels as well. Powell's reluctance to reintroduce these characters is an ascetic move that heightens the sequence's self-contained feel. Not only is it a fictional world of its own, cordoned off from "reality" as well as the fictional worlds of other novelists, but it is even isolated from the author's other fictions. This self-containment counterbalances what is a thoroughgoing realism in the sequence. For all the accusations of snobbery its cast of characters has prompted, *Dance* is unpretentious. If there is any signal aspect to *Dance*'s relationship to its own material, it is this lack of pretense.

The anatomy of the individual works proceeding below focuses on the themes at play in each of them. The humor of the sequence is a major part of this, but the humor only resonates because of the intricate scaffolding behind it. Sometimes this intricacy seems to involve clairvoyance. The philosopher Arthur

Danto remarks on this when he notes that, in "the roman fleuve of Anthony Powell, the last volume of which narrates events the author could not have known about when he begun his work. . . . Widmerpool meets his death in the last volume through an involvement with figures from the counterculture of the 1960s, and Powell could hardly have known that when he designed the character of Widmerpool. So the novel has a kind of improvisatory quality and with regard to the historical events themselves, the author is more in the position of a chronicler than a narrator, and the writer shares the ignorance of the characters of their own futures."[6] Similarly, when he first interjected Dr. Trelawney into *The Kindly Ones,* published in 1962, Powell could not have known of the resurgence of cults in the late 1960s and early 1970s. Thus the use of Trelawney as character was at its best impressively prophetic, at its least a narrative gamble that worked. The answer to Danto's paradox may be that the roman-fleuve as a genre has a peculiar capability, by its dilating to and fro in time, to if not anticipate the future, then at least not to be constrained by the too-rigid certainty of the present.

The final significant structural feature of *Dance* is the role of the four seasons. The packaging of the books into four separate trilogies, familiar to the American reader, is less so to the British. In Britain, the books were originally published separately and only recently have become available in the tripledecker format. The only explicit use of "Spring," "Summer," "Autumn," and "Winter" as titles for the four sets of three was part of the packaging superintended by Patrick O'Connor for the Popular Library paperback editions of the 1970s.[7] These have not been followed by the 1995 University of Chicago edition, which arranges the trilogies as "First Movement," "Second

Movement," and so on, implying that the overall framework is a sort of symphony while avoiding more melodramatic or allegorical overtones. As it is uncertain whether Poussin intended the seasons to be represented in the painting, the Chicago decision was perhaps prudent, although the seasonal analogy does provide a way of understanding how Jenkins, as narrator, approaches his own experiences. When David Thomas, then the editor of *Punch,* remarked to Powell in 1989 (*Journals,* 29 June 1989) that he was in the "*At Lady Molly* stage" of his life, he was relying on this analogy, with the fourth book as the beginning of "summer." The seasonal frame provides a way for the reader to negotiate, on their own terms, with the sheer mass of data contained within the sequence's confines.

A Question of Upbringing (1951)

A Question of Upbringing starts at school (very obviously based on Eton, but unnamed. (Eton is named explicitly in *Military Philosophers,* when Colonel Chu, the Chinese attaché historically doomed for his support of the Kuomintang in 1949, expresses a wish to go there.) Our narrator, Nicholas Jenkins, is an adolescent, on the verge of adult situations and responsibilities. Three fellow schoolmates loom particularly large to him: the charming Charles Stringham, the bluff Peter Templer, and the indescribably monstrous Kenneth Widmerpool. The first major narrative incident occurs when Le Bas, the housemaster of Jenkins and his school friends, is, through a prank of Stringham's, arrested as the criminal "Braddock alias Thorne."

The first section of *A Question of Upbringing* shows the sequence's beginning in narrative time (with the flashback to school days) and in subjective time (youth, "starting out" in life).

But there is a key element in the first section that also shows us how the sequence begins in literary-historical time: the scene in which the three boys (Jenkins, Stringham, and Templer) come upon Le Bas, lounging and reading poetry, and shortly afterward decide to stage the "Braddock alias Thorne" prank. The incident is the first piece of drama in *Dance,* and as such is very significant. But so is its prelude. Le Bas recites some lines of verse and asks the boys to guess the author. The answers given do much to reveal the characters of the young men. Templer's answer, Shakespeare, indicates his heedless yet amiable abstention from high culture. Stringham's interjection of Oscar Wilde shows his rebelliousness and his disinclination to lead the conventional life expected of him. Jenkins's reluctance to venture a guess shows his strategic reserve. Widmerpool's absence from the scene indicates his complete unwillingness to even consider aesthetic questions, a constant through all twelve volumes, as Widmerpool, able to change his social and political views at the drop of a hat, remains throughout resolutely opposed to the arts. (Would a Widmerpool of the early twenty-first century be quite the same in this regard?)

The various poems provided—including those by Matthew Arnold, Andrew Lang, and, controversially, Oscar Wilde—tap into a rich vein of *Dance*'s humor provided by changes in artistic taste, by literary and artistic works that become humorous once they seem dated or old-hat or seem to be about a certain aspect of human character rather than a general artistic truth. Le Bas, in narrow terms, knows the answer to his own question; yet he is unaware of the time-bound nature of his entire set of assumptions. The poem he quotes is "Ballade to Theocritus in Winter" by the astonishing Victorian polymath Andrew Lang, a much underrated figure. This poem is not about the third-century B.C. Sicilio-Alexandrian pastoral poet as much as it is an address to him. Lang, who also wrote a volume called *Letters to Dead Authors,* longs for the rural innocence conjured, if not experienced, by Theocritus, but the postlapsarian nature of the modern world intervenes. Theocritus represents an ideal of quietude, if not quiescence, for which both Lang and Le Bas yearn. There is some hint that Le Bas may be more sentimental about this ideal than Lang himself. But both are confined within the conventions of Victorian nostalgia, and Le Bas does not have an adequate grasp of the proportions of this nostalgia.[8] When Stringham guesses Arnold, Le Bas thinks it a good guess and says, "There are descriptive verses by Arnold somewhat similar in metre that may have run in your head, Stringham. Things like:

> The clouds are on the Oberland
> The Jungfrau's snows look faint and far;
> But bright are these green fields at hand
> And through those fields comes down the Aar.

"Rather a different geographical situation, it is true," continues Le Bas, "but the same mood of invoking melancholy by graphic description of natural features of the landscape." This, to me, is one of the most hilariously funny moments in the first volume. It is a humor perilous to anatomize as it is so pitch-perfect as to resist inspection, but one will try. The homophone between "Aar" and the plural form of the verb "to be" makes the Swiss riparian name sound silly, more a pun than a real place. The melancholy and pessimism of the mountainous snow is given a kind of Victorian, buck-up-your spirits boost by the minimally scenic invocation of river and fields, providing a stoic

consolation that counters the morbidity that Arnold feared. In
Le Bas's performance of the poem, both the melancholy and the
heartiness are mannered, and the incongruity of this is quite
funny. And, of course, "rather a different geographical situation" is an understatement. It is not just that Switzerland is
colder than Sicily, but that is Teutonic, at a time when any
romance of the "cousinly Teutonic" is long gone in England due
to the First World War (whose resonance is audible through this
volume even if its most direct treatment in *Dance* is in the opening chapter of *The Kindly Ones*). Instead of distant classical
lucidity, we have Teutonic clunkiness. Le Bas, in fact, despite his
English nationality and French name, is described as "curiously
Teutonic" (26). The near-complete lack of drama in the quoted
stanza is highlighted even more when we look at the original
poem, "The Terrace at Berne" and see that it is a love poem to
the famous Marguerite, and the Swiss topographical stanza is
atypical and surrounded by mournful amatory incantations to
which Le Bas is totally deaf.

Now Stringham, the bad boy of the scene, comes into play.
He suggests a villanelle ("triolet" in the 1951 Heinemann edition) by Oscar Wilde as a comparison, very reasonably, as it is
called "Theocritus" and also evokes ancient Sicilian memories:

> O singer of Persephone!
> In the dim meadows desolate
> Dost thou remember Sicily?
> Still through the ivy flits the bee
> Where Amaryllis lies in state;
> O Singer of Persephone!
> Simaetha calls on Hecate
> And hears the wild dogs at the gate;
> Dost thou remember Sicily?

A line that is not quoted, "And still in boyish rivalry," could potentially, in the spirit of Powell's jottings in *A Writer's Notebook*, be the title of a novel of adolescence, though not this one. In any event, Le Bas reacts very defensively, saying that Wilde, whom he only reluctantly acknowledges as the poem's author, is "not a very distinguished versifier" (41). Obviously, Le Bas's grievance against Wilde is not due to his distinction, or lack thereof, as a versifier but for his homosexual notoriety, particularly an issue, of course, for a housemaster in a boys' school of that era. The Wilde embarrassment is smoothed over by the mention of the thematically cognate "Heraclitus" by William Johnson Cory, who spent much of his career associated with Eton in some context, Stringham thus manipulating Le Bas back to cultural terra firma (albeit by the verse of someone he sees as far less modern than himself). It is Stringham, the most ostensibly aristocratic of the three boys, who presents the challenge; for all his naughtiness, he knows how to maneuver out of a parlous situation just before a crisis. The supreme irony is that presumably in 1951, when the book was published, and verifiably fifty years later, the Wilde poem is reasonably well known, but the Lang is utterly obscure. The Arnold, too, will not bring instant recognition, even on the part of a well-schooled reader of Victorian poetry.

One of the points here is that the older generation is out of touch, a major theme in Powell's prewar novels and the first few volumes of *Dance,* and one perhaps generally undertreated in the extant Powell criticism. The blitheness of the Aar reference, in particular, shows that Le Bas has not understood the impact of the First World War, which the boys inferentially have, although they are much too young to have been involved in it. Le Bas's carapace of Victorian classicism is all too eminent, despite his own attempts to break through it. Along with Uncle Giles's earlier appearance, Le Bas's self-presentation epitomizes the preposterousness of adulthood. This preposterousness is dramatically teased out by the Braddock-alias-Thorne arrest, an event that, since it is the first dramatic occurrence in the sequence, has resonances well above its immediate impact. (This perhaps is testified to by the fact that Powell's son, Tristram, when he himself was at Eton in 1958, made a short film, *Manhunt,* dealing with the Braddock episode; until the 1997 television version, this was the only part of *Dance* that had ever been adapted for visual media.) But the limits of Le Bas's adulthood and the ambiguous potential of the boys' youth are already manifest in the poetry-quotation scene. The three boys may wish to become adults, as is shown by their excitement at Templer's sexual adventures in London, but they do not want to become *these* adults.

The poetry scene shows us something not only about the book's characters but also about its narrative stance. We are used to first-person narratives, especially those starting in adolescence, being essentially about the narrator's personal development and starring the narrator in a featured role. During the poetry scene, we begin to see that this will not be the case. The fact that it is *Stringham* who ventures the closest guess of the poem's author is telling, as really, Jenkins should have made this guess. After all, Jenkins will become a writer, and Le Bas notes when he briefly reappears at the end of the volume that Jenkins was "keen on English" (224). Based on textual evidence alone, however, he would have to had learned this through osmosis. Jenkins does not make any literary observations within Le Bas's earshot. In the volume's fictional world, either Jenkins has been reticent in literal terms or, perhaps, is deliberately underrepresenting his role in the incident as recollected. Traits that could be those of the narrator are spliced off and given to Stringham. In this way, Stringham becomes the fraternal twin of the narrator, his complementary adjutant. We know that this narrative will not be one of self-aggrandizement or at least one that, in conventional autobiographical terms, stresses the self.

The poem-guessing episode also plays more than a setup role in relation to the Braddock-alias-Thorne episode. In both, Stringham not only mocks Le Bas but also openly challenges his authority. Here the narrator is not totally on Stringham's side. Although he passively watches the plotting of the Braddock hoax, and makes no attempt to stop it, he does not take part in it himself. There is a palpable sense that Stringham has gone too far, has been too rebellious. And this overrebelliousness heralds both Stringham's troubled relationship with his mother and stepfather and the increasing irresponsibility he will show in his university career and adult life. But it is Widmerpool, monstrous where Stringham is merely flawed, whom the Theocritus episode helps us understand the most, even though he is absent for its duration. The three boys, in guessing at the poems, are willing to create some distance between themselves and their housemaster. Their lack of automatic deference is, in proportion, an asset, as it allows them have some sense of individual integrity.

Widmerpool is shocked to hear Le Bas has been arrested, not so much because of any personal regard for the man but because his entire schoolboy identity has been built on an unquestioning deference to authority, a trait that later will be transmuted into a craven acquiescence to whatever he perceives to be the prevailing power of the day. Widmerpool is determined to be in step with whatever authority prevails at any given time, whether with respect to the Captain of Games or to the more sinister, in all senses of the word, authorities with whom he traffics in future volumes. He aspires to be a man of his age but can only read that age's symptoms, not anything deeper. Despite the excess of Stringham's prank, his playfulness is to be preferred to Widmerpool's ambition. Yet Widmerpool and Le Bas's poems are linked by the way they can attain a certain "spirit of the age" and nothing more. In a way, each book is divided into its Widmerpool action and its rereading action. This is because Widmerpool is so memorable a character (many people have heard of Widmerpool without even knowing what books he comes from) that he tends to dominate the first reading of the sequence. Where will Widmerpool turn up next? What outrageous fad will he be following? What will he do and in whose people's lives will he meddle? Having come out of the mist, having oozed and scraped his way through adolescence, where will he go next? The first-time reader, preoccupied with these questions, tends to ignore the weighted literary allusions or the significant minor characters. As with the Theocritus passage, they will have to wait for a second reading.

Widmerpool's school career—his masochistic lack of complaint at having Budd smear a banana on him, his shock at the arrest of Le Bas, his turning in of Akworth on grounds of moral turpitude, and even his wearing the wrong overcoat—defines him for the reader, and, in a sense, defines Widmerpool for himself. All his later triumphs over his schoolmates are designed as revenge for his being seen as a figure to be mocked and abused. At the 2001 Anthony Powell conference, James Tucker wondered whether Eton, or its fictional calque, made Widmerpool by mocking and excluding him. Is what Tucker calls "the judgments and protocols and taste of the top public school" simply ratified, uncritically, by Widmerpool's villainy in *Dance*?[9] One could riposte, in the words of an Etonian of the eighteenth century, the poet Thomas Gray, that the unjust obscurity in which the rural poor lived did not disbar just the deserving but unrecognized but also the evil but uncredentialed: "nor circumscrib'd alone / Their growing virtues, but their crimes confin'd." Widmerpool's upper-class education is an opportunity for him, helping give him a stage on which to parade his self-aggrandizement. But he would have been the same person without it. Tucker's observation is part of a more general objection to *Dance* as a whole—that it is unfair to Widmerpool, that the decks are stacked against him. Quiggin, who makes a deliberate fetish of his (exaggerated) unpromising origins, is made fun of by the sequence, but in a benign way, and he is, when the chips are down, a good person. Widmerpool is not; he is a maleficent schemer, and that, not his class origins, are what is wrong with him. Widmerpool himself, as he expounds to Jenkins at La Grenadière, is fully aware of the advantages given him by his education and is only too eager to scrape acquaintance with the imagined elite, the "right people" (135). In many ways, one might ask what Widmerpool would do without his humiliation as a teenager. It seems to drive his ambitions well beyond his later revenge against his tormentors.

The overeagerness, in fact, the preternatural ambition of Widmerpool (and, failing that, the raffishness of Uncle Giles) will draw most of the attention of readers new to this first chapter of *A Question of Upbringing*. Few of them will concentrate on the Theocritus scene. But the salience and, in particular, the humor of this scene emerge strongly upon rereading. The reader going through the first time is spurred by curiosity about who these boys are, what will happen, what the book is going to be like—and does not really notice the poems themselves. A first reading will usually miss the literary in-jokes. Most good reading is in fact rereading, as Powell's many rereadings described in the *Journals* indicate. It is only on a second, more leisurely ramble through the book's pages that we notice the humorous and serious implications of the poems themselves. The critic Matei Calinescu refers to the process of rereading as "to-and-fro, back and forth, broadly circular."[10] If reading impels the forward march through time, what the American classicist Steve Nimis writing about the *Iliad* calls a mode of "forward propulsion," rereading suggests a more latent sense of time's rhythms, not necessarily circular or even nonlinear, but certainly not straight-forward.[11] If a reader sets out to reassay the entire sequence, it is perhaps during the Theocritus scene that this reader will fully realize that what on the first run-through was seen as narrative complication in fact possesses richer and more reflective strands. This realization will guide the entire rereading of *Dance,* a work that, at least for its admirers, can be read a myriad of times without any diminution of pleasure.

Powell is not only telling us something about Jenkins, Stringham, Templer, and, in absentia, Widmerpool through the poem quotations, but helping frame the way the knowing reader, the rereader, responds to his work. The poems work in tandem with the action of the first section in telling us a lot about the character of Le Bas and thus setting up the preposter-ousness and incongruity of his being confused with a wanted criminal. Le Bas is both a classicist and a romantic, or more aptly, he is romantic about classicism. He thinks he has seen through earlier renditions of sentimental classicism, that he is more "modern" than his predecessors. He supposes he is half mocking Lang's poem, when to the boys, its self-consoling

purpose is more obvious. But to the younger generation, especially Jenkins the retrospective narrator, Le Bas's literary and
cultural assumptions seem both outdated and impracticably
protective of an old order, a Hellenic paradise upon which the
realities of modern life will not infringe. Even though Jenkins
and the other boys have not known very much of life so far,
their future will be different and will occur outside the realms of
Le Bas's "Theocritus."

In a way, both Jenkins's and Le Bas's stance are classicist,
romantic, and modern all at once; but they are so in different
proportions, and proportion is the key here. At the end of the
first section, before virtually anything has happened in the
sequence, Jenkins's narrative has situated the reader in time and
context as well as giving them a foretaste of the complexity—
and hilarity—in the action to come. And Le Bas's poems being
connected with the Greek language's leading pastoral poet renders moot any simple nostalgia, any merely Arcadian picture of
school days, perhaps expected at the beginning of a long first-
person narrative, even one written by an author whose nostal-
gias for the past were "by no means automatic" (*Infants,* 43).
The picture of school days is Arcadian enough, but it is not particularly the retrospective stance that provides this atmosphere.
The narrator is only minimally nostalgic as Le Bas's pastoral
projections have preempted this within the story. Without the
advantage of the printed page, the television adaptation makes
a similar point. When the boys are in the school chapel following the Braddock-alias-Thorne incident and Le Bas's arrest, a
lesson is read from 1 Kings, chapter 1 that deals with the old age
and death of King David and his succession, after some intrigue,
by Solomon. The message here regards generational succession
—the young boys on the rise with new assumptions and values.

Thus Le Bas's poems are clues not just the to the characters in the book we are reading but also to the nature of the book—or sequence of books—we are reading. *Dance* is a classic in ways that the poem samples by Lang, Arnold, and even Wilde are not. What makes *Dance* not a reliquary of time when these other works have been consigned to that status? Yes, the poems are not their authors' best, but that is almost beside the point. One answer might be to say *Dance* is open to rereading in a way that the other works are not; indeed, the poems are, subjectively, more interesting when embedded in *Dance* than on their own. These "classical projections" (*Question of Upbringing*, 2) bring us close to that other word, "classicist"—what Le Bas is like it or not, in the judgment of Jenkins, and an adjective frequently used of Anthony Powell. But how is Powell a classicist? The twelve books of *Dance* clearly echo the twelve of Vergil and twenty-four of Homer. The memory that impels the story is prompted by "classical associations" (*Question of Upbringing*, 2). Powell's style is Latinate, though Latinate in a ruminative and eccentric way, not in the sense of Ciceronian balance. Yet Powell is not a classicist in the sense of using classical forms or striving for classical diction in the manner of Victorian classicists such as Lang, Arnold, and A. E. Housman. (Wilde uses a comparatively modern—or at least late medieval—French form, the villanelle. Whether the triolet/villanelle confusion in the 1951 edition was Le Bas's, Jenkins's, or Powell's, both forms are similar not only in shape but also in their postclassical emergence; thus even as a literal "mistake" is made, a larger point is reconfirmed.)

Powell is not, at least strictly speaking, an acolyte of Theocritus or any other ancient writer, pastoral or no. (See *Journals*, 11 April 1990, for his unenthusiastic response to the actual poetry of Theocritus—translated by Andrew Lang.) He is less a classicist in the "passing on the classical tradition" sense, the Le Bas sense, as in the "taking no one thing too seriously, as the ancients did" sense. This sort of classicism both values tradition —without doubt, that of the ancient world—and takes heed of its own time, but it does not throw such a disproportionate weight behind its engagement with either of these that it does not have sufficient "lift" to be appreciated by the future. Like Le Bas, the narrator of *Dance* often makes classical references and parallels; however, these are leavened by citations of the art and manners of the narrator's own generation and a wide and truly comprehensive range of references to what we might term "European *civilization*," a European civilization not unpunctuated by mentions of most other parts of the world and one not limited by a polemical position in any "quarrel of the ancients and moderns." Like Le Bas, the narrator is aware of the dangers of not confronting experience and seeking refuge in a golden past. Unlike him, the narrator manages to interact with the outside world in a meaningful way. In addition, the narrative possesses self-awareness, and the narrator does not shrink from self-scrutiny; he turns his analytical rigor on himself and his own assumptions in a way that Le Bas never can. This may be what gives *Dance* its air of freshness, of counterpoint, of liveliness—qualities that Le Bas's poems for the most part lack. This may be why *Dance* yields so fruitfully to rereading. The aforementioned second, "non-Widmerpool" reading is a "Theocritus" reading, more interested in the jokes, references, and minor characters. This does not simply separate the "art" strand of the book from the "power" strand. For instance, in the tenth book, the doomed novelist X. Trapnel is, by dint of his affair with Widmerpool's wife, more part of the Widmerpool level, whereas less flamboyant representatives of the imaginative world, such as Lord Huntercombe, Dr. Brightman, and Le Bas himself, are at the hub of the Theocritus level.

Powell values aestheticism, but he does not idealize it. Thus, to get back to the Theocritus scene, he can have his fun with the poems without completely ridiculing or disavowing them. And here Le Bas's second appearance in *A Question of Upbringing* becomes consequential. This operates, provisionally, as a form of narrative closure, and achieving narrative closure is especially pertinent in the first volume of a long sequence, in which most of the characters and situations have been brought on to foreshadow future action. Le Bas's reappearance gives the reader a sense of just having finished a self-contained volume, not a mere antechamber to future chronicles (on this point, see also *Writer's Notebook,* 86). Le Bas had earlier seemed preposterous to the narrator; now he seems to represent almost a sort of innocence. For instance, Le Bas does not even have a glimmer of an idea that Widmerpool's worldly ambitions are in any way feasible, whereas Jenkins has, in his stay at La Grenadière, sensed some of the future reality of what might seem ludicrous aspirations.

Le Bas says he hopes Widmerpool will find his level in life, as if there will be many levels above his, while Jenkins already has some sense that, as far as possible, Widmerpool wants to take over the world. Yet some of Le Bas's innocence is commendable—the fact, for instance, that he has not heard of Donners-Brebner is admirable in contrast to the more Machiavellian Sillery, the university counterpart to Le Bas at school, for whom Donners-Brebner is as crucial a part of his world as any classical text. In this way, Le Bas's poems (and the Cory poem is once again referred to at book's end) represent a kind of respite, and their outdatedness and provinciality should not be rejected out of hand. In the manner of Le Bas's parting admonition to Jenkins, "It takes all sorts to make a world" (*Question of Upbringing*, 224), it takes all sorts of books to make a reader, and this is no doubt why the actual texts of the poems, as opposed to the notional literary-historical idea of them, are included—because Powell wants us to read them, to mock them to an extent, but also to read them.

For a book to be relevant for all time does not mean it has to disarticulate itself from the ephemerae of its context—and the literary past valued in different times and ways by that context. Powell's classicism is not just a reverence for a series of irreproachable monuments.[12] If "books do furnish a room," then, as in any room worth living in, the furniture must be to scale, must look like it belongs in a room, not a museum. And in this way, Le Bas's affection for second-rate Victorian classicism is not entirely misplaced. In *Dance* we have a classicism that does not repress mirth or, for that matter, melancholy in Arnoldian stoicism, but delights in humor and the idiosyncrasies it reveals. In between the writers who in his *Journals* Powell refers to as "the big shots" (19 April 1992), there is room for the minor, the quirky, the offbeat, the sidelined and outdated. There is romantic quirkiness here, though channeled within the boundaries of classical restraint. And there is even room for Le Bas himself, despite all the measured ridicule directed his way. What the Widmerpools of the world use as symptoms, the narrative of *Dance* preserves as oddities. It takes them less seriously than the consensus at first but remembers them keenly afterward—and proportionately values them. In terms of literary taste as well as personal development, it does, Powell implies, indeed all come down to "a question of upbringing."

The persistent European undercurrent in the pleasingly ineffable Englishness in *Dance* is given winsome rendition in the La Grenadière section of *A Question of Upbringing,* the fourth major venue we have seen in this first installment of *Dance.* In between, Jenkins has visited the homes of both Stringham and Templer and found things other than one would might have expected. Stringham's home, dominated by the rival, if differently benevolent, monitors of his stepfather, the urbane Commander "Buster" Foxe, and his mother's a secretary, the compassionate if indomitable Miss "Tuffy" Weedon, is somehow more sad than Jenkins seems to have anticipated. As so often in *Dance,* aestheticism is a close cousin to melancholy. Jenkins has found more in Templer's household, not because of Templer himself but out of those he encounters there. He seems to have a greater affinity with Stringham; for instance, when Stringham leaves school, Jenkins worries that his departure will "alter the orientation of everyday life" (63). Indeed, he wonders how he and Templer will get along without the bridge of Stringham, which previously had linked them. Yet he finds himself "settling down with Templer" (67). In fact, to our surprise, it is Templer's world of business and sex, not Stringham's milieu of bittersweet aristocracy (even though "Templer" as a name, with its overtones of "Knights Templar," sounds more aristocratic), that brings Jenkins genuinely new possibilities. It is from the Templer household that Jenkins finds people who will recur in his life (Jean, Stripling, Farebrother); the only equivalent from the Stringham world would be Miss Weedon, who is at a further remove from Jenkins. Lady Gwen McReith, who is a fairly openly flaunted lesbian interest of Templer's sister, Babs, gives Jenkins a brief sexual thrill on the dance floor, which primes him for the appeal of Peter's younger sister, the surly but viscerally attractive Jean. On a separate level, the rivalry between Babs's husband, the auto racer Jimmy Stripling, and the positively portrayed businessman "Sunny" Farebrother—Powell makes the reader feel that they would like to meet this man for lunch this very day—a man with a valiant war record who is an associate of Templer's father (a relationship that the sequence reveals is not nearly as happy at first appears), give Jenkins a glimpse of both the stable and eccentric side of adult life. But it is Jean who makes the biggest impression on Jenkins, and he continues to think of her as he goes to France. The account of the uncomfortable rail journey to France, with Jenkins's direct statement of his continued concentration of Jean ("most of all I thought of her while the train traveled across France to Touraine" [*A Question of Upbringing,* 106]), has a directness that stands with the best sentences of Hemingway.

The La Grenadière section is perhaps the most freestanding section of *Dance;* because most of its characters never appear anywhere else, it is almost like a short story and is the segment of *Dance* most feasible for inclusion in the *Norton Anthology of English Literature,* which event would indeed be a sign of the apocalypse. What we first notice is the theme of doubling, of duos. There are Suzette and Berthe Leroy, as young girls (and Suzette and Madame Dubuisson as people toward whom Jenkins manifests erotic interest), Rosalie and Marthe, both servants, Paul-Marie and Jean-Népomucène (why a French boy is named after a Czech saint we do not know; it is not an uncommon name in Catholic countries, but it is probably a Venusbergian in-joke of Powell's, and the need to write the accents correctly is funny). Other duos are the Scandinavians Örn and Lundquist, even the dogs, Charley and Bum. There is some humor here, in the enumeration of every aspect of a newly encountered household; but there is also a subtle indicator that we should look carefully at the mega-duo, as it were, of Jenkins and Widmerpool.

It is at La Grenadière that Widmerpool first turns up unexpectedly, as a fellow French-language student ("We must talk in *French*, Jenkins," which occasioned the unuttered riposte, "Oui, Widmerpool"). We first grasp Widmerpool is to be a recurring character in France; perhaps aptly, as the French novelists Balzac and Proust surely were Powell's key precedents in constructing the recurring-characters aspect of *Dance*. Widmerpool's recurrences serve several functions. He knits together disparate aspects of experience, gives them a common totality other than that they happened to Nicholas Jenkins. Everybody's experience, especially in the twentieth century and after, is so inherently ramified that a picaresque this-happened-to-me ramble will no longer suffice. Widmerpool always being there, like a choric undertone, makes the world of *Dance,* which for all the accusations of its restrictedness is astonishingly diverse, far less random. There also is a psychological aspect, as Jenkins realizes Widmerpool's inescapability. Widmerpool will always be with him, as a kind of double: ambitious where Jenkins is reticent, socially maladept in contrast to Jenkins's courtesy. But Jenkins also learns at La Grenadière that Widmerpool's social skills, or at least social potency, should not be underestimated. The spat between the two tennis-playing Scandinavians, Monsieur Örn and Monsieur Lundquist, also there to learn French, has to be understood in light of Norway, like the more imperilled Lithuania, being, in the 1922 of *A Question of Upbringing,* a "new country," independent from Sweden only in 1905, the year of Powell's own birth (Norway's late king, Olav V, who reigned from 1957 to 1991, was a Balliol colleague of Powell, as seen at

Infants, 123). The contest between Örn and Lundquist is not just fraternal but what we would today call postcolonial. And Widmerpool realizes this. He is playing the role of diplomatic mediator, not just household smoother-over, and the high he gets from his successful resolution of the dispute is one of power politics. Widmerpool, in fact, outdoes Monsieur Dubuisson, who had amused the reader earlier by saying he wrote in three areas: empirical accounts of current events, more sweeping overviews about same, and reflections on "the growth of the social idea in English literature" (125). (This is dramatic literary-historical irony, in that we know the social idea in English literature has no place to go but down from 1922. As with the Theocritus incident, an attention to what Hugh Massingberd has called "phases in art and taste" is crucial for fully realizing how funny this line is.)[13] Monsieur Dubuisson is indeed, despite his Widmerpudlian social views, a Theocritus character, in the sense of one best appreciated on rereading and of belonging to the aesthetic side of the novel. In his reconsideration of *Dance* in the *Journals,* Powell mentions that Monsieur Dubuisson was "intended to play some role in Second War Free-French Affairs" (10 January 1989). This not only indicates that Dubuisson was originally intended to reappear, but that he would reappear on the right side, morally and politically. Even though overbearing and caught up in himself, Dubuisson is friend, not foe. This accords with the benign feelings we are made to have about the vast majority of the denizens, permanent and temporary, of La Grenadière. The pastoral element is stronger here than at school, where it might be more expected.

Furthermore, the sketchily described Suzette Leroy comes across as the most objectively attractive of all of Jenkins's early girlfriends. After having been foiled by Widmerpool in the summerhouse in an especially poignant scene, Jenkins gets up his nerve to make a romantic gesture to her at the end of his stay (prompting the Powellian speculation that perhaps this sort of thing might be easier rather than harder in a foreign language) only to find, after successfully making his declaration of love, that he had spoken it not to Suzette but to Madame Dubuisson. This incredibly farcical scene has a strange pitch because Powell's tone is so low key; it is as if you were playing the loudest piece of music available but turning the volume knob down to near zero. It does not, therefore, dominate the scene as it otherwise might. In fact, it is doubled, as with the pairs of Charley and Bum, Paul-Marie and Jean-Népomucène, Widmerpool and Jenkins, with the mystery of who drew the crude drawing of Widmerpool in the bathroom. In both episodes, we are not sure who did what to whom, or what the intention was; we assume one of the young boys drew the picture, we assume that Jenkins's address of Madame Dubuisson was a mistake, not a Freudian slip, but we do not know for sure. There is even a very faint, and probably untrue, suggestion that Suzette herself drew the picture, somehow setting off a chain reaction that makes Jenkins flub his lines, but there is the danger here of overreading. Jenkins's unintentional overture to Madame Dubuisson is an indication that intentions do not always achieve consequences. Jenkins looks silly, but he has also gained insight into the inevitable silliness of human behavior, the way the most noble thought may become preposterous. These are lessons different from those Le Bas has attempted to teach him about classicism and poetry, but their result—the amused, reserved acceptance of what happens—is similar.[14]

The last chapter of the book transpires at Jenkins's university. There is nothing to rival the drama of the Braddock-alias-Thorne controversy; the machination of Sillery are fascinating, though, and prepare the way for what later volumes will regard as the power, if not the acceptance, world. The most interesting new characters are the strangely linked literary figures, one bel-letristic, one aggressively political—Mark Members and J. G. Quiggin. That Members is early singled out for promise by the then-septuagenarian Edmund Gosse makes a point similar to the plagiarism of Captain Pimley's work in *Waring,* that what is hailed as new in fact meets the dictates of an aging establish-ment.[15] Quiggin's pouting exegesis of the phrase "Public School Verse" (the magazine in which Members publishes the promis-ing poem "Iron Aspidistra") brings to mind one of the ways in which the 1997 television adaptation helped establish a social situation needing to be explained to the viewer. When Quiggin is making his uneasy visit to Sillery, Thomas Hardy's *Jude the Obscure* is mentioned. This book, which most educated readers will know deals with the attempts of a working-class young man to enter Oxford, illuminates Quiggin's sense of being an outsider to the elite world in which he now finds himself, or at least his self-dramatization as an outsider. This interesting technique, of importing learned references not in the original novels to bring across points made at length and discursively on the printed page, may at first seem odd considering how many allusions in the novels the filmmakers obviously had to prune. But in both these instances, it works very well, helping the intelligent but non-Powellian viewer understand what is going on.

Quiggin's affected working-class resentment and his weird enmeshment with Members contribute to the many comic amusements in the university chapter, such as the disastrous car ride with Templer's unsightly friend Jimmy Brent, there mainly to set up Brent's future role in Jenkins's love life and take second place to Stringham leaving university for Donners-Brebner. Sim-ply put, this is a betrayal of art for commerce, though Powell, unlike a nineteenth-century writer, will never hit the reader over the head with it or even overtly point it out.

As unhappy as Stringham was at university—whether he found the social life too stifling, or was unable to adapt his somewhat dilettantish intelligence to academic protocols, or found his radically individual charm too unassimiable to the conformist mediocrity to be found even in the very best academic institutions, we do not know—he made a mistake by leaving it. Stringham is never the same afterward, and only during their accidental rendezvous in wartime does his friendship with Jenkins totally recover. By going to Donners-Brebner, Stringham resigns the aesthetic pride of place he had during the Theocritus episode. It is only after Stringham's defection that Le Bas recalls that Jenkins was good at English, whereas before, Jenkins's literary interests were far in the background to Stringham's aesthetic brio. Stringham is supposed to represent an independent-minded unconventionality, an alternative to the apple-polishing, ladder-climbing Widmerpool. But then he ends up working for Donners-Brebner, the epitome of corporate conformity in *Dance*, a firm satirized with unremitting scorn. Ironically, Stringham's would-be protectors, Miss Weedon and Mrs. Foxe, and his academic counselor, Sillery, lead him down the wayward path of corporate mediocrity. Buster, Stringham's *soi-disant* tormentor and designated bane, rigidly and reflexively but nonetheless rightly takes the other position, that he should stay.

The book ends with Jenkins reencountering Le Bas, Stringham, and Uncle Giles, both to round things out and to let us know that, in the course of one book, the status of Widmerpool and Stringham has changed. Le Bas has underestimated Widmerpool, as has Jenkins. As the Theocritus incident signifies, Le

Bas is behind the times; this insulates him from bad things as well as good, as, for instance, he has "evidently never heard of Donners-Brebner" (222). He still does not understand that Widmerpool will surpass many of the boys who had mocked him at school; when he says, "I hope he will find his level of life" (223), he does not see Widmerpool as, for instance, ever being elected to Parliament or becoming a member of the House of Lords. Interestingly, what time does seem to have given Le Bas is greater recognition of Jenkins's abilities. It is here that he recognizes Jenkins is good at English, though it was Stringham who had, on camera (also seen in Jenkins's memory of the de Tabley quote at *Military Philosophers,* 62–63), as it were, displayed that ability. This combines with Stringham standing Jenkins up for dinner a few pages later, and Stringham's defection from the realm of art and learning to the mundane environment of Donners-Brebner to cast a medium-dark cloud over Stringham's aura of charm. In the short scope of two hundred–odd pages, the characters in *A Question of Upbringing* have entered into adulthood—a world not only drastically different from former generations but one that changes them from the people they formerly were.

A Buyer's Market (1953)

The meticulous compendium to *Dance* as provided by Hilary Spurling proves more valuable than many more abstract commentaries in isolating the salient feature of *Dance*'s second book: a good portion of it is set in the course of one evening in 1928–29.[16] This has implications for the narrative, but the most obvious connection to be extrapolated from this fact is the way it so clearly alludes to Joyce's *Ulysses* (1922), both as literary influence and as object of narrative reference. Powell's one night in London is, arguably, even more phantasmagoric, if less technically innovative, than Joyce's one day in Dublin. It is inconceivable without the Joycean precedent, and is also an act of deliberate homage to Joyce. Powell tacitly defines the modernism of *Dance* in *A Buyer's Market;* if *A Question of Upbringing* was taken up with last-ditch romantic attempts (posing as classicism) to stop modernity, *A Buyer's Market* plunges straight into the marrow of not only modernity but also that far more specialized arena, modernism. In a key passage in chapter 3, Jenkins reflects on Barnby's paintings possessing "a rather deceptive air of emancipation that seemed in those years a kind of neo-classicism, suggesting essentially that same impact brought home to me by Paris in the days when we had met Mr. Deacon in the Louvre: an atmosphere I can still think of as excitingly peculiar to that time" (174). There are affinities here with cubism in France and the Neue Sachlichkeit (new objectivity) in contemporaneous German painting. What these tendencies had in common was a renewed sense of objectivism and an interest in classical forms—the idea being that modern abstraction, in its starkness and interest in fundamental lineaments of form, has a kind of classical poise to it even far removed from the kind of realistic classical scenes practiced by Deacon. Barnby's is a kind of art that has the novelty of being free from any kind of normative realist canon but at the same time is not merely frivolous in its use of modern techniques, anchoring them to a deeper aesthetic mission.[17] This passage indicates the substantial degree to which Powell sees his own vision as coming out of modernism. As the passage indicates, he did not see modernism as a priori emancipative, as socially or sexually liberating (of the so-called major modernists, only Lawrence would have had anything to do with this vision; Eliot, Woolf, and Joyce cannot be so simply defined). Powell, though Jenkins's description of Barnby's painting, sketches a vision of modernism as ironic, cerebral, resisting excessive emotion. Barnby's painting, in this way, is at once more abstract and more classical than Deacon's symbolism, even if the latter refers often to classical subjects such as the emperors Cyrus and Diocletian. This aesthetic crosses media: the music of Moreland and the art of Barnby are indeed its chief exemplars, given that, aside from his narration of the sequence, little idea is given of the writing of Jenkins. (An example of this sort of mixed-media collaboration in real life can be seen in the musical and artistic contributions to Powell's poem *Caledonia* by Constant Lambert and Edward Burra respectively.)

The personal life of the narrator is unexpectedly, and for *Dance,* unusually at the forefront of this second novel in the sequence. *A Buyer's Market,* indeed, is largely about Jenkins's unspectacular love life. Jenkins wants to become sentimental with Barbara Goring and, later, Gypsy Jones, and his romantic ardor in this book reveals that the characters, even the narrator, of *Dance* are capable of passionate subjective feelings. The romantic, or perhaps antiromantic, theme of *A Buyer's Market* is lent depth by the appearance of the painter Ralph Barnby. As Spurling comments, he is mentioned in *A Buyer's Market* long before "the reader has the faintest idea who he is" (xviii). It is, as far as the action of *Dance* is concerned, typically unexpected that Jenkins meets Barnby, the consummate theorist of heterosexuality, in the largely homosexual milieu of Mr. Deacon. Barnby's storehouse of apothegms about women lend context and meaning to Jenkins's dealings with the opposite sex.

These dealings are captured vividly in the diptych of parties that occupy one day in time and take up the first half of *A*

Buyer's Market. The phrase "A buyer's market" is a term from finance, one by now familiar in application to all areas of life, which signifies that the buyer of a given commodity has an advantage over the seller. Presumably, the buyers are the streams of aspiring young men in their twenties flooding London society; more generally, the title refers to the opportunities of life as such, beyond those protected areas—school, French guest houses, houses of friends—seen in the first volume.

A Buyer's Market moves from these enclosed, pedagogic spaces to more open areas. Its great metaphor is the party. We go to two parties in one night. One is the debutante party held by the Huntercombes, where Jenkins's love for Barbara Goring ends after his beloved pours sugar over Widmerpool's head. The next is the far more raffish party held by Mrs. Andriadis, the older woman who has taken on Stringham as her lover, in a house rented from the ever-so-bourgeois Bob Duport, collector of appalling Victorian seascapes who has married Jean Templer. This social whirl of this book does not end at Andriadis's soiree on Hill Street, as we go to another party at Stourwater and then conclude with what must be called another party, even if the dingiest one possible, at the house of Widmerpool's mother, where, to the reader and literature's everlasting regret, Jenkins and Mrs. Widmerpool never get to have their talk about books. But the two-party night in London remains memorable. The reader is probably as exhausted as Jenkins is at the end of it, though not quite as frustrated by Uncle Giles turning up at the small hours after midnight and detaining Jenkins with conversation about "the Trust."

Powell is barely mentioned in Christopher Ames's authoritative work on parties in twentieth-century writing, but he is one of the great chroniclers of parties in world literature. This may seem to ballast Powell's reputation for writing about upper-class society, but in fact, Powell observes parties with a detached eye, more reminiscent of the sociologist or anthropologist than of the gossip columnist. Even at occasions where Jenkins has a personal stake in what goes on, such as at the Huntercombes', when he is in pursuit of Barbara Goring, he is able to observe other people, and the collective hum of the gathering, more or less disinterestedly. This is what is behind a parody of Powell quoted by Bevis Hillier (*Spectator,* 17 May 1997): "Across the room, at Lady Elspeth's party, I caught sight of Deirdre, to whom, I recalled, I had once been married." This is overstating things, but the grain of truth in this joke testifies to the restraint of self-aggrandizement in Jenkins's account of parties.

Powell does not mean just to describe. The fact that half the book is devoted to one long night of parties is an obvious allusion to *Ulysses,* James Joyce's multilayered account of one day in Dublin in 1904. Powell testifies, in both his memoirs and *Journals,* that Joyce was a writer he had read in his twenties, and that, though not advocating Joyce as a role model for either his own writing or that of others, he found Joyce's modernist procedures liberating. If not quite approaching the raucous badinage of Joyce's Nighttown, the Huntercombe-Andriadis evening, with its painter-pamphleteers, physical assaults with sugar-shakers, and parade of homosexuals and pacifists comes close to its convulsive anarchy. Another great party in modernist writing is recalled by the Huntercombe-Andriadis evening: Mrs. Dalloway's in Virginia Woolf's novel of that name. Though Powell is acerbic about Woolf in particular and the Bloomsbury group in general, General Conyers's point that "the woman can write" (*At Lady Molly's,* 80) must be respected. In many ways, we start the evening at the Huntercombes home, preceded by dinner at the Walpole-Wilsons, in a Dalloway-esque environment, and then descend into Joyce's Nighttown at the Andriadis event. What Powell is doing here is complex. He is acknowledging his predecessors in depicting modernity and, in a book depicting the 1920s, paying homage, and allusive respect, to the seminal modernist writers, all the while making the point that Jenkins is of a generation born into modernism and the twentieth century, seeing it from a ground eye's level, not Stephen Dedalus's Martello Tower. There is also a T. S. Eliot connection. The phantom drama of the limned but unincarnated characters in part 1 of *The Waste Land* (Madame Sosostris, Belladonna, Mrs. Equitone) is in many respects incarnated at Mrs. Andriadis's party with Mr. Deacon, Max Pilgrim, "the young man with the orchid," and Miss Jones. (This kinship with the Eliot of the 1920s is captured in Roy Fuller's parody-poem, pseudepigraphically ascribed to the character Mark Members in *Dance,* "Iron Aspidistra," which includes the couplet "Beyond the gates a glimpse is seen / of Mrs. Sutton-Coldfield in her limousine.") The entire Andriadis party is a fantastic admixture of lived reality and images glimpsed in books, or perhaps the confirmation of the unlikely realism of the latter by the former. As in most modernist works of any quality, bohemia, even if surveyed, is not presented as liberating or redemptive. In fact, bohemian circles often appear in *Dance* as horribly banal, even if their artistic experimentation offers an interest not to be found in the old-money venues preferred by one Zouch.

The reappearance of Stringham in *A Buyer's Market* provides a glimpse of Powell's ability to braid old characters in with new ones. Powell gives the feeling that everyone in Stringham and Templer circles, even unrelated persons such as Miss Weedon, Farebrother, and Stripling, is part of that milieu, so there is a frisson, a sense of crossed boundaries, when they appear in an unexpected circumstance. The unexpected reappearance of Widmerpool, on the other hand, almost becomes expected. The reader waits for it. It is in *A Buyer's Market* that we see how the Widmerpool leitmotif will operate during the entire sequence. We have Sir Gavin Walpole-Wilson's question, to Jenkins, "Have you met Mr. Widmerpool?" (29), plus the muffed announcement of his name as "Mr. Winterpool" (57). As readers, we know Widmerpool already, know Winterpool is Widmerpool, even if Jenkins makes no overt comment. We see that Widmerpool's reappearances will be hallmarks in the series, that what happened at La Grenadière was a portent. We also see that Widmerpool's strange relation with Jenkins now extends to their relations with the opposite sex. Both he and Jenkins are in love with Barbara Goring. With Widmerpool, this love has a more marked tinge, as it emerges that his late father had supplied liquid manure to Barbara's grandfather, Lord Aberavon, and thus his courtship of Barbara is somewhat, in Widmerpool's mind, like the ambitious churl courting the princess in the tower. (Barbara is only half aristocratic in the genuine sense, as Lord Aberavon was a nouveau riche entrepreneur who had been raised to a peerage only near the end of his life.) There is also a third participant in the pursuit of Barbara, Tompsitt, a young diplomat who is a very effective character, one often passing under the radar screen of commentators. With a kind of anticipatory dramatic irony, we sense that the promise seen in Tompsitt, not to mention Bill Truscott, by their elders, such as the prominent and cashiered diplomat Sir Gavin Walpole-Wilson, is misplaced. They seem to be young men in a hurry. But as with the travel books of T. T. Waring, they are just what the older generation wants to see, not representing the actual forces at work in their generation. They are thus doomed to supersession. But, alas, the agent of that supersession is Widmerpool.

The sugar-pouring incident is one of the most celebrated, and funny, incidents in the sequence. Powell faces a big challenge as the incident is *almost* too preposterous for the relatively realistic social frame of *Dance*. It is moored to earth by the punctilious description of the people at the dance, including even spare men such as Archie Gilbert. A touch of realism is also added by Jenkins's evident disgust at Barbara Goring after the incident. In fact, he turns from loving Barbara to suspecting that he hates her. So as gratified as we are to see the slimy Widmerpool humiliated, especially as he had been importunate and pestering toward Barbara, we do not see it to Barbara's credit that she has done so. After the same night, Stringham is also humiliated by a woman, in his case, Milly Andriadis, the much older former mistress of royal figures and many others who has installed Stringham as, more or less, her kept man. Although Stringham still appears a far less risible figure than Widmerpool, he is clearly unhappy, visibly drunk, and, though instantly able to amiably reconnect to Jenkins, does not give any clue that the closeness of their old friendship is able to be resurrected.

After this night of mega-partying, it is individual meetings that count the most for Jenkins. Jean's brief appearance at Stourwater, followed by Widmerpool's preternatural manifestation in the (seeming) dungeon where "the girls who don't behave" are put, serve the narrative function of keeping these two crucial characters in the game. Two encounters with more newly met people are also remarkable.

Jenkins's initial actual meeting with Barnby is hilarious. "What name?" "Jenkins" (*Buyer's Market*, 165). Barnby obviously thinks Jenkins is one of Deacon's homosexual confreres.

Barnby is the first friend of Jenkins who is a fellow creative artist, presaging the sort of friendship that he will have with Moreland in *Casanova's Chinese Restaurant* and after. His relationship with Barnby's bête noire, Gypsy Jones, shows, in its unexpectedly passionate denouement, how two people who fundamentally dislike each other can still feel a powerful if ephemeral sexual attraction. Although the language in which it is written about is clear, the actual import of what transpired between Widmerpool and Gypsy is much more clouded.

It is likely that Widmerpool did *not* have sex with Gypsy, "forking out" for her abortion out of, in descending order of likelihood, (a) hopes of having sex with her in the future, (b) just being a hapless chump, as he was later with Mrs. Haycock, or (c) misplaced social responsibility or a vicarious thrill at being on the wild side among the lower, or at least less well behaved, orders. And by contrast, or apposition, we have Jenkins's sex scene with Gypsy, the first recorded example of his sexual activity in *Dance,* in a scene so opaquely written that an eminently intelligent critic, Robert K. Morris, thought that things had gone the other way. Morris laments that Jenkins ended up "cerebrating away the first serious opportunity to lose his virginity" when in fact he was cerebrating *while* losing his virginity, a more exacting endeavor.[18] So the blatant Gypsy is involved in two enigmatic conjunctions with men crucial to the narrative of *Dance.*

Jenkins and Widmerpool, with such different personalities and values, are attracted in *A Buyer's Market* to the same women, themselves very different from each other—Barbara Goring and Gypsy Jones. It is as if Jenkins is being pulled into Widmerpool's vortex, finding himself less and less able to distinguish his own desires from those of this loathsome figure. Only Tompsitt blocks a direct Jenkins-Widmerpool competition over

Barbara. Not just Jenkins and Widmerpool, but four men, including the unforeseen eventual winner, Pardoe, vie for Barbara's affections at the ball. Following that, Widmerpool and Jenkins never approach Gypsy Jones at the same time. This conjunction seems to be an aspect of the London party world. At La Grenadière, for instance, Widmerpool, despite hanging around Suzette Leroy so that Jenkins could never really make himself know to her, did not manifest any overt interest in her the way Jenkins at least attempted to do. Similarly, Widmerpool shows no interest in Jean Templer; indeed, he never meets her throughout the book, even though he eventually is the effectual agent of Jenkins's breakup with her by transferring Duport to South America and therefore giving a new lease on life to Jean's marriage. In this latter instance, we assume that Widmerpool does not know he is harming Jenkins, unlike his later sending of Stringham off to death in Singapore. Nevertheless, Widmerpool does ruin Jenkins's love life. His constant presence seems to be a metaphor for the sense of unmistakable personal futility that Jenkins feels in his early London years.

The presence of Tompsitt in the Barbara Goring episode allows an entre into the diplomatic world of Tompsitt's patron, Sir Gavin Walpole-Wilson, and thus gives us a sense of interwar diplomacy and European politics as part of the subject matter of this portion of the sequence, not just as backdrop. Christopher Hitchens has remarked upon the 1990s pertinence of Sir Gavin's sister, Miss Walpole-Wilson's, "article about the Bosnian Muslims."[19] What needs to be glossed, especially in light of millennial assumptions about modern Eastern European history, is that the Bosnian Muslims had sympathized with the Central Powers during the First World War and felt underprivileged in the Serb/Croat/Slovene (not yet Yugoslavian) kingdom created after the Versailles treaty. So Miss Walpole-Wilson was in essence making trouble for the Allied settlement, in a no-good do-gooder kind of way reminiscent of the meddlesome Miss Kilman in Woolf's *Mrs. Dalloway.* On the same note, it is worth reading up on interwar European diplomatic history to appreciate just how unintentionally and tragicomically funny is Sir Gavin's remark about his "fundamental reciprocity of thought" (*Buyer's Market,* 222) with Sforza and Károlyi. Sir Gavin is totally unsuspecting of the coming wave of European history, which will have no time for men of the moderation of Sforza and Károlyi, both of whom represent countries, Italy and Hungary respectively, eventually on the Axis side in the Second World War. (There is some sport being made of Sir Gavin here. In another irony, Sir Gavin later becomes mildly pro-Soviet.) He also makes his remark virtually to thin air. No one is listening; no one is interested. The Sforza-Károlyi remark is merely an orotund *obiter dicta,* almost a piece of discontinuous dialogue in the style of Ivy Compton-Burnett. So often in *Dance,* conversations are not mutual. Indeed, the most mutual are those conducted in terse, Hemingwayesque, *Afternoon Men*–style dialogue, such as Jenkins's and Jean's clipped, stichomythic exchanges during their love affair. The longer and more rhetorical the uttered statement in *Dance,* the less likely anyone is listening—the best example being Widmerpool's speech at the Le Bas dinner. The most meaningful talk in the novel is compressed, economical, and conducted in a blended spirit of concise poise and nervous asperity.

Sir Gavin is a survivor of an elder generation, a figure more in the orbit of Jenkins's parents than of the narrator himself. This is originally true of Mr. Deacon as well, but in making a renewed acquaintance with the elderly artist in London Jenkins claims Deacon for his own social orbit and finds something valuable in his admittedly eccentric company. Deacon has stopped painting for, presumably, two reasons. His painting is so transparent an expression of his sexuality that, once that has been stated, there is little left to do: there is only one meaning, and Deacon's art lacks the mystery and plurality of motivation great art must have. Second, his painting is only comprehensible as a reaction against Victorian academicism. Once that has been achieved, there is no further prompt. And even in that achievement, there is a certain decorum, a self-censorship in unconscious emulation of its adversary, displayed by Deacon's anxiety that Max Pilgrim's "Tess of Le Touquet" song will give strength to "the puritans" (*Buyer's Market*, 149). So Deacon's painting, on a far less artistically elevated plane, finds itself with the same problem as the work and assumption of the Bloomsbury group. Deacon nonetheless is a major character in *Dance;* the reader is glad that Widmerpool's and Barnby's initial disapproval of the friendship did not ward Jenkins off from pursuing it, and it is surprising for the reader to remember he died so early in the sequence. The final scene in the Henderson gallery would have been inconceivable without Deacon's paintings being present— a sign that even the survival of mediocre art can contribute to a just and harmonic outcome of time's dance.

A *Buyer's Market* itself is far more implicated in a modernist world than is Deacon. It is profoundly conscious of modernist predecessors such as *The Waste Land, Ulysses,* and *Mrs. Dalloway,* though it lacks the despair of the first work and the measured affirmation of the latter two. It stays within a comparatively controlled comic milieu, intent to inhabit the cerebral, quasi-classicist side of 1920s modernity. But as the final paragraph, with its imagery of raised stakes, of things finally

mattering, indicates, the consequence of life, and of the twentieth century, cannot be forever postponed.

The Acceptance World (1955)

At the beginning of *The Acceptance World,* Jenkins, alone of his
initial cohort at school, is unmarried. In fact, Stringham, already
married and divorced, automatically assumes Jenkins is married
(200). His generation is not only "accepted" in various aspects
of society—the professions of all those at the Le Bas Old Boy
dinner—but is beginning to "accept" definitions of themselves.
Jenkins, by contrast, remains uncommitted. Even his affair with
Jean Templer is tentative, although passionate. And it is surrep-
titious—not even her husband, who, it turns out, is aware of
other affairs she has been having, is aware that Jean is having an
affair with Jenkins. Nor is Jean's brother and Jenkins's close
friend, Peter Templer, aware of the liaison.

The precise beginning of Jenkins's romantic relationship
with Jean Templer tells us a little not only about what kind of
literary character Jenkins is but also what, as narrator, is his
literary approach to life. During the drive to Templer's house
in Maidenhead on the Great West Road (the contemporary A4
road), Jenkins takes Jean "in my arms" (65) and feels that "at
once everything was changed" just a "few hundred yards" (64)
beyond where "the electrically illuminated young lady in
a bathing dress dives eternally through the petrol-tainted air."
This is, in other words, a roadside sign. When the American
reader, or indeed any reader familiar with American literature,
comes on this detail, they are not wrong to think immediately
of the T. J. Eckleburg sign in Fitzgerald's *The Great Gatsby.* To
Nick Carraway, the narrator of that novel, the Eckleburg sign

signifies the course or not one but three romances—Gatsby's
with Daisy Buchanan, his own with Jordan Baker, and on an
imaginative level, his romance with Gatsby, the "romantic-
hearted gangster" (*Books,* 217). In the "valley of ashes" (27)
scene at the beginning of chapter 2 of *The Great Gatsby,* the
eyes of Eckleburg are described as "blue and gigantic—their
retinas are one yard high. They look out of no face but, instead,
from a pair of enormous yellow spectacles which pass over a
nonexistent nose. . . . His eyes, dimmed a little by many paint-
less days under sun and rain, brood on over the same dumping
ground" (27–28). In both cases, advertisements are adapted
from their original, mercantile or attention-getting purpose to a
more inward, romantic meaning. Both are described with an initial humor, even disdain, that yields to a sense of spectacular
awfulness that, in its sheer squalor, can maneuver itself in position to aspire to epic or at least romantic mock-epic dimensions.
The advertisements, not only functional but also tawdry and
commercial, become strangely numinous, unique symbols of
young and enabled love. Both Powell and Fitzgerald, noticeably,
do not rail against modern commerce. These sorts of signs only
appeared on roads during their lifetime. They were an aspect of
the public experience that only their generation of all novelists
known to them were able to chronicle. These love affairs take
place under the aegis of modernity, and they are not falsely
taken away from a modern context and immured in great
houses or among the gentry in hunt season (cf. the comparison
between Persepolis and Battersea Power Station at *Harmonies,*
250—not to the latter's disadvantage). Jenkins achieves a more
truly, albeit temporarily, satisfying passion then does Zouch in
From a View (or, in *At Lady Molly's,* Widmerpool with Mrs.
Haycock at Dogdene) because he takes experience as it comes,

rather than waiting for a suitably aristocratic milieu to conse-
crate his erotic expectations as visible action.

Both Maidenhead and West Egg are modern suburbs, even
though Gatsby, at least, dreams of the past, in both personal and
collective terms, in a way in which the closest approach in
Dance is, again, Widmerpool's interest in Dogdene. Both Powell and Fitzgerald are interested in the past, in lineage, heritage,
and all it represents culturally and spiritually. But this interest is
neither rigid nor disablingly nostalgic. Both their major protagonists, Nick Jenkins and Nick Carraway, for instance, are interested in their own genealogy but do not romanticize it. Powell
and Fitzgerald both know they are of their own time, and their
greatest valor is to face this squarely and not dissimulate, as
one could argue that the Evelyn Waugh at least of *Brideshead
Revisited* did. Powell's encounter, both in person and through
reading, with Fitzgerald was pivotal to his work, and not just
because both men went to prestigious universities and min-
gled, intermittently, with high-society figures. They share an
ironic but observant stance toward their own world. And in
both cases, this stance is expressed in tone and language as well
as in narrative perspective. Speculation about the reason for
Jenkins being named Nicholas can be directed toward Nicolas
Poussin, painter of the work that gives the sequence its title,
whose perspective upon the world seems characterized by an
aloof tension similar to that of his putative Jenkins namesake,
or, a far darker but not ineligible horse, on Nick Adams of Hemingway's stories, who, though far more rough-hewn than the
impeccably urbane Jenkins, manifests a similar stoicism, a refusal to be defeated by experience that, in any conventional
terms, is not rewarding. But as has been noted by several commentators, most recently and eloquently James Doyle on the

Anthony Powell Internet mailing list, surely the most crucial precedent of the same name is Fitzgerald's "Nick" Carraway, who, in *Gatsby,* is the narrator but not the hero of his own story, drawn like a moth to the flame to "the abortive sorrows and short-winded elations of men," people more outsized than he, who yet represents the conscience of the book and incarnates the morality of tact and reticence.[20] That Jenkins does not have a Gatsby but a Widmerpool indicates the far darker tone of *Dance* (masked by Fitzgerald's having had a more tragic life than did Powell). Nor, other than the uncharacteristic final paragraphs of *A Buyer's Market* and *Casanova's Chinese Restaurant,* does Jenkins come up with the sort of elevated, diagnostic coming to terms with the condition of his world that Carraway manifests at the exact moment of his thirtieth birthday. But the two Nicks are similar, not just because they are observers, but because both are moved by their intelligence to come to a moral reckoning with regard to those around them, while their social poise makes them profoundly aware of the arrogance that often accompanies suggesting solutions to the world's problems. Carraway's reluctance, as proclaimed to Jordan Baker, to "lie to myself and call it honor" has its parallels, for instance, in Jenkins's realization that any "but the most crude indication of my own personality would be . . . hard to transcribe" (*Acceptance World,* 33). If Jenkins is not the mythologizer that Carraway is (he does not idolize, say, Stringham or Trapnel the way Carraway, at one time, does Gatsby), the two Nicks are alike in not mythologizing themselves.[21]

Early in *The Acceptance World,* while waiting in the lobby of the Ritz for Mark Members to discuss St. John Clarke's prospective introduction to the book his publishing firm is producing on the art of Horace Isbister, Jenkins sees a group of South Americans (who may or may not include Colonel Flores, the future husband of Jean Templer herself). He begins,

> To brood on the complexity of writing a novel about English life, a subject difficult enough to handle with authenticity even of a crudely naturalistic sort, even more to convey the inner truth of the things observed. These South American sitting opposite, coming from a Continent I had never visited, regarding which I possessed only the most superficial scraps of information, seemed in some respects easier to conceive in terms of a novel than most of the English people sitting round the room. Intricacies of social life make English habits unyielding to simplification, while understatement and irony —in which all classes of this island converse—upset the normal emphasis of reported speech. (32)

Other than the last sentence, Jenkins's musings seem confirmed in how many novels British writers have subsequently written about South America (for instance, Louis de Bernières's trilogy on the continent) or based on South American precedents (most of the oeuvre of Salman Rushdie), but it is the last sentence that is most pertinent. What Jenkins, and his creator, are trying to avoid are the clunky certitudes of the nineteenth-century novel, without being limited by procedures, such as those used in Woolf's *To the Lighthouse,* that are brilliant but, because they are so solidly premised on an evolution beyond the Victorian, can only be used once. Powell finds his solution to the dilemma limned as Jenkins waits in the Ritz and mulls on the milling Americans through American precedents—though from North, not South, America. Fitzgerald, born in the 1890s and not, like

Joyce, Woolf, and Eliot, the 1880s, is closer to Powell's generation and his generation's assured relationship to twentieth-
century culture. (The same could be said, in a different manner,
of Hemingway, whose early work impressed Powell with its
innovation, reliance on clipped dialogue, and lack of self-pity.)
Neither Powell nor Fitzgerald, for instance, ever knew a world
without the automobile, which enables both to notice roadside
signs. The car is a motif in *Dance,* from the Great West Road
incident to General Conyers arriving at Stonehurst in 1914 to
the vintage-car parade at the end of *Temporary Kings,* in which
the automobile, and modernity itself, are so much second nature
as to become the object of the kind of nostalgia Le Bas, in 1921,
was evincing for Victorian, if not classical times. (Maidenhead
is more or less "beyond" Eton on the same road, and the person who drives from London to Maidenhead will also pass the
town of Goring. Powell's strong sense of place, and his interest
in transposing place names to personal names, not to mention
the symbolic resonances of "Maidenhead" itself, surely come
into play here.)

Powell and Fitzgerald can reach the heights of romanticism,
as in Carraway's search for "something commensurate to his
capacity for wonder" or Jenkins's bleak but passionate vision of
the Ghost Railway at the end of *Casanova's Chinese Restaurant,*
or the scalding extremes of satire, as in Fitzgerald's portrait of
Myrtle Wilson or Powell's of Gypsy Jones, because they are at
home in this world. They do not have to compensate for being
estranged from it by disbursing lofty platitudes. As Matthew
Bruccoli says in his preface to the revised textual edition of *The
Great Gatsby,* Fitzgerald's novel "does not proclaim the nobility of the human spirit. . . . It does not reveal how to solve
the problems of life; it delivers no fashionable or comforting

messages. It is just a masterpiece."[22] Ditto *Dance*. Also pertinent is the "concision" of *Gatsby*, a feature to which Powell cast attention in his 1998 selection of the book as a *Daily Telegraph* Book of the Century. For all its epic scale, *Dance*, in language and perspective, is economical, down to earth, content to be quirky rather than prescriptive, to sketch rather than to bloviate. Both writers manifest a kind of high whimsy capable of registering straightforward romanticism, an epic reach. In fact, *The Great Gatsby* is both an epic and a self-deflating title, resembling the title of *Dance* in the former respect and those of the individual books in the latter. This discursive charm, this predilection for the beauty of innuendoes, is a trait no doubt inherent in Powell's talents yet one he found reinforced by Fitzgerald's winning and plangent example.

Fitzgerald's allusive ghost is succeeded in *The Acceptance World* by the momentarily more palpable one of Karl Marx. Aside from the affair with Jean (and hints that Templer's wife, Mona, is attracted to Quiggin), the highlight of the weekend visit to Templer's house is the séance, provided over by the uncanny Mrs. Erdleigh, in which the Ouija board produces the gnomic saying "Karl is not pleased" (94). This utterance, which, when the oracle goes on to say, "Nothing to the Left" is recognized as a reference to Karl Marx, would have been a winning newspaper headline indeed on 10 November 1989, or indeed a good entry in Powell's *Journals,* although he would never be this obvious. It is interesting that Quiggin would suspect Jenkins, not so much that Jenkins has actually staged the incident (although there is a kernel of truth for this, as Jenkins's alter ego, Powell, has), but that he would think that Jenkins, somebody self-depicted as not a political activist, would know a tag line from Marx. Jenkins, though indifferent to and baffled by the

Marxist turn his milieu has taken, nonetheless keeps himself up to date on it. The "good" people in *Dance* are often, though not always, the people who bother to keep up with things in the arts and culture: Pennistone, Conyers, Moreland, Trapnel, and even Short, who keeps up with interesting people, and of course Jenkins himself. Jenkins, though the furthest thing from being a Marxist, has kept up with things enough for Quiggin to suspect that he, and certainly no one else at the table, has manipulated the Marxian answer that is received.

Even though the séance later gives Quiggin news that St. John Clarke is ill, leading him to find out that Members is once more back in the novelist's confidence and forcing Quiggin to scurry back to London to (unsuccessfully) firm up his power base, Quiggin is the long-term beneficiary of the weekend, as shortly thereafter Mona, who had at first appeared to see him as a ludicrous specimen whose very absurdity would lend color to the house party on the weekend, leaves her husband for him. In not too bald a way, this signifies the eclipse of the man of pleasure, Templer, in favor of the abstemious exponent of class struggle, Quiggin.

Notwithstanding Quiggin's working-class reverse entitlement, and Monsieur Dubuisson's vague progressivism, in *A Question of Upbringing,* it is in *The Acceptance World* that Marxism enters onto the stage of *Dance.* It is one of the sequence's great villains, and chief sources of amusement. Not even someone skeptical of postcommunist euphoria will argue that this is all, in the vast majority of its incarnations, Marxism actually was. Powell's attitude toward it, though, is either gently or coldly ironic, not feverishly polemical. The immediate occasion of the rise of Marxist visibility is the economic crisis of the 1930s. Although *The Acceptance World* is set after the onset of the Great Depression, and characters speak of "the slump," we do not feel a change in atmosphere in *The Acceptance World* the way we do in the next book, which features Jenkins's marriage. The spectacle of the ultra-bourgeois middlebrow novelist St. John Clarke suddenly attacking the "bourgeois" and falling under the secretarial sway of Members, Quiggin, and the dour German Trotskyist Werner Güggenbühl (later the urbane British academic Vernon Gainsborough) is a sign of the times. Even more so is the changed conduct of Widmerpool. Widmerpool, who eventually swings over to Quiggin's political views, even in the wake of the Depression is still the good soldier of Donners-Brebner. In other words, he is as enthusiastic about corporate capitalism in the 1920s as he is about communism in the 1930s and after. This illustrates that whatever Powell's vendetta, for the most part justified, against the Left of his own time, his creation of Widmerpool was to show up not simply the Left but also political opportunism in general. No doubt, had Widmerpool lived on into the 1980s and 1990s, he would have rediscovered, with gusto, his enthusiasm for capitalism; indeed, he would have been irrationally exuberant about it.

At the Old Boy (reunion) dinner for former students at Le Bas's house, a number of people who have achieved success in various fields speak about their areas of interest. After these, Widmerpool, unexpectedly and without invitation, arises: "'You have heard something of politics and India,' he said, speaking quickly, and not very intelligibly, in that thick, irritable voice which I remembered so well. 'You have been asked to join the Territorial Army, an invitation which I must heartily endorse. Something has been said of county cricket. We have been taken as far afield as the Congo basin, and as near home as this very hotel, where one of us tonight worked as a waiter while acquiring his managerial training. Now I—I myself—would like to say a word or two about my experiences in the City'" (*Acceptance World*, 190–91). Widmerpool's aggressive self—manifestation is presented not just as an effluence of personal ego. In representing himself as the voice of "the City," Widmerpool is acting as if everyone else at the dinner is a dilettante muttering clichés about Theocritus. In fact (and for all of his defense of Le Bas against his student tormentors in the first book), Widmerpool's speech is an attack on Le Bas's values, and it is not surprising that Le Bas suffers a stroke, though much of his discomfort must have been as a result of sheer boredom, not a sense of being the target of hostility.

Widmerpool's speech is, on the narrative level, an appalling specimen of tedium and, on the authorial level, a masterpiece of satiric wit: "Now if a governmental policy of regulating domestic prices is to be arrived at in this or any other country, the moment assigned to the compilation of the index number which will establish the par of interest and prices must obviously be that at which internal e economic conditions are in a condition of relative equilibrium. So far so good" (*Acceptance World*, 193). This alternation of pompous and obscure economic jargon with reassuring phrases such as "All that is clear enough" measures the increasing distance between Widmerpool's monologue and any possible interest in the part of his audience. It is a performance of incredible megalomania, and so embarrassing that we almost feel sorry for Widmerpool. The amazing aspect of this is, unlike as would have happened when both Jenkins and Widmerpool were teenagers, Widmerpool does not feel set back by his humiliation. In fact, he is empowered by it. When Jenkins and Stringham are walking to Stringham's home from the dinner, Stringham is mocking Widmerpool in much the same way as he had done at school. Then suddenly they meet Widmerpool, and Jenkins is forced to explain to him that Stringham is drunk. The power equation changes before the reader's eyes. Widmerpool, as it were, has become the agent, Stringham the patient. No one realizes this more than Widmerpool; his aggressive participation in putting Stringham to bed reveals his satisfied, almost gloating comprehension of the changed circumstances. Widmerpool's strange mastery over Stringham, his exultation at turning the tables on the boy who had looked down on him at school, is distasteful in its obviousness. Jenkins, quick on the uptake, registers the change in the power equation.[23] "Widmerpool, once so derided by all of us, had in some mysterious manner become a person of authority. Now, in a sense, it was he who derided us" (209). This is as evident, as symptomatic, a shift as, say, Quiggin's replacement of Members as St. John Clarke's secretary, or of the economic slump's correction of the previous boom. The public nature of Widmerpool's triumph over Stringham, the way it is as staged and deliberate an act of aggression as was Widmerpool's speech at the dinner, contrasts with the private, clandestine nature of the affair between Jenkins and Jean.

We are never totally convinced that Jean is as attractive as Jenkins thinks she is. As compared with Jordan Baker in *The Great Gatsby* (which, if Jenkins is Nick Carraway, would be the equivalent figure, and the initial letter is the same), she is a rather pallid character, although the actual rendering of her relationship with Jenkins is intense in its economy of means. It is striking how invisible this relationship is to the other characters in the sequence—in a fictional world where everyone is constantly talking about what everyone else is doing. Barnby and Dicky Umfraville, it is assumed, know of the nature of Jenkins's relationship with Jean when she accompanies him to Foppa's and then on the visit to Milly Andriadis, but the affair does not percolate beyond these somewhat bohemian and disreputable circles. Jean's affair with Jimmy Brent is well known to her husband, Bob Duport, and eventually Jenkins, and Jean takes delight in taunting Jenkins with her affair with Jimmy Stripling. There is a technical explanation to this invisibility, similar to that Powell will later give about the lack of detail given about Jenkins's marriage, in that if Jenkins's relationships are too visible to the other characters he will not be able to act so smoothly as a recording observer; he would seem more an interested party, in the thick of the dance rather than, as he often though not always is, on the sidelines.[24] The undertone of bitterness that is always there as a substrate of the intense passion of Jenkins's affair with Jean makes clear, by the end of the book, that their relationship will not last. The world in which Jenkins "seemed to find himself" (214) at the end of *The Acceptance World* is poised in an almost exact balance between satisfaction and sorrow.

At Lady Molly's (1958)

The even balance achieved at the end of *The Acceptance World* changes decisively in the fourth book, and virtually the sole agent of this change is Jenkins's marriage to Lady Isobel Tolland. This is easily missed, as Jenkins in narrative terms is not lavish about his courtship and reticent throughout the course of the sequence about his marriage. Jenkins's marriage provides the perspective from which he sees the past, the assured set of convictions that allow him to retrospectively assess his experience in such confident and sophisticated terms. Because of this, we, as readers, feel exhilaration at Jenkins's marriage, which indeed gives a new spring, a bounce, to the entire sequence. This is not just because we have come to like Jenkins and want to see him happy, especially after the negative and unromantic way his affair with Jean ended. When Jenkins sees Isobel, he instantly knows that he will marry her. Just as instantly, everything comes into focus, and any potential for meandering or loss of purpose is forestalled. Isobel's entry means that *Dance* will not end up like the prewar novels, because marriage to her makes Jenkins into someone that the protagonists of those previous books could never become. There are only two events that could have this effect, of dividing the world in two, before and after their occurrence: the outbreak of the war and Jenkins's marriage to Isobel. The sense that conditions in society are not always going to be what they are in Jenkins's recollections is a result of the war. But Jenkins's sense of who he is, of standing at a vantage point from which he can make retrospective assessment of individuals, comes from his marriage.

Though Jenkins meets his future wife at Thrubworth, the home of her raffish, leftist brother Erridge (Lord Warminster, who is still addressed by his siblings with the courtesy title), his courtship of her is conducted very much under the aegis of Lady Molly Jeavons, as can be seen in the book's title. As mentioned before, the reader might first suppose Lady Molly to be an upper-class hostess, much like Madame de Guermantes in Proust. In fact, this Lady Molly is a maverick and something of an outcast. Formerly the Countess of Sleaford, after her husband—Chips Lovell's first Sleaford uncle—has died, she no longer has the status accorded the chatelaine of Dogdene and is a superfluous figure in the world of the landed aristocracy. "Lady Molly" is called that because she is the daughter of Lord

Ardglass. If she derived her title from the Sleaford connection, she would be called "Lady Sleaford," presumably the dowager Lady Sleaford. This superfluity is compounded by her startling marriage to Ted Jeavons, a man not only of undistinguished ancestry but also of no particular artistic talent or ambition. He does have a distinguished record in the First World War, but his wartime experience tends to trap him in the past rather than, as with General Conyers's far earlier army experience, giving him strength to face the present. Though many of the characters find him uncomfortable to be with, Jeavons, in his honesty, lack of pretension, vulnerability, and genuine love for Lady Molly, emerges as a kind of unobtrusive moral center in *Dance*.

So Lady Molly's is not a fortress of the aristocracy. It is a kind of "contact zone," a phrase defined by Mary Louise Pratt as denoting "social spaces where cultures meet, clash, and grapple with each other, often in contexts of highly asymmetrical relations of power."[25] A contact zone is a liminal space where the different worlds of *Dance*—bohemia, the military, the aristocracy, the Socialist Left—meet and mingle. The Lady Molly zone is precisely what the unknowing reader does *not* think it is, and in this way the title tricks the reader. Lady Molly's household includes the creepy butler, Smith, and a monkey, Maisky (named, we presume, with some sense of facial resemblance, after the Soviet ambassador), whose fates eventually become intertwined in a grotesque incident. Many relatives in their twenties flock to her house as an encouraging venue free from the stuffiness of the alternative, yet the most senior generation, too old even to serve in the First World War, is made welcome there as well.

Once Lady Molly's eccentricity, amiability, and social adaptability are understood, the reader has to ask the questions necessary of all literary characters: Why is she in the book? What role does she play in the life of the narrator? Notice that for all the attention lavished at second hand at Dogdene, including the hilarious fake Pepys passage, the narrator actually never sets foot in Dogdene. Widmerpool does, and Chips Lovell of course has, but there is no narrative record of Nicholas Jenkins ever crossing the threshold of the Sleaford manse. But Jenkins does go to Lady Molly's, and the kind of "contact zone" atmosphere of the Jeavons household also defines the range and curiosity manifest in Jenkins's own social relationships. Concomitant with this is General Conyers—a veritable one-man contact zone between generations, a Boer War veteran, far too old to lead troops at the Somme or at Passchendaele, yet "young at heart" enough to read Virginia Woolf.

It is deeply significant that Jenkins never goes to Dogdene. Dogdene, not the down-at-heel Thrubworth or the menacing Stourwater, comes closest of all the houses mentioned in *Dance* to be the archetypal Great House, inhabited by a conventional Tory aristocrat, a place aspiring young men making their way in society want desperately to visit. But it remains completely offstage; Jenkins never sees it, and its denizens are not only opportunists such as Widmerpool but also people such as Chips Lovell, who, even though Jenkins likes him, are presented as intellectually and aesthetically limited. There is no sentimental romance of the great manor here—not only in the twentieth century but also in past centuries. The pastiche of the diary of Samuel Pepys narrates a tawdry incident that is never likely to be used in the copy for a tourist brochure.

All the quotations in *Dance* by well-known writers that refer to ancestors of personages mentioned in the narrative were written by Powell himself, or as Spurling wittily puts it, "seem to be known only to Nicholas Jenkins" (246). In other words, Powell did not take a real letter or diary entry from Byron, Gronow, or Pepys containing a given personal name and then spin a consequent narrative from it. Some commentators have been taken in by the Proust, thinking "Prince Odoacer" is a historical personage, but it is clear that "Odoacer" is a retrospectively coined takeoff on Prince Theodoric, Odoacer being Theodoric's predecessor as barbarian administrator of fifth-century Italy. Thus the putative Proustian Odoacer is a back formation on the part of Powell rather than his Theodoric being a latter-day homage to Odoacer.

Even with a faux Pepys in its past, Dogdene cannot hold a candle to Lady Molly's far more modest establishment. The logic of the Jeavons' marriage is interesting, particularly when compared with the proposed alliance between Widmerpool and Mrs. Haycock, née Mildred Blaides. What Widmerpool wants to do is "marry up," to make a marriage that will cement his social upward mobility, and he is willing to take an older woman with two teenage children in order to accomplish this. Of course, General Conyers would be the first to note that this is an inadequate psychological generality. The flip side of Widmerpool's opportunism is his need for humiliation, which his involvement with Mildred seems to satisfy. Indeed, the unpredictability of Widmerpool's motivation, the murkiness of what Jenkins at one point styles his "theoretical side," is one of the chief agents of the sequence's comic suspense. But Jenkins's sense that it is important that Widmerpool, even if registering pseudonymously in a hotel, was entitled by virtue of Mildred's background to style the couple "Mr. and the Hon. Mrs. Smith" seems to ring true and tallies with Widmerpool's intuition that Dogdene would be an appropriate venue for the premarital consummation of his relationship with Mildred. That this turns out to be an embarrassing farce indicates the extent to which Widmerpool has overreached himself.

The Jeavons household is both the displacement of Dogdene and its antinomy. For Widmerpool, it is the very poor relation of the Sleaford household, where he hopes to "prove" himself as lover and social aspirant. But Widmerpool might have taken a closer look at the Jeavons marriage. Jeavons has, in a way, realized Widmerpool's dream—he has "married up." But that is not how he understands his relationship with his wife at all. Chips Lovell's description of how they came together gives the flavor of their association:

"At the Motor Show. Went to Olympia in her widow's weeds and saw Jeavons again. He was acting as a polisher on one of the stalls. I can't remember which make, but not a car anyone would be proud to own. That represented just about the height of what he rose to in civil life. They were married about six months later."

"How does it go?"

"Very well. Molly never seems to regret the Dogdene days in the least. I can't think what they use for money, because, if I know the Sleafords, she didn't give much in the way of a jointure—and I doubt if she has a hundred a year on her own. The Ardglass family have been hopelessly insolvent since the Land Act. However, she manages to support herself—and Jeavons—somehow. And also get some fun out of life." (18)

Molly does not regret the loss of the great-house prestige to which Widmerpool aspires. And Jenkins's narrative perspective endorses her take-life-as-it-comes attitude. In fact, the Jeavonses are the married couple of the former generation portrayed most positively in the first four volumes of *Dance* (compare Commander and Mrs. Foxe). And the book's thematic exploration of marriage takes their very eccentric marriage as its offhand and unobtrusive moral center. So many of the characters introduced or further observed in the fourth volume—General Conyers, Dicky Umfraville, Jenkins—share the Jeavonses' crossing of social and attitudinal boundaries. They rebuke conventional assessments of social status. And of course, the most visible and surprising rebuke to Widmerpool's conventional assessment of social rank comes when the reader, if not Widmerpool, finds out that Mildred and Ted Jeavons had a torrid wartime affair. Thus the coveted "aristocratic" wife is associated with a liaison that Widmerpool would have found even more regrettable than his own with Gypsy Jones.

At the beginning of *At Lady Molly's,* the plot centers on Widmerpool's marriage, which never occurs. And the marriage that does occur in the book is unanticipated at the beginning. Jenkins meets the Tolland family in dribs and drabs, of course first encountering Uncle Alfred at the Le Bas Old Boy dinners, where he is a holdover from an archaic previous regime, but perhaps the key meeting is with the eldest of the Tolland sisters, Lady Frederica Budd, at Lady Molly's. When Jenkins shows his social polish by knowing who the Edwardian dandy "Brabazon" was (87) and behaving with just the right mixture of curiosity and reserve vis-à-vis the lesbian ménage of Norah Tolland and Eleanor Walpole-Wilson, he shows himself as compatible with, if never entirely absorbable by, the "world" of the extended Tolland family. Those few pages can be seen as the epitome of Jenkins's social education and aplomb. We realize

that Jenkins, who had in the earlier books seemed a man possessed of little particular talent—lacking Stringham's charm, for
instance, or Widmerpool's go-getting—has a tremendous ability
to be interested in people, a talent that comes in handy in social
situations. Jenkins's behavior is almost a vade mecum of social
forms and graces. *At Lady Molly*'s is one of the few volumes in
the sequence in which Jenkins's fortunes outpace Widmerpool's,
and part of this is attributable to its social terrain being Jenkins's
home turf.

The interaction between Frederica and Jenkins maps the
territory where Lady Molly Jeavons dwells. The book is called
At Lady Molly's even though Jenkins meets his future wife at
her brother's house, Thrubworth. Yet note that he does so as a
guest of the raffish lord's leftist co-conspirator, Quiggin, hardly
a scenario to be found in conventional annals of aristocracy.
Quiggin has invited Jenkins for a weekend in the country for
opportunistic reasons, hoping Jenkins, whom he falsely supposes to have Hollywood connections simply because he works
as a writer for film, will help make Quiggin's paramour, the former Mona Templer, into a film star. Quiggin, in essence, introduces Jenkins to Isobel, and this gives the lie to the idea of
Dance just being about Tory toffs who rightfully spurn grasping
leftist wannabees. The novel, not just this novel but the novel as
a genre insofar as it is successful, is about individuals, not types
(the critics who act as if Powell was writing Theophrastan characters could not be more wrong), and Quiggin is represented
as an individual—one with the wrong politics, with a reverse-
snobbish personal myth that in many ways masks conventional
snobbery, but still an individual Jenkins likes, whose presence in
Jenkins's life is, despite all, to the good. This sort of acceptance
of all but the unacceptably uncivilized on their own terms is a

hallmark of Lady Molly's conduct, and it is one adopted by Jenkins as well.

Just after Jenkins's first glimpse of Isobel, Quiggin sets the tone of harmony, concord, and politeness by the way in which he congratulates Susan on her engagement to the young Conservative politician Roddy Cutts:

> Quiggin, however, came to the rescue.
>
> "Much as I hate the Tories," he said, "I've heard that Cutts is one of their promising young men."
>
> Everyone, including Susan Tolland herself, was surprised by this sudden avowal on the part of Quiggin, who was showing at least as much enthusiasm on the subject of the engagement as might have been expected from Erridge himself.
>
> "I grant it may not be my place to say so," Quiggin went on, switching at the same time to a somewhat rougher delivery. "But, as you know, Alf, you really ought to celebrate rightly in a bottle of champagne. Now, don't you think there is some bubbly left in that cellar of yours." (140)

Quiggin, the surly leftist, acts with a social grace that his aristocratic, if eccentric, patron Erridge lacks. For that matter, Quiggin is ahead of the usually far more adept Jenkins. His rare and unpredictable grace catalyzes the moment in which Jenkins is able to attain personal happiness. Jenkins's situation at Thrubworth is unlike Zouch's in Passenger Court, or indeed Widmerpool's at the Dogdene, which Widmerpool has, essentially, borrowed for himself to stage the same process to meet girls. Despite the fact that Jenkins has, in the immediate past, met several of her siblings, Isobel is only encountered through the medium of a dour agitator—Quiggin. To some extent, this is

Quiggin returning the favor, as Jenkins, through the latter's friendship with Templer, has introduced him to Mona. Thrubworth is in shabby shape, and as a house it is not inherently attractive. In addition, it is subtly made clear that the Warminster family is not just a bourgeois person's fantasy of aristocratic perfection. The second marriage of Lord Warminster to the demanding Katherine, a union characterized on the earl's part by extensive travel abroad, is clearly not idyllic. In addition, this branch of Tollands has only inherited the peerage because Erridge's grand-uncle, the Chemist Earl, had died unmarried. The Tollands are subject to the same happenstance as any other family, and Jenkins's marriage into them does not change who he is. He is not Zouch, nor was meant to be.

Although Jenkins's politics are to the right of Erridge, he comes into the family through Erridge's political side, not his aristocratic aspect. Ironically, it is Widmerpool, whose empirical politics are closer to Erridge's, who cannot imagine the owner of a great house being different in character from Chips Lovell's second Sleaford uncle. But it is Jenkins who actually engages with Erridge to the extent that he is in place for his fortuitous and consequential meeting with Isobel.

Yet Thrubworth is not the key great house here. One is tempted to say the key great house is Dogdene in absentia, but Dogdene in absentia is tantamount to Lady Molly's house, as a kind of dingy, casual Sleaford court-in-exile, like the equivalents in Shakespeare, considerably more attractive and interesting than the actual seat. The likability of the Jeavonses provides a sunny atmosphere for Jenkins's courtship, for Widmerpoo's humiliation, and for the unexpected revelation of the octogenarian General Conyers as a commentator on modernist literature and psychoanalysis. And all these fortunate, and fortuitous,

events somehow transpire under the sign of the net of relationships Jenkins has established and explored "at Lady Molly's."

Widmerpool's courtship of Mrs. Haycock, an older woman
with two teenage sons, shows his relative lack of interest in sex
and his zealous pursuit of power. Like Sir Magnus Donners, he
does not ever produce children. There is no Widmerpool Junior,
and the extremely rare instances when he actually achieves
physical relationships with women make this no surprise. It is
thus to be expected that Widmerpool's sexual performance at
Dogdene is disastrous. The pursuit of Haycock also indicates
Widmerpool's premature aging. His interest in making an acquaintance with older people such as Sir Magnus, and the fact
that his fiancée is a former girlfriend of Ted Jeavons, throws him
back into the previous generation. It is noted once or twice that
Widmerpool is slightly older than Jenkins, and this is a small but
crucial detail, as for all Widmerpool's bumptious zeal to keep
up with the times, he is always trying to get inside a slightly
archaized power structure that Jenkins more passively regards
in a manner less illusioned, more distant, and with more of
an understanding of its imminent passing. Widmerpool's conformism means that he is always slightly dowdy from the perspective of people his own age. In this way, a criticism made by
some viewers of the television version of the portrayal of Widmerpool by Simon Russell Beale—that Beale often appeared too
old for the age Widmerpool was supposed to be—was in reality
an aspect of the character of Widmerpool. In fact, Conyers is the
less conformist of the two. Widmerpool, whose mother, also his
aesthetic conscience, is still talking about Thomas Hardy, would
never read Virginia Woolf as does the Conyers.

Neil McEwan chooses the final scene of *At Lady Molly's*
to represent Powell in his anthology *The Twentieth Century,*

1900–Present, an intelligent choice, as the Jeavons household is at the heart of the social world valued by the sequence. But the La Grenadière scene in *A Question of Upbringing* is preferable precisely because of the nonrepeated nature of all characters other than Jenkins or Widmerpool. It provides the reader an unusually bare canvas on which the truly salient aspects of the sequence can be easily seen.

Casanova's Chinese Restaurant (1960)

The idea of "Casanova's Chinese Restaurant" expresses a contradiction in terms, an incongruity, something "recklessly hybrid" (*Casanova's,* 28), as well as a sense of layering of one era over another. In an era when ethnic restaurants even of the noncompound variety were rarer than now, there is also an air of the exotic and the unheard-of about it. The "Casanova" reference also implies erotic content, of which there is some, although a lot of this is conducted within the un-Casanovan format of marriage.

The cryptic beginning of *Casanova's,* with its retrospective look from after the Second World War, has vexed readers for decades. Perhaps the only way to make sense of it is to note that Powell had originally envisioned ten books, had seen the beginning of *Casanova's Chinese Restaurant* as the halfway point, and had felt the need for some narrative recalibration—not realizing he would discover a more apt and effective way of doing this at the beginning of *The Kindly Ones,* the sixth book and true halfway point. (Letters Powell wrote while working on *The Kindly Ones,* such as the ones to Bernard Bergonzi held by the archive at the Eton College Library, are the first to formally announce a twelve-volume length.) So it is something of a red herring, aside from representing the reality that there was mid-sequence revision, that *Dance* was not conceived as a wholesale, perfect edifice from the start.

This is the "musical" book of *Dance*, and this is notable not just in music being one form of the imagination but in it being a structural metaphor for the sequence as expressed in its title. In the first chapter, we are introduced to a gallery, or more aptly a quartet of musical personages—the composers Moreland and Maclintick, the performer Carolo, the critic Gossage—who between them run the gamut of all the roles in the musical world. Something fairly stunning for the reader in this exposition is the fact that Jenkins had known these people in the days when Mr. Deacon was still alive, in other words, during the action of the second book. This is jolting in a way that the introduction of General Conyers in *At Lady Molly's* was not, even though Jenkins had known the General before this and not told us, because Jenkins's first acquaintanceship with the general was as a child, and we only met Jenkins as narrator as a teenager. But with the musical gang we feel slightly disconcerted, as if Jenkins had held out on us during *A Buyer's Market*. Powell no doubt had many reasons for delaying the advent of the musical coterie until *Casanova's Chinese Restaurant*, from the prosaic one of his perhaps not having thought of them yet to the more formal possibilities of balance, pacing, and variety. But surely part of these characters only being revealed in the fifth book proceeds from what we might call "second-book carryover." As we have mentioned, a great portion of the second book is taken one with one day's events, the consecutive Huntercombe-Andriadis parties. In addition, a good portion of the latter half of the book is taken up with Jenkins's first visit to Stourwater with the Walpole-Wilsons. We do not see much of his London life—his boss at work, his colleagues, his friends outside from those that happened to be at one of the two parties. There is a reserve of unexplored territory in the setting of *A Buyer's Market* that is drawn out here and even up to the eleventh volume (the flashbacks involving Glober and Mopsy Pontner and also the revelation that Tokenhouse had been Jenkins's boss in publishing). There is a symmetry here, as both the fifth and the eleventh volume, like the second, are the middle volumes in their respective trilogies. So in all the nonwar trilogies, there is action taking place in the late 1920s, either on the present level or in flashback. But it is less likely that Powell deliberately structured this symmetry than that it is the consequence of the second-book carryover generated by the deliberately modernist and allusive tack of having so much of the action of *A Buyer's Market* in one long night. (Note that *Ulysses,* the chief recipient of this allusive thrust in *A Buyer's Market,* is actually mentioned in *Casanova's Chinese Restaurant* at 212, by Maclintick.)

At first, Hugh Moreland does not seem to stand out of the musical coterie. Soon, however, he becomes a pivotal figure. Moreland is adduced by Spurling as perhaps Jenkins's "closest friend."[26] This is at first surprising because Stringham is sentimentally established in the reader's mind as the original "best friend" of Jenkins and Moreland is initially presented as one of a musical milieu. This is unlike Barnby, who is the only painter of Jenkins's generation mentioned prominently in the sequence, Isbister and Deacon being much older. Moreland and Jenkins have biographical similarities. They are both in the arts, and they are exact contemporaries (implying a kind of spiritual kinship; witness how many others among Jenkins's contemporaries are just slightly older than he is, symbolically indicating a noncoincidence of temperaments). Jenkins and Moreland are able to maintain their friendship because they are neither too similar to, nor too different from, each other. (This was well expressed in physical terms in the portrayal of Moreland by James Fleet in the television version of *Dance*.) Although Jenkins is in many ways Widmerpool's structural opposite, it is Moreland who most tangibly represents the romantic, aesthetic counterpart to Widmerpool's opportunistic values. Whereas "Widmerpool" implies viscous, watery instability, "wetness" in the most squishy, indistinct sense, "Moreland," literally "more land," implies we are "moored" on solid ground. Notably, Jenkins remarks that, though in principle he and Moreland liked the same sort of woman, "never . . . did we find ourselves in competition" (41). This is interesting when we remember that Widmerpool and Jenkins did compete for women. That Moreland is not too similar to Jenkins sustains the remarkable sympathy they have with each other. In one of the most affecting descriptions of friendship in modern literature, Jenkins reflects, "With only a month or two between our ages, some accumulation of shared experience was natural enough. . . . There were, however, in addition to these public spectacles, certain unaccountable products of the zeitgeist belonging to both childhoods, contributing some particle to personal myth, so abundant in their way that Moreland and I sometimes seemed to have known each other long before meeting for the first time one evening in the saloon bar of the Mortimer" (*Kindly Ones,* 82). We are reminded of the moment when Jenkins "knew" he would marry Isobel upon seeing her for the first time. Isobel and Moreland incarnate what Jenkins sees as admirable in a person. This honor is suggested, as always, very indirectly, because one of the key ways Powell is different from novelists such as Evelyn Waugh or Ford Madox Ford, who might be said to have similarities of theme and approach with him, is that he shows rather than tells the reader who the good guys are.[27] Despite the passionate outbursts that punctuate his life, with Moreland we are on terra firma. Not so with Widmerpool. Moreland and Widmerpool encounter each other once, not only in *Casanova's Chinese Restaurant,* but in the entire sequence, excepting their both being present at the Seven Deadly Sins scene in *The Kindly Ones,* which occurs in chapter 2 of *Casanova's Chinese Restaurant,* when Moreland is at the hospital when his wife is about to have a baby, whereas Widmerpool is being treated for boils (one of several light touches in the sequence suggesting that Widmerpool's evil has allegorical overtones). Moreland gets on with Widmerpool no better than he does with Isobel. Indeed, without Brandreth, a doctor who had been a school contemporary of both Jenkins and Widmerpool, to make musical chitchat, their meeting would have been tense indeed.

By the fifth book, Powell has to find more ingenious ways to stage Widmerpool's reappearance than merely being at a party or even being somebody's unlikely fiancée, for it is of the essence to Widmerpool's structural role in the novel that he has to disappear and then crop up again, and in a circumstance that brings surprise and laughter. After his hospital reintroduction, Widmerpool's main feature in *Casanova's Chinese Restaurant* is his oblique reference to the love affair between the recently ascended Edward VIII and the American divorcee Wallis Warfield Simpson, for whom he eventually had to renounce the throne. This abdication crisis undoes Widmerpool's careful cultivation of the woman the king loves and shows both the callousness and desperation of Widmerpool's opportunism. The rapidity with which Widmerpool allies himself with forces he sees as rising ones is amazing, especially since his physical bearing and manner seem to suggest someone, though not slow-witted, ponderous and not necessarily quick on the uptake (as when he is bamboozled by Gypsy Jones). But Widmerpool is no doubt catalyzed into celerity by his opportunism, which is the only motive behind his thrill at proximity to royal circles; he certainly has no respect for the institution of monarchy itself or a personal liking for the couple involved. Even if the causes themselves are judged wrong, either by history or by the narrative, it is not the causes but the opportunistic manner of Widmerpool's adherence to them that is negatively assessed. For instance, Quiggin and Erridge's politics are clearly judged preposterous by the narrator—but both men are, in a human sense, decent if severely imperfect people. On another level, not everyone who supported Edward and Mrs. Simpson has been mocked by history. Winston Churchill, no righteous man's Widmerpool, was one of the doomed king's most ardent backers. Widmerpool is the most allegorical character in *Dance*. Sometimes he seems to be Evil incarnate, but at other times, he is a being living in a civilized, social world, subject to political tergiversations as are many in such a world.

It has been remarked upon, and accurately, that one of the preoccupations of *Casanova's Chinese Restaurant*'s social world is marriage. We see little of Jenkins's own marriage, for reasons Cathleen Ann Steg has adduced: "Isobel may be hidden; she does exist, nonetheless, as a vital personality to be reckoned with in *Dance*. Part of the challenge in making her acquaintance, of course, is that the only source of revelation about this woman is a narrator who happens to be her husband as well" (*Proceedings*, 91). In other words, if the narrator would speak too intimately about his marriage, it would weaken the objectivity, or at least the fictive stance of objectivity, with which

Jenkins sees the other characters in the novel, who are, after all, just as much its prerequisite in subject as the narrator is its prerequisite in stance. But we do see plenty of Moreland's marriage with Matilda, which in many ways becomes the paradigmatic marriage of the sequence. We see Moreland's relations with his wife in full view, whereas Stringham's with Peggy and Templer's with Mona and Betty, are only seen through reportage or in cameo. A far darker vision is provided by Maclintick's marriage. Of all the artists' careers in *Dance,* Maclintick's is the most naturalistically presented, partly because Jenkins's lack of friendship with him, and Powell's need to indicate what qualities make the other artists congenial to Jenkins, make him emerge more frontally. Maclintick and Moreland are two of the few characters whom Powell openly concedes are based on real people: in the case of Moreland, Constant Lambert (1905–51), and in the case of Maclintick (described, however, as primarily a critic, not a composer), Peter Warlock (1894–1930), a pseudonym for Philip Heseltine, who was also the model for Julius Halliday in D. H. Lawrence's *Women in Love.* There may, incidentally, be a gradation between character models mentioned in the memoirs and those in the *Journals,* that those mentioned in a work published when Powell was still producing and many of his contemporaries were still alive are more obviously and uncomplicatedly based on real people than those mentioned in a work originally intended to be published posthumously and was, in any event, released when the author was ninety and all his significant contemporaries were dead. But it should not be supposed that Powell sat down, wrote what he would have written about Lambert, and simply crossed out the name of Lambert and replaced it with that of Moreland when it came time to publish. Nor, most likely, did he conceive of Moreland as explicitly premised on Lambert and take care to make the portrayal as accurate as possible. Most plausibly, he decided that a musician friend would play a similar role in Jenkins's life as Lambert had done in Powell's. It is the *role* that is based on Moreland in this hypothesis. Then aspects of Lambert's personality may have seeped in insofar as they were compatible with the character of Moreland as it had emerged in the book—inevitably taken on, as even the most realistic art takes on, an autonomous pulse. Powell, for instance, concedes in *Messengers* (60) that Moreland shared with Lambert a liking for the music of the nineteenth-century French composer Emmanuel Chabrier. This, though, is not so much simply replicating a detail of individual taste as developing the similarity between Moreland's own artistic preferences and those of Jenkins. Chabrier fits in with the image of classical, witty, self-aware modernism adduced in *A Buyer's Market*, whereas Maclintick's brand of music is presumably emotionally deeper, more romantic, more on the expressionist, or at least the introspective, than the classicist side of modernism. The divergence in taste is not all that marked, however, as the Chabrier book is in Maclintick's house. And Maclintick is certainly very realistic in his rigorous assessment of the quality of Moreland's symphony (*Casanova's Chinese Restaurant*, 149).

Maclintick's house, not to mention his marriage, is not a happy one. One assumes that the basis for its unhappiness is economic, unless Maclintick, like his real-life counterpart Heseltine/Warlock, was "simply tired of the business of living" (*Messengers,* 149). The underside of the high social life we see, for instance, Barnby aspire to in his liaison with Baby Wentworth, or the dancer/actor Norman Chandler in his allegedly nonsexual friendship with Mrs. Foxe, is the harrowing financial realities faced by artists in a world without today's foundation grants or university appointments, without such aristocratic sponsorship. Another is Mrs. Maclintick's seeming lack of appreciation for Maclintick's work. This philistinism, slightly astonishing in a woman who has consecutive romantic liaisons with two composers, presents a problem in the Maclinticks' marriage that does not exist for the Morelands and the Jenkinses.

The marriage theme borne out even in the minor characters. Isbister is said to have refused a knighthood "so as to spite his wife" (*Casanova's Chinese Restaurant*, 191). There is also the historical background of the momentous marriage of the eventual duke and duchess of Windsor. In addition, the marriage of Commander and Mrs. Foxe is an underlying, if sub rosa, problem at the Stringham-Moreland party. The theme of marriage brings up the question of the treatment of women in *Dance*. Powell is often accused of not creating compelling women characters. (Ironically, this is not far from the accusation Jenkins levels against Trollope in the glare of General Liddament's incredulous face: "Women don't analyze their predicaments as there represented" [*Soldier's Art*, 46]). Since it is hard to say that Pamela, at the very least, is not a compelling character, what one assumes this means is that Powell is said to not include *sympathetic* women characters. It is definitely true that there is no female Stringham or female Templer in the sequence, no woman who sympathetically represents a discrete sphere of life. Jenkins's early amorous interests—Barbara Goring, Gypsy Jones—represent respectively opposite poles of conformity and dissension, each found unsatisfactory, and in any event are too tainted by their involvement with Widmerpool.

Miss Weedon sustains Stringham, even at the cost of de-energizing him, and is a devoted mate to two very different men,

General Conyers and Sunny Farebrother. The sequence's chief woman character, Isobel, is, for strategic reasons, in the grain of the narrative rather than a directly represented object of it. This does not mean that she is not a sine qua non for the entire narrative. Rosie Manasch is a minor portrait that might be mentioned, as is Frederica; neither are exactly "the perfect woman" for the narrator, and both have perceived limitations, but they are three-dimensional characters.

The reader notices that the women, except Billson, a maid and therefore understood to be one of the lower classes, are not called by their last names. The men, on the other hand, are routinely called by their last names, even Moreland after he has been Jenkins's best friend for two decades. The one exception is Albert, whom Jenkins is astonished to find even has a surname, also understood to be of the lower classes. This may be seen as a constraining privatization of women, a barring from full participation in the public sphere, or it may just reflect social customs of that era. Powell should not be pilloried for such a reflection. Though women such as Barbara Goring and Gypsy Jones are certainly mocked (remember, though, that they are seen through the point of view of a still immature narrator), the character of Pamela cannot be seen as an attack on women; indeed, in devising a sort of female Widmerpool, Powell is perhaps giving equal time to the opposite sex. To attack Powell as patriarchal would be beside the point. The problem is that the novel is set in the near past, which perhaps is the kernel of truth in the old adage that great novels, George Eliot's *Middlemarch* being the obvious example, are set in the near past, free of the consensus truths that undergird our sense of both the constituted present and the stable past. Surely a novel written in the twenty-first century about the 1920s would not garner objections, nor would a novel written in Powell's era about the Victorian epoch.

Yet another theme of the book is death. Maclintick's suicide is the most harrowing of any death in the sequence; even Biggs's suicide in *The Soldier's Art* has a morbidly comic touch, in its cricket associations, utterly lacking in Maclintick's. Despite Jenkins's personal lack of warmth for Maclintick, and the distance that almost inevitably comes with a "friend of a friend" relationship, Maclintick's death is profoundly registered. Another more indirectly canvassed death is that of the writer emeritus St. John Clarke. Jenkins feels oddly affected by Clarke's death, even though the only time he had ever met the novelist was at a party held, in *Casanova's Chinese Restaurant*, by his mother-in-law, Lady Warminster. In this sunniest scene of a generally depressing book, it emerges that several years earlier, Clarke had given Jenkins's novels "carefully hedged praise" (*Casanova's Chinese Restaurant*, 182), in other words, in a list of names of younger authors recited like a mantra to give a sense of currency, with no additional interpretive insight demanded or wanted. One can see it now: "Other important younger writers are: Mark Members, J. G. Quiggin, Nicholas Jenkins . . . ," as the litany trails off into names Clarke has even known less well. This is, at least to anyone with experience of reading general literary journalism, one of the most drily funny moments in the book. Aside from that, Clarke had been known only as an off-stage figure in the antics of Jenkins's contemporaries, Members and Quiggin. Yet Clarke soon dies, retrospectively casting the pall of death over even Lady Warminster's bright and cheery party. For Jenkins, a benchmark is gone. In combination with Maclintick's death, soon to unfold, there is a sense that the older generation, which had been there as a departure point, even if ridiculed, is no longer material. Jenkins's generation is no longer protected from death by youth and optimism.

Symptoms of a more collective death also begin to appear. Nearly every character in *Casanova's Chinese Restaurant* takes sides over the Spanish Civil War. Given that the vast majority of British intellectuals favored the Republican cause, which quickly became tainted by Soviet influence, Erridge's quixotic expedition to Spain falls well short of the inflated leftist rhetoric of "the struggle." Hugo, the sexually and vocationally uncertain youngest Tolland son, and the dour Maclintick are in favor of Franco, or at least say they are to outrage trendy leftists. Powell is clearly more sympathetic to Franco than to the Communists. But in his *Journals* and his correspondence with John Monagan, he makes clear his distaste for Franco in a more than ceremonial tone.

Death, though, does not close all in *Casanova's Chinese Restaurant*. A less morbid, even if perhaps no less horrifying, scene is the party that Mrs. Foxe, as musical patron, holds for Moreland's symphony. As with Widmerpool, Stringham and Moreland encounter each other once—at this party. But Stringham's attendance is not at all anticipated. Stringham and Moreland are Jenkins's two closest friends at different point of his life, come into contact. Despite an enormous difference—Moreland has achieved something in his music that Stringham has not, in terms of not only a career but also a creative raison d'être—they are similar. They personify art. They are "men of imagination." Just as Moreland's happiness is punctured by the uncreative Sir Magnus in *The Kindly Ones,* so is Stringham strangely ruined by his inability to fit into the conventional life represented by his father-in-law, Lord Bridgnorth—a situation he refers to again and again. They die early and tragic deaths after ending up in unlikely relationships with domineering women. Indeed, with a bit of narrative irony, we later see that both of these controlling women, Mrs. Maclintick and Miss Weedon, are present at this very party. Spurling describes both Stringham and Moreland as "romantics" (xvii). In their doomed fates, they are like the subjects of great English elegies such as Spenser's *Astrophel* (cited at *Military Philosophers,* 180) or Milton's *Lycidas,* men who die prematurely, deeply mourned, while the reader wonders what has enabled the mourner (Jenkins, in this case) to survive while the one mourned has died.

Neither Moreland nor Stringham are dead yet. Indeed, their ascribed fortunes at Mrs. Foxe's party vary considerably. On the surface, Stringham's appearance at the party would seem to oppose Moreland's success to Stringham's failure. Moreland is a promising young composer, having the premiere of his symphony and afterward the object of a celebratory party at the house of a prestigious upper-class hostess. Stringham, on the other hand, is divorced, not gainfully employed, in the care of a keeper who does not permit him to go out of the house carrying any cash and not particularly welcome at his mother's own party. Moreland seems to be one of life's winners, Stringham one of life's losers, a ne'er do well, a "being past serious credence" (*Casanova's Chinese Restaurant,* 145). But what we see at the party casts doubt on that simple equation.

First, neither Commander nor Mrs. Foxe seem in particularly good shape, or at least their marriage does not. Commander Foxe clearly either made a mistake in leaving the navy for the business world or left because he was given no prospect of serious promotion, one that would have given him the sort of command that the reader knows his generation, born in the 1880s, will have in the upcoming war. When the war does come, Foxe reenrolls and is given the rank of captain, but his work in

intelligence, though vital, does not match the kind of self-impor-
tance he previously had exuded. In fact, his work is only one
step above that of Jenkins's father, whose military career is seen
as, in the scheme of things, unsuccessful. Nor does Commander
Foxe seem as much in control of the situation as his dispatch
of Miss Weedon to remove Stringham might indicate. This is a
tactical, not a strategic, victory, as Stringham has shown he can
still function brilliantly, if eccentrically, in a way that Buster's
"Poor old Charles" (*Casanova's Chinese Restaurant,* 145) rhetoric to Jenkins would foreclose. Mrs. Foxe's weird liaison with
the flamboyantly homosexual Chandler, and her cultivation of
other creative artists such as Moreland, is in a way a broaden-
ing of interests from her previous, more narrowly high-social
world; but it is also a clear indication that something has gone
wrong in her marriage, that she feels short of options in her
immediate family circle. (As Stringham points out, Chandler
does all the things "Buster fails at so lamentably" [165].) When
we stand back and look at the canvas or, more aptly, listen to
the music, we see neither Commander nor Mrs. Foxe have aged
particularly well. When Jenkins first encountered them in *A
Question of Upbringing,* they seemed middle-aged, but neither
then was much over forty. Now their lives have taken, if not
a turn for the worse, then at least one the younger Jenkins, coming to the house as a friend of Stringham, could not have expected.

Moreland, far from exulting in his symphony's proclaimed
if not unanimously applauded success, is making a fool of himself in his affair with Priscilla Tolland, both undermining the stability of his marriage and short-circuiting his ability to follow up
on his moment of perceived musical triumph. Stringham, on the
other hand, attempts to stage something of a comeback at the
party from the rumored state of disrepair ascribed to him. For a

while he is resurgent. Or is this an illusion? Is this, in fact, the final embarrassment, a publicly humiliating debacle that exposes what Stringham has become to the world?

Powell's description of the party is a triumph of stage-management. Just as the Maclinticks are threatening to erupt in complete rancor over Mrs. Maclintick's exaggeration of her husband's reserved remarks about Moreland's work, just as Jenkins begins to worry about the overtly manifest nature of Moreland's affair with Priscilla Tolland, the depressing, not-really-Italian, former child prodigy violinist Carolo walks in. This provides a break in what was becoming very intense action and gives a genuine impression of a party, where many things are happening, not all in the narrator's purview or the mainstream of the story. Very few novelists know how to deploy characters in given situations so that their presence there seems natural and unforced and their physical progress from one scene to another does not seem mundane, procedural, or manipulated. Powell brilliantly braids his characters movements, physical and social, and thus avoids the gawkiness and the overly algorithmic programming from which many novelists moving a character from one place to another burden themselves. In this way, musical techniques, not just references, come into the marrow of *Casanova's Chinese Restaurant,* and the "dance" and "music" references in the title are here not structural metaphors for the entire work but a concrete indication of how the action in the work takes place. There is a symphonic element in scenes such as the Stringham/Moreland party, in which different conversational strands are analogous to different instruments or themes. And there is a balletic element, not just in the obvious trope of "changing dancing partners" as applied to the various love affairs that occur in the book, but also in the discrete and nearly anonymous movements that take place in any given life situation, which are, like balletic movements, both spontaneous and stylized. When we find out, at the end of an abstract, reflective conversation between Jenkins and Moreland's wife, Matilda, on marriage, that Matilda was formerly married, not to Sir Magnus Donners, whose one-time mistress she is well known as being, but to none other than Carolo, it is an astonishing revelation—but one that shifts the weight of the balance of the scene rather than bringing it to a cathartic culmination. During the abstract conversation, Jenkins had worried that it would be particularized by reference to Moreland's affair with Priscilla. It is indeed particularized, but by Matilda's revelation of the relationship with Carolo. Now we understand why Carolo (from the narrative point of view) is at the party. The information about the Matilda marriage is like a concluding chord at the end of a symphonic movement. But it is not a melodramatic revelation such as explicit unearthing of the Priscilla problem would have constituted. It is a stoppage, a drawing of breath, a representation as final of something perhaps in other circumstances temporary. Carolo does not really matter to Jenkins or figure in any of the greater total action of the sequence. An aura of impersonality is drawn over the party, a sheen of sheer plurality, a reassuring knowledge that everything in the world does not have relevance to oneself, which overt highlighting of an affair between Jenkins's friend and his sister-in-law would have done much to dispel. There is a sense of an unmanipulable reality beneath Powell's surface action, even if that reality is only a substrate accessible by fictive evocation.

Shortly thereafter, Stringham arrives. This is one of the most enigmatic episodes in *Dance*. Does Stringham really find Mrs. Maclintick attractive? Is his "Little Bo-Peep" (166) remark sarcastic or genuinely flirtatious? When he asks her to a night-club, is he being at all serious or is he just being ironic? That Jenkins sees Stringham's manner as "horseplay" (167) indicates a combination of all these alternatives, admitted on the surface by Stringham and presented aggressively to Mrs. Maclintick. But why does Stringham do this? Is this an unexpected angle in protest against a family script that has rendered him a marginalized, helpless failure? Is his attraction to this domineering, not conventionally feminine or attractive woman a testimony to the role played by dominating older women in his own life—his mother, Milly Andriadis, and, as we shall see, Miss Weedon? Mrs. Maclintick is the bane of her husband's existence. If not the sole agent of his suicide, she certainly did not help the situation. Yet later on, Moreland, a more solid, moored version of Stringham, becomes involved with her as well. She seems to embody some sort of chthonic life-force, some bracing assertiveness, some mesmeric termagancy, that makes these men feel they need her. The tone of her badinage with Stringham may best be described as mutually sardonic.

Miss Weedon's behavior is also not straightforward. On the one hand, Weedon, we learn, has been deputized by Buster Foxe to extricate Stringham from the party. Thus in a way she is a secret agent of Stringham's enemy while posing as his great friend. But in one of the most emotionally direct passages of the entire sequence, we are told that she has rescued Stringham because she "loved him" (*Casanova's Chinese Restaurant,* 280), though Jenkins thinks this before it is learned that Buster was behind her presence. Is Miss Weedon's first loyalty to Stringham or to, such as it is, the Foxe family? And why does Priscilla blush upon Miss Weedon's entrance? Is she embarrassed about the public display of her affair with Moreland? Or is she embarrassed on Stringham's behalf?

The anticlimactic way in which this particular scene ends —Lord Huntercombe suddenly materializing to tell Mrs. Foxe,

"Amy, are you aware this quatrefoil cup in a forgery?" (189)—
is resonant with implication for such a throwaway line. Lord
Huntercombe's fixation on Mrs. Foxe's china shows how it is
possible for someone at a party where such a climactic event as
the Stringham incident occurs to not notice it at all. People live
disparate lives, have disparate agendas, and notice disparate
things—a kind of deflationary counterpoint to the web of coincidence and mutual acquaintance that often envelops the characters in *Dance*. The diminutive, dapper, slightly absurd Lord
Huntercombe is completely wrapped up in his own preoccupations. But his kind of innocent delight in focusing on small
details in a work of art to the exclusion of more worldly considerations—surely Mrs. Foxe could not have liked being told that
a valued possession was in fact a forgery—is, in a minor key,
admirable. Walter Huntercombe does not have the emotional
depth, the genuine artistic greatness, of someone like Maclintick
(who, we realize with surprise, is one of the most creatively talented people in all of *Dance*). There is a pettiness about Huntercombe's obsessive interest in minor pieces of china. The
technical burglary of his bringing out "a small penknife in his
pocket" (170) in order to gain access to Mrs. Foxe's china is preposterous. Yet the narcissism of connoisseurship is vastly preferable to the narcissism or self-infatuation or self-aggrandizement
that a melodramatic ending—say, Matilda walking out in denunciation of Moreland's affair with Priscilla or Stringham
giving Buster a deserved punch in the nose—would have lent.
Huntercombe, an unobtrusive aesthete, pursues his own mission,
benignly oblivious to the clatter of the dance around him.

This minor victory for art is, as far as determining the
book's tone is concerned, more than counterbalanced by the
horrific defeat represented by Maclintick's suicide. The sadness

of Maclintick's end is partially muffled as neither Jenkins nor, most likely, we particularly like Maclintick. Yet there is genuine shock here. When Jenkins describes expecting Maclintick, even though recognizably depressed, to recover, musing that "people found their way of out depressing situations" (216), he expresses the reassuring component of the action of *Dance:* with no illusions as to the innate goodness of the human soul or a general optimism about which way history might go, there is yet a sense that, given that life is a dance, there are always possibilities for new conjunctions in the next step, ones that may be less gloomy than their predecessors. Maclintick's death cuts off the possibility of change. It is a bracing reminder that the consolation offered throughout the sequence can be forestalled altogether in certain individual cases of ineradicable pain.

Even what is, comparatively speaking, the comic relief of St. John Clarke leaving all his money to Erridge—ironic in that the former has all his life been some sort of middle-class liberal, the latter a radical peer—cannot stanch the mournfulness of the book's conclusion. The somber and stately ending of the book as it muses on the "Ghost Railway . . . fingered by spectral hands, moving at last with dreadful, ever increasing momentum towards a shape that lay across the line" is one of the most tonally elevated passages in all of *Dance.* Its tone is unrelievedly grim, and even if readers have been able to convince themselves through the first four volumes that this is light social comedy, at the end of the fifth, this mistake is inconceivable.

The Kindly Ones (1962)

The opening section of *The Kindly Ones,* which flashes back to Jenkins's childhood in 1914, is among the favorite parts of the

entire sequence for many readers. It is noteworthy that this is
a flashback from 1921; the same chapter would have been read
differently had it appeared at the sequence's chronological
beginning. As mentioned before, we do not begin in Jenkins's
childhood, which makes *Dance* different from a characteristically Dickensian narrative such as *David Copperfield* but gives
it some of the old epic virtues of beginning in the midst of
things—a technique that enables the sequence to dip back into
the past in its Herodotus-on-the-Scythians-style accounts of Mr.
Deacon and General Conyers. But the first subdivision of *The
Kindly Ones* is set entirely in 1914, seven years before the narrative proper of *A Question of Upbringing* begins, an approach,
as John Russell observes, "antedating all other material so far."[28]
Critics have tended to see this as a narratological move stressing, through analepsis, the mutability and manipulability of time.
As Widmerpool himself might say, this is all well and good. But
notwithstanding the frisson of the heretofore withheld prequel,
it is the specific time to which the narrative goes back, not the
backward move itself, that is determinative.

The title of the book refers to the Eumenides, actually the
Erinyes (the Furies) in Greek myth, who in a placating manner
were referred to euphemistically as "the Eumenides," meaning
"the kindly ones," "flattery intended to appease their terrible
wrath" (*Kindly Ones,* 2). The Eumenides were, of course, particularly prominent in 1914 and 1938–39, the years *The Kindly
Ones* with its unusual, exceedingly effective two-part structure,
represents, and the title is, of course, ironic.

The scene at the Jenkins family bungalow, Stonehurst, is
like that of La Grenadière in the ingenuity with which a dramatic ensemble is assembled. Both scenes are astonishing portraits of complex societies of ten or so people relating to one

another against a defined background of context and situation. The first chapter of *The Kindly Ones* would indeed make a good one-act play or an effective *Norton Anthology* excerpt, much like the France episode in *A Question of Upbringing*.

There is some readerly delight in seeing the seemingly imperturbable Jenkins, for all his diffidence, possessed from his first adolescent entry onto the stage with an adult poise and confident in judgment, as an eight-year-old child. Similarly, we approach Jenkins's parents, whom we have never seen on stage before, through the prism of Uncle Giles—the reverse of the traditional story of growing up, where we would usually meet the parents first before some raffishly undesirable uncle. Despite the memorable portrait of Jenkins's father, both here and, at one remove, in *A Question of Upbringing* (his "occasional and uncontrollable desire to tell Uncle Giles to his face what he thought of him, a mood that rarely lasted more than thirty-six hours, by the end of which the foredoomed efficacy of such contact made itself clear" [18]), Uncle Giles seems to be a figure more susceptible to narrative approach in *Dance* than his younger brother, Jenkins's father. James Tucker comments on Giles's resentment toward people in authority that "if he cannot win, the game must be wrong." But even though Giles excites the severe dissatisfaction of Jenkins's father, we can see underlying similarities between Giles's opposition to "all established institutions on the grounds that they were entirely—and therefore incapably—controlled by persons whose sole claim to consideration was that they could command influence" (*Question of Upbringing,* 67) and Jenkins's father's "hatred of constituted authority" displaced onto an even more severe hatred of hearing "constituted authority questioned by anyone but himself" (*Kindly Ones,* 38). Jenkins's father is one of the most fascinating minor characters in the sequence and is underrated because he does not come into the main action, being somewhat like Monsieur Dubuisson in this respect. Hilary Spurling, for instance, should have listed this rather distinguished *officier de carrière* (*Military Philosophers*, 89) not as "Captain Jenkins," which puts him at the same rank as his disreputable younger brother, who has more or less breveted himself the title, but as Lieutenant Colonel Jenkins, the highest rank the senior Jenkins attained and apparently the highest military rank ever attained by the Jenkins family. The two Jenkins brothers, though uneasy with each other, have underlying similarities. The egoism, the sense of grievance, the aura of personal lack of fulfillment, combined with a kind if unshakeable faith that the social order was describable and determinate, and operated in a predictably hierarchical manner, is a familiar or generational feature shared by the Jenkinses. It transcends Jenkins's father being more conventionally successful and in a position to lord it over Giles both morally and financially.

We must differentiate Uncle Giles from Widmerpool. There are certainly some similarities in their politics and their determination to cause trouble for what they see as an Old Boy network that stands in their way. Both appear at the very beginning of the first book, and, in a fascinating structural symmetry, Uncle Giles dies in the sixth book and Widmerpool doubles him by undertaking what he at that point might have been more apt to term synthesis or transformation in the twelfth. But Uncle Giles has nothing of the ambition of Widmerpool. Nor does he have the vindictiveness. If he had ever, to the astonishment of his relatives, married, settled down, and pursued a respectably conventional career, he would have puttered around for a while and then quietly died in a more decorous but essentially similar manner to what "actually" happened. There would have been none of the preening, the exultant mastery over his previous circumstances and those who had determined them, indulged in to such excess by Widmerpool. Jenkins also has a reluctant affection for Uncle Giles, perhaps because his uncle is a less demanding version of his father. When Jenkins unexpectedly sees the Huntercombes' party through Giles's eyes in *A Buyer's Market,* not knowing he will actually encounter Giles in the flesh at the end of his long night, he does so to satirize Giles's pretentious dismissal of pretentious occasions and to leaven any self-conscious fanciness about his own description of the ball, to lend an air of distance from the event by seeing it through the prism of someone bound to be hostile to it because of his sense of exclusion. Nicholas Jenkins is conscious of the self-serving nature of his uncle's outsider rhetoric, his pose of being a bit of a radical, but it comes in useful for him as a monitor when he does not want to be too much of an insider. There is also the sense of the intimacy of family relationships being a fortifying reminder of more immediate human ties when Jenkins is embarking on the complicated social minuet entailed by attendance at occasions such as the Huntercombe ball.

Uncle Giles, along with General Conyers, is one of the characters ready-to-hand in the analeptic first section of *The Kindly Ones.* Both Giles and Conyers have been established as members of an older generation within Jenkins's family orbit. From the older characters already mentioned in the first five books, we have a potential stock of individuals conceivably active in 1914. There is something pleasing in seeing these characters, familiar from a later milieu, reappear in a younger guise. Then there is the triangular mini-drama of Albert, the imperturbable servant, who is loved by Billson, the maid, who in turn is loved by the soldier-servant Bracey, whose unrequited affection for Billson—made unrequited by the mere fact of his being a soldier—sets off his legendary "funny days," which awareness of their coming manifestation does nothing to forestall. When Billson finds out Albert is marrying someone else, she stages her resentment openly by appearing naked in front of the assembled house party—at the same time as the assassination of Archduke Franz Ferdinand, which will set off the First World War, is announced. As the domestic drama has percolated, so have the wheels of impending war begun to turn, with Conyers musing on Liman von Sanders, the German general sent to command the Turkish military and keep an eye on the envisioned construction of the Berlin-to-Baghdad railway, demonstrating Skobeloff's dictum that "the road to Constantinople leads through the Brandenburger Tor" (*Kindly Ones,* 56). Again, as we have seen these sorts of references to politics of the time occur in the books representing the 1920s and 1930s, there is a frisson of fun in seeing this sort of prequel effect, with the same kind of references made to events that had preceded the references to President Wilson and the Versailles peace conference in *A Question of Upbringing.*

To give a full overview of the twentieth century, the First World War must be directly represented in *Dance.* The seemingly idyllic opening of the first book, and Le Bas's attempt to encapsulate that idyll in poetic quotation from Theocritus, cannot conceal the conflagration that has just recently ended. The war has a more direct, "menacing" (*Infants,* 19) effect on Jenkins's generation. So many of their elder brothers—figuratively if not literally—have been killed off in the war or otherwise maimed or traumatized, like Ted Jeavons, Dicky Umfraville, or, tacitly, Jenkins's own father. Because of this, there are more openings in society for those too young to have served in the war, for whom "'the Armistice' was a distant memory" (*At Lady Molly's,* 171) than otherwise would have been the case. Thus the tales of early achievement in *Dance,* such as Mark Members's rise as a poet, Tompsitt's rise as a diplomat, or Bill Truscott's early promise as a cog in the machine of Donners-Brebner, have an aftertaste of melancholy to them, as if these goals of "getting on in life and making a 'good marriage'" (*At Lady Molly's,* 13) are pursued amid echoes of "onerous acts of service and sacrifice" (*Kindly Ones,* 74).

The occult practices of Dr. Trelawney are another portent of war. "The Essence of the All Is the Godhead of the True" and its cryptic rejoinder "The Visions of Visions Heals the Blindness of Sight" evoke a vague, spiritual pantheism. Of course, on the verbal level, they become unmoored from any such reference, so that Powell fans can repeat the phrases to each other as part of the fun of their own coded communication in a secret fraternity —thus, paradoxically, the lines as manifested in a novel have the same sort of magical quality as they do in the presented real life of the Trelawney cult, though surely a less literal, more benign one. The Trelawney cult, along with the far more sketchily presented movement of the Elect, adhered to by the housemaid Mercy, are of course harbingers of the Eumenides, of the furies of war, in their madness, their doggedness, and their sense of military determination, and of a general sense of crisis signaled by such spiritually intense claims. Powell's prescience, in presenting a cult existing in 1914 in a novel published in 1962, not knowing that a cult existing in 1968 would serve him very well in a novel published in 1975, has already been noted. But it would be wrong to see Scorpio Murtlock's essentially far more menacing version of Trelawney's cult as the only analogue of

Trelawneyism in *Dance* (Trelawney himself is a comic, farcical character, to all evidence far less menacing than his obvious model, Aleister Crowley). So many people in *Dance* draw adherents, have hangers-on. This is true, in very benign fashion, even of the straightforward Templer, to whom less confident men such as Bob Duport and Jimmy Brent adhere. It could even be said that Jenkins is a member of the Stringham cult at school. Mr. Deacon's entourage has aspects of a cult, and Pamela Flitton is definitely the fulcrum of a sort of erotic cult of death to which Russell Gwinnett attaches himself as priest. And the great ideological menaces to the world of *Dance*—fascism and communism—were of course metastasized cults themselves, laden with all the mumbo-jumbo and catch phrases of Trelawneyism, though managing to gain control of armies and large, industrialized multinational empires, not just a ragtag band of dropouts.[29]

As self-contained as the first chapter is, it is not categorically separated from the rest of *The Kindly Ones*. This is not only because of the First–Second World War linkage but also because the second chapter takes up a comparison of Moreland and Jenkins's childhood. In fact, even if we did not have the 1914 chapter, we would find out more about Jenkins's childhood from the second chapter than from anywhere else in *Dance*. This helps ease the experimental structure of *The Kindly Ones,* with one chapter set twenty-five years before any of the others. Because of the segue provided by the second chapter, the dovetailing back to childhood is no more disconcerting than to find Herodotus proceed from the general background of the Scythians to their precise interaction with Cyrus, to mention a name whose infrequent occurrence in ordinary discourse so heartened Jenkins (*Buyer's Market,* 15).

The later portion of *The Kindly Ones* is dominated by the pageant of the Seven Deadly Sins at Stourwater. It is in this scene that we first get a full view of Sir Magnus Donners, one of the major secondary characters in the sequence and, arguably, its most menacing besides Widmerpool and Scorpio Murtlock. Sir Magnus is a "man of affairs," and his first encroachment in the novel is as the person who draws Stringham away from Oxford —and the world of Jenkins—into the "acceptance world" in which he so markedly does not prosper.[30]

Sir Magnus, when falsely told he was about to die, tries to rectify his felt cultural inadequacy by holing himself up in the country seeking out "the best" (*Temporary Kings,* 271) of everything—the best books, the best art, the best music, even, perhaps, the best sexual practices. Donners's last-dash aesthetic binge is a much more vulgar version of Le Bas's classicism, though both are attempts to take shortcuts to the hard task of being a serious student of the arts. Of course, finding the "best" in all these areas is, in essence, listening to other people's recommendations of what the best is, which inevitably will be more or less conventional. Donners, however, does not seem to have bad taste in the visual arts—certainly better than Bob Duport.

Sir Magnus, like Widmerpool, is a man of unorthodox sexual inclinations; unlike Widmerpool, though, who complements his zeal for power with a strain of masochism, Donners appears to be exclusively sadistic. His sadism is channeled through voyeurism—what today we would call the "male gaze." The voyeur holds power by observing rather than acting (cf. Donners never marrying, not having children), in a mode analogous to Sir Magnus's political and business machinations, where he is always acting behind the scenes, arranging pieces on the chessboard (sending Duport to Turkey for chromite), and has both women and men at his disposal in different capacities. Also, there is Henchman in *The Fisher King,* in which photography is associated with literal impotence, metaphorical power.

Sir Magnus also has a more unconventional relationship toward bohemian figures. He has mistresses in common with them. Whereas General Conyers represents a "contact zone" between the power world and the world of art, it is through Sir Magnus's mistresses that the worlds of art and money meet:

Sir Magnus—Matilda—Moreland
Sir Magnus—Baby Wentworth—Barnby

These love triangles, structurally of the same sort of the more socially prosaic Albert-Billson-Bracey one, involve a classic opposition between the rich but ignoble suitor and his poor but noble rival, as both the composer Moreland and the painter Barnby are, whatever their occasional raffishness, presented as fundamentally good people, whereas Sir Magnus is presented, rather straightforwardly, as an immoral man. The contest here is not as lopsided as the conventional supposition might have it. Barnby, with a jaded, counterintuitive confidence, observes that "a poor man competing with a rich one for a woman should be in a relatively strong position if he plays his cards well" (*Buyer's Market,* 172). But most of the time it does not turn out that way in *Dance.* When Matilda leaves Moreland for Donners, she is betraying art for commerce—when Moreland says she has "gone back to Donners" (*Kindly Ones,* 242), it is a relapse in taste, not just a recidivism in sentiment. That Powell is so unmoralistic a writer as to never play up these oppositions in any way that would involve sentimentality does not mean that, tacitly and subtly, they are not there in the book.

There is a difference in nomenclature between the name given "Sir Magnus" and most of the other characters. Powell's matchless onomastic technique takes names from the existing stock of English and, for that matter, Welsh nomenclature and, stretching credibility if at all then very gently, reshuffles them to fit his idiosyncratic cast of characters. (As a matter of fact, he does this effectively with the French and Belgian names in *The Military Philosophers;* the Polish names in the same book, though plausibly Polish, do not seem to have the philological wit the other names do.) "Sir Magnus Donners," though, is an outsized, hyperbolic name. It is of a sort more typical of nineteenth-century writers from George Bernard Shaw to Charles Dickens to W. S. Gilbert, or of Restoration comedy. "Donners" comes from the German word for "thunder" and "Magnus" from the Latin for "great," though Magnus is seen as a Scandinavian name. The ethnic roots of "Donners" make the name seem more plausible than it would for someone alleged to be of English descent; Powell's names, no matter how preposterous, are never implausible. But the difference in onomastic resonance does make Sir Magnus a more "stock" character and puts him on a less realistic plane of representation. There are cartoonish elements (*Buyer's Market,* 136) and those of the stage tycoon (*Buyer's Market,* 137), even though, as Jenkins notes, these do not exhaust his character's potential. Of course, one could argue that this is true of Widmerpool as well—that he is less "round" a character than, say, Stringham.

Donners is not a self-made man, in that, as that consummate diplomat, Sir Gavin Walpole-Wilson, puts it in *A Buyer's Market,* he "did not start life barefoot" (181), not that Sir Gavin finds anything wrong with that. So he is more a twentieth-century magnate than a nineteenth-century entrepreneur.

Compared with the aristocratic families in *Dance,* though, he is an *arriviste.* Stourwater is the only great house mentioned in *Dance* not historically associated with hereditary nobility. In generational terms, Donners (born ca. 1874) is slightly older than the generation of Jenkins's father and Uncle Giles, born in the 1880s. He is similar in age to Winston Churchill (1874–1965), and like Churchill, he is not totally averse to economic planning, to government having a role in the economy. Donners in fact is the representative of "capitalism" and "high finance" in *Dance* and is a living rebuke to those who claim that Powell satirizes only the Left. Granted, Donners had "advanced" sexual and, to a far lesser extent, social views more characteristic of the Left, but basically he seems to be a moderate Tory (cf. the party loyalist Tory Fettiplace-Jones speaking well of his organizing abilities), certainly serving in the wartime government of national unity as a Tory. When Stringham leaves university to work for Donners Brebner (we never see Brebner at all; a typically Powellian joke, whose ancestor is perhaps "Judkins and Judkins" in *Waring,* where the protagonist is perpetually being asked for which Judkins he works), it is a betrayal of art to corporate careerism. Stringham, who at the beginning of *A Question of Upbringing* is talking about villanelles and Theocritus, at the end works for what Quiggin mocks as a "big concern." Even though the Left-leaning Sillery sees Sir Magnus as at least an enlightened despot, Sir Magnus is a figure of the conventional Establishment. It is as such that both the congenitally conventional Bill Truscott (only he would call Sir Magnus "the most unconventional man in the world") and the eager-beaverish Widmerpool gravitate to him. Though Widmerpool nominally comes afoul of Donners in *The Acceptance World* and to some extent speaks disparagingly of him thereafter, they retain a fundamental kinship; they are after the same goals. Powell's point here is that seekers of power will find common ground with one another whatever their surface political labels. The Widmerpools of the world will gravitate to whoever seems to represent the rising tide, whether it be Donners in the roaring twenties or Murtlock in the swinging sixties.

Unlike Widmerpool, though, Donners has traffic with the arts. Not only is he a patron of the arts as an aspect of his image as corporate magnate, but he takes a dilettantish and very conventional interest in them himself. As a patron, Donners wields power through the arts, unlike Widmerpool, who keeps his distance from them (even through Tokenhouse's Socialist realist painting in *Temporary Kings,* which he disregards as Glober quirkily admires it). In staging the Seven Deadly Sins, Donners shows his zeal for power—arranging the tableau and assigning a sin to each person present—as well as his interest in the arts as a mode for enacting that power. Many people find this the most disturbing scene in *Dance.*

Stourwater becoming a girls' school in *Temporary Kings* and *Hearing Secret Harmonies* is a clear hearkening back to the imprisonment of "the girls that don't behave" in *A Buyer's Market* (202). It is also an ironic rejoinder to Donners's aggressive hypermasculinity. The ambiguous relationship with the arts persists after his death as well. The Donners prize goes to one eccentric, Gwinnett, for his biography of another eccentric, Trapnel, both of whose intellectual interests would have been incomprehensible to Sir Magnus. Thus the asymmetrical relationship between art and power continues even onto later ages. This relationship generates some of the sequence's least reserved assessments. Jenkins, so often neutral or reticent in his observations of other people, always giving himself time to take their measure, seems to come to a more immediate opinion of Sir

Magnus than most others—"the sledge-hammer impact of his comment left, by its banality, every other speaker at a standstill, giving him as a rule complete mastery over the conversational field" (*Kindly Ones,* 111).

As a scene, the Seven Deadly Sins is potentially stagey. Therefore, Powell, with his unerring sense of occasion, clamps down on any portentousness by having several of the participants—Anne Stepney, Matilda, and the crazy Betty Templer, with her memorable statement that her first husband was "in jute" (119)—be essentially minor players. (Think if Stringham or Gypsy Jones had been involved.) Intriguingly, Widmerpool arrives just too late to participate in the Seven Deadly Sins masquerade. Perhaps this is because he incarnates all of the sins, perhaps because he represents an Eighth Deadly Sin—opportunism (if not, as Lady Donners suggests in *Hearing Secret Harmonies,* humbug).

The second trilogy, merely by virtue of its setting in the 1930s, raises political issues of a particularly serious sort. Christopher Hitchens has recently called attention to a possible problem in Powell's representation of the 1930s, when, in the midst of a generally highly laudatory essay on Powell, he notes that there is no depiction of the "Fascist or crypto-Fascist element in upper-class British society" in *Dance,* presumably of the sort so memorably provided in retrospect by Kazuo Ishiguro in *The Remains of the Day* (1989).[31] There has been general concern that Nazism and its supporters among the English upper class do not come in for their fair share of skewering by the satirist's wit. Powell might respond that a novel, by its generic nature, cannot be comprehensive and necessarily relates events from a given angle. The narrator's milieu (or its real-life model) may have happened to include more communists, or this particular focus might have served the structural and formal aims of the novelist. There is no evidence that Powell knew the Mosleys or the Cliveden set (his relationship with the Mitford family was pretty much restricted to the novelist Nancy Mitford and Deborah, the future Duchess of Devonshire, the youngest Mitford daughter), and Jenkins thus does not meet characters based on these people in the novel. Julian Allason, a writer for the *Financial Times* who is active in the Anthony Powell Society, is of the opinion that an upper-class fascist such as Sir Oswald Mosley actually drew "little support" from "his own echelon of society." Another riposte to the Hitchens argument would be to argue that characters are indeed represented as flirting with Nazism. Widmerpool, for instance, suggests in *At Lady Molly's* that Göring be given the Order of the Garter, as a way of allaying tensions between Britain and Hitler's Germany, and is of the deluded opinion that the anti-Semitic aspects of the Nazi platform will be dropped. He also hints at a friendship with Edward VIII (later duke of Windsor), a figure often accused of pro-Nazi views. Uncle Giles, a raffish character who is viewed in the sequence as generally being up to no good, says in *At Lady Molly's,* "I rather like that little man they have in Germany these days." Widmerpool, in the course of a speech suggesting all manner of appeasement of the Nazis, including Göring being given the Order of the Garter, says, "I myself possess a number of Jewish friends, some of them very able—Jimmy Klein, for example" (63), an unwitting reenactment of the banality "Some of my best friends are Jewish." (Note that Jenkins does have Jewish friends—Feingold, Rosie Manasch—who are not referred to self-consciously as Jews.) Perhaps what upsets some people is that the Nazi sympathies are attributed not to hereditary aristocrats but to an opportunistic social climber.

The similarity in spelling between Göring (Goering in the book, spelling out the umlaut) and Goring as in Barbara

Goring, has to be deliberate on part of Powell since he made up one of the names, and might indicate some sort of subconscious connection between the values of the family of Lord Aberavon and some of the Nazi hierarchy. (The Goring name is also evocative of the Lord Goring in Oscar Wilde's *Ideal Husband,* particularly given Frederica Budd's bantering about "Lord" Goring in *At Lady Molly's.*) Yet Powell had fewer links to the aristocrats who were Nazi sympathizers than some of his contemporaries; for instance, he talks about how little he had to do with the Mitford family. Compare the experience of James Lees-Milne, the superb diarist and renowned historic preservationist, who was a good friend of Tom Mitford and acquainted with the rest of the family. Lees-Milne's politics during this era were very different from Powell's. A pacifist, he also had some sympathy with the Franco regime in Spain, though certainly not for the Fascist governments in Italy and Germany. This is not to Lees-Milne's detriment but does show how generally centrist and interventionist Powell's prewar political views were.

There is, though, a small kernel of truth in Hitchens's complaints, in that in one respect *Dance*'s view of the late 1930s does not entirely agree with the usual historical verdict. A clue to this can be seen in *Temporary Kings,* when Tokenhouse and Jenkins's father, once old friends, are said to have fallen out in a "political disagreement of the bitterest kind" (58) over "Munich," that is, over the agreement between Adolf Hitler and British prime minister Neville Chamberlain in September 1938 that gave Germany the German-speaking portions of Czechoslovakia in return for an exceedingly chimerical promise of continued peace. But it is not explained just what positions Tokenhouse and Jenkins senior took. If, though, we assume that Tokenhouse was as much a Soviet sympathizer in 1938 as he was in 1958, he would have taken the pro-Soviet position in

1938, which (far contrary to that which Stalin would take when he signed the nonaggression pact with Hitler a year later, an event which sends Tokenhouse to a psychiatric breakdown) was very much belligerent and urging the West to fight for the Czechs, though the Soviets were certainly not going to take any action on their own.[32] So the position of the senior Jenkins must then have been for the agreement. This was absolutely not as a form of appeasement but out of a sense that, as his son puts it in *The Kindly Ones,* the country was not ready for war, that "there's no point in going to war if we're not going to win it" (98). Jenkins père and fils, however drastic their temperamental differences, seem to have had similar politics. Though this is still not the majority opinion of historians, it is a wholly legitimate one from the pro-Allied ideological position. It is given support by the historian Gerhard Weinberg, who fled Germany as a boy in the 1930s. Chamberlain, he notes, "tricked" the Nazis "into negotiations" when their army was much superior to Britain's.[33] As a result, Britain gained a year's time, which might have meant the difference between defeat and victory. Not everyone will buy this interpretation—certainly Winston Churchill did not, and even in *Dance,* Ted Jeavons wants to attack Hitler in 1934.[34] But it should not lead to either Jenkins or his creator being seen as anything but thoroughly antitotalitarian, with regard to both Nazism and communism. That there were people of good will on both sides of this difference can be seen in the conversation between two conservative members of parliament, Roddy Cutts and Fettiplace-Jones (the latter's first name is never revealed during the sequence) in *Kindly Ones* (92), where, un-like as in the portrayal of Rex Mottram in *Brideshead Revisited,* one of the participants is not seen as a deviator from the true faith. This debate between Cutts and Fettiplace-Jones, replayed so many times in later historiographical discussion, can have none other than an interim verdict at this point, as the twentieth century, a tumultuous one, is unlikely to be the subject of permanent historical consensus anytime soon.[35]

As the last few paragraphs indicate, even though *The Kindly Ones* lacks the personal tragedy of Maclintick's death in *Casanova's Chinese Restaurant,* the storm clouds of war make a gloomier canvas than in many of the previous books. The Seven Deadly Sins scene is particularly dark and disturbing. All the more reason why we need the sunny glimpse of the young Jenkins, before either world war had transpired, in the first chapter. But there is another chink of light even after the war has begun. Like the happy events of *At Lady Molly's,* it transpires in the Jeavons household.

Stanley Jeavons, Ted's even less noteworthy brother, gets Jenkins into his preferred regiment. Thus the agent of this process is not Jenkins's own career officer father, not General Conyers, not Sir Magnus Donners, not any of the great and the good who Jenkins had encountered through the preceding six volumes (certainly not Widmerpool, who is unmoved by Jenkins's pleas for help), but a totally prosaic and previously unencountered figure. Stanley Jeavons is somebody of completely no glamour in ordinary life, an accountant without any remarkable personal features or any notable contacts, somebody who floats into Jenkins's life only randomly and at first seems inconspicuous. The streak of good luck associated with the Jeavons household is intact. Movers and shakers like Donners do not, it turns out, have the field to themselves.

The Valley of Bones (1964)

The title is taken from the Old Testament, Ezekiel 37. Here the point is not just the desiccation of the dry bones themselves but their potential to "come to life" (Ezekiel 37:3, AV), as their sudden animation is a portent of the Jews' return to "their land" from exile by the waters of Babylon. So the import is as much prophetic and optimistic—in fact, almost connoting a new creation—as despairing. Powell indicates the association of the Welsh troops with a biblical mentality in their singing of the originally Welsh hymn "Guide me Thou, O Great Jehovah" (Cwm Rhondda), which is the first instance of overt institutional religiosity since school in *A Question of Upbringing*. In fact, in some ways book seven is as much going to school for Jenkins as book one is, although this time it is the school of war. The food motifs—porridge, galantine—also give a sense of people living in community, forced to eat whatever food is available and in general live by a corporate code, much the same way as the boys did at school. Both books one and seven also begin with snow falling, so the return to the snow image at the end of *Hearing Secret Harmonies* caps both the twelve-book sequence as a whole and the final six-book half of it.

Jenkins, however, is not as at home in the army as at school, though he respects both institutions equally, if not to the point of idolatry or to being unwilling to make fun of them. By his own admission, he is not a sterling military officer. He is a second lieutenant, one of two along with Idwal Kedward, responsible for a "section" of thirty or so men. Their immediate superior is Captain Rowland Gwatkin, in charge of the company as a whole, whose unit strength is about 120 men. Jenkins serves his company commander, Gwatkin, the regimental officer, Colonel Davies (the regiment really being the operative unit to which Jenkins, in essence, belongs), and General Liddament himself (who commands the division) with all the good will in the world. But the play-it-by-the-book Kedward, far less intelligent and experienced in worldly matters than Jenkins, impresses his superiors much more. Kedward is named to succeed Gwatkin when the latter suffers his humiliation over botched code words and Maureen the Irish bar girl. But Jenkins's relative mediocrity is presented comically and without any displacement of it to resentment against the army as an institution. Especially when the regiment is posted to Castlemallock in Northern Ireland, disillusionment can set in: "Like a million others, I missed my wife, wearied of the officers and men around me, grew to loathe a post wanting even the consolation that one was supposed to be brave" (171).

Gwatkin, though, is presented positively. His gift of an entire piece of chocolate to Jenkins is one of the most genuinely generous actions taken by anyone in the entire sequence. His dreams of glory in both war and (adulterous) love are not mocked. Yet there is an upward limit on his idealizations. Another writer might have lionized Gwatkin as a man of action as compared with Jenkins's man of words, or at least presented him as a gracious model warrior, much like Gwatkin's fellow Welshman Fluellen in Shakespeare's *Henry V*. But Gwatkin, though admirable, is a person, not a kind of glimpsed martial or, in light of his first name, epic/courtly, ideal. Similarly, it is overdoing it to call Kedward "a Widmerpool in miniature," as Robert Morris does.[36] Kedward is soulless and self-serving but not monstrous; if he is Widmerpool, then most people who do well in organizations are, and Widmerpool, unmistakeably, is not meant to be a prototype of the medium-successful organization man. Also, Kedward does not recur of his own accord. In fact, in *The Military Philosophers* Jenkins has to really work to make an uncooperative Kedward remember him at all. Regimental service does not inspire the same mesmeric yoking as Widmerpool seems to possess vis-à-vis Jenkins.

Kedward's attitude epitomizes the difference (in broad terms) between the characters in the third trilogy of *Dance* and those who populate the books before and after it. The "war trilogy" composed of the seventh, eighth, and ninth books of *Dance,* though theoretically on the level of the other three trilogies, has from the beginning had a quasi-independent existence in the minds of Powell's readers; witness John Russell subtitling his early book on Powell, *A Quintet, Sextet and War.* As with the other books, new characters are introduced in each, and in milieus more substantially different from what had come previously as to guarantee the war books a self-sufficient quality. This does not mean we should expect a sudden switch from drawing-room conversation to battlefield skirmishes. Powell's war, as opposed to most of the novels written by men who had served in the war, involves minimal combat. As James Tucker comments, "we do not see the enemy."[37] All the combat deaths are offstage, and the only wartime casualties seen onstage are civilian victims of aerial bombing (the terrible evening in March 1941 when, in separate incidents, both Chips Lovell and his estranged wife, Lady Priscilla Tolland, are killed by German air raids).

There is not, for instance, a battle scene with the clarity and vividness of the Dunkirk passages in Ian McEwan's 2002 novel *Atonement.* Yet Powell's war, though undramatic and unsanguinary, was his own. The war trilogy of *Dance,* written a mere twenty years after the events they chronicled, simmer, beneath their measured prose, with the intensity of firsthand experience. Powell uses the *Servitudes et Grandeurs Militaires* of the nineteenth-century French writer Alfred de Vigny—introduced to Jenkins by David Pennistone, who turns out to have been present at the Milly Andriadis party in *A Buyer's Market*—as a prototype for stressing the routine and drudgery of military life, not its dash and valor. This emphasis on routine, even boredom, means that the war trilogy is not disconcertingly more exciting than the rest of the sequence. It would be a mistake to confine the theme of "war" in *Dance* to the three books taking place between 1939 and 1945. Beneath its placid surface of gossip, humor, and serene social forms, *Dance* is very much a sequence colored by war; *The Kindly Ones,* as we have seen, depicts the onset of both world wars, *A Question of Upbringing* is tinged by war's aftermath, and *Temporary Kings* is set at the height of the cold war, whose beginnings, as well as the aftermath of the Second World War, are seen in *Books. Dance* depicts, throughout its reach, a nation engaged in war and people who have been, are, or will be affected by war.

It may be going just too far to say that *Dance* as a whole is a war sequence. Powell's tone, if nothing else, is too serene, assured, and consoling for this. But war is never far away. There is also a hidden war in *Dance:* the war between Widmerpool and those of different values, which, though not presented as starkly as those who accuse Powell of favoring some characters at the expense of others tend to imply, nonetheless rages throughout the duration of the sequence. Even aside from this, so many personal relations are presented as conflicts, as situations where first one party then the other has the upper hand—the relationship between Stringham and his stepfather, as noted by Hilary Spurling, is one, as is the all-too-little-noticed relationship between Sunny Farebrother and Peter Templer's businessman father, where Farebrother can only reveal, or admit, his loathing for Mr. Templer after the latter is long dead.

It is not, then, war that gives what we will still call the war trilogy its unity, but an alteration of the nature of the cast of characters as a result of Jenkins being in the army. Previously, when we had met new characters in one book, they had, by and large, recurred in the next. Barnby, presented in the second book as part of Mr. Deacon's artistic milieu, recurs in later books, as does General Conyers, who appears in *Lady Molly's,* then, staying alive for much longer than the reader suspects he will, recurs as well. Even far more local characters, like the musical figures Gossage and Carolo in *Casanova,* recur in later books. The only exceptions are characters in the two "special" venues, Stonehurst and La Grenadière, who, with the exception of characters previously established, do not recur. But with the war trilogy, we have a situation in which Rowland Gwatkin, in many ways the major character in *Valley of Bones,* a character whom the reader comes to know and view sympathetically, never comes back in the flesh. Only his obituary is mentioned. "One returned to a different world" (*Books,* 94). Jenkins's reintroduction of him in *The Military Philosophers* in his conversation with Kedward is hamstrung by Kedward's own unclear recollection of Jenkins himself, which surely stands for the reluctance of people outside Jenkins's extended social circle in London to gossip or keep up with what has happened to each other. If Kedward has people about whom he talks about this way, Jenkins is outside that circle. Jenkins desperately wants Kedward, and through him Gwatkin, to recur. But Kedward will not consent. Far from the snobbish Jenkins not extending his social circle to depict the ordinary Kedward, it is Kedward who will not step inside the circle, perhaps because he has genuinely forgotten Jenkins, whether through the demands of duty or simple incuriosity, or whether he sees Jenkins as such a nonstarter in terms of military career gamesmanship as to be a waste of his time.

Jenkins, though, also limits himself from drawing too many connections between army and civilian life. A clue that this limitation is intentional on the part of the author is seen in *Writer's Notebook* (65), where Castlemallock seems to have been envisioned as the Ardglass seat. This connection to the debutante world of the early novels of the sequence was eventually rejected by Powell once he actually wrote the book, for Castlemallock is a drab place without *Dance* antecedents, although with literary ones in terms of Lord Byron's (again fictive) visit there. The brief apparition of Greening, the aide-de-camp to General Liddament in *The Soldier's Art,* in the Christmas shopping scene in *Hearing Secret Harmonies* (141–43) is an exception to this, as of course is the reappearance of Bithel, the unreliable and bibulous lieutenant posted to the company just after Jenkins's arrival, as a member of Murtlock's cult. To this could be added the way Cheesman appears in *Temporary Kings* to give news, in an unaffected manner that is somehow uncommonly moving, of Stringham's death at Singapore. But as the last example indicates, all the reappearances of wartime characters in later books are to bring news of some of the London characters. They operate as what Henry James might call *ficelles* and are not of primary importance in their own right.

It is through the motif of nonrecurrence that here, in *Valley of Bones,* we finally come to the subject the reader has surely long awaited: social class. The readers who castigate Powell for not writing about the lower classes seem to elevate, as a kind of normative, baseline plot, the romance of the poor boy struggling against the odds, as in Dickens. But most twentieth-century novelists do not write according to this norm; certainly, on the American side, Faulkner, Fitzgerald, and Hemingway do not. Some of Powell's contemporaries, such as Henry Green, George Orwell, and W. H. Auden, took a deliberate interest in the lower classes, but this interest was both part of a deliberate aesthetic and political design on their part. It would be underrating these writers to see them as dutifully affirming some social consensus against which Powell snobbishly held out. Virginia Woolf used to receive the same sort of criticism, but at some point she became immune to it, perhaps through the rise of feminism, but, one suspects, not entirely so. The class-bias accusation may be a displacement of annoyance at Powell's conservative politics. If *Dance* had featured people from exactly the same background taking impeccably liberal positions on issues of the day, it would not have received the sour criticism that so often was Powell's reward. That Powell does not display these sorts of liberals to good effect, and sometimes satirizes them (as does Virginia Woolf in *The Voyage Out* and *Mrs. Dalloway*), is perhaps his real "upper-class" offense.

Even before the war begins, it would be a mistake to assume every character in *Dance* sees himself or herself as upper or even upper middle class. Uncle Giles does not, and though his rationalizations of his own personal failure as a result of class prejudice are somewhat lampooned, it has to be noticed that he is a blood relative of the narrator, who finds Giles's perspective almost a consolation at times when he feels lost in intimidatingly upper-class environments. The creative artists in the sequence—Barnby, Moreland, and Maclintick—are hardly of upper-class background, although their work does involve them with the upper classes as consumers of the arts. To the extent that the criticism about class comes from outside Britain, it is perhaps a result of an overexaggeration or a melodramatizing of class differences. Virginia Woolf writes well on this with respect to class assumptions in American Anglophilia, particularly in the fiction of Henry James. "The more sensitive, or at least the more sophisticated, the Henry James, the Hergesheimers, the

Edith Whartons, decide in favour of England and pay the penalty by exaggerating the English culture, the traditional English good manners, and stressing too heavily or in the wrong places those social differences that, though the first to strike the foreigner, are by no means the most profound."[38] Criticism of Powell on class grounds by Americans is in a way the complementary obverse of these attitudes.

The class issue becomes inescapable in *Valley of Bones,* where Jenkins finds himself in the midst of a group of middle-class South Welsh bank officers, clerks, and miners, few if any of whom have attended university or had any exposure to metropolitan life. The shift in social milieu, to a largely Welsh regiment far from the more socially prestigious metropolitan regiments into which, presumably, others of his circle have been inducted, is taken in stride. There is no overt nostalgia for Stringham, Templer, Barnby, or Rosie Manasch. Jenkins is an observer who likes taking account of people; he will pretty much take account of anything, anywhere.

But the reader, who is used to those characters, who has continued reading the sequence because the characters are found of persistent interest, feels deprived. We probably breathe more of a sigh of relief than Jenkins does when he goes on leave and sees the Tolland family and, at the Aldershot training course, meets the odious Jimmy Brent, whose affair with Jean Templer while she was also having a romance with Jenkins was revealed in the previous book by Bob Duport. Bob Duport and Jimmy Brent are in the same boat, as nonintellectual as the soldiers, but they are of the same social class as Jenkins, at least they were in competition with Jenkins for the same woman, more or less the only interest they had in common. So the problem is as much that the soldiers are not intellectual as that they did not go to the same university; Bithel's admiration for Jenkins as a "varsity man" is in fact made to seem a misplaced arrogation of virtue. This sense is confirmed by Evelyn Waugh's legendary discontent over being stationed in Yugoslavia with "Randolph Churchill and Freddie Birkenhead" (*Journals,* 27 January 1986) because of the limited intellectual stimulation this afforded Waugh; when one considers that the two men were, respectively, the prime minister's son and the second earl of Birkenhead, surely prestige was not the issue here. The division between those who cannot live without books and those for whom books do not matter preempts all others. Jenkins feels temperamental kinship with Gwatkin, but all that the captain reads is *Puck of Pook's Hill,* a children's book by Rudyard Kipling, albeit one admired by Powell, and Gwatkin has trouble understanding the simple, balladic verse about the devotees of Mithras, the sun deity, keeping themselves pure until the dawn. Whatever alienation or dissatisfaction Jenkins feels with the regiment, it is prompted by his loneliness for his loved ones and for literary badinage, not snobbish petulance.

Jenkins's service with the regiment is completely cut out of the television films, in which his wartime service begins at divisional headquarters. There is no Gwatkin, no Sergeant Pendry, no Corporal Gwylt. This decision by the adapters, Alvin Rakoff and Hugh Whitemore, is understandable, but it does show that Powell did not have disdain for those not of exalted background, as he deliberately sought service with them in wartime and, in his fiction, went out of his way to give a thorough and sympathetic portrait of that service. But the adapters' decision also underscores how detachable a lot of the war material is from the main line of the sequence.

This immiscibility of the wartime characters with those who populate the other parts of the sequence is also demonstrated by the fascinating appearance of Macfaddean at the training course. Macfaddean's assiduity, his pleasure at actually being there, as opposed to Jenkins's and Brent's gossip, brings a kind of military reality check to bear on Jenkins's social whirl. One of the most self-effacing and winning aspects of Jenkins's self-portrait as narrator is how readily he admits he is not the ideal army officer. In fact, Jenkins, Brent, and Stevens, who all have ambitions of one sort of another, clearly do not intend to manifest those ambitions within the bureaucracy of the regular army. In this way, it is as if all the men other than Macfaddean are on a different plane. Macfaddean must have wondered why so many of the other men in the Infantry Training School were behaving as if they were characters in a novel. The war trilogy does not rely on the romantic myth of characters, befuddled in civilian life, finding their true calling in war; the only possible candidate for this is, ironically, Stringham, whose service with the Mobile Laundry is not the stuff of neo-chivalric fantasy. Those who do particularly well by the war range from people with limited imaginations to those with moral flaws to downright monsters: Macfaddean, Odo Stevens, and Pamela Flitton.

Macfaddean is not a humorous character, and the reader looking for obvious jokes or for news of Widmerpool may miss his significance. The same is true of the genealogical passages at the beginning of the book. Malcolm Muggeridge derided these passages as Powell's attempt at "Stonehenge Revisited," a remark that helped end the once close friendship between Muggeridge and Powell.[39] There is more here than pedantry or historical background, however. Mention of the Jenkins forebears heading off to India to "lay twenty-year-old bones in the cemeteries of Bombay and Mysore" (2) is one of the few references to "the British Empire" in *Dance,* and not a particularly romantic one. And the mention of Cunedda, the late-fourth- to early-fifth-century Brythonic chieftain who is seen as a figure in both Welsh *and* Scottish history, as an ancestor in the female line of Jenkins is fascinating. "Cunedda" equals "Kenneth," and Widmerpool's paternal ancestry is said to be originally Scottish, of the name of Geddes. So there is a sense that Widmerpool and Jenkins have a common ancestor, a vertiginous reverberation that is missed if this passage is just seen as Jenkins trying to impress us with his pedigree.

Widmerpool's long-awaited reappearance occurs at the end, when he is suddenly revealed as Jenkins's superior, the DAAG (deputy assistant adjutant general, a post with influence beyond its manifest rank because of its occupant working closely with the divisional commander on logistical issues). Widmerpool, as a matter of fact, had deliberately selected Jenkins from a number of names ("I allowed the ties of old acquaintance to prevail" [241]). This turn of events is the nadir of the fortunes, not of Jenkins as a person, but of the anti-Widmerpool cause. Widmerpool, waxing in vindictiveness and self-righteousness, has Jenkins under his "power" (203). As far as the values of the sequence are observed, it is the valley of bones indeed.

The Soldier's Art (1966)

As with the Theocritus poems in *A Question of Upbringing,* it is a good idea to read the Robert Browning poem "Childe Roland to the Dark Tower Came" beyond the lines that supply the title, "Think first, fight afterwards, the soldier's art." This promises an intellectual mode of soldiering, maybe heralding the momentous literary debate Jenkins is shortly to have with General Liddament. But reading further we see "one taste of the old time sets all to rights."[40] Can nostalgia quell the unease of wartime? In both Browning and Powell, it cannot. In the poem, the speaker remembers only scenes of old friends proving to be miscreants and traitors. Similarly, there is no nostalgia in *The Soldier's Art*. Despite the horror of wartime conditions, there is no road home to a time before calamity. The tragic double loss of Chips Lovell and his wife Priscilla (to compound the pathos, while they are estranged and she is having an affair with Odo Stevens) leads to Jenkins's poignant memory of Lovell saying, "The chief reason I want to visit Aunt Molly's is to take another look at Priscilla Tolland, who is quite often there" (166), the most emotionally affecting of all chapter conclusions. The single most traumatic incident Jenkins witnesses, therefore, is when he is back in London with his old friends. And Jenkins's (putative) rapprochement with Stringham is the exact opposite of retrieving comfortable old images. Tastes of the old time certainly do not set all to rights.

Meanwhile, Jenkins is stuck in a dead-end army job while his country fights for its life against an implacable and evil enemy. He is uncomfortable being Widmerpool's subordinate, although, as we have seen, perfectly happy being Gwatkin's subordinate despite the latter's lack of literary knowledge, social polish, or metropolitan sheen. In *The Soldier's Art*, Jenkins comes to actively dislike Widmerpool in a way he never has previously, finally catching up, in a way, to what the reader has always thought of Widmerpool. Jenkins does not seem particularly disturbed by Widmerpool being his superior. In fact, he takes it initially as just another amusing, or fateful, coincidence. In the closest American equivalent, in this respect only, to the war trilogy, Anton Myrer's *Once an Eagle* (1968), the Widmerpool figure, Courtney Massengale, is for a time the subordinate of Sam Damon, who though certainly not a Jenkins is maybe an ultra-successful Gwatkin, and comparatively, this position is even more odious for the protagonist. There is some hope when Jenkins, caught in a literary discussion with General Liddament, commander of the division, posits Balzac as an alternative. Jenkins's derogation of Trollope, which had made the General kick a chair, demands an explanation from Jenkins, who can only come up with such ineffectual lines as "Women don't analyse their own predicaments as there represented" (*Soldier's Art,* 46). Whereas in Jenkins's usual circles, Balzac is a perfectly reasonable alternative to Trollope, in relation to a career military officer whose reading is largely for leisure, "Balzac" is as refined and obscure as any of the more patently recondite answers— Svevo, Lermontov, Choderlos de Laclos—Jenkins has rejected. The joke is that the general's full name, H. de C. Liddament, reveals that he is probably of French ancestry despite his apparent Francophobia. (This was brought home with renewed force in March 2002 when I had lunch with Powell's friend the Hon. John Monagan, who pronounced the General's name Leed-a-MENGH in the most emphatic French way.) Powell is also telling the reader that his own work is more like Balzac's than Trollope's, and especially that it partakes in a European, not just an English, tradition. It is also part of the entire French-language motif that starts at La Grenadière and continues through Jenkins's admitted inability to "harangue" (*Soldier's Art,* 102) a Vichy regiment in Lebanon to the point of convincing them to come over to the Free French, disappointing the general, who thought he had found the army a most useful man.

Even more than in *Valley of Bones,* the first-time reader feels the scenes set at Divisional Headquarters to be dry compared with the vivid scenes of the London bombings. But without the dry scenes, the dramatic scenes would have far less impact. As a writer, Powell is fully aware that not all writing can be at the same high pitch, that there must be mundane passages as well as memorable ones, both humorous and sad moments. The intrigue between Widmerpool and Hogbourne-Johnson over Ivo Deanery is more sketched than dramatized, for instance, though the interplay between Hogbourne-Johnson and Pedlar is highly amusing.[41] Two scenes at the headquarters, though, do stand out. One is Biggs's suicide, which would have been more affecting had Biggs been given more stage time as a character, but in its mute spareness is a passage that makes the reader pause. (The reference to the "cricket pav" is one of the few references to sports or any kind of athletics in all of Powell's work, outside of the first school scenes in *A Question of Upbringing*.) Biggs has not been presented sympathetically. But his death makes us realize that what had been acerbity on his part had masked a lonely desperation. Jenkins, in a way, is taught by the Biggs incident that even he is able to underestimate people.

The second moving scene at divisional headquarters is the reappearance and departure of one of Biggs's targets for abuse —Stringham—as a mess-hall waiter, one of *Dance*'s most astonishing reappearances. In fact, it is the only reappearance of a character other than Widmerpool that packs the punch of a Widmerpool reappearance. (At *Soldier's Art*, 75, Jenkins is stunned by this reappearance, whereas Stringham finds it plausible, showing Jenkins, as narrator, as somewhat blind to the technique of his narrative.) It is often remarked that readers of *Dance* speak about its characters as if they were real people. Though this happens no doubt with any work containing compellingly drawn characters, it should be recognized that this is, as much as the result of the author being able to simulate flesh-and-blood individuals, a result of the way the characters represent *conceptual* questions in dramatic form. For some reason, of all of *Dance*'s characters, it is Stringham who seems most spoken about in this way. Stringham is *Dance*'s most substantive presence, as well as its greatest enigma.

The central event of *The Soldier's Art,* not necessarily immediately visible in all the bureaucratic machinations and wartime details of the book, is that Widmerpool sends Stringham to his death. True, he does not know the Japanese will take Singapore, as few did. But he did know that the Middle East was where the British were doing their best in military terms (having uprooted the Italians from Ethiopia, forestalled the pro-German coup in Iraq, and held off the Afrika Korps from Egypt) and that the Far East was far more exposed to the as-yet-unbelligerent Japanese. Widmerpool revels in his power, what Hitchens calls his "bureaucratic fiat," over Stringham, still deriving emotional energy from schoolboy incidents of two decades earlier.[42] Whatever his sufferings at the hands of Stringham in adolescence, however blithe and complacent were Stringham's assumptions that Widmerpool would forever remain the ineffectual buffoon he was at school, Widmerpool's inability to get over this perceived slight is pathological. Widmerpool, usually more masochistic than sadistic (see his relationships with Budd, Barbara Goring, Pamela, the Soviet Union, and Scorpio Murtlock), is at his most sadistic with Stringham. He can never forget Stringham's sense of superiority at school, even though, as in the case of Budd smearing him with a banana, he had often enjoyed bullying by other schoolmates. (The closest parallel would be Widmerpool's relationship with Colonel Hogbourne-Johnson, whom, at *The Military Philosophers,* 112, he still cannot resist taunting, and against whom he is still seething with resentment at being "abominably rude" despite trouncing the Colonel over the Diplock fiasco. This public display of temper, never seen in relation to Stringham, may yet provide clues with respect to the earlier relationship, as might Widmerpool's unnecessarily cruel treatment of Bithel, associated with Stringham by virtue of being the latter's commanding officer.)

What is Stringham's reaction to his reduced position? That it is reduced is seen even by those such as Biggs who do not quite know what he was originally. If Stringham is comfortable with anyone at headquarters, it should be Jenkins. But Stringham's reaction to Jenkins's presence (this, rather than the most narratively immediate reverse, is what is in question here) is problematic. He is not angry at Jenkins but seems to want to just get on with life and not make an issue out of the difference in rank with his friend Jenkins, an officer, albeit not exactly a glamorous one. But eventually the two old friends settle into something like their original routine, and Stringham makes a crucial remark. On hearing that Jenkins is very familiar with General Conyers, who is in the midst of the second world war of his active retirement, Stringham says, "My dear Nick, you know everybody. Not a social item escapes you" (*Soldier's Art,* 80). Jenkins's urbanity, polish, and sympathetic interest in others represents not just civility but citizenship. As funny as it to see the unbombastic Jenkins, in his role as vice commander of the company, toasting "the king" (180), as much as he mistrusts that sort of public role, his formal toast to George VI's ceremonial and benign sovereignty is the visible manifestation of the thousand small acts of citizenship Jenkins performs in observing, describing, noticing, and listening. It is no accident, by the way, that it is Conyers that occasions Stringham's reflections, as it is Conyers's reentry into Jenkins's life that is coeval with the introduction to

Lady Molly Jeavons and thus is part of the ambience in which Jenkins meets his wife, Isobel. Conyers, like Farebrother, is one of those good-luck tokens people have in life. Their presence always means something good for Jenkins and for the world of the novel's characters. Jenkins tries to save Stringham. But Stringham, it seems, does not want to be saved. Is he too far gone for saving? Does he mistrust the heroic narrative this would imply? Is he less romantic, more resigned? Is he guilty over the mess, as it were, that he has made of himself and his life? There is a passage in *Soldier's Art* in which Stringham, in talking to Widmerpool, seems to address the latter's sadistic script: "'It's interesting to recall, sir,' he said, 'the last time we met, I myself was the inert frame. It was you and Mr. Jenkins who so kindly put me to bed. It shows that improvement is possible, that roles can be reversed. I've turned over a new leaf. Stringham is enrolled in the ranks of the sober, as well as the brave'" (185).

Despite the inevitable slight sarcasm here, Stringham is behaving in the absolutely best manner. He is being respectful to Widmerpool, as befits an attitude toward a superior officer. More than that, he is being reasonable and arguing for a sensible healing of the grudge between the two of them. To paraphrase his meaning, we might construct it as "Look here, Widmerpool, let's talk man to man. I know you felt looked down upon me at school. I am sorry about that and I realize I underestimated you. You have come much further in your career than I imagined and are in general a far more serious figure. You have worked hard at your life, whereas I have frittered away mine in drink and silliness. So let's square that out. In return, it would be nice if you could get over your sense of nurtured grievance and realize that I, Stringham, have changed too.

Wartime has invigorated me and given me a new sense of purpose. We are all fighting a common enemy—Hitler. So let's end this pointless rivalry." Jenkins does not stay to hear Widmerpool's response, and we have to conclude that there is none. Widmerpool will not realize that there is new potential in Stringham (which appears to have developed after the departure of Miss Weedon, although the valence of her role is one of the most open questions in all of *Dance*). Widmerpool perpetrates the same injustice he has harbored against Stringham for two decades, that Stringham had unfairly underestimated him, and he now wields this underestimation against Stringham himself. For Widmerpool, Stringham will always be the rich boy who failed, the no-good drunkard. That scripts can be revised, that the notes of the music or the steps of the dance can change, that "improvement is possible and roles can be reversed" is unthinkable to Widmerpool after a certain point, that is, his vindication as "successful Widmerpool," the bill-broker, the sudden friend of Templer's, the man of affairs, the superior officer. So Widmerpool sets up a pseudohistorical logic against which the entire narrative logic of *Dance*—that there is always one more turn on the wheel of time—is arrayed. It is surprising that someone of Widmerpool's intelligence does not realize that he is not tapping Stringham's own potential, which, as a military officer in command of troops during a war in which his nation is fighting for its survival, he should be more than anxious to harvest.

With Stringham's loss, gone is that person who most effectively derided Widmerpool and whose life and manners most directly contravene those of his rival. Without Stringham, Jenkins is all there is left to oppose, or at least monitor, Widmerpool. Jenkins's personality does not equip him to maintain such a stance with the brio and charm possessed by Stringham. What

Robert Selig terms the "social sadness" of Jenkins's relationship with Stringham never regains the intensity of their boyhood friendship in *A Question of Upbringing,* but both Stringham's increasing remoteness as a friend and then his tragic loss reverberate profoundly for Jenkins.[43] As at Mrs. Foxe's party, Stringham seems at once to have declined and rallied. It is unfathomably appalling, even for a reader not at all concerned with individual social status, that someone of not only Stringham's education and background but also his charm and intelligence is serving only as a waiter. Even though, as Milton put it, "they also serve who only stand and wait," surely, merely from the pragmatic standpoint of the war effort alone, Stringham could have been of more service somewhere else in the military.[44] In his position as waiter, Stringham is not only once again the subject of Widmerpool's vindictive punishment of him for ancient schoolboy mockery but also the object of general jabbing, by various officers dining at the mess, for his cultivated manners. On the other hand, Stringham has given up drink. He is genuinely dedicated to his work and even seems to enjoy it. Indeed, it is Jenkins, not Stringham, who displays overt unease about the lack of dignity of Stringham's job, although this may be just good manners on Stringham's part. His joke about being General Fauncefoot-Fritwell's aide-de-camp (*Soldier's Art,* 175) shows some of his old sparkle. Perhaps Stringham, confessedly not at home in the great-house ambience of his Stepney in-laws, finds the less exalted atmosphere refreshing. (And perhaps, if the war trilogy had been told from the viewpoint of Stringham, it would have been transformed into the Henry Green novel some seem so urgently to want.) We are also never sure whether the people in Stringham's life help him or not. Not only is Miss Weedon both caretaker and captor, but Mrs. Foxe's relationship with the much younger Chandler, overtly a strike against her naval husband, also is something of a rejection of Stringham. Stringham may absorb this as a setback even if he does not seem to register it on the conscious level. Stringham's sister Flavia, shown to us in *Valley of Bones,* is never on stage with Stringham at the same time, nor indeed with any blood relative of her own, and is an enigma. She does not seem able to help Charles out. In fact, she seems to have as many problems as he has.

Stringham's raffish, intermittently unreliable character does not make his eclipse inevitable in the world of *Dance.* Dicky Umfraville, always described as much like Stringham, survives until the end, long after the reader expects him to disappear from the scene. *Dance* is generally fond of eccentrics and people who are different from the conformist stereotypes. As Cathleen Ann Steg puts it, Jenkins "consciously aligns himself with the men of art and not of action," the former almost by definition either nonconformist or those who do not reflexively conform.[45] This leads to Powell desisting from demanding only one model of behavior, one sort of person (which a surprising amount of novelists do; both Hemingway and Henry James, for instance, have this problem, though in very different registers). For instance, Powell's positive, though not humorless, depiction of gays and lesbians—Heather Hopkins, Eleanor Walpole-Wilson, Norah Tolland, Hugo Tolland, Mr. Deacon, Max Pilgrim, and Barnabas Henderson, among others—has been widely noted. The way Max Pilgrim tells the story of the death of Bijou Ardglass in the March 1941 bombings shows that gays and lesbians are included in the citizenship mentioned earlier in relation with the toast to the king. Whatever social disapproval Pilgrim's outré behavior—not just his sexuality, but his very public display of it —may excite, Pilgrim is a member in good standing of the society of *Dance*. Analogously, Lady Molly Jeavons's pure daffiness is her most winning quality, and her loss in the March bombing, unendurable for her husband Ted, is also hard on the reader.

But despite these tragedies, the mood in *The Soldier's Art* is not entirely pessimistic. The book ends in June 1941, when Germany invades the Soviet Union, meaning Britain will no longer be the lone great power standing in the way of Nazism. Hogbourne-Johnson is defeated by Widmerpool, but we sense Farebrother will not be, despite the setback over Szymanski in *The Military Philosophers*. Considering the weight given to Farebrother's predicted reappearance in *A Question of Upbringing*, he does nothing dramatic in *The Soldier's Art*, or for that matter the rest of the sequence, leading to inevitable speculation that perhaps, as with M. Dubuisson, a more dramatic role was planned. But even so, he stands as a positive force. Barnby's death, which has to mean more to the narrator than that of Chips Lovell, is slotted in inconspicuously at the end of the book, much like the way a sculptor will distribute the torsion of his piece in such a way as to make sure every part of the artwork is in equilibrium. This should not lead us to suppose that Barnby, always more present aphoristically than dramatically, was any less of a friend to Jenkins than was Stringham. The wording of the Barnby sentence—"That same week the plane was shot down in which Barnby was undertaking a reconnaissance flight"—repositions Barnby away from being the subject of the sentence. The dogged obliquity of this wording somehow intensifies the piquancy of the sadness.

The Military Philosophers (1968)

The Military Philosophers starts with perhaps the most deliberately "stately" writing in all of *Dance*:

Towards morning the teleprinter's bell sounded. A whole
night could pass without a summons of this sort, for here,
unlike the formations, was no responsibility to wake at four
and take dictation—some brief unidentifiable passage of on
the whole undistinguished prose—from the secret radio Spi-
der, calling and testing in the small hours. Sleep was perfectly
attainable when no raid intervened, though recurrent vibra-
tion from one or both machines affirmed next door the same
restlessness of spirit that agitated the Duty Officer's room,
buzzing all the time with desultory currents of feeling be-
queathed by an ever changing tenancy. Endemic as ghouls in
an Arabian cemetary, harassed aggressive shades lingered for
ever in such cells to impose on each successive inmate their
preoccupations and anxieties, crowding him from floor and
bed, invading and distorting dreams. (1)

Despite the Powellian qualifiers—"on the whole undistinguished," "perfectly attainable"—there is a sense that what is
being described is inherently significant. This is a man and a
nation at war, and what is being done is, even if implausibly,
vital in conducting that war. It is a grim situation, not one to be
taken lightly. This is the only passage in *Dance* in which the
events of the twentieth century, on their own, are allowed to
inform the writing purely through the weight of their historical
significance.[46] This passage succeeds, but it is good the rest of the
book is not written in this style. This is especially true of the
description of the Victory Service commemorating the positive
outcome of the war at the end of the book. A lesser writer, or a
writer of lesser discipline, would have been decoyed by the
undoubted historic sense of ceremony and moment of the victory service to be pompous or self-aggrandizing.

In *The Military Philosophers,* Jenkins is out of the imagination-sapping environment of the regular army and stationed where he can take more advantage of his intellectual abilities and knowledge of the world, serving as military liaison officer to several of the governments-in-exile that have taken refuge in London after Germany overran Europe. Powell portrays the Czechoslovaks ("Czechs" in the book), Poles, and Belgians with amused affection (like Pennistone, "getting as much amusement out of the job as possible"; *Military Philosophers,* 33) and for the most part makes up convincing names for them. They generally are based on the real people Powell knew in similar positions during the war. This makes *The Military Philosophers* the great exception, whether in terms of being the only book most of whose unique characters are based on real people, or the only one where the author is prepared to admit this. The army books, by virtue of their subject matter and the need to introduce so many new characters based, more locally than previous ones, on real people who, even if eventually funny, cannot be uproariously so at first, are less seamlessly funny than the first six books, yet many of the funniest one-liners in *Dance* occur in *The Military Philosophers:* "*old bitch wartstone,*" (122), "please amplify" (45), Major Prasad's "religion" (161), even, in a lower key, "*c'est bien le mulberry*" (169). Powell, of course, has to make up his own names; these are convincing but, because of the language barrier, without the puns and in-jokes found in so many of the British or even Franco-Belgian ones. As *Writer's Notebook,* 124, shows, Powell rejected more archaic or Germanic-sounding names like Gondibert or Theodomir, leaving him with Bobrowski, Philidor, and Kielkiewicz (Sikorski and Anders being of course real people). These characters do not fully join the dance. Szymanski, for instance, the most potentially comic character among the Poles, never really gathers momentum. Powell seems to have realized this and did not have him recur, although, in his colorful, ne'er-do-well nature, he is far more a likely a recurrent character than the various functionaries who populate the ninth book. He operates as a bridge between the largely historical world of the politics and personalities Powell had to deal with and the core interlocking characters of *Dance,* who are given new, if menacing, redress with the arrival of Pamela Flitton, with whom Szymanski has an affair (as does seemingly every heterosexual male in the sequence other than Jenkins himself). Szymanski also helps impart a sense of drama to Powell's portraits of officials driven from their nations by invasion and trying to work to free their homelands.

The deliberately novelistic character of Szymanski, despite his name being based on a real-life individual, suggests the significant differences between the effects, if not the essential natures, of the difference between military attachés in *The Military Philosophers* and in the third volume of Powell's memoirs, *Faces.* In the memoirs they are simply people encountered along the way, just as so many are. There is not the separation between wartime and civilian experience in the memoirs that there is in the novel. In fiction, the military attachés connote comprehensiveness, allowing Europe and the rest of the world to register, as referents, within the sequence's inclusive frame. Powell's military career may have supplied the data, but the need for such an ambitious work to encompass the world in a century of what would today be called "globalization" yields the novelistic meaning. This is the rationale for the particular French, Eastern European, Scandinavian, and Latin American strands in the sequence (indeed, all these areas are provided with far more systematically patterned swatches than the United States, which, the Catholic Flannigan-Fitzgerald in the first book aside, does not begin to enter the sequence until wartime, and only prominently in the last three books). And it is the Eastern European strand that surges to particular prominence in *The Military Philosophers.*

Hitchens sees Powell's genuine interest in these countries as based on his identity as "a Welshman" and indicating "a sympathy for the predicament of small nations."[47] This statement, written in 1998, at the height of misguided euphoria about Welsh devolution, could not be more ludicrous. What comparison can be made between, say, Belgium and Wales in 1943— a country independent for 110 years, immorally invaded and occupied by its totalitarian neighbor, which subjugated it ruthlessly and allowed it no rights, and a country governmentally interlinked with England since the thirteenth century, formally united to it in the sixteenth, which has always had just as much democratic input into the unified government as any part of England and whose people speak, willingly, the English language more than their own, which has had its population intermarry with that of England's so that personal ties between the two are little more extricable than those between New York and Pennsylvania? This defies belief.[48] In addition, Powell, though possessed of a Welsh name and interested in his Welsh forebears, was born and raised in England and had, when it came down to it, more English ancestry than Welsh and always identified himself with England. But it certainly is true that Powell's interest in cultural history and genealogical research made him curious about small European countries. There is also the cosmopolitanism associated with the upper classes, which cosmopolitanism's inherent, if not limitless, virtues Powell does his best to accentuate.

The centerpiece of the foreign liaison officers is the tour to Normandy toward the end of the book, with the memorable incident being the episode when Norwegian general Asbjørnson has to give up his room with a bath to Major Prasad, an Indian, because the lower-ranking officer needs it for religious rites. But its moral heart is the speculation, leading to horrific revelation, concerning the 1940 Katyn forest massacre, in which, while the Soviet Union was still tacitly allied with Germany as a result of the nonaggression pact, over ten thousand Polish officers were brutally massacred. The "large deficiency" (as Q [Ops.] Colonel puts it at *The Military Philosophers,* 103) of the Polish officers taken prisoner in the Soviet Union as part of the latter nation's bounty for its role in the Hitler-Stalin pact becomes an issue when both the Poles and the Soviets are on the side of the Allies and the Poles have some leverage for inquiries about their missing officers. The Polish officers are at first supposed to be transferred to Franz Josef Land above the Arctic Circle, in the area of the "hyperborean seas" (*Harmonies,* 272). Incidentally, the British government tried to discover the fate of the Polish officers by talking to Maisky, the Soviet ambassador, who, as might be expected, was unhelpful. If only Maisky, the monkey, was still alive, having not received a sentence of capital punishment for his fatal assault of Smith, the shared Jeavons/ Thrubworth butler, the "tenacious ape" (*Military Philosophers,* 78) no doubt would have shed some simian clarity on the situation. The particular, in strict aesthetic terms disproportionate, space accorded to Katyn in *The Military Philosophers* is an act of testimony, of witness, one all the more impressive in 1968, when, for the most part, even after the suppression of the Prague Spring, the Western literary intelligentsia did not want to listen to criticism of the Soviet Union. This may not have been the only reason for the neglect of Katyn, reasons that may have ranged from honest confusion or actual ignorance about the massacre and its implications to motivations rooted in ideological bias. But that it was neglected there is no doubt.[49]

There are objections that Powell emphasizes Katyn while not seeming to mention the Holocaust. This can be answered empirically by the statement that Powell's work during the war involved Katyn but not the Holocaust, so blaming him for underplaying the latter would be like blaming him for not writing a sufficiently vivid account of D day. Also, when the book was published in 1968, the Holocaust was in nearly everyone's consciousness, whereas Katyn was, outside a small, marginalized group of Poles and conservatives, unmentioned by the intelligentsia or the media—in any country, West or East. The Katyn massacre finally became publicly aired in the mass media, not just in Eastern Europe but in the West, in the late 1980s. (The Soviets, just before they disappeared from the scene, admitted their guilt at a Kremlin ceremony on 13 April 1990.) Powell clearly felt that in making such a point of Katyn, more or less twenty years ahead of the curve, he was drawing attention to an atrocity that was underdiscussed. It is interesting how massacres "have their day," as the sudden "discovery" of the Jedwabne slaughter of Jews by Poles in 1941, only ventilated at all publicly in the early 2000s, indicates.[50] In any event, the same process of disbelief and rationalization that led British military intelligence, as portrayed in *The Military Philosophers,* to ignore the obvious signs of mass slaughter also occurred, just as lamentably, in the early response to the barbarity of the Nazi death camps. We should not also forget that the Japanese army's atrocities at Singapore are responsible for the death of Stringham. To accuse *Dance* of focusing on the atrocities of Britain's allies at the expense of those of its enemies is wrong. Powell, like Churchill, and unlike a fair amount of other Tories, including people of good conscience such as James Lees-Milne, was only too glad of the Soviet Union's involvement in the war.[51]

There is a larger suggestiveness, though, in the coverage allotted to Katyn. The Poles killed at Katyn were the intelligentsia, not just high-ranking military men but people interested in, and active in, culture and the arts. They were military philosophers, and no doubt someone killed at Katyn knew Vigny almost as well as did Pennistone. What if everyone from Jenkins's prewar London life who later joined the army proved to have been killed by a country later an nominal ally? What does it mean for an entire class or sensibility to be extinguished?[52]

These resonances are only enabled by Powell's far greater than normal political attentiveness; politics, for him, is not simply furniture to fiction; in its historical unfolding, it touches the central fabric of narration. Powell's friend, Robert Conquest, refers to Powell as someone "without special interest in politics."[53] Unless what is meant by "interest" is "political ambition" or "use of politics to further one's own personal aims," one is hard pressed to understand this comment. Especially when it is, reluctantly, realized that most novelists are interested in little more beside their own sales and career, Powell's scrupulous attention to political issues that did not directly concern his own immediate personal interests is remarkable. Powell's treatment of the Katyn massacre is a product of this attention. Of course, Powell is neither a propagandist nor a party hack, and the politics are always balanced with something else. In a way, the political references are complemented on the other side by the visual arts/music/dance references, which between them support the literary and social world that is *Dance*'s most familiar ground.

On the other hand, that politics, the arts, and social relations are not entirely distinct spheres may be suggested by the way Powell's interest in Katyn stems from the same fundamental interest in other people that energizes *Dance* as a whole. It may seem either petty or supernumerary to have to draw a connection between responding to such atrocities as occurred at Katyn, Auschwitz, and Singapore and simply caring about other people on a one-to-one level, but this linkage is braided into the very chronological notation of *Dance*.[54]

The deaths of the Polish officers are not the only ones in *The Military Philosophers*. We learn from Pamela about Stringham's captivity and likely death at Singapore. Also, Peter Templer is lost on a mission to supply the resistance in Prince Theodoric's never-named former country. (Previously, it seemed likely this country was Bulgaria, based only on the German dynasty ruling the Slavic country, although in *The Military Philosophers* it is much closer to Yugoslavia, with Widmerpool's selling-out of Templer paralleling the switch in Allied support from Mihailovich's Chetniks to Tito's Partisans. Later, in *Temporary Kings*, it seems once again to be Bulgaria as Yugoslavia was out of the Soviet bloc by this time, but Powell wants us to see it as the same country for consistency's sake.) Templer has never been the most magnetic character in *Dance;* his company, always relaxing, never tense, was not ultra-stimulating, and Jenkins was not thrilled with Templer's own choice of friends (Duport, Brent, and later Widmerpool). But with Peter Templer's death, winter has come. Like Stringham, Templer seems daunted and scathed by the war; also like Stringham, he has given up women, though that gesture is recanted for one last disastrous fling with Pamela. Pamela says, in her climactic confrontation with Widmerpool, that he was the "the nicest man I ever knew. He just had him killed" (*Military Philosophers*, 221). This statement, incredibly, made by Pamela to Widmerpool before the couple had gotten married, is striking for its emphasis, as of the "original three" friends Templer is the one the reader has thought the least about, whereas, in different ways, Stringham and Widmerpool have been constantly on the horizon, even though in some of the volumes (*Lady Molly's* and *The Kindly Ones* for Stringham, *Casanova* and *Valley of Bones* for Widmerpool) they are virtually absent. Even though it is true of Pamela that "emotional warmth in her was directed only towards the dead" (*Temporary Kings,* 102), the statement nonetheless rings true. Oddly, Templer, less charming, than Stringham, is more deeply missed by the narrative. While there may be a tendency to canonize Stringham, to see him in his misfortune and cruel death as St. Stringham, it is hard to see Templer not only aesthetically indifferent but a man who has alienated his first wife and driven his second mad, as St. Templer. Yet Peter Templer's departure changes the tone of the narrative as does that of no one else. Part of this emanates from what must be called Jenkins's survivor guilt, with respect to not only Stringham and Templer but also the many victims of the war and its attendant catastrophes.

Stringham and Templer die, Widmerpool remains. Robert Selig comments that "worthwhile human beings whom we love and respect can drop out of our lives, but despicable persons can cling to us like leeches."[55] But there is a public dimension as well, as Britain and the world lose men of Stringham's and Templer's caliber and retain those of Widmerpool's. This leads to a crisis in public culture, not just in the personal friendships of Nicholas Jenkins. This is underscored by all the political parallels and references, never forced but always informing the action on the private level. Some readers consider *The Military Philosophers* the best of all the books, but for others it has its *longueurs;* John Russell, for example, refers to its "cluttered" quality.[56] Yet *Military Philosophers* also introduces a significant larger-than-life character, Pamela Flitton. Pamela is the most significant female character in *Dance,* and it is understandable why that alone could lead to the impression that *Dance* is a misogynistic work (which is not true). When Pamela first comes on stage, we are sympathetically disposed to her. She is, after all, Stringham's niece, and the reader is still reeling from Stringham's loss. Her early escapades with various Polish officers and other uniformed personnel seem no more than an expression of youthful erotic high spirits. It is only when she becomes, successively, involved with Templer, Duport, and Widmerpool. Her interest in older men (Trapnel—and Gwinnett, who actually is a few years younger—are the only men her own age with whom she takes up) connotes an interest in power, yet she has absolutely no interest in any of the responsibilities that come with power—even less than Widmerpool or such arcane esoterics as Trelawney and Murtlock, which prevents her from being totally comparable with many female politicians of whom she would otherwise remind us. The product of a broken home, the daughter of a woman who has led a shattered life, Pamela, like all unpleasant people, obviously came from somewhere. The looming specter of her alliance with Widmerpool, at first glimpsed with horror by the reader, becomes a travesty whose realization is looked forward to with a kind of appalled inevitability.

Jenkins himself is one of the few men not to feel Pamela's allure. Witness his remark to her mother in the last book that he knew Pamela; he was about to say that he knew Pamela well, but he realized any man saying that of his relationship with

Pamela would inevitably give the wrong impression. Two others immune to Pamela's charms are, respectively, Jenkins's superior and colleague at military intelligence, Finn, whose overly Hellenistic first name, Lysander, Finn wisely tries to suppress, and David Pennistone. Pennistone, based fairly obviously on Powell's friend (and Evelyn Waugh's brother-in-law) Alick Dru, introduces a note of Continental thought into *Dance* with his references to Kierkegaard and so on, in many ways a more serious incarnation of what was represented by the psychoanalytic and German references in *Agents*. Both Pennistone and Finn do their jobs well but with a sense of personal flair and style; they do their duty, but with none of the forced or procedural air of people deliberately intent on letting their co-workers know they are doing their duty. If the intellectual side of being a military philosopher is represented by Pennistone, who allows his intellect and wartime job to inform each other, not either merging or separating them, the procedural side is represented by the larger-than-life Blackhead. Though Powell sends up wartime bureaucracy in Blackhead's fussiness about "supply of straw for stuffing medical establishment palliasses" (*Military Philosophers*, 32) for the Polish army-in-exile (we must remember, a serious fighting force that helped the Allies win), he does not have the sort of sentimental excoriation of wartime bureaucracy visible, in different avatars, in the work of his contemporaries Evelyn Waugh and George Orwell. Blackhead, "beyond age; beyond or outside Time" (42) is such a satiric character that he cannot recur. But his one moment in *Dance* is matchless. Pennistone's hoist-on-his-own-petard response to Blackhead's impenetrable memos, "Please amplify," is one of the funniest lines in the entire sequence, and recitation of the phrase has virtually become second nature to Powellians. Powell takes particular gusto in providing abbreviations and acronyms, which has a satiric aspect but also a delight in the sheer complexity of reference that these designations afford. In fact, the wartime bureaucracy provides endlessly fertile fields for the satirist's literary roving. Powell not only lampoons bureaucracy but also renders the lineaments of each bureaucrat's preposterous self-maintenance, as well as the way they are seen by others as immovable cogs in the machine, the minor character of Q (Ops.) Colonel being a good example.[57] Also, there is a suggestive association in *The Military Philosophers:* "Q (Ops.) Colonel? Mime? Widmerpool?" (218).

After all these tribulations, we have the gratification of the victory service. Yet as D. J. Taylor points out, for all the emotional release, pride, and sense of deliverance Jenkins feels at the service, his demeanor there is not exultant: he is uncomfortable with the ceremony's pomp and conspicuous display, he yearns for "a humbler yet more satisfying patriotism," and he feels "unease over the public celebration of victory."[58] Taylor is the only critic to grasp the dynamic between core belief and rhetorical asseveration, how they balance each other out the way dialogue and discourse, politics and the arts do in other aspects of the narrative. The victory service passage itself is highlighted by Powell's no-holds-barred quotation of all three verses of "God Save the King," including the second verse on the king's enemies ("confound their politics / frustrate their knavish tricks") later sidelined out of political correctness. There is no doubt that this cause—for whom, after all, victory did not come easily—has been worth fighting for, and that the Allied cause is a righteous one. Also, we remember that the war was fought over whether humanity, as it had been known, would continue to exist, and not the bureaucratic self-advancement yearned for by Widmerpool.

Dance is indeed more black and white in its values than many other novels (though less than quite a few other works considered great), and even a supportive critical guide to it should admit this and also concede that it is good that not all novels are as black and white to the same degree, just as, for example, it is good that all historians do not have the same sometimes contrary relation to what we see now as ascertainable fact as did Herodotus, or that not every later biographer followed the gossipy predilections of John Aubrey. But this does not mean *Dance* is flawed on this account, just that its particular perspective on life is one on which people have substantively different moral stances. *Dance,* as said before, is not far from being a war sequence and represents conflicts between moral positions, as masked and screened as these are in comedy and social forms. There is no reason why people should look down on *Dance* for this reason. Most of those who do look down on *Dance* surely respect Virginia Woolf's *To the Lighthouse.* Yet Woolf's great novel relies upon a dichotomy between sensitive, artistic souls and people of affairs that is as moralistic as any dichotomy in *Dance,* whether the similar one between men of will and men of imagination or (what *Dance*'s negative critics perhaps do not like, as they somehow see themselves as Widmerpool) the contrast between Widmerpool and Jenkins. Indeed, Woolf and the Bloomsbury group associated with her are justly seen as being at the center of British modernist literary production. But it is as easy in Woolf's work as in any other to tell who are intended to be "good" and "evil" characters, and this is not to its detriment; novelists have the right to express their own values. All the reader can ask is that these values are expressed with subtlety, nuance, and self-awareness. Both Powell and Woolf, whose values, for the most part, are very different, meet this standard.

Dance, for instance, believes unequivocally that there are good people and evil people, good values and evil values, but within civilized forms. Without a blurring of the opposites, there is an anchoring of them within complex social patterns. Sometimes Widmerpool takes the same position as people who are good (as when he joined the Territorials in the peace-besotted interwar years). Despite its comic attributes, *Dance* resides on the level Northrop Frye termed the "high mimetic." Normally associated with tragedy, this level transmutes "fear without an object . . . into a pensive melancholy."[59] Both Powell and Woolf are writers of the first rank, and both should be valued on their own terms; whatever political differences their particular incarnations of what Frye calls "favorable and adverse moral judgment," and those who follow those judgments, may have had in their lifetimes, there is nothing to preclude the twenty-first-century reader from enjoying both writers.[60] The only difference, perhaps, is that the collective Bloomsbury ambience in which Woolf dwelled fostered a certain moralistic, we-are-always-on-the-right-side complacency. But as will be seen in chapter 6 on the *Journals,* non-Bloomsburyites are also fully capable of this reductive posture. Because there is no action at the front, the war trilogy of *Dance* is not in that genre of Second World War novel that, though fully convinced of the superior merits of the Allied cause, not to mention its defense of humanity, finds any war appalling because of the horrors of combat. What is represented of the effects of war, aside from the bombings in London and the offstage depths of so many characters, is how war irrevocably disrupts normal social routines, so that, win or lose, they will not be the same afterward. "Everyone was by now so tired" (*Military Philosophers,* 217), Jenkins reflects. "The country . . . was absolutely worn out."

But seconds later we are back listening to music, "Holst, Elgar, Grieg, finally Handel's 'Water Music'" (218), as direct public observation eddies back into aesthetic distance, into passive yet alert receptivity.

Just this sort of relationship between literature and public attitudes is on Jenkins's mind as he listens to hymns and recitations at the victory service. Jenkins begins to compare four particular writers, Abraham Cowley, Alexander Pope, William Blake, and Edgar Allan Poe. As a classicist, he would in categorical terms prefer Cowley and Pope (though, as the discussion in the passage reveals, Pope himself would not have preferred Cowley) but cannot deny that Poe and Blake are great writers, whatever romantic excesses they inspire. Blake had "come out on top in the end" (*Military Philosophers,* 224) from the status of at best, maverick, at worst, raving lunatic to an official status as bard of national celebration. This victory is not begrudged, even though Jenkins might find, say, Cowley a more immediately, though not completely, congenial temperament. For Jenkins, taste is not the same as dogma. A respect for the rules does not mean that small instances of rule breaking are not allowed, a principle seen in the extraliterary sphere with Finn's sanctioned delight in the unauthorized salmon from Scotland because "after all, we've won the war" (228). In a way, what is being said here is that the English-speaking tradition in literature, whose maintenance the Allied victory in the war assured, has many different styles, and that this is how it should be. This sentiment would hardly inspire the men slogging through the Ardennes in December 1944, but between this and "God Save the King" we get Powell's image of why we were fighting the war. The line from Poe also is a perfect illustration of the way narrative surprises are gently anticipated for the reader. It prompts memories of Jean Templer's gray eyes—just a few pages away from Jenkins's reencounter with Jean, now revealed as Madame Flores. Jean's reappearance at this climactic moment, which some might think overly coincidental, adds a needed private dimension to the public victory, underscoring D. J. Taylor's point about the passage's urgent desire for qualification of its own forthright assertions. Jean's appearance both confirms the euphoria of the moment (a happy reunion) and deflects it (a sense of limitation in what can be aired, a remembrance of a failed romance).

We are meant to understand that Jean's new husband, Colonel Flores, "an officer wearing a heavy gold aiguillette" (*Military Philosophers,* 219), represents a Latin American nation that had just joined the Allies under the wire for the deadline to be a part of the victorious coalition in good standing and, therefore, a charter member of the United Nations. Later on, Flores becomes not "much short of dictator" (*Harmonies,* 253) of his own country. A couple of years before Powell died, fiction became prophecy, as a Carlos Flores, albeit a democratically elected one, was inaugurated president of Honduras in 1998. It is this sort of calm, uncanny percipience with respect to what is past and what is to come that enables Powell to so imperturbably present a war so convulsive in its effects and so far reaching in its consequences.

Books Do Furnish a Room (1971)

The tenth book of *Dance* sees Widmerpool in literal political power. He is a member of the majority party in Parliament, speculation on his precise politics ranging from being "fellow-travelling" to "Right-Wing Labour" (93). This does not mean his private life is assured. His marriage to Pamela, unsurprisingly if gratifyingly, does not turn out to be a storybook one. Pamela takes up with the young bohemian novelist X. Trapnel, who first borrows money from Widmerpool then has an affair with his wife. (When Widmerpool complains about the money borrowing after the affair has been revealed, we feel some rare, albeit mild, sympathy for him). Trapnel, who at first sees Pamela as his great muse, discovers she is in fact a kind of literary succubus, who throws his cherished manuscript, "Profiles in String," into the Maida Vale canal, in effect ending Trapnel's career as a writer and, soon enough, his life.

As mentioned before, the novel's title connotes a provisional postwar recovery.[61] Most particularly, it is an apt caption for the postwar (and early cold war) sense that literature, as a cultural sphere, had to be resuscitated ("constant talk of 'little magazines' coming into being" [*Books Do Furnish a Room*, 35]) in order for Britain, and the West in general, to prove its resilience in a changed world. Thus the funding available for *Fission,* the periodical on which Jenkins and many of his friends work in the late 1940s, a rare circumstance in any literary period.

With Stringham and Templer dead, there is a need for new characters, though the hollow their loss leaves in Jenkins's life can never be filled. Stringham, one might argue, is in some way replaced by Trapnel as Jenkins's faintly unreliable, alcoholic friend, but Templer is never replaced. Templer is even in some sense irreplaceable, which might help explain the odd intensity of Pamela's mourning for him, even over her uncle Charles, when otherwise she does not seem the sort to excessively mourn dead lovers—witness her cavalier response to the demise of Ferrand-Sénéschal in *Temporary Kings*. As a personality,

Ferrand-Sénéschal (whose name is a humorous one, as "sene-schal" was a kind of manorial undermanager plenipotentiary in medieval Europe) is basically a combination of Boris Souvarine and Maurice Merleau-Ponty, with a dash of Jean-Paul Sartre thrown in; the name owes something to Claude Levi-Strauss (mentioned at *Wheel,* 59). After Stringham and Templer's departure, there is an atmosphere of "bare ruined choirs where late the sweet birds sang" (Shakespeare, sonnet 73), a wintry aspect, stemming from more than chronological age given that Jenkins is only in his early forties when the last trilogy begins.

The new characters in *Books Do Furnish a Room* are largely literary ones. Indeed, these characters are known largely for the books they produce, and one of the resonances of the titles might mean that, if the loss of Stringham and Templer leaves a vacancy, that vacancy will be filled not so much by new people—such as the eponymous "Books-do-furnish-a-room" Bagshaw, said to have made the comment in the aftermath of a seduction—but by the books they produce. There is an avalanche of books mentioned in the tenth volume. We see *Moss off a Rolling Stone* (3), *Slow on the Feather,* L. O. Salvidge's *Paper Wine,* Bernard Shernmaker's *Miscellaneous Equities* (to which Powell's own book of collected criticism, *Miscellaneous Verdicts,* is an obvious ironic homage), Sillery's *Garnered at Sunset: Leaves from an Edwardian Journal* (whose dullness did not augur the extreme interest in Powell's own journals, similarly published when the author was in extreme old age), and, most lucrative of all for its publishers, Ada Leintwardine's sexually suggestive *I Stopped at a Chemist*'s (the innuendo of whose title, comprehensible to American teenagers in the late 1970s, needs no transatlantic explication). The origin of the idea of fictive book titles in novels is, no doubt to General Liddament's horror from Balzac's *Les Illusions Perdues* (*Lost Illusions*), where our somewhat more Blore-Smithian than Jenkinsesque hero, Lucien de Rubempré (mentioned in *Books Do Furnish a Room,* 216), publishes two books, a historical novel, *The Archer of Charles IX,* and a book of poems, *Marguerites.* But no one has done it more funnily than has Powell, and it is hard to imagine anyone ever will. The world of books is hilariously rendered, and its grim side is revealed in the episode concerning Odo Stevens's *Sad Majors* (a play on a line from Shakespeare's *Antony and Cleopatra*), which is almost quashed by Communist sympathizers, a needed reminder of the threat of censorship, overt or tacit, that always arises in any sphere of public culture, no matter how ostensibly liberated that sphere feels itself to be. But even this sordid episode is balanced by the nearly endless cavalcade of funny literary moments. For instance, there is the tremendous gratification when Salvidge, Shernmaker, and Shuckerley are mentioned together, in glorious alliterative succession (*Temporary Kings,* 214), the three literary denizens never previously having been cited in sequence.

In this welter of literary examples, there is one character who represents the life of a writer in what Balzac might call its full splendor and misery. X. Trapnel is based on Julian Maclaren-Ross, a legendary bohemian figure of postwar London, whose eccentricities are well detailed by Powell in *Strangers.* Just as Widmerpool is riding high on the hog, with his marriage to Pamela and his prominent place in a Labour-dominated party, Trapnel comes out of nowhere to seduce Pamela, as if art was making a sudden guerrilla attack on opportunism. Trapnel, though, is not romanticized—certainly not by Jenkins, nor for that matter by Pamela—as neither one, whatever their many differences, are apt to romanticize people. Trapnel is feckless, irresponsible, sponges off people, and is self-centered. Yet we are persuaded that he is a good and original writer and that his remorse when Pamela tosses "Profiles in String" is a lament not just at the loss of a part of himself that had been alienated or abstracted into the manuscript but out of an objective sense that the world has lost a great novel. Pamela's motives for throwing away the manuscript are unclear. It could be that she had just tired of the affair and did not want Trapnel to write about her, fearing that, perhaps, it would embarrass the reunited Widmerpool couple. Or she could be acting as literary critic and felt the work did not achieve her high standards, just as Trapnel himself did not. Intriguingly, Pamela seems to rebel against being a character in someone else's novel, although not realizing that she is just that in the work of, if not "Nicholas Jenkins," then Anthony Powell.

Books Do Furnish a Room's concern with literature is not just on the level of trivia, as seen in quirky book titles and publishing gossip. Trapnel's speech about naturalism is a lengthy literary credo, a statement of principles, and has been recognized as such by Spurling, who titles her foreword "The Heresy of Naturalism," and by sundry other critical commentators, most of whom make the mistake of treating Trapnel's views as if they were entirely Powell's. It is true that Powell seems generally sympathetic to Trapnel's views, which, in stating that naturalism is "just a way of writing a novel like any other, just as contrived, just as selective" (217), repudiates a rhetoric of authenticity, of there being a true or more apt subject or style for a novel. The fact that Trapnel, not Jenkins, makes these statements can be seen as similar, in its non-egocentric splitting-off, to having Stringham, not Jenkins, make the guess of Oscar Wilde for Le

Bas in the Theocritus scene. But that Powell echoed some of
Trapnel's statements—for instance, that Tolstoy's *Anna Karenina*
is "a magazine story of genius" (226)—in his nonfiction
writing should not lead to an automatic conclusion that Powell
threw his full weight behind every word Trapnel said. Trapnel is
not an idealized character; even more than Stringham, he is
unreliable, emotionally unpredictable, and not always in control
of himself or his impulses. He is seen as a good writer, and certainly personal flaws would not, for *Dance,* preclude correct
aesthetic judgments. But Trapnel, far more, for instance, than
characters such as Barnby and Pennistone, who are to some
extent objective monitors because they never significantly encounter Widmerpool, is in the fray of the game, in the thick of
the action. His infatuation with Pamela Flitton certainly casts
some doubt on his taste. At the beginning of chapter 3 of *Hearing Secret Harmonies,* Trapnel and Jenkins are shown debating
the role of character in the novel, in which Jenkins, perhaps
playing devil's advocate, takes the less "naturalistic" position,
the statement "the very concept of character in a novel . . . is
under attack" (85) clearly referring to something like the French
nouveau roman.

Notwithstanding the Trapnel question, there is the problem of "naturalism." Naturalism, as a term, is overwhelmingly
associated with realistic writers of the political Left, figures
such as Zola, Dreiser, and the early Dos Passos, writers with a
social conscience who aim by a rigorous observance of existing
conditions to change them, or to simply reflect the mechanical
injustice of life. This characterization cannot be said to apply
to Powell, although something like the mechanical injustice
of life is presented, very artificially, in *Afternoon Men.* (The writers Powell most admired—Proust, Dostoevsky, Fitzgerald,

Hemingway, and Joyce—have seldom been described as naturalists.) Powell several times seems to shy away from applying the term "naturalism" to himself, for instance, stating of V. S. Naipaul that his work has a "directness, a naturalism" (*Strangers,* 163), that "English writers do not always find easy, one eye always swiveling in the direction of fantasy." Presumably Powell is including himself here, and "swivelling in the direction of fantasy" is a good description for the books' feel— like those of Jane Austen—of a self-contained world. In an interview with Paul Gaston, Powell asserts, "I am not absolutely bound to naturalism."[62] Combining Trapnel's comment that naturalism often manifests himself in "grotesque irrational trivialities" with Powell's comment, cited in chapter 2 of this book with regard to *Agents and Patients,* that it was with regard to his fourth novel that he began to see alternatives to naturalism, that in his view, *Dance* was less naturalistic than the early works. Naturalism, to Powell, seems to consist of a near-anarchy of incident (the reverse of the overarching ideology with which naturalism is associated). In his memoirs, Powell traces the softening of this anarchic naturalism and his gradual conviction that "human brings are rarely, if ever, naturalistic" (*Messengers,* 116). Whatever definition of naturalism we use, we can see that, despite the realism of Powell's work, or at least the way it matches the world as seen by the author in his nonfiction to a reasonable degree, *Dance* is not naturalistic in any definable sense. Its great achievement, that it creates a world of its own where everything in it is true in its own terms, is, as mentioned before, comparable to a good science fiction or fantasy book; it surpasses naturalism in supposing that there is a central moral purpose to life, even if never explicitly rendered, that naturalism can never assume.

Another instance of Powell shying away from naturalistic precepts can be seen in the Ritz Hotel scene already mentioned in the context of F. Scott Fitzgerald, where it is stated that English writers are more or less incapable of producing the straightforward realism that is conventionally expected, at least from writers of other countries. The dialogue between Trapnel and Bagshaw on fiction (actually more of a monologue on Trapnel's part, and one in which Bagshaw, perhaps still quasi-Marxist aesthetically, though certainly no longer politically, is the great advocate of realism) rebukes certain truisms of literary criticism but enshrines no new truisms. Its emphasis is on the inevitable variety of literary practice and, most interestingly, in literature that does something truly new being able to impart information that is "not necessarily what the reader wants to hear" (215).

Given the emphasis on literature in *Books Do Furnish a Room,* it is apt that we see more of Nicholas Jenkins as a writer than ever before. In fact, it is in this book that we learn of the only actual book title of Jenkins's writing career that is ever known: *Borage and Hellebore,* his biography of Robert Burton, the author of *Anatomy of Melancholy,* the seventeenth-century quasi-encyclopedic treatise. At this point, the sort of question about the status of *Dance*'s narrative of fiction arises that has not previously come up. We know that the contours of Jenkins's career parallel that of Powell. As John Gould puts it, "Both men were born midway through the first decade of the twentieth century. Both were the sons of military officers; both attended Eton and Oxford; both worked for film companies and book publishers before World War II; both served during the war in a Welsh unit and later did liaison work with the Poles, and so on."[62] We also know that Powell, just after the war, wrote a biography of a seventeenth-century prose writer whose works straddle genres and are studied as much by literary scholars as by anyone else—not Burton, but John Aubrey. Powell stated that Jenkins's Burton book "stands for my book on Aubrey."[64] Burton is the more reflective writer of the two, or at least the more philosophical one.

Aubrey is not mentioned in *Dance,* although he could have supplied several apposite examples or parallels. This is to make sure the two worlds, Powell's and Jenkins's, are sealed off from each other. (This procedure is not universal in *Dance;* for instance, John Galsworthy is mentioned by name [*Question,* 66], even though his "real" presence in the sequence is as St. John Clarke. Similarly, Fitzgerald and Joyce are overtly mentioned, although, as this book has argued, they are also covertly present in passages of *Dance.*) The pastiche passages of Pepys, Byron, and Proust suggest a fictional universe that can even produce fictional versions of past writers, much less contemporary characters, but this is never pursued so systematically as to change or distort our views of these writers themselves.

A similar proximity exists between Powell and his fictional analogue, Jenkins. As Christopher Hitchens puts it, "Jenkins follows all the steps . . . traced for Powell."[65] Yet there are minor differences between Powell and Jenkins. "Jenkins," for instance, a name now found largely in Wales, is thought to be originally a Flemish name (son of Johan) that came over to England at the time of the Norman Conquest; thus Jenkins would have had some ancestry in common with some of the Belgians with whom he liaises during the war. Jenkins is not as markedly Welsh a name as "Powell," which stems from a Welsh patronymic, ap Hywel, son of Howell. Notwithstanding this, in *Question* (24), Jenkins begins to give a reluctant Uncle Giles genealogical information similar to that of Powell's own paternal line. Spurling, intriguingly, has Jenkins born in 1906 or 1907.[66] Powell was born in December 1905, so there is not all that much difference, but Spurling is on to something here. Jenkins several times refers to being slightly younger than nearly exact contemporaries such as Widmerpool and Erridge. Jenkins seems less successful than Powell. Often he is just scraping by, and his achievement as a novelist is acknowledged but not excessively praised by the other characters. This might just be self-effacement on Powell's part. But the autobiographical portrait he gives in the memoirs and *Journals* cannot help but reveal a more widely appreciated man.

Writing comes up in *Books Do Furnish a Room* in another way as well. The novel is the space where *Dance* could announce its self-reflexivity, as it comes closest in approach to 1951, the year *Dance* was actually launched. In other words, Jenkins could announce to the reader in *Books* that he was writing a long, sequential novel, carrying a number of characters over a period of time and including requisite social and cultural background—in essence, the very work the reader is reading. Self-reference of this sort, associated with such late modernist masters as Borges and Nabokov, can in fact be traced back far earlier—to Shakespeare's Sonnet 74, for instance, in which "this" clearly indicates the poem that we are in the act of reading. Robert Selig, in mulling over this issue, states that the absence of any reference to the writing of *Dance* in *Dance* means that Jenkins is not represented as the internal author of *Dance*, that in a rather phonocentric fashion, he speaks it but does not write it. But surely this is going too far. Jenkins is not an oral bard, chanting ancestral tales like the Serbo-Croatian singers so often referenced in oral-formulaic theories of Homeric poetry. All that the nonpresence of *Dance* as written referent in *Dance* really means is that Jenkins and Powell inhabit different worlds, as is instanced by the Aubrey/Burton displacement.

But the real question is, Why does not Powell insert references to the composition of *Dance* as a part of writing from what John Gould calls "the unpainted piece of wall" that lies between "the narrative past" and "the narrative present"?[67] Powell shies away from this because he is simply not interested in these literary pyrotechnics—not necessarily incapable of or insensitive to them, simply not interested. This is seen in the *Journals* (1 January 1990), where, in this case at the suggestion of the Austrian academic Peter Kislinger, Powell read Henry James's short stories "The Figure in the Carpet" and "The Lesson of the Master"—usually, even by the most orthodox critics, read as a parable of aesthetic meaning, the process of making fictions, or the elusiveness thereof—as pieces of straightforward realism about human relationships. Nonetheless, the fact that the "bridge" novel, in other words, the novel where the sequence's own potential conception is bridged, has *Books* in the title might be a slight, graceful gesture toward this potential opportunity. But only a very slight one.

References to writers that have been mentioned in this book as allusive presences—Balzac, Fitzgerald, Joyce—are always made far from where the possible allusions occur, as if Powell means them to be in the reader's awareness but does not want to be obtrusively suggestive. Despite Powell's reference to the music and politics of his own era, or eras, there are no references to writers of his own generation, such as Greene, Green, and Waugh. The mention of "Orwellian overtones" (*Military Philosophers,* 215) is the only instance of a literary contemporary of Powell actually mentioned in *Dance*. Perhaps this is because, of all of Powell's major intellectual contemporaries—excepting

Robert Byron—only Orwell was dead in 1951, when the representing time of *Dance* begins. Similarly, it is very surprising that the Poussin painting, after which the sequence is named and in many ways upon which it is premised, is only mentioned in the first and twelfth books (and not in the tenth book), and that Poussin himself is not endlessly reiterated as an aesthetic indicator; the novelist who wanted to give his references more weight would, for example, have used Poussin where Tiepolo is used in *Temporary Kings,* although this might have meant not setting the scene in Venice, or used another Poussin painting instead of the Bernini sculpture, *Truth Unveiled by Time,* especially since Bernini is often said to have been an artistic rival of Poussin.[5] Witness the extent to which the television version, which *has* to make the Poussin visible in order to explain the concept of title to a fresh audience, has to go to foreground the Poussin, actually having the characters attend a museum lecture where its meaning is elucidated by a docent. This is required because there is so little Poussin in a sequence premised after a Poussin painting. Part of this reluctance to be flagrantly self-conscious about the "artiness" of *Dance* is because Powell is already so aesthetically self-conscious that there is no need for splashy special effects. There is, finally, a rigor in Powell's approach, an unwillingness to be distracted from the task at hand, a reluctance to let generalizations about self-references distract the reader from the mundane tasks of actually, in one's own inevitable subjective and unstable judgment, getting the book right. In this way, the very material nature of *Books Do Furnish a Room*'s portrait of the world of books is apropos.

Even Kingsley Amis is puzzled by the Poussin question, mentioning in his memoirs that, surprisingly (given the far more jocular, less literary surface of his work), he, Amis, might be a "more literary" writer than Powell, as Amis had asked about the aesthetic function of the "card-reading stuff with Mrs. Erdleigh" in *Dance*. Powell had replied that people had been interested in "that sort of stuff" at the time, so including it was a social reference, not an aesthetic gesture.[69] This may be what Evelyn Waugh had in mind when he spoke of *Dance* as occurring "all on one level."[70] Waugh meant that *Dance,* unlike other novels of its day, does not present certain characters as Christ figures or symbols for sacrifice, alienation, or other abstractions. Nor does it propagate, in an allegorical or even symbolic manner, a doctrine or ideology. But to totally endorse Waugh's opinion would be to say that there were no rereadable subtleties, no "secret harmonies," only a Widmerpool level and no Theocritus level, or variations thereupon.

Nor is *Dance* without small playful gestures of its own. Amis himself, for instance, is the object of a small, playful gesture, as the English professor in Swansea whom Gwenllian Breeze married, in preference to Gwatkin, in *Valley of Bones* is a reference to Amis's teaching at Swansea in the 1950s. Similarly, "Angus and Iris," as George Tolland's stepchildren, refers to Powell's fellow novelists Angus Wilson and Iris Murdoch. The one small bit of self-reference to "Powell" in *Dance* is in *Hearing Secret Harmonies,* when Jenkins is attending the Magnus Donners Prize dinner and is seated next to the wife of one of the firm's directors. The Director's Lady asks him, "What do you think of Enoch?" (*Harmonies,* 105), the reference being, not to the biblical personage but to Enoch Powell, the maverick Tory politician whose anti-immigrant comments were then at their most notorious. One could easily reconstruct a real-life scene as the basis for this: a woman at a party assumes Anthony Powell is Enoch Powell, and on realizing he is not, asks him,

"What do you think of Enoch?" Similarly, Cutts and Widmerpool's discussion of "2½ % Treasury Stock Redeemable after 1975" (173) may be a self-referential allusion to the year the last volume of *Dance* was to be published (the production of *Books Do Furnish a Room* in 1971 ensuring the possibility of this prediction being reasonably reliable). Also, as narratologically minded critics have noted, *Books* was published in 1971, the year the action of the sequence's final book, *Hearing Secret Harmonies,* ends.

Whether or not these examples are significant, they are not obtrusive but braided into the fabric. Gould summarizes the question well when he says of any overt reference to *Dance* in *Dance,* "We never hear of it."[71] *Dance* is characterized less by overt self-reference then by a serene, presiding literariness, a sense of resemblance of all action to motifs to be found in art. This literariness, though, is not arch or coy. As Hugh Massingberd puts it, Powell "took a robust approach to the Arts. Real aestheticism called for toughness, discipline."[72] This aesthetic discipline can be seen in the account of Erridge's funeral, in which, within the space of four pages, there are references to George Herbert, Dostoevsky, Burton, and Walter Ralegh. Some of these (Herbert and Ralegh) occur as part of the funeral service itself, whereas the others are products of Jenkins's own musings. But these references illustrate the most profound way that "books do furnish a room" in *Dance,* by providing the widest possible canvas for conversation and reflection, bringing a shield of civilization to sad and tumultuous times and providing a background of nuance and depth to the passing show of life. The literary influences also underscore how nuanced is the action of *Dance.* At the end of his life, for instance, Erridge finally does something about raising the memorial window to his father, the previous Lord Warminster. Erridge has, late in life, done the right thing, risen to the demands of duty. As with *From a View,* though, there is no sense of a tidy or harmonic restoration of the past order. The presence of Siegfried, the former German prisoner of war, as well as Pamela's vomiting in the Chinese vase, make sure of that. In addition, we are reminded that the Thrubworth estate only retains the wood because of the ever-so-bourgeois St. John Clarke's "fortuitous legacy to Erridge" (*Books,* 65). Erridge's belated surge of responsibility is not a recuperation of the past but a personal gesture of valor. It is interesting that Erridge had so little to do with Widmerpool, even though both had many friends in common and traveled in leftist political circles. The independence and eccentricity of Erridge, as well as his strange sense of saving immaturity—his never having fully become an adult, unless perhaps at the late memorial homage to his father—has prevented him from being absorbed in adult machinations. A revitalized Erridge might have resembled the final, pathos-filled return of Lord Marchmain to Brideshead in Waugh's novel. Powell avoids both this and its opposite, farcical extreme of having the obviously homosexual Hugo inherit the peerage, which ultimately goes to Jeremy, posthumously born son of Erridge's younger brother, George. Neither comic degeneration nor rousing recovery are in the cards. Powell can present these subtleties and still keep the jokes coming and the narrative rolling because the bulwark of all the literary references keeps us alert to how ramified experience can be.

Temporary Kings (1973)

There is a ten-year gap in setting between the tenth and eleventh book (1948 to 1958, ending in 1959), which is more or less repeated between the eleventh and twelfth (1959 to 1968, ending in 1971). The immediate occasion of 1958 as the setting was probably the Life Peerages Act, whose passage in that year enables Widmerpool to make his unlikely ascension to the House of Lords (receiving a hereditary peerage would have been too ludicrous; in any event, no one would inherit, as Widmerpool's marriage, which does not produce children, is also not necessarily the sort that would). The peerage is conferred by the Conservative government of Harold Macmillan and cleared by the opposition leader, Hugh Gaitskell, in order to balance out the upper house with sufficient Labor peers so that it will not be accused of being unrepresentative. Widmerpool's business connections (notable in that they prevent him from just being a caricature of a leftist; he is not Quiggin) make him acceptable to both parties, if unadmired by either. But the substantial gap between *Books Do Furnish a Room* and *Temporary Kings* has an abstract purpose as well. It lets us known that the last two books are in a different era—one of television, nuclear weapons, and global ideological competition. Many readers have spoken out against the last two books, feeling that Powell's grasp on these later years is not as assured as on the earlier ones, and wishing the author had stayed within a more defined compass. But the straying into another era is precisely Powell's point. *Dance* covers the bulk of the twentieth century. In fact, if one accepts the rather Eurocentric conventional historian's definition of "the short twentieth century" as being between 1914 and 1989, *Dance* covers nearly all of it, and the *Journals* make up the rest. The eleventh and twelfth books expand the reach of *Dance* well beyond adding mere chronological duration.

Temporary Kings, called by Powell (*Journals,* 10 January 1989) "perhaps the best constructed volume of the sequence," is faultlessly choreographed, considering its by-now huge cast of characters who have to be moved on and off stage and positioned in relation to one another without any sense of labor or contrivance, the best moment in this respect being when Jenkins's wife, Isobel, as a kind of external oracle, notifies him from London by telegram of the gossip about Ferrand-Sénéschal's death. For the first time, this large cast includes American characters in major roles. The cold war is at its height, and as a consequence, all sorts of money is available for the funding of cultural congresses to debate the writer and society, the future of culture in the West. It is at one of these conferences, a particularly opulent one in Venice (the Biennale is in progress, which mandates an even year, thus 1958 instead of 1959), that Jenkins finds himself at the beginning of the book. The conferees, living the high life at Venetian palazzi, are merely "temporary kings."

But one of the principal presences in the book is not a person, but a painting. The Tiepolo, from a painter too late and too narrative, as Herodotus is a historian too early and too narrative, is fascinating; along with the risqué theme, it achieves a rare combination of complete cultural legitimacy and outrageous eccentricity.[73] The Tiepolo painting—like the literary pastiches, imaginary—of the story of Gyges and Candaules is the cynosure of *Temporary Kings*'s artistic edifice. It is interesting, then, that although superbly described, it does not come across as exceptionally beautiful. Powell does not want to put art on too high a pedestal. Despite the opposition, particularly intense in this book, between power and art, Widmerpool and Theocritus, Powell takes care to keep it on what, returning to the terms of Frye, we might call a high mimetic, not an epic, level. Not that the starker epic positions are to be condemned, but Powell, as an artist, does not choose to employ these in his work.

The story of Gyges and Candaules starts off the *Histories* of Herodotus. It is the opening anecdote, and it has to be, as it explains how Lydia became such a strong state that it attracted first Median and then, when the latter people, headed by M: Deacon's best-known subject, took over Media, Persian attention, thus bringing Persian power into an area where it could encounter the Greeks, the confrontation between these two people being Herodotus's story. As the opening anecdote of the first reliable historical account involving any part of Europe, the Gyges-Candaules story is in a way the founding tale of "European history," that is to say, the history written by Europeans rather than European history as such, even though the events described, of course, take place in Asia Minor. It is in this capacity that the Gyges and Candaules incident received its now more famous mention in Michael Ondaatje's novel, *The English Patient* (1992). It is Ondaatje, not Powell, who inflects Herodotus as European and the founder of European narrative, rather than just a storyteller who gets some things right, some other things wrong, but is entertaining and informative in the process. This of course could be explained as a product of postcolonial consciousness. But it is notable how Powell is more interested in the European as human rather than the European as European in his work. Herodotus provides a similar mixture of history, anecdote, and myth to *Dance*. It is only modern generic distinctions, plus the fact that Herodotus uses names known to be historical and Powell uses names known not to be, that puts them in different bookstore shelves and library classifications.

As Moreland, in his last scene in *Dance,* and Jenkins admit at the end of *Temporary Kings,* the Gyges-Candaules analogy is inexact in diagnosing the reality of the Widmerpool-Pamela situation. Widmerpool is, most plausibly, Gyges, in that it is he who looks on while his wife has sex with other men (even though in the original story the queen is, of course, Candaules' wife). In his eventual role as self-elevated Lydian strongman, Gyges perhaps is what Widmerpool dreams to be. But in publicly exhibiting his wife to other men, Widmerpool also possesses strong aspects of Candaules—in a way both flaunting his power and, self-destructively, rendering it vulnerable. *Dance* is interested in voyeurism. This is a case where a complaint of contemporary critics, one that has contributed to the sequence being kept out of the postmodern canon, despite its greater suitability for such than many works that are included, namely, that the narrative perspective is so set against Widmerpool that he is simply targeted and lampooned by it, is simply wrong. Widmerpool, in his sexual life, is a voyeur. But so, in other capacities, are Jenkins and Moreland, and so, in another capacity, are we, the readers. In terms of voyeurism, every entity involved in this literary transaction is a voyeur, and nobody is free from Widmerpool's warped perspective. In addition, the spatial, visual element of *Dance* (unmentioned in the sequence's title, with all its implication of flow and movement) is in a way its mainstay. It is surprising, that, for all the interest of postmodern theory in voyeurism, *Dance* has been so little analyzed under this aegis—especially in the way that Pamela is the conceiver of the applicability of the Gyges-Candaules precedent to her own case—so here the object of the voyeuristic gesture is also its agent. The actual description of the false Tiepolo, protracted and rather harrowing to read, is notable for its evocation of the bedchamber as managing to "float out of whatever building it was normally part—some palace on imagined—to remain suspended, a kind of celestial 'Mulberry' set for action in the upper reaches of the sky" (*Temporary Kings,* 83). The witty reference to the mulberries, the artificial harbors used in the Normandy invasion, also, on a deeper level, alerts us to the false Tiepolo's actual invented status as postwar art.

Temporary Kings, with its cold war setting and its chronicling of the fall of Widmerpool from his swaggering peak, is to Powell's work what, as it were, the battle of Salamis is to that of Herodotus. It is in a way the grand finale, even though there is another book after it, *Hearing Secret Harmonies* being the extended epilogue to *Temporary Kings.* This mirrors and offsets the way the death of Trapnel is not actually chronicled in his own book, *Books Do Furnish a Room,* but in its successor. Its position in *Dance,* not to mention its particular content, makes it of paramount importance. The eleventh volume is another second volume—not only the second volume of the final trilogy, but the "penultimate" volume (as the 1973 Little, Brown book jacket calls it; I remember reading this at thirteen and thinking it a term of praise, not enumeration). Just as the second volume was where the artists and bohemians of *Dance* were really introduced, in the eleventh volume they achieve the purpose the sequence intends for them—to entertain, yes, but also to fend off Widmerpool. A sort of rackety (as Powell might put it) aesthetic "coalition of the willing" forms in *Temporary Kings.* This coalition includes Gwinnett, who as biographer of Trapnel is trying to walk in his footsteps, out of a mixture of research and quasi-idolatrous adulation. But he is also out to avenge Trapnel. And surprisingly, he does. Trapnel loses to Widmerpool. He has a brief moment of triumph when Widmerpool's wife runs off with him, but he ends up with his manuscript and death's-head stick gone, reduced to drink and ruin. In fact, Widmerpool's victory over Trapnel (albeit with a major assist from Pamela) is the last in his string of victories over, successively, Truscott, String-ham, Hogbourne-Johnson, Duport, Templer, and Trapnel, with only the imperturbably confident ("his blue eyes always smiled out bravely on the world"; *Military Philosophers,* 14) Fare-brother interrupting the string. But Pamela and, in his own way, Widmerpool do not survive their encounter with Gwinnett. This revenge, with its operation through the least romantic aspects of sex and, for that matter, death, is unattractive. It is certainly not simply a heroic putting of things to rights. But it is in key with *Temporary Kings*'s theme of how art or artistic intentions that are not ideal nevertheless have their role to play. The unlikely quartet of Gwinnett, Glober, Tokenhouse, and Dr. Brightman, all in their different ways hard-nosed aesthetes, manage to con-tain the new peer's ambitions, if not roll them back. It some-times seems in *Dance* as if anyone involved to any extent in the arts has some good in them. This is not true in the real world, even the real world as imaged in Powell's *Journals.* But it is one of the vertebral conceits of *Dance.*

Another one of these unusual aesthetes is the filmmaker Louis Glober. As in *Casanova's,* Powell deftly deploys flash-back technique in bringing Glober's past with Mopsy Pontner and the Lilienthals. For Glober, about whom the 1920s remi-niscences lend a sense of being weathered in the world of *Dance,* does not seem like a new character, even though he is one, and therefore does not disconcert the reader, who is already having to stretch to include Americans in a cast that, aside from the desig-nated "foreigners," has been, in all nontrivial aspects, exclusively British.

Relevant also here is the strange figure of Daniel Token-house, Jenkins's former boss in publishing (though never men-tioned in those early volumes in which Jenkins works as a publisher, another instance of second-book carryover). Token-house may be the "humorless egotist" Neil McEwan discerns, but he is more than that.[74] He is on the spectrum of permissible, tolerable humanity in a way that Widmerpool and Pamela are not, even if he is not someone Jenkins admires. Formerly a conventional businessman, sufficiently conventional to have been friends with Jenkins's none-too-experimental father, Token-house has gone over the edge and become a raving Communist. Self-exiled to Venice in protest against British policy, reconceiving himself as a socialist-realist artist, Tokenhouse yet holds on to his residual status in British society, writing letters to the London press in which he affirms his army rank as a retired major. There is an odd ebullience about Tokenhouse, even if he is otherwise a curmudgeonly, insane Stalinist. Tokenhouse quickens the tempo, not only of *Temporary Kings* but also of the entire sequence. A militant atheist, he is similar to a figure in the next book, *Hearing Secret Harmonies,* the Christian cleric Canon Paul Fenneau, in combining utter intellectual confidence with utter self-infatuation, although Fenneau has more grounds for at least the former than does Tokenhouse. Tokenhouse also seems to genuinely like Jenkins, to not, as others might, hold the split with the senior Jenkins against the son. Tokenhouse's contempt for "Lord" Widmerpool, though reflexively left-wing, does prevent him from becoming a pawn in Widmerpool's plans.

As much as Tokenhouse's paintings (*Four Priests Rigging a Miracle*) are made fun of, seen as exemplars of an aesthetically unsustainable Socialist realism that collapses into a parodic crudeness, his practice of socialism is infinitely superior to that of Widmerpool; as with Quiggin, Jenkins maintains amiable personal relations with Tokenhouse. When Glober buys Token-house's painting, it is basically because the painting is so bad as to intrigue Glober, already bemused by Tokenhouse's living situation, his very existence, in fact. There is a graciousness in Glober's flattery of Tokenhouse. Even if out of pretense, posture, or a sense of fun, Glober has managed to take a boring, isolated eccentric of extreme views and make him feel wanted and admired. Glober is somehow deliberately interested in "saving the situation" (*Temporary Kings,* 144), a phrase with a weight beyond a merely procedural one, as Glober's gratuitous interest in Tokenhouse's art is symptomatic of the way in which Widmerpool's power schemes, his intrigues with Dr. Belkin, will inevitably fail, out of their obviousness and lack of taste, if nothing else. Glober buys the Tokenhouse painting not out of a profit motive but from what must be termed a sense of fun. Under the shadow of the (fictive) Tiepolo, a notable picture by a great painter, Glober's appreciation of a terrible picture by a third-rate painter strikes one of the most significant blows in the entire sequence on behalf of art—and courtesy.

"Tokenhouse" as a name is also perhaps the capstone of the game Powell has been playing all along with names as compound entities, rearranging plausible prefixes and suffixes, rarely reusing any, avoiding both caricature and meaninglessness. This is true in *Dance*'s names of people—Stringham, Bagshaw, Shernmaker, Pontner, Mountfichet, Tokenhouse—and of houses: Thrubworth, Dogdene, Castlemallock. Care is taken in the arrangement of the two compound elements to make sure that neither, as an individual component or in synch with its counterpart, is so broad and comic as to make the reader doubt its actuality. This is a task all the more difficult with a name like "Tokenhouse," both of whose elements mean something in ordinary language, but the name succeeds as simulating the name of a real person, even though there are few, if any,

Tokenhouses in phone books worldwide. Tokenhouse is a place name (Tokenhouse Yard in London), but it is resituated convincingly as a personal name. This is why Powell's names are so much better than, to use a case upon which he often remarked (see *Journals,* 23 July 1991), those of Henry James. And yet the end product, so funny in a dry, subtle way, is one some readers, unattuned to or uninterested in name humor, will not get.

Glober, Gwinnett, and Tokenhouse represent three different approaches to art: Gwinnett a darkened classicism, Glober a touch of the outrageous mixed with a necessary acknowledgment of the profit motive, and Tokenhouse a sheer battiness, a constriction by outlandish dogma that possesses at its core a scintilla of integrity and honor. This coalition to some extent includes Polly Duport, daughter of Jean, who is depicted unsentimentally, given that, if Jenkins had married Jean, as he surely one day wanted to, she would have been Jenkins's stepdaughter. Polly Duport is presented as reasonably ignoble, if affable, and pretty much possessed of the conventional actress's temperament. Yet she also stands out against Widmerpool—more immediately, against Pamela—and is proof that the world is constantly producing new possibilities, that those people like Widmerpool and Pamela who would want to bend it to a monolithic, not to mention maleficent, shape for their own ends are eventually ground down by the endless fecundity of life. These rogue aesthetes are tough-minded and are more effective against Widmerpool than the admirable, but *au fond* rather sentimental, Trapnel. Widmerpool is defeated not by one valiant opponent, but by a thousand small acts, intentional and unintentional.

On a Widmerpool reading of *Temporary Kings,* we notice Gwinnett mainly as biographer of Trapnel. But on a Theocritus reading, we notice Gwinnett as himself—the American academic. Turning from, for instance, Widmerpool to Russell Gwinnett is, for all of Gwinnett's strangeness, like a breath of fresh air. Emily Brightman feels this attraction, and so does Pamela; in fact, Pamela's erotic suicide, her life-in-death, may be somehow morally preferable to her death-in-life with Widmerpool. Gwinnett is a descendant of Button Gwinnett, the Georgia signer of the Declaration of Independence who gave his name to a prominent county of that state and was the first of the signers to die, in 1777, and therefore has the rarest signature. Powell is showing he can display his onomastic and referential brio on the others side of the Atlantic as well as his own. He makes the American reader—who likely will have heard of Button Gwinnett if they have taken a couple of college-level American history courses—feel included. The American reader gets the joke, and in that way the reference is effective. Opinion is more divided as to whether Gwinnett is an accurate portrait of an American academic, one born circa 1925, coming to intellectual maturity in the 1950s. In trying to explain him to Jenkins, Dr. Brightman says, "If there is a superfluity of Edgar Allan Poe brought up to date, there is also a touch of Edwin Arlington Robinson" (*Temporary Kings,* 48). This would indicate a combination of bourgeois repression and gothic morbidity, which is a hard combination to render so specifically and at such a cultural distance (as Jenkins admits, "You outrun my bounds").[75] Certainly the interest in Jacobean drama is typical of Gwinnett's generation, who in so many ways took their lead from T. S. Eliot. One could have, relatively recently, gone to, say, the cash bar of the Tudor-Stuart society at the Modern Language Association convention and seen several aging Gwinnetts. His politics, though, seem strangely liberal for this generally, though not invariably, conservative group, if one assumes that when the then-upcoming 1972 presidential election is discussed in *Hearing Secret Harmonies,* Gwinnett is advocating the Democratic candidate.

But if the question is whether Gwinnett would be the average American academic, even of his generation, the answer would have to be no, although it must be remembered that Powell was basing him on his own experience and on the particular strain of American academics he would have encountered in the course of his own work, which strain likely would have been more Anglophile and eccentric than the norm. Gwinnett is a mixed character. He does not charm us as do Stringham or even Trapnel, although he is much more efficient an aesthete than either of them. Certainly Gwinnett is no paladin of virtue, as Flavia Wisebite demonstrates when she calls him "dreadful" (*Harmonies,* 227). But he is interested in literature, not in power. Thus his dreadfulness, which is, despite Flavia's undeniable hysteria, undoubted, is able to be accommodated within social forms. Glober, as a Hollywood tycoon, is more of a type, though based on people Powell actually met (*Journals,* 23 March 1991). But Glober is not caricatured; he is a real person, and when it comes down to it, a sympathetic one. Gwinnett and Glober, part of the aforementioned coalition of unlikely aesthetes, also have their Americanness, not to mention their common initial "G" (which links then with the Welshman Gwatkin, also in his own, limited way a practical aesthete). But what else are they doing?

Why are these Americans in *Dance,* and why only from the eleventh volume? In some ways, the idea of Americans in *Dance* is inconceivable, as the sequence is so classical, so ceremonial, so archaizing. But on the other hand, there is a converse sense in which Americans, of the 1950s and 1960s especially, could not be more apt as characters in *Dance,* as the sequence also has a modernity, an openness to the future, a New World sensibility, a delight in what the course of time hurls forth. The cynic might explain this on the basis of American sales; a more generous explanation would see Powell, grateful for the support and enthusiasm his works had a perceived from so many Americans, is giving a sort of homage of thanks. But this does not seem to be the case, either in intention or effect. Most American readers do not find Gwinnett or Glober at all recognizable as Americans. Even Powell's friend, Congressman John Monagan, was unenthusiastic about the American characters.[76] Michael Henle, grandson of the American publisher of *From a View,* commented on the Anthony Powell e-mail list that the far more obscure Colonel "Courthouse" Cobb, the American assistant military attaché in *Military Philosophers* who does not have much of a presence, is "a more attractive example of an American."[77] The nature of the Americans might suggest the purpose to which Powell is deploying them. Unlike Cobb, these two men are not military officers; they are not businessmen, lawyers, diplomats, or engineers. They are associated with the cultural side of American prominence after the Second World War, not the political side. But this obscures the precisely political purpose for which they are being used. Widmerpool is, more or less, on the side of the Soviets in the cold war. Jenkins, and Powell, are on the side of the Americans in the geopolitical standoff, or realize that American power is the only viable counter to the Soviet threat. Powell is conscious, though, of anti-American stereotypes, coming as much from the Right as the Left in Europe, that Americans were or are boorish, uncultured, preoccupied with finance, and morally innocent. These are stereotypes writers have dispelled from the time of Henry James, if not earlier. But they persist today, much less in 1973, when the book was published, or 1958, when the book is set. Powell, in trying to defend Americans from these geopolitically contumacious characterizations, *has* to come up with Americans who are eccentrics and aesthetes, people familiar with the dark and miserable aspects of existence whom Americans, perhaps not infelicitously, tend in both others' perception of them and their own official ideology to sideline. Gwinnett and Glober are artistic in a way that dispels politically motivated anti-American rhetoric. As the stakes are raised in the eleventh book, culture and power, art and geopolitics become ever more tightly wound. The rival musics of art and politics, sometimes clashing, sometimes contrapuntal, sustain and undergird the action of *Temporary Kings*. One is not sure why both Americans have such peculiar sexual habits, unless it is again to disprove Daisy Miller–vintage myths about American innocence in this sphere, which end up, as James perceived, being somehow invidious to Americans despite their moral desirability on the purest level. If anything, the stereotype might be said to run the other way (who knows about the reality?). Gwinnett's tastes, at least, come into the plot, whereas Glober's remain somewhat more gratuitous.

These Americans form part of the backdrop against which Widmerpool's cold war tragedy is played out. Widmerpool is exposed, ironically from within Eastern Europe, as part of the post-Stalinist "thaw." The non-appearance of Dr. Belkin means his political goose is cooked. Widmerpool's monstrosity is also conspicuously adorned with small unkindnesses, as he has not even attended his mother's funeral, after she had died a few short years after her son had trundled her off, safely away from Pamela, into grim internal exile in Kirkcudbrightshire. The location (reverting to the alleged Scottish ancestry of the Widmerpool clan, although presumably this was on the father's side) is meant to be a joke, as Kirkcudbrightshire, in southwest Scotland, is one of the more obscure Scottish shires, and because "K" names for some reason come off as funny in English, like "Kalamazoo" or "Kokomo," frequent subjects of humor in the United States. Widmerpool's relegation of his mother to obscurity at the end signifies that he lacks virtue in either the public or private spheres. A Communist agent, he betrays his country —but also his friend (Templer, for instance, truly regarded Widmerpool as a friend) and his mother. He does not even have the virtues of a mama's boy such as Robin Jilson in *Fisher,* although he does think about setting up his mother with "Marshal Stalin," a match from which no doubt neither party would have emerged unscathed. In this book, Widmerpool's dreams of cold war glory, or notoriety, lead him to behave with inhuman callousness.

The most interesting historian of the cold war, Derek Leebaert, says of the 1956 to 1961 period, amid which *Temporary Kings* is set, that it was characterized by "that ancient wisdom *one ignotum pro magnifico,* 'Everything unknown is taken as formidable.'"[78] This aphorism, conceivable as uttered by Mrs. Erdleigh or Dr. Trelawney, also characterizes Widmerpool's dealings with the Soviet Union. His interest in communism, is, if anything, *less* idealistic than that of the Cambridge spy ring. (The "Third Man" of that ring, Kim Philby, was exposed in 1958; the "Fourth Man," Anthony Blunt, former keeper of the queen's pictures, was exposed in 1979, too late for Powell to use what is a bizarre conjunction of *Dance*'s interest in cold war politics and modern European painting; what John Banville did with this theme in *The Untouchable* [1997] will have to suffice.) Note that after *Temporary Kings,* Widmerpool seems to lose all interest in communism, even though communism itself goes on.

Perhaps this was prudence, as the deal that let him off presumably had a proviso that he would have nothing more to do with communism. The interests in youth and the occult take over. But this also might reflect an awareness on the part of Widmerpool, who does not need to be a weather man to know which way the wind blows, that the power of communism, as communism, had waned and he would have to hitch his horse to the apparently more promising youth culture, whether as another incarnation of communism or, as constructed by Widmerpool, not in reality, as its own endogenous malice. The Swedish electronic journal *Contra* (www.contra.nu; its motto "För frihet—mot socialism") maintains a list of heroes of the cold war. Powell should be on that list. As a writer who opposed the Soviet Union at the time it existed and waxed mighty—there are all too many literati champing at the bit to denounce it now that it is dead—Powell showed not only discrimination, not only what we might call political taste, but true nobility of spirit. *Temporary Kings* is a substantial contribution to the literature of anti-communism. If there is a college English course on Western anti-Communist literature, it should be among the texts read (along with such works as Arthur Koestler's *Darkness at Noon*), all the more so in that its modus operandi are, in true Powell style, tacit and implicit.

This reluctance to graphically parade incident is also seen in the book's more personal dramas. The death of Pamela is very circumspectly described. Indeed, one of the reasons Delavacquerie asks Jenkins so graphically about the "necrophilic professor" (*Harmonies*, 75) is that many readers of *Temporary Kings,* on publication, no doubt asked Powell the same question. But remember that the post-opera confrontation is also not directly witnessed by Jenkins, only reported by Moreland and Stevens.

This material is so grisly, so horrific, the narrative cannot look at it straight on.

But the immediate impact of Pamela's death is as a turning point in the public career of Widmerpool. He will remain on the scene, making mischief or making a fool of himself, but any sense of his roving at will in the corridors of power is completely gone. He will remain in the House of Lords, but in no role of public prominence. The evidence against him as a spy is just short of enough to prosecute, and presumably Widmerpool knew enough secrets about other people in the government to remain safe himself. But he is discredited and is no longer the coming man, the man of the future, just a partially deflated left-wing windbag. Until the last three volumes, Widmerpool's identity as a man of the Left was not predominant or even sure. But in *Temporary Kings,* both Widmerpool's public vices and Pamela's private ones (also sampled by Widmerpool) are "sinister" in every sense of the word.

On the other hand, despite manifest eccentricities, Glober and Gwinnett are "good guys." They stand for art, for imagination, for continued creative life. They are not like Widmerpool, with his endless intrigues and love of power for its own sake. In that respect, Powell's pro-American position in the cold war resounds on not just a geopolitical level but on the level of the individual personality. "I always liked Gwinnett. I liked Glober too" (*Temporary Kings,* 269). These simple, declarative sentences belie a teeming complexity underneath. Jenkins seems to be replying to some implicit adversarial contention in saying he likes these people. Why "always" with respect to Gwinnett when he has only been in for one book? Any why the "too" with respect to Glober? Is it because as a Hollywood figure he is someone the obviously uncommercial Jenkins is expected *not* to like, to look down upon from a disdainful, ivory-tower perspective? The link between the two Americans is probably the point here. Jenkins is saying that, whatever their individual or collective failings, he likes Americans, welcomes them as participants in, and readers of, the *Dance*. And in a book filled with decadence and morbidity, this makes the reader feel optimistic not only about America but also about the world, that whatever the continued prevalence of Widmerpools and Widmerpoolism, the world will continue to produce Pollys, Gwinnetts, and Globers enough to stand in their way.

American or no, the rogue aesthetes of Venice do not exhaust the storehouse of fascinating minor characters in *Temporary Kings*. The senior Bagshaw, who witnesses Pamela's strange rendezvous with Gwinnett in his son's house, is reminiscent of Captain Pimley in *Waring*, though with a better head on his shoulders. He is like some sort of portentous limit figure in Greek mythology, a door warder, a signal of Pamela's approaching death and doom. Bagshaw, as well as a character in the following book, the countryside stalwart Mr. Gauntlett, show that even at the end of the sequence there are still people older than Jenkins and his contemporaries. We tend to think of *Dance* as a book about a generation—Jenkins, Stringham, Templer, Members, Quiggin, Widmerpool—that grows up, goes through war, and dies or grows old together. But so much of *Dance* is devoted to Jenkins's encounters with those older than himself, to his efforts to analyze them in their own terms and in his, to use them as exemplars for his education. This education continues even when Jenkins is in his weathered mid-fifties and the older people are ancient and frail. Another index of the increasing age of the characters and the length of the sequence is the vintage car craze that takes over so many characters at the end of

Temporary Kings. The sequence is entirely within modernity, and its most moving scene of nostalgia is not in fact Le Bas's yearning for a never-existent classical pastoral but the nostalgia of these fiftyish men for the vintage cars of their mechanized youth. The vastness of *Temporary Kings*'s character menagerie becomes a point in itself. When the taxi driver says, "None of you gentlemen Sir Leonard Short, by any chance?" (265), we laugh, because Short is the least conspicuous of all the characters, the one we always tend to forget about, even if he was necessarily the point of contact for the befuddled taxi man.

The manner of Pamela's death, never really explicitly gone into, has troubled some readers profoundly. Even the way Widmerpool dies is more reassuring (especially the way it dovetails back into his emergence in *Question*) than his wife's premature and squalid death. Few can find reading about this enjoyable, however just Pamela's desserts, or Widmerpool's, and Powell may be out to deliberately make the reader uncomfortable, much as with Maclintick's death in *Casanova's Chinese Restaurant* (*Temporary Kings*'s analogue as the second book in an even-numbered trilogy), which bursts the bouncy, optimistic mood coming from the fourth book. Having such a grim ending to the penultimate book, though, does afford Powell the opportunity, in terms of aesthetic balance, to convincingly achieve the relatively consoling ending to the twelfth book. As unsettling as Pamela's death is, it removes any sense that *Dance* is set in a sheltered world where bad things do not happen to people and happy reaffirmations are guaranteed.

Hearing Secret Harmonies (1975)

The title *Hearing Secret Harmonies* comes from the seventeenth-century occultist Thomas Vaughan, a.k.a. "Eugenius

Philalethes," whose mention continues the seventeenth-century submotif that becomes increasingly prominent in the sequence's later books, with the mention of Robert Burton and several other figures of that era, not always even those that were in general twentieth-century fashion after the John Donne revival of the 1920s. The phrase "hearing secret harmonies" is actually first mentioned by Mrs. Erdleigh in *Temporary Kings:* "the liberated soul ascends, looking at the sunset towards the west wind, and hearing secret harmonies" (246). So the reader who has not read the previous volume will have missed not only much of the significance of the events in the twelfth book, such as the Gwinnett-Widmerpool relationship, but also that of the title. This balances out the fact that, for readers unattuned to the opaque, the blunt description of Pamela's death by Delavacquerie—"Tell me, Nicholas, did not Pamela Widmerpool take an overdose so she might be available to the necrophilic professor?" (*Harmonies,* 75)—is not given until the final book. To hear secret harmonies is to die. Death, even if sometimes described by the Mrs. Erdleighs of the world as blending, synthesis, and transition, matters in *Dance,* whose most emotional moments are, it cannot be stressed too much, the deaths of Stringham and Templer.

The country opening in *Hearing Secret Harmonies* is one of the few scenes in situ, not set in a mobile, metropolitan audience, and this gives Powell his chance to do something with local dialects, such as that of Mr. Gauntlett when he makes remarks like, "Many a year since I went out after crayfish. Used to as a boy. Good eating they make" (22). This brief exposure to the countryside milieu of the Jenkinses, perhaps an unnecessary impediment in a Widmerpool reading, grasps our attention upon a Theocritus reading. The opening is also a scene shifting and a slowing of pace after the frenzied allegretto of the conclusion of *Temporary Kings.* The opening image of the "duck flying in from the south" (*Harmonies,* 1), paralleled in the next chapter by a quote from Harington's translation of Ariosto mentioning ducks and mallards rising from the brook and sardonically troped by the "retired kestrel" reference (14), imparts a lyric quality, an interruption of the hectic narrative pace on which the eleventh book had operated. There is a pause, a sense of leisured resumption that allows the narrative to rally its forces while marking a clear break from what has gone before, particularly the "squalor" of Pamela's death. Later on, the quarry hearing in chapter 5 also allows a break from the accumulating drama of Murtlock and company, permitting Powell to do four or five pages of regional dialect in Mr. Gauntlett's speeches, something he does with unexpected facility and interest. This is one of those small revelations in *Dance* where we see Powell try his hand at practices usually associated with very different writers. The birds, though, are the paramount emblem of this preparatory pause. As mechanisms of augury, they presage the entire dilemma of "wrapping up" the series, in which the author, whatever his revulsion at the occult practices of Scorpio Murtlock and their gang, will find himself relying on similar coincidences and discerned meaningful patterns. The pastoral/ esoteric beginning of *Hearing Secret Harmonies* also helps fend off any sense of Victorian plot contrivance, of a neat bundling of the strands. This is a real concern for *Harmonies,* as it has to satisfy the demand of the reader who has read through all twelve volumes for a payoff, a satisfying ending, a resolution fully compatible with the experiences and expectations of the reader in the previous eleven volumes. The Sir Magnus Donners prize dinner also helps provide a refreshing reorientation. The presence of the Director's Lady in the television films, when so many more prominent characters have been eliminated, indicates her importance as an external monitor who helps refocus a scene increasingly frenzied by the passage of time and the proliferation of characters. By introducing this new minor character, having her there as a distraction while Russell Gwinnett, as biographer of Trapnel, is reintroduced to the scene after he has been given a rest for the first fifty pages or so, Powell is announcing a fresh perspective.

All this scene shifting both accentuates and helps contain the figure of Leslie "Scorpio" Murtlock, a young, charismatic guru, in some ways Trelawney *redivivus,* though whether literally we do not know, *Dance*'s interest in recurring characters not extending so far as reincarnation, though the resemblance of the young Lord Warminster to the earlier Chemist Earl may, if it is not simply inherited, provide an augury of the latter. Scorpio Murtlock (his sobriquet an accurate reflection of Scorpio's status as the most menacing sign of the zodiac; Powell is once again manifesting the knowledge of horoscopes he shares with his subject John Aubrey) is a cesspool of dynamic, evil energies. Murtlock runs through a couple of overmatched church officials, then meets Widmerpool. Indeed, Widmerpool has sought him out. Both men think they can use each other. Murtlock values Widmerpool's established position in society and, perhaps as much or more, the fact that he owns a cottage and a reasonably substantial piece of property Murtlock can hijack as a base for his fanatic cult. Widmerpool, with his age-old symptomatic disease of wanting to be "in" with the "in-crowd," is gratified by potential associations with Murtlock's youth and the seeming currency of his mystical ideas. Perhaps also, realizing that he is getting old, he sees some sort of youthful injection of potency.

Potency is not lacking in Murtlock. Murtlock is not a charlatan. He has genuine occult powers, as is told in his correct advice to Mr. Gauntlett to "seek the spinney" when the latter's dog, Daisy, is missing. Gauntlett, a self-consciously stagy countryman, is impressed by Murtlock's powers but unaffected by them; unlike the less genuinely "heathen" Widmerpool, he is presumably used to such things.

Hitchens criticizes the "elderly" intonations in Powell's putting "pop star" in quotes and finds Powell's stance toward the 1960s "vaporous."[79] Many readers of Hitchens's generation have had similar reactions, claiming that Powell does not get the 1960s, that his portrait of it is either a caricature or is just completely off because it was written at such a remove from the depicted milieu. Powell's major point about the counterculture, that its leaders wanted power as much as anybody in the Establishment, surely is less controversial today than it might have been in 1975. His comments in his memoirs about its role in the "international cult of self-pity" (*Strangers,* 102) can hardly be controversial now. Certainly, his depiction of the subordinate role played by the women, Fiona Cutts and Rusty, in Murtlock's cult very much squared with the continued maintenance of gender hierarchies by the so-called rebels of that era. Another aspect of some readers' discontent with the Murtlock scenes is not so much that Murtlock is portrayed as evil but that he is defeated. He may have harassed Widmerpool into death, but he has been foiled. This is no more signaled than by Bithel's successful lifting of the Modigliani painting. Murtlock has lost the battle for the control of art, always the crucial battle in this twelve-volume sequence. Murtlock cannot be an occult Donners, bridging two worlds with power. He is at best going to live out his life as a diminished Trelawney.

So much attention is paid, both within the book and by critics, to Murtlock that the other two "new" characters introduced in the twelfth book, Fenneau and Delavacquerie, have received short shrift. Part of the reason for this is the paradox implied by the previous sentence: if they are new characters, not much use can be made of them; they are like people coming on the scene at the end of a party, or indeed, like Colonel Flores being accredited as military attaché to Britain at the very end of the war. But if their dramatic visibility is thus limited, their figurative importance is not. Aside from the brief appearance of the Rev. Iltyd Popkiss (Iltyd, appropriately, being a Celtic Christian saint), Fenneau is the first cleric to appear in *Dance*. There has been much controversy about Powell's religious belief. Some, simply by virtue of his being the brother-in-law of the seventh Lord Longford, a prominent convert to Roman Catholicism, have seen Powell as a Roman Catholic, which he was not. Most of the references to churches in his work, both in fiction and non-fiction, are to Anglican ones, and Powell generally seems to regard an Anglican religious procedure as a kind of default position, admittedly no rare event in England, but something that distinguishes his work from Waugh's.[80] This does not necessarily indicate any manifest Christian piety. Hugh Massingberd quotes Powell as saying he was basically "non-croyant," in other words, nonbelieving, and at one point in the *Journals* (29 June 1989), Powell seems to refer to himself as "agnostic."[81] There are indeed many pagan and occult references in *Dance*. Yet there are also many citations of Bible passages and hymns, many of which are crucial.

For instance, Bithel sings a later verse of "Guide Me Thou, O Great Jehovah" (*Harmonies*, 238), both recalling his and Jenkins's wartime experience and somehow putting their entire odyssey in the context of religious experience and pilgrimage. Similarly, Akworth's recitation of 1 Corinthians 13 at his granddaughter's wedding is a keystone for a series of introspective self-measurings. There is no sense that any of these amount to religious assent, but the secret harmonies of the end of the sequence do not entirely exclude a Christian perspective. Fenneau, who Neil McEwan calls a "sleek, fashionable London cleric," tacitly, in his article on Chaldean magic and the worship of Isis and Osiris, makes an "exception" (242) in his own case to his previous aphorism that "we go through life lacking understanding of many things." While manifesting a fascination for the many gods of antiquity, Fenneau evinces a belief that Christianity can more than hold its own with respect to them.[82]

Canon Fenneau, however excessive his infatuation with the occult, seems able to keep on the right side of it. Indeed, he is pictured as one of the most intellectually confident people in *Dance,* and his article seems likely to faze the erudition of most of the other characters, especially Sillery, if perhaps not Dr. Brightman. There is also a certain alignment between Fenneau's thought processes and those of *Dance* itself when the cleric commends Jenkins for bearing out "a deeply held conviction of mine as to the repetitive contacts of certain individual souls in the lives of other souls" (*Harmonies,* 128), that is, to interactions of recurrent characters, as the reader of the previous eleven and a half books has witnessed. Another revealing instance regarding religion is when Mr. Gauntlett, instructed by Murtlock to make an offering, a pagan sacrifice, if the latter's prediction as to the location of his dog is correct, responds by saying he will put something extra in the church collection plate that upcoming Sunday—an acknowledgment by Gauntlett, clearly acquainted with the power of nature, of the devotional claims of the church.

Though no one would doubt that ultimate answers are deferred in *Dance*, it is with (unintentional) acuity that Malcolm Muggeridge spoke of Powell's viewpoint as "Anglican in its flexibility and tenacity."[83] Some critics have found it mechanical that Fenneau is the undergraduate Paul whom Jenkins had met as a student at Sillery's salon. We can assume that Powell did not, when writing the first volume, intend Paul to reappear as an elderly canon eleven books and forty-five narrated years later. But perhaps the vague outlining of the original Paul was meant to provide a template for an as-yet unspecifically envisioned recurring character, which is, in the twelfth book, plugged into "Fenneau" for purposes of narrative economy.

Delavacquerie's role is less easily explicable. Powell, in his 10 January 1989 *Journals* entry on *Dance*, feels unsure about whether Delavacquerie comes off, and the first-time reader probably shares this sentiment, although further readings reveal more subtleties, in fact, too many to go into in this introductory survey. Delavacquerie's name alone is of considerable interest. One of the devices in *Dance* that shows we are dealing with a fictional world is how people do not share first names. Peter Templer is the only Peter in *Dance*, Charles Stringham the only Charles, Nicholas Jenkins the only Nicholas, even Derrick Hogbourne-Johnson the only Derrick. This kind of protection of the first name, interesting in that nearly all the characters are known by their last names, is a non-authenticating device, because in the real world there are many Charleses, many Peters, and so on (this issue is semiacknowledged at *Soldier's Art*, 175). But if this procedure is used, there will have to be a "Gibson" or similar name somewhere along the road by the twelfth book. "Delavacquerie" itself, as good an Anglo-French hybrid as "Liddament," with a characteristically Powellian interaction of prefix and proper noun, is pleasing as a name. One also gets the sense that Powell, fascinated by nomenclature, simply wanted to use this sort of slightly Anglicized French name, just as with "X. Trapnel" he wanted to have a character with "X" in his name, the idea of it being short for "Francis Xavier" being the easiest way to execute this.

Powell, in the 10 January 1989 entry of his *Journals,* writes of "the suggestion" of his friend the poet Roy Fuller as a source for Delavacquerie was intended, but that Fuller had supposed the character based on "a certain Canadian poet." Presumably this poet would have been George Woodcock, who wrote on George Orwell and would have been, more than any other Canadian poet, in Fuller's milieu.[84] But the principal importance of Delavacquerie is to show the deterioration of Jenkins's once matchless ability for social prognostication. When his sister-in-law Susan informs him that her daughter Fiona, a former member of the Murtlock cult, is getting married, Jenkins assumes it is to Delavacquerie, only to have Susan find this preposterous—to her, Delavacquerie is only her daughter's landlord. Jenkins has to admit, "I never knew what Delavacquerie really felt about the Fiona business" (242). The lessening of Jenkins's social acuity, almost like the waning of an aging athlete with suddenly soft reflexes, tells us the curtain is about to fall. Jenkins misdiagnoses the entire Delavacquerie-Fiona-Gwinnett imbroglio. He is getting old, or at least too far removed from the social scene. He is beginning to wrongly assess situations that earlier he would have intuitively analyzed at once.

When Jenkins, previously infallible in social terms—recall Stringham's praise in *Soldier's Art* for knowing everyone, even the octogenarian general Miss Weedon had married—begins to get things wrong, to mistake Fiona's landlord for her lover, we sense that this increasing distance from the hubbub of life is part of the sequence's drawing to a close. Another instance in which people have sensed Jenkins's reaction to events as somehow off is at the Cutts-Akworth wedding, when Widmerpool begs to leave Murtlock's orbit and Jenkins, as a bystander, says or does nothing until Widmerpool finally "made no demur" and "accepted defeat" (*Harmonies*, 238).

Peter Kislinger's words about the final encounter between Jenkins and Widmerpool are valuable:

An interpretation that reproaches Powell (the author) for Jenkins' . . . passivity asks from the author to do what a character in the narrative for whatever reasons is not capable of doing. It requests from the author a moral statement that has, in accordance with the novel's upholding of individuality and individual moral accountability, been left to the reader. . . . What this amounts to is requesting from an author to do away with harsh realities, like snobbery, inhumanities of all sorts etc.—at least in literature. That kind of reading falls prey to a "prejudice" (again one of the Dance's themes)—the expectation of a protagonist/"hero" whose development—at the level of the action—steers once and for all and unmistakably away from, say, snobbery. In the scene of Akworth's reading from Paul irony is leveled against Jenkins (the experiencing self). Jenkins starts daydreaming and reminiscing about the past. I understand the verses quoted and, more important, those not quoted, as an indirect (or "ironic" in the truest sense of the word) commentary on Jenkins' behavior.[85]

Akworth, who actually reads the lesson, was personally injured by Widmerpool in a way Jenkins never was; Jenkins's grievances against Widmerpool are all on behalf of other people and thus have an impersonal aspect about them. Akworth finds the lesson from St. Paul's epistle "a beautiful passage" and "a great favorite of mine" (227). It could be said that Widmerpool, who is ostensibly begging forgiveness, is actually holding on to the grievance more than the genial, urbane Akworth, who perhaps has semiforgotten his schooldays and is somewhat befuddled by the entire drama. That Akworth's manner may be motivated by generosity and forgiveness finds a corollary in the attitude of Sunny Farebrother when Jenkins accidentally meets him on a train early in the book. This, one of the last of *Dance*'s coincidental meetings, is a particularly elegiac one. Farebrother, as reencountered, is a fragment shored against the ruins of Jenkins's world. But there is also hope of moral and emotional growth. Farebrother has just come from Jimmy Stripling's funeral. The two men had started out the sequence as bitter enemies, trying to make fools of each other. But now Farebrother (who, we must remember, is eighty if he is a day at this point) feels he has been "uncharitable" (83) and, while still speaking of Stripling irreverently, realizes that he and his old nemesis are, fundamentally, in the same boat.

Farebrother's inscrutable survival demonstrates how the twelfth book conveys the triumph of time, the way time, merely by its rolling, mute persistence, will overcome inequity and bring right to light. But it is the triumph of *time*, not of Nicholas Jenkins. If the deaths of Stringham and Templer are, to quote Shakespeare in *Twelfth Night*, "revenged in the whirligig of time" (and the frequent references to Jacobean revenge tragedies in *Harmonies* are apposite in this respect), Jenkins is not a direct beneficiary, or even an agent, of this revenge, which in a way has already begun before *Harmonies* even commences its narrative.

Jenkins is not time's master, nor can he decisively intervene within its frame. Furthermore, Jenkins's nonintervention is not the sole cause of the Widmerpool calamity. From the volume's first page, Widmerpool is not in good shape. In *Hearing Secret Harmonies*, according to James Tucker, Widmerpool may hope to stage a "withdrawal from conventional politics meant to precede a coup come-back" like Tucker's example of Hitler or the fictional one of Shag Whipple in Nathanael West's *A Cool Million*.[86]

But more realistically, it is visible at the beginning of *Harmonies* that Widmerpool is on his way down. Though he was not prosecuted for his involvement in Soviet spy mischief, his political career is over. Short of a literal Soviet takeover, in which he could play a Vichyesque role, he will never be prime minister, as might have been feared. His wife has died in a sordid, scandalous manner. The posited illusion, for the public record, of domestic stability is forever shattered, however ludicrous it might have been to anyone who knew the couple.

The question, perhaps, is less why does not Jenkins help his friend than why is he not more vindictive. Widmerpool is behind the death of Jenkins's two closest friends. He has made sure that despite Jenkins's success and personal happiness, Jenkins's world is never quite what he wanted it to be. For what Widmerpool has done to Flavia Wisebite alone, he deserves punishment according to traditional fictional justice. The reticent, rarely seen Flavia is a kind of hidden hinge of *Dance*'s narrative. Of a "sandwich generation" between a flamboyant mother and daughter, not to mention brother, she suddenly emerges as a kind of index of justice. Indeed, Flavia's forthrightness about Widmerpool's awfulness, after twelve books of apologetic acceptance, faint mockery, circumlocutory tolerance, is refreshing—as much in its own way as Jenkins found the "confound their politics" verse of "God Save the King" at the victory service. Not just Flavia but also others who had been silent about Widmerpool—Lady (Matilda) Donners, for example, and Duport—are now not afraid to speak loudly. The tide has turned. As per the Bernini sculpture referred to several times in the sequence, truth is unveiled by time. In the wake of the failure of aggression, time realizes its slow triumph through perseverance. Widmerpool's decline, from ridiculously up-to-date school chancellor to patron of the young occultists then their abused victim to one dissolving back into the mist from which he emerged—and Powell, who has not often in this sequence given in to reader expectations, gratifies them spectacularly with this last gesture—makes the bespectacled, portly peer indeed the object of pity. For a while, indeed, we feel that Murtlockism is the greater evil, and that whereas Widmerpoolism can be contained within social forms, Murtlockism, with its obedience to absolutes such as the Essence of the All, cannot. But can or should Jenkins, who could not save Stringham from a cruel death during wartime, intervene? There is also Flavia's reaction to consider. Flavia is frightened by Widmerpool almost to the point of terror, so much so that the ordinary banality of the Alford-Greens becomes, for the moment, a saving normality, a stay against the "dreadful" Widmerpool (*Harmonies,* 227). The "detestation" that Flavia feels for Widmerpool and all his works is not one excessively demurred from by either Jenkins or the reader, both of whom have come to know Widmerpool rather too well over the preceding twelve books.

Widmerpool is often seen, like Malvolio in Shakespeare's *Twelfth Night,* as a comic buffoon whose aspirations have exceeded his circumstances and is rightfully rebuked at the end of

the drama. Not entirely true even with respect to Malvolio
(whose excessive punishment is acknowledged, though admittedly not redressed, at the end of the play), it is certainly not true
of Widmerpool because he gets so much further than Malvolio
does. In *Books Do Furnish a Room,* he is probably about ten
steps, ten calculated moves, away from being prime minister. He
becomes a force on an international scale. Malvolio sent no one
to their deaths, nor did he engage in intrigue with evil foreign
powers. If *Dance* took place in a great house, and Widmerpool
was a Zouch-like intruder, then the Malvolio scenario would
work. But Widmerpool and his world involved factors and
threats not seen in Shakespearean comedy. However, to see the
dominant note of the English comic tradition, going back to
Shakespeare or even Chaucer, as squelching an importunate
challenger to the given order is to drastically simplify, and Powell thus participates in a long line of writers manifesting comic
complexity.

Comic happiness usually connotes harmony. But in this
book harmony also means cultic conformism, eldritch reckoning, and death. There is a bad side and a good side to harmony.
Harmony can mean artificial conformity, the slavelike obei-
sance into which Murtlock prompts his followers, or it can
mean supererogatory differences being smoothed out (Farebrother and Stripling's late reconciliation, Akworth's bygones-
be-bygones approach to Widmerpool's repentance). Murtlock
is an apostle of harmony. But Widmerpool is so only reluctantly,
and as Murtlock in this case correctly asserts, inefficiently. Widmerpool and Murtlock are different in temperament and are
two different kinds of menacing talents. Murtlock is not able to
be accommodated within society as is Widmerpool, and unlike
Widmerpool, he does not press his agenda within accepted social

forms. But formidable as both are, and though there is not one charismatic "good" figure (something never to be found in Powell's works) to oppose them, both are vanquished by the end of *Hearing Secret Harmonies*. Not only is Widmerpool dead but Murtlock is losing his influence with the defection of Barnabas.

There is the feeling that the menace has been turned back. Nevertheless, there is no victory lap for Jenkins. Cool, passive, calculating, in the most benign possible sense of that adjective, Jenkins, in all central respects, has not changed, and this is apparent in no greater way than in his consistently nonjudgmental, non-interventive character. For instance, he does not take advantage of Flavia Wisebite's willingness to reveal all about her and her daughter's life, even though these revelations might help solve some of the mysteries of the Stringham family and their tragic fate. Also, the final meeting with Jean Templer, though deeply moving in its evocation of "lost love" and satisfying to both Jenkins and the reader in Jean's finally acknowledging publicly their romance, has an odd, undeniable bitterness about it, as well as a sense of issues left unexplored. These three encounters—with Widmerpool, Flavia, and Jean—between them conjure nearly all the significant personages in Jenkins's life. Yet in no case does he take any action. The Widmerpool incident cannot be singled out as an unusual act of callousness. Another factor here is that Widmerpool is not really on the same level as Jenkins or the rest of the characters in the sequence. He is a preternatural, abnormal force (his origin, and end, in the mist contains more than a hint that he literally came from there). Despite all the twinning, mutuality, and doubleness of his relationship with Jenkins (in some ways they are each other's Members and Quiggin), Widmerpool is on his own plane. For Jenkins to

intervene in his story would be like for a good human protagonist in the *Iliad* or *Aeneid* to intervene in the doings of a wrath-
ful deity.

The determinate end of the Widmerpool saga does not end
the time of *Dance* as a continuum. Widmerpool has affected
that continuum beyond his own actions, and not only Jenkins
himself but the world of *Dance* as a whole has to reevaluate and
renew itself. The initially opaque series of references to the
Renaissance poet Ariosto have to do with self-evaluation and
altruism ("Orlando" Furioso recalling "Rowland" Gwatkin;
Astolpho's pilgrimage to the moon in order to regain his friend's
wits is, perhaps, echoed by Jenkins, who is on a mission to
retrieve the dignity, memory, and, for lack of a better phrase,
integrity within time, not of Widmerpool, but of the friends
Widmerpool had caused to come to their doom. There is also a
sense in which Gwinnett is Trapnel's Astolpho, rescuing, albeit
posthumously, his wits from the dispersion into which they had
been thrown by the combined forces of Pamela and Widmerpool. In this way, Gwinnett's Americanness is connected to the
American moon landings in 1969 and after, cited as summoning
thoughts of Astolpho's journey to the moon. Astolpho's mission,
though, does not just emblematize journeys into outer space.
It also has to do with the revival of lost reputations, a principal theme in *Hearing Secret Harmonies,* ranging from the fiction of St. John Clarke to the paintings of Mr. Deacon, to the
neo-Trelawneyism espoused by Murtlock himself. The very
scope of the roman-fleuve gives space for eternal recurrence,
assumed in a pragmatic, not metaphysical, sense. The fact that
it ends in 1971 gives scope for the reappearance of previously
discarded styles. Had the sequence continued for twenty more
years, a latter-day Uncle Giles could have reported more trouble

in Sarajevo, and so on. Even in 1971, much time has elapsed. Not only is there a new, now-grown-up earl of Warminster of a younger generation, but there is a new monarch (the significance of the mention of the Annigoni portrait of the queen at Stour-water), a new era. It is striking to reflect that, even though Powell lived to ninety-four, half of his life had passed before Elizabeth II ascended the throne. In fact, had the date span of *Dance* been any longer, any sense of historical significance or progress would have been lost, as any attempted overview would have been overwhelmed by continuous change. The nar-rative of *Dance* emanates from a decided perspective, even if Jenkins is sometimes so detached that, though we never leave his vantage point, we also rarely if ever feel it to be controlling.

The reappearance of Duport's seascapes—about which Pen-nistone, aesthetically indignant, says, "The pictures—My God, the pictures!" (*Buyer's Market,* 140) at Milly Andriadis's party —is also under the sign of eternal recurrence. But Duport, no longer jealously disregarded by Jenkins as a rival in love, has now joined the category of unlikely aesthetes including Glober, Tokenhouse, and, in his delivery of the Modigliani to the gallery, Bithel. As William Empson pointed out in a gesture extraordi-narily in touch with the sinew of Powell's prose, Duport's "inter-est" in South American aluminum has its correlate in a genuine, if limited, aesthetic interests in the seascapes—on which he has also made a good deal of money.[87] Time smooths out former gradations among those who value and honor art. Duport's savagely virulent denunciation of Widmerpool in the gallery scene not only proceeds from an old wartime grudge but also signifies his full enrollment in the rather anarchic and melan-choly ranks of the aesthetes in their perpetual contest against the men of will. As John Gould succinctly puts it, "Art survives. Ego perishes."[88] Everything has a way of coming back, even the hawk near Jenkins's home in the country reminding him of a "retired kestrel" (*Harmonies*, 14) from a 1930s poem, the allusion being to the attempt of W. H. Auden and his contemporaries, never favorites of Powell, to look at the English landscape in a more grittily lyrical, less constrainedly romantic light. This is, however, somewhat like what *Powell* is doing here, as well as in the Great West Road scene in *Acceptance World*. We feel that there is a danger, if the sequence goes on, of an interfering recursiveness, as already inscribed historical motifs come back as myth or symbol. The reader, who might be hungry for more of the sequence, is finally convinced that it has to end because otherwise it would just be extended into an orbit where everything referred to previously would randomly resurface.

The reemergence of Stringham's signed Modigliani drawing is not random. It is particularly weighted and marked. The way it is mentioned at the end of the book, in fact, would lead the reader who has read only the twelfth book to think that Stringham's Modigliani is a recurrent symbol of art, when in fact it is barely mentioned before the last trilogy. As always, this underweighting serves the mechanics of the sequence well, as individual tokens are not overladen with significance; we do not hear the welling of sentimental violins when the Modigliani is mentioned, only a sober awareness of art, its vicissitudes, and the narrow margin by which it is materially and figuratively preserved. Modigliani was an Italian artist of wholly Jewish descent, a draftsman, a man always in precarious health (physical, in his case, more than emotional, although Stringham's alcoholism can be seen as a physical illness). His date span, 1884 to 1920, is analogous to Stringham's presumed date span of, say, 1905 to 1943.[89] Associated with the modernity that Le Bas had tried to exclude against Stringham's anti-Theocritan mischief, but also possessed of a classical restraint, a sense of line, and a carved poise, Modigliani is a sober, unflamboyant artist whose work does not require an extravagance of means for its execution. Nor does it surround itself with classical or historical associations. How much more melodramatic, how much tighter and more stage-managed, would it have been if Bithel had recovered Stringham's Poussin, even if one could conceive of a Poussin floating around people's private possessions, as one can, only just, conceive of a Modigliani so doing? When Widmerpool marries Pamela and inherits the Modigliani, first seen during the scene in which Stringham is drunk and Widmerpool is sober, we are made to feel that this is the supreme in-justice. Not only is Stringham humiliated and dead, but his property devolves onto the person he had most despised. But Henderson's retrieval of the Modigliani from the cult means that, in a way, "Stringham," or what he represents, has once again repossessed the property. Technically, the Modigliani is stolen property. It does not legally belong to the Murtlock cult that has occupied Widmerpool's house, unless he has legally signed the house over to them, which is doubtful. Yet it belongs to Widmerpool's estate. (Does Flavia Wisebite inherit as mother-in-law?) It does not belong to Barnabas Henderson, even if Henderson fears that Murtlock will eventually destroy or discard it. But in a kind of magnification of Walter Huntercombe prying open Amy Foxe's china cabinet in order to ascertain the authenticity of her pieces (or for that matter General Conyers not actually being "officially attached to the formation" at the time of the charge across the Modder River in the Boer War; *Lady Molly's,* 235), the legal irregularity, just for this specific occasion, is, through some sort of narrative equity, pardonable in aesthetic terms.

Though doubtless to be resold to a moneyed individual or institution for a tidy profit, the Modigliani is out of the world of death, released to the world of life and a dance that is continuing, even if, for Jenkins, the steps are drawing to a close. What survives Powell's "short twentieth century" is art, and here, art that, because of the Jewishness of its creator, might have been obliterated forever not only by Murtlock but by the twentieth century's most loathsome menace.

Barnabas Henderson, somewhat of a cipher to Murtlock's dynamo, is pivotal to this final scene. He acts as a kind of serene stabilizer, a manager of concord, subject of a happy deliverance himself an agent of another one for art and for memory's sake. Henderson, Murtlock's quondam saner deputy, is, in fact, much more interesting as an actual person than is Murtlock. Henderson represents a more matter-of-fact aspect of the coming generation: not an occult menace, but a rather ordinary man who finds the aging Jenkins far less interesting than his own prejudices about the past and confidently guesses that Jenkins does not know Madame Flores because she has been out of the country so long. When ruminating over other people's pasts, he takes the map for the territory, which is the only way someone his age can do it but is nonetheless disconcerting for Jenkins. In refusing to believe that *Boyhood of Cyrus* had ever been owned by Sir Gavin Walpole-Wilson, Henderson makes Jenkins realize that his memory is the only real vehicle for recording all that has happened to him. The core truths may get put down correctly, but the multiple subjectivities that buzz semiharmoniously in his consciousness will go when he goes. Henderson represents, with respect to the denouement of *Dance*, both the things that do go well (Widmerpool is defeated, Murtlock is on his way out, art survives as time turns out to be on its side) and those that do not go well (Jenkins and his generation are fading, and the texture of the life they have shared is sadly impermanent). There is no culminating sense of concord. Jenkins's meeting with Jean is like Blore-Smith's experience in *Agents and Patients*. Jenkins gets no more out of it than a confirming sense that his life has really happened to him, but this is enough.[90] Barnabas Henderson— benign, vulnerable, just self-centered enough to make assumptions about people, just altruistic enough to realize when he is proven wrong (as when Jenkins *does* know Jean)—is not an ideal symbol for the end-time of *Dance*. But he will have to suffice.

As Jenkins reflects on the past half-century, there is purity, there is self-discipline, there is a sense of a pilgrimage well made and of a victory for the principles that matter. But this is victory sans complacency or self-congratulation. The bracing clarion call of the "hyperborean seas" (*Harmonies*, 272), of the utter- most north (north even of Spitsbergen or Franz Josef Land, where the Polish soldiers killed at Katyn were wrongly thought to have been taken), is cleansing, cathartic, but also chilling. It represents a kind of elemental purity transcending the steps of the dance and breaking through only when they have, at least for a measurable moment, stopped. We see a kind of pure layer of reflective awareness extended above the tumult.

CHAPTER 4

Man's Permitted Limits
Understanding Powell's Fiction of the 1980s

O, How the Wheel Becomes It! (1983)

The two decades of the twentieth century in which Anthony Powell published freestanding novels are the 1930s and the 1980s. *Wheel* is the first of the two novels Powell published during this latter decade. For this novel, Powell continues the practice, initiated earlier in his previously published memoirs, of deriving a title from a semi-obscure line of Shakespeare's, although *Wheel*'s source, from Ophelia's mad speech in *Hamlet,* will strike more of a bell to the mildly acculturated Shakespearean. What precise relevance Ophelia as such has to the plot is unknown, unless Isolde Upjohn, like Ophelia, is a woman caught between ambitious men, a thin analogy to say the least. Perhaps the "wheel" is a reference to the wheel of life (dance of time) or wheel of fortune, on which our protagonist, Shadbold, takes a couple of spins. In any event, the *Hamlet* reference is carefully explained at the beginning of the novel, which sets the tone for the discursive, expository, and erudite nature of the narrative. *Wheel* has never been well understood. Powell commented that, in Britain, all but four or five reviewers "absolutely hated it." Even in the United States, where the reception was much more positive, the book's reception was muted by being embedded in huge oeuvre reviews of Powell's entire life's work, one of which, in the then-countercultural *Village Voice,* Powell found "rhapsodic" (letter to the Hon. John Monagan, 4 September 1984).[1] Such a small book could not bear the weight based on it by these comprehensive, often compensatory (i.e., making up for earlier, often politically motivated neglect) reassessments of Powell's career.

On the other hand, there is perhaps more to be said about *Wheel* than any of Powell's non-*Dance* novels. With *Wheel,* we are back to the protagonist as more or less Jenkins manqué. In fact, considering the forty-four years' distance, *Wheel* is surprisingly like the early novels, if possessing far more of *Dance*'s discursiveness. G. H. W. Shadbold is an elderly writer in the early 1980s, unquestionably a remaining if minor figure of the "*Brideshead* generation." He is married to Prudence, a formidable woman, a generation younger than her husband, who writes detective stories under the classicizing and determined name of Proserpine Gunning. Perhaps his most intense emotional involvement, however, is with long-dead, long-forgotten literary rival Cedric Winterwade. (Shades of the relationship between Members and Quiggin—and note that the scansion of the two names, the trochaic SHAD-bold and the dactylic WIN-ter-wade, matches JEN-kins and WID-mer-pool.)

Everything bad that could possibly happen to Shadbold in this novel does. By absentmindedly arranging for Shadbold's former youthful love, Isolde Upjohn (now, having spent much time in the Middle East, Mrs. Abdullah) and the television personality Rod Cubbage (an apt bookend, in terms of the kind of name it is, to the music critic Gossage in *Dance*) to come on the same day, bringing about just what he has tried to avoid, Shadbold falls prey to the law of unintended consequences, and perhaps also for some sort of unconscious desire for self-revelation or, possibly, to put himself, even in a bad light, into a glare of publicity that his mediocre career had not provided him. For whatever reason, calamity occurs, as all Shadbold had tried to repress comes out with a vengeance. Winterwade, author of that forgotten, St. John Clarkian realist masterwork, *The Welsons of Omdurman Terrace*—whose clear mediocrity is another suggestion that Powell is not a wholesale adherent to the heresy of naturalism—is far more lionized than he ever had been because of Isolde's appearance and Cubbage's manipulation of the interview (something Powell himself complained about with respect to his interviews by television journalists). Powell spoke of the idea of television personalities having "passed into myth," become totemic presences larger than their actual importance.[2] "Accustomed to carry his brusqueness of demeanor into private life (if he could be said to have any private life, the furthest extent of which being sometimes to be encountered at functions if that kind) Cubbage was easy enough to dislike" (62). The smooth and, for all his outgoing bonhomie, self-absorbed Cubbage sees what he wants to with regard to the residue of the Shadbold-Winterwade feud.

So does Jason Price, schematizer, a kind of young-fogeyish version of Barnabas Henderson. Price shows the limits of any comprehension of the past when that can be achieved when he is reminded on seeing Mrs. Abdullah at the funeral, "Looking at her in church just now . . . I was reminded of that line in one of Wilde's plays to the effect that women kneel so divinely" (*Wheel*, 136). Price, for all his knowledge of the past, has no real specific comprehension of the life circumstances of Winterwade, Shadbold, and Isolde (particularly the extent to which Shadbold had been in love with Isolde, which, for all his later humiliation, and his knowledge of Winterwade's greater precedence in her heart, still remains the strongest emotional connection in the novel), comprehension that can be had *only* by those people themselves. Instead, he has a mental box of contents consisting of indifferently applied apothegms, catch phrases, and period references, which can be no more than a pastiche of the past. This is not so much a flaw of Price as an epistemic lapse endemic to the historical process. The very idea of Shadbold and Winterwade being "contemporaries" means that, for all their envy and mutual dislike, they have shared a climate, an awareness, a sense of being alive that can no more be conveyed to a later generation than can eras of history no longer remotely within living memory. Herodotus and John Aubrey wrote of their own time, and that of the generation immediately before them. After them may come sounder or more comprehensive historians. But the process of the handover of the past to the Jason Prices of succeeding generations is inevitably accompanied by something lost in translation. Price does not get it. The 1920s, or even more the 1890s, can never be reinvented. The only true memories are held by the era's rapidly aging survivors. No matter how much the young may try to recapture or schematize the past, even as they think they are succeeding in it, the old are dying off and bearing the essence of that past away.

Unlike the younger generation as presented in *Harmonies,* this young man is not in search of sex, drugs, rock and roll, and neopagan rites. But he does not really penetrate any further into the fabric of his elders' lives than Henderson does when he refuses to believe that Jenkins had known an "Edgar" Deacon. Once Isolde dies (and considering the diaries remain undeciphered), the story of her relationship with Shadbold and Winterwade will be lost forever. Once again, Powell absorbs the lesson of *The Great Gatsby:* the past cannot be brought back, and even nostalgia has its limits.

Another minor character of note is Jock Crowter, a retired Second World War infantry major who delivers the supreme rebuke to Shadbold, one that seals his fate, asking him to repay the sum he, Crowter, had lent Winterwade before he died of a sexually transmitted disease in Bombay. Shadbold has lost almost his entire self-esteem. It is now revealed that Winterwade had always been there before him: a better war record, greater love from the women Shadbold had always attempted to love, and now, posthumously, as a result of the arbitrary and expediently fashionable currents of publishing and academia, rescued as a novelist while Shadbold continues to sag. But Shadbold still has the loyalty of the redoubtable Prudence/Proserpine, and as much as all the revelations hasten his death (we must remember he is pushing eighty), somewhat like Blore-Smith in *Agents and Patients,* he ends humiliated and exposed, but not without honor.

Shadbold is given all sorts of attributes directly contrary to what we know of Powell. For instance, Shadbold has never really written a central work, he dresses shabbily, he is averse to anything to do with the military, and he particularly enjoys public speaking. It is as if Powell, annoyed by the constant suppositions that Nicholas Jenkins is himself, has decided to create a protagonist of which this could never be said; or, alternately, that he is returning to the idea of the Jenkins manqué of the prewar books. Despite all this, Shadbold's intellectual performance with respect to Horace Grigham at the latter's "new" university is brilliant. Grigham, the trendy academic (somewhat conflating several different critical trends of the early 1980s that would not have been combined so cavalierly by someone who knew what they were talking about), has more or less developed a cult around his own trendiness. He is suspicious of the noncontemporaneity of seventeenth-century drama and sees Arthur Conan

Doyle's Sherlock Holmes stories as retrograde in their lack of social concern (an acute portrait, as one of the hallmarks of that generation of leftist academic was a bizarre hostility to detective fiction).[3] Shadbold comes back by noting possible references, or premonitions, of Heidegger and Marx's son-in-law Edward Aveling in Doyle's stories, and he speaks of the "repressed homosexuality" (52) of Holmes and Watson. Shadbold, in fact, has a freer, less stuffy relationship to "the classics" than does Grigham, who illuminates the ever-present truism that, with regard to would-be academic innovators, new presbyter is but old priest writ large. Shadbold's rout of Grigham is his moment of glory in a book in which, otherwise, he endures humiliation upon humiliation and, finally, an anticlimactic death. Shadbold, though not a great writer, is a true intellectual. Who else would be called on to review a book on the eighth/ninth-century intellectual majordomo Ealhwine, a.k.a. Alcuin? No charlatan.

Because he knows that a reasonably intelligent man such as Shadbold can handle this little specimen of academic arrogance in stride, Powell does not become hysterical about Grigham. Grigham is not presented as a threat to Western civilization, more as a minor buffoon, to a certain extent an object for Powell's weirdly impartial though doubtless appalled authorial glance. Grigham is just another operator; the world has seen them before, will see them after. Grigham is not the apocalypse. The true coup de grâce to Grighamism comes when Proserpine Gunning entitles her new detective story *Culture-Code of Samphire*. The new jargon neither wins nor loses. It is assimilated into the mainstream, into as conventional a genre as the detective story, the very genre Grigham has bashed as conventional. Whereas the standard "campus novel" of the 1980s satirized academic excess, Powell places it in a more comedic context, comedic in the sense that the genre of comedy resolves absolute differences and integrates them into an ongoing fabric.[4] They are braided into the fabric, made into subthemes in a music of time that can include what Powell called, at the end of *Writer's Notebook,* "academic tones"—and that academic studies such as a fictional study of a melancholy encyclopedist and a real-life study of a gossipy antiquarian have helped orchestrate. These things pass. Penelope writes *Culture-Code of Samphire;* the innovative suffers, or is blessed by, reabsorption in the conventional. Grigham is a target for Horatian rather than Juvenalian satire. Samphire, as referent, may have no more solid a basis in reality as do culture codes, as the samphire gatherers in *Lear* do not "really" exist within the play but are fictively described (act 4, scene 6) by the feigning Edgar to his blind father, Gloucester.

Strikingly, the symbols in Winterwade's diary are also codes, decipherable only by those of his own generation (not a latecomer like Price) who hold the rapidly dissolving key to the living past. Since Winterwade's son, in Australia, never quite realizes the commercial viability of the diary, he ends up destroying it, and the encoded content is lost forever—just as the past is lost as anything else *but* history. *Wheel* is in so many ways a novel about misunderstanding—perhaps why the Ophelia quote provides the title. Misunderstanding certainly pervades the fatuity of the novel's protagonist. Shadbold messes things up, as he always does. Unlike Jenkins, he does not have any magical capacity to smooth things over, to steer himself from one potentially dicey situation to the next.

The Fisher King (1986)

The Fisher King's interlocking menagerie of characters— Robin Jilson and his mother, Lorna Tiptoft, Gary Lamont, Saul

Henchman, and Barberina Rookwood—provides a more fully satisfying plot than does *Wheel*. But the atmospheric minor characters are the first feature of the book that fully strikes the reader. For instance, there are the two Americans, obviously, though never explicitly revealed, a homosexual couple. Called by their t-shirts, "Basically Bach" and "Marginally Mahler" (inspired by a Mostly Mozart t-shirt Powell saw on an actual cruise, presumably without knowing this referred to a festival), they engage in musical discussions. These are possibly lineal, if attenuated, descendants of those Gossage, Moreland, and Maclintick would have undertaken at a certain restaurant. "More than once Lamont caught the name of Boulez" (*Fisher,* 50). However, this is not a musical observation but one about the nature of conversation, how meaningless it can be if abstracted from the immediate motives of its participants (this point, one of Powell's favorites going back to *Afternoon Men,* shows him to be more alert to the minutiae of communication than critics have realized). Powell's view of dialogue is that it does not convey truth. If truth is to be found, it is in discursivity, although discursivity for Powell is always a move away from naturalism—what we might term the naturalism of artificiality.

Wheel takes place against the background of history, *Fisher* that of myth. In the case of *Wheel,* this is not just in the sense of references to contemporary figures such as Gaddafi (Qaddafi), but in the overall way *Wheel* is set in ongoing time; whereas the voyage motif, along with the title itself, shrouds *Fisher* in an atmosphere of an age-old, oft-repeated quest. In many ways Valentine Beals is a better mythic novelist—in his speculations about the sex life, and mythic reverberations, of the renowned photographer Saul Henchman—than he is a historical novelist, his actual trade. Beals is able to perceive events "outside of his own terms of narrative" (*Fisher,* 105). Powell's own image of Henchman going off to America at the end (the mention of "Oregon City" [*Fisher,* 7] to which Henchmen is supposed to have headed is a tribute to the "American City" of Henry James's *Golden Bowl*) brings to mind Aeneas as depicted by Vergil in his great epic, forsaking his doomed homeland and striking out for distant western shores. This example marks the thrust of *The Fisher King*—how mythic patterns can be projected onto perfectly ordinary people or situations. It is not whether the projections are accurate or plausible that is the point, but the very fact that the myths can be projected at all, their *applicability.* Powell, in both *Dance* and the *Journals,* constantly compares people to unlikely prototypes—for instance, Stringham to Veronese's Alexander and Glober to a young Byzantine emperor.

But just what is the Fisher King? By giving the novel this title and not giving any extended exposition, unlike as in, say, *The Kindly Ones,* Powell is assuming the reader knows the referent. The canonicity of the idea of the Fisher King comes from the notes to T. S. Eliot's *The Waste Land,* which cited several books on myth, ritual, and anthropology that reinterpreted the motif, from the medieval Perceval and later Arthurian legends, of Amfortas, the Fisher King who is paralyzed by impotence. (The Fisher King parallels implied of Jake Barnes in Hemingway's *The Sun Also Rises* may well also have contributed; yet again, Powell's sources are more American than conventional Anglophilic stereotype assumes.) The canonical modernists were fond of using the "mythical method," by which the *Odyssey* would undergird the daily adventures of Leopold Bloom in Dublin in 1904 or Shakespeare and Spenser would stand behind Eliot's description of the rotting banks of the Thames in *The*

Waste Land. The Fisher King motif was avowedly used by Eliot as a mythical framework of just this sort. Powell expects the reader to know the Fisher King reference not only as a myth but as a mythic literary motif within modernism. Indeed, this title is Powell's consummate definition of himself as a second-generation modernist.

The Fisher King concept balances power and impotence. The aphoristic first sentence, "Exile is the wound of kingship" (*Fisher,* 7), connotes the way the possibility of the loss of power is always the underside of its exercise. Like the original Fisher King, Henchman is sexually impotent; in a way, the sadistic, controlling aspects of his photographic technique have usurped more conventional sexual energies. The more literal cause of the impotence is a war wound, much in the manner of Henry James's "obscure hurt," which also disables his legs so he has to use crutches. This recalls the physical and psychological maimings of the war trilogy of *Dance.* The photographer has the capacity to not only objectify others but also gratify them: "Even those still uneasy as to whether Henchman's summing up of them was what they inwardly wanted, departed thinking better of themselves, full of praise for Henchman's art" (*Fisher,* 68). Unlike other late-twentieth-century novels about photographers (Paul Theroux's *Picture Palace,* Delia Falconer's *Service of Clouds*), the photographer is kept well away from the narrative perspective; Henchman is the narratee, he who is discussed. While not moralistically denouncing photography, with which Powell is clearly fascinated (witness the generous display of photographs in the memoirs and *Journals,* as well as Powell's approval of the *Album* project and his frequent mentions in the *Journals* of himself photographing people and cats), Powell suggests that photographers, with their capacity to use imagination to (far more than as claimed by other media) convincingly represent reality, are to be very closely watched when it comes to letting them attain *narrative* power.

The situation between Henchman and Barberina seems fixed, almost as if it were a photograph, and his mastery seems unopposed. Powell is giving us a lesson in the dynamism of what we might suppose were static situations. Like Widmerpool, Henchman is undone, not by his own tragic flaw, or even a kind of cosmic justice, but through the unveiling of truth by time. Time has run out on his control of Barberina, and once Barberina can find another option, she liberates herself, as emblematized by the way her dancing again, in its dynamism, breaks the stasis, as of a photographic object, in which she had been encased. She is no longer fixed by Henchman's scopic, voyeuristic drive. This is actually one of the few situations in Powell's novels that leads to an achievement of personal liberation, as we are made to feel that Barberina's new situation, however preposterous, is a quantum improvement over her subjugation to Henchman.

Of course, voyeurism is a double-edged sword in Powell's work. Powell himself admits to being a voyeur, not an exhibitionist (*Strangers*, 79), and Gwinnett's voyeurism with respect to Pamela, as grisly and morbid as it is, is nonetheless not as maleficent as whatever Widmerpool wants out of his relationship with Pamela. A trait such as voyeurism is not repressive in itself; it is what one does with it, and Henchman has allowed his voyeurism to become static and domineering. The name "Henchman" suggests not a martinet but somebody who is an adjutant of a martinet (e.g., how "henchman" is used of Corporal Curtis at *Military Philosophers*, 28). Perhaps this connotes that Henchman desires the authority of power without being willing to carry its responsibilities, to be anything more in practical terms than a "henchman" of power.

Barberina, formerly a promising ballet dancer, has had her personal growth stalled by Henchman's erotic possession of her. Barberina is enrolled in Henchman's own cult of himself, of which the photographer is also high priest. The way Jilson, the underestimate Mama's boy, outfoxes the suave Lamont to not only win Barberina for himself but, for all Jilson's self-infatuation, liberate her from the control of both Henchman and, potentially, Lamont. There is a detachment in the way this denouement is enacted, almost as if Powell believes that, having established these characters as psychologically viable and evoked some intimacy and interplay between them, that the novelist's next step must be detachment. In this respect, it is notable how many commentators or analysts there are in this book: not just Beals and his auditor, Middlecote, who occasionally does some analysis of his own, but Professor Kopf, an unexciting character (though in this way a far more typical American academic than Russell Gwinnett) who is there is a kind of foil for Beals. Beals's speculations about Arthurian legend are actually more interesting than Kopf's, which are larded with a kind of melancholy, constrained dryness. But the speculators are as present as the participants; the gallery is as much in view as is the stage.

As a historical novelist, Beals writes such bestsellers as *Nell o' the Chartists* (*Fisher,* 169). That Beals is not just a trashy novelist but a trashy *historical* novelist is worthy of discussion. Powell, who studied history at university, who wrote a biography of a seventeenth-century antiquarian, and whose major outside interest was genealogy, might have been thought the prototype of the writer of the historical novel. But he was not, at one point consenting to the definition of the historical novel as "an obsolescent genre of literature" (*Infants,* 127). Interestingly, defining a historical novel as set more than fifty years back from the date of publication, neither did Evelyn Waugh, Graham Greene, or Henry Green, despite, in differing degrees, their capability for writing such a book. One would have to go to Alfred Duggan (*Infants,* 127; his brother Hubert was to some degree the model for Stringham) to find a contemporary of Powell who wrote (actually very good) historical novels, some covering Celtic-medieval terrain of potential interest to Powell. (Beals is modeled not on Duggan, but on Dennis Wheatley, a writer Powell respected as a person, if not a literary figure, and with whom he maintained a steady correspondence, including a kind and compassionate note to his widow.)[5] So Beals is not a fool, and indeed his judgments about the events on the *Alecto,* though somewhat hypothetical, are more reliable than their hypothetical aspect may indicate. But it is worthy of note that the historical novel as a genre, to whose siren song so many writers in the 1980s and after responded, is apparently a genre of little inherent interest to Powell, despite his great interest in both historical content and historical technique. (Nor are historical novels among the works he frequently rereads in the *Journals;* Powell seems more interested, for example, in Sir Walter Scott's poetry than his fiction, even though that may be attributable to his Marmion descent.) Beals is just the sort of novelist, "prone to laborious simplification" (*Fisher,* 25), Powell was not. In Beals, Powell has perhaps found the happy medium between Jenkins and Blore-Smith, between a point-of-view character who is almost definitely Powell and one who is definitely not him. But Beals's insights into history do not make him more insightful in to the characters he meets; that insight, though there, is basically from a different part of his mind than that from which emanates the second-rate fiction.[6]

The final paragraph, as Joanna Motion has noted, has a valedictory air to it.[7] "On the far side of the waters, low rounded hills, soft and mysterious, concealed in luminous haze the frontiers of Thule; the edge of the known world; man's permitted limits; a green-barreled check-point; beyond which the fearful cataract of torrential seas cascaded down into Chaos" (*Fisher,* 256). As with the end of *Dance,* we are in the North, though literally this time at least in borean, if not hyperborean, seas. The classicism of "man's permitted limits" is obvious and compelling, as, more subtly, is the use of colons and semicolons to both distend and suture semantic meaning. There is certainly a sense that man must or should remain within his limits, along with an elegiac if stringent regret that he has to, that chaos is indeed so all-consuming. A fitting sentence as coda for Powell's novelistic career, it can stand as a summation of the values for which Powell stood. It is a rare concession on the part of the novelist that the imagination cannot conjure everything, that its limits are as evident—and in a way as valuable—as its capacities.[8] There is also an affirmation of British nationhood. As the boat circumnavigates the island, it reconfirms a sense of the unity of Great Britain, even in this corner of Scotland as much Norse as Celtic in antecedents. We are once again reminded of Virginia Woolf's village pageant of English history at Poyntz Hall in *Between the Acts.* Powell is not given to patriotic reaffirmation. But here he provides this as much as he possibly can.

Fisher, set on a cruise around Britain and ending up on the remote Orkneys, is a novel of circumnavigation. It is potentially a national novel, perhaps the chrysalis of a Condition of

Britain novel, written in a lush, magical-realist style, with lots of whimsical tales and full of gazeteering descriptions of recondite portions of the island. Had one of Powell's much younger contemporaries written this sort of book in 1986, it would have had sales that would have made Valentine Beals proud. Powell, analytic rather than synthetic, comic rather than ludic, will not write this sort of book. (On this general point, see Lady Violet Powell's mention at *Journals,* 21 December 1989, with respect to a novelist of the younger generation, of "many Digest readers," no doubt even more avid consumers of Beals's sort of work than of the writer specifically mentioned in the comment. *Fisher* is a second-order modernist book. It is not a postmodernist one, although there are incipiently postmodern elements in its plot and conception. The action has to be after 1979, as there is a reference to Henry Kissinger's memoirs *White House Years* (not *My White House Years,* as at *Fisher,* 50, unless that was the British title). There is little other social reference in the book, except the character of Lamont, obviously based on the newspaper and book editor Harold Evans. He models a quintessential 1980s–90s figure; indeed, the elderly Powell could not have picked better if he wished to extend his social reach up to the millennial verge. Powell's mild and genial rendition of the "eminently hateable" (*Fisher,* 43) Lamont (note the similarity to the evocation of Rod Cubbage in *Wheel*) is a late masterpiece of description.

For many readers, Powell will have saved the best for nearly last. This is the reference to Isbister, the "portrait painter" (205), the one connection between the *Dance* and non-*Dance* works, the one positive link. (Unless one counts the reference to Robert Burton at *Fisher,* 204; incidentally, Henchman's subsequent laughter could well be to Isbister, not as a real person in the real world of this novel, but as a character in the novels of Anthony Powell, read and enjoyed in the world of the cruise ship.) Many readers no doubt wanted to read the further adventures even of minor characters such as Ada Leintwardine or Delavacquerie. Powell mentions several times that his readers demanded this (see *Journals,* 7 June 1989). The Isbister reference is as far as he will go in yielding. It is significant that Isbister is chosen. He is so minor a character that he will not disturb the balance between worlds. And as a portrait painter, he incarnates voyeurism, what recent literary theory might call "the gaze." Considering how intricately the individual volumes of *Dance* are connected to each other, it is remarkable that until this point there are no connections between any other of his novels. With readers desirous of a *Dance* pendant, Powell, ever-scrupulous, refused to make the kind of artistic compromise this would inevitably entail. But he relented in this one small respect.

Gary Lamont is defined by his encounter with the battered hobo, Mr. Jack—comparable to Bithel in *Dance*—when the latter dramatically asked in the funniest line in *Fisher,* "Ever fallen in love with a tart?" (42). "Gary" as a first name is ingeniously prescient about the valence of a certain name; compare Kingsley Amis's comment about Powell's clairvoyance, at least as early as the *second* book of *Dance,* in picking "Kenneth," a name that can, by "trendy truncation," be shortened to "Ken," for Widmerpool's forename just before a torrent of British politicians named "Ken" erupted onto the public sphere.[9] The suave Gary finds Mr. Jack an aspect of humanity that he cannot quite master. Mr. Jack later replaces Barberina as Henchman's assistant, an almost total reversal of fortune for all concerned. Yet this is somehow plausible with respect to the interaction among tightly drawn ensemble aboard ship. Mr. Jack is a fun character and is depicted with zest. Of all of Powell's novels, this is the one in which the character of the most dubious social origins and status is the most noticeable and, despite himself, likable. With regard to Mr. Jack, Neil McEwan has written the best single sentence of extant Powell criticism: "The wrecked figure of Mr. Jack is more appealing than those of characters living on pure will: Lorna Tiptoft, Jilson, Lamont."[10]

These two late books are rarely discussed. The prewar books, though neglected, have their own intra-canonical role, standing for skepticism of tone and anarchy of incident as opposed to the more transcendent and organized *Dance*. The late books do not have even this. *Wheel* was not carried, but buried, by the flood of praise for Powell's other work upon *Wheel*'s release in the United States, a fate that bears out Powell's apparent puzzlement at this exceedingly positive reception. (No writer was ever more realistic about his reception, even at its most adulatory, than was Powell.) *Fisher* received four or five very perceptive reviews in Britain. But it did not win any prizes, even though "the late work by an acclaimed master" is a class of book that *does* tend to win prizes, and somehow did not make a splash in America.[11]

This neglect is unfortunate, not only because they are interesting books, but because they are short, not part of a twelve-novel sequence, and therefore teachable. Either could well be the Powellian equivalent of Joyce's *A Portrait of the Artist as a Young Man* or Thomas Pynchon's *The Crying of Lot 49*, a short-to-medium-length "teaching text" that can represent the author in a survey course and give students a taste of their approach. Certainly readers of Powell would want him to avoid the fate of Proust, as perceived by Lieutenant Kernevel in *Military Philosophers,* as being "a writer not taught in the schools."

Wheel, because of its concern with literary reception, and, more essentially, because it is such a charming and generous book, is ideal for the classroom.

CHAPTER 5

The Other Side of the *Dance*
Understanding Powell's Memoirs

Infants of the Spring (1976)

The reader's spontaneous reaction to the news that Anthony Powell was publishing his memoirs was, "What was there left to write?" The presumed thrust of *Dance* was autobiographical, however much in spirit rather than letter, and any memoir might well take the shape of a cryptology manual, telling the reader who was really who (much like Shadbold's envisioned role with respect to Winterwade's diary in *Wheel*).

But the memoirs are much more than this, although, at both the times of their publication and subsequently they have been among the most underappreciated aspects of Powell's oeuvre. The memoirs are also a sequence, called *To Keep the Ball Rolling*, and as with *Dance*, its volumes are individually titled. So one would speak of *Messengers of Day,* the second volume of *To Keep the Ball Rolling,* the same way one would speak of *A Buyer's Market,* the second volume of *Dance. To Keep the Ball Rolling,* its immediate pertinence being because it is a quote from a Joseph Conrad novel that mentions a character named Powell, is also a comment on *Dance* and its relation to Powell's life. By keeping the ball rolling, by providing further elaboration and reflection on issues raised in *Dance,* Powell does not allow his sequence to stand alone as an imposing, monolithic monument. It is for this reason, to emphasize the sequential nature of the memoirs, that the four-book version is used as the object of this discussion, not the one-book abridged version that appeared in 1984, even though it was abridged by the author himself, is currently in print, and, according to Powell, made "a better book."[1]

The *To Keep the Ball Rolling* title signifies that for Powell, there is life beyond *Dance* (whereas a plausible interpretation of the end of *Dance* could indeed be that Nicholas Jenkins is about to die, after he has finished telling his story). Powell, who published eleven books (and one further posthumously) after finishing *Dance,* should not have his reputation restricted to what is unquestionably his great work. For a writer so renowned as a novelist, and as the author of a twelve-book novel sequence at that, it is surprising how much nonfiction Anthony Powell wrote. Reading only the fiction of Anthony Powell—and even more, reading only *Dance*—is somewhat like reading only the fiction of Thomas Hardy, or, if you like, reading only Hardy's poetry. Those who thus limit themselves miss not only the memoirs and *Journals* but also the two critical books, some of whose components (the pieces on Tolstoy and Rilke in *Review,* those on Sir Iain Moncrieff of that Ilk, American first ladies, and Ivy Compton-Burnett in *Verdicts*) are among the finest and most perceptive concentrated pieces of writing Powell ever did. In addition, Powell's fiction, although participating in so many respects in the historical trajectory of the novel, reads particularly like nonfiction. The roots of its narrative structure, as we have seen, go back to a figure like Herodotus, and its audience is much more like the traditional audience for prose history. Powell's temperamental closeness to nonfiction can also be seen in his more occasional writing: he never wrote short stories, excepting his D. H. Lawrence parody, *A Reference for Mellors,* and no lyric poetry; *Caledonia* was an energetic jeu d'esprit, although the embedded songs and poems ("Tess of Le Touquet" at the Andriadis party in *Buyer's Market,* the takeoff on Walter Savage Landor as adapted to the life of Barbara Skelton at *Journals,* 8 October 1987) are quite good. Powell's forays into drama were short and, if not disastrous, then certainly not ipso facto deserving of laurels. But he wrote extensive journalism, essays, introductions to reissues, remembrances, and testimonials and seemed to enjoy doing so; he makes clear in the *Journals* that this writing was not done for financial reasons. Furthermore, as Powell's reviewing career went on, he increasingly *reviewed* nonfiction (see *Journals,* 4 September 1992). Powell is certainly not one of those novelists who are magicians in their fiction but rank amateurs as nonfiction writers. He takes nonfiction very seriously as a form of writing, not just as a genre reluctantly engaged in to support, in one way or another, his career as a fiction writer. In a less obvious manner, Powell's work raises similar questions as to when fiction ends and nonfiction begins, as does the later career of his friend V. S. Naipaul.

A writer for whom nonfiction is this important will not follow conventional patterns when writing nonfiction. This is no more true than in the memoirs. Our conventional ideas of autobiography see personal narratives as chronicling a journey, an odyssey, a story of something attained in the course of life. Great stress is placed on self-consciousness (though not, conventionally, self-irony) and metaphors of maturation. These are for the most part not applicable to Powell's life, much less the way he chronicles it. Far from displaying the self-advertising brio that characterize many examples of the autobiographer's practice, Powell, as Robert Selig notes, makes "a kind of apology for writing memoirs at all."[2] Most subjects of autobiography relate how, in essence, they became themselves, narrate the coming-to-be of their present identities. St. Augustine of Hippo, an improvident heretic in his youth, became a pillar of the church who drew some of the authority of his "retrospective introspection" from his former heresy.[3] Rousseau chronicled his "agonized self-awareness," his somewhat circular process of coming to be in order that he can discern how he came to be himself.[4] In this context, the passage from Powell cited below is disconcerting:

Good-natured, easygoing, by all accounts without outstanding vices of any kind, Edmund Lionel Welles *alias* Wells-Dymoke (1814–1892) contrived—unlike his father—to be called to the Bar. There the matter rested. His most energetic endeavors were represented in early years in service in the Royal Cumberland Militia, in which he rose to the rank of captain. Far from military in his tastes (unlike my Powell grandfather) he had doubtless been roped in by his brother-in-law. Roland Pennington, of the Fifth Fusiliers (Northumberland's regiment) a Peninsular veteran; one of the first up the ladders at Badajoz. (*Infants*, 188)

Powell starts out his autobiography (in the original British edition; the American publishers saved this material for the end) with three chapters of genealogy, including both his immediate forebears and family atmosphere as well as distant forebears in medieval Wales. This gives the narrative not just a sense of history but one of reverberating memory; Powell, for instance, may be the youngest English writer for whom the Napoleonic wars, even by genealogical echo, seem to personally matter. But by the standards of Rousseau and Augustine, this excerpt will not pass muster. There is no sense of coming to be, no agonized conversion away from heresy to the sober and true doctrine of maturity. Powell was pretty much always who he was, and, therefore, his autobiography provides no Augustinian conversion proceeds. As with Jenkins in *Dance,* as seen in the car ride with Lady Frederica in *At Lady Molly's,* Powell "matures" through understanding contexts and mastering social conventions. Furthermore, he is as much interested in other people than himself—indeed, the memoirs are often little but accounts of the people he met and the books he read—so there is little opportunity for Rousseauesque cathartic self-discovery. As Laurie Frost points out, Powell prefers "social life" to "private life."[5] Thus he breaks the mold of the customary chronicle of the usual story. Powell certainly believes there is such a thing as growing up; such an assumption is inherent in the idea of a question of upbringing, and a belief in "adulthood" as a state is necessitated by the grim endings of *Buyer's Market* and *Casanova's Chinese Restaurant.* But achieved adulthood is not the consequence of a growing-up process that is concentrated primarily on the self.

There is another dimension here, though, unique to the twentieth century: the political valence expected of most autobiographers. In a recent book on twentieth-century autobiography, *Threads of Life* (subtitled, significantly for *Dance*'s distinction between men of will and men of imagination, *Autobiography of the Will*), Richard Freadman covers, among others, Arthur Koestler, Stephen Spender, and Lionel and Diana Trilling. These are all intellectuals who started out on the Left and ended up on the Right, or at least to the right of their imputed initial political position. Freadman takes this trajectory as a base for analyzing his subjects' processes of moral education, the way they repudiate what Spender referred to as "the new religion of pseudo-science," to arrive at a mature stance full of negative capability and a knowledge of one's own limits.[6] Powell certainly ended up on the Right. But he did not start out on the Left. Nor did he ever believe in any pseudoscientific religion, not even that of Aleister Crowley, the obvious model for Dr. Trelawney, much less than of Lenin or Hitler. Therefore, his life pattern is outside the box of the usual sequence for people of his generation—and after. All this both explains the memoirs' cold reception and adds to their intellectual interest, even when compared with the autobiographical works of Powell's contemporaries. Muggeridge and Auden, among Powell's contemporaries, obeyed the Left-to-Right script (and Muggeridge's late conversion to Catholicism subscribed to the script even more), though Auden, unlike his friend Spender, never wrote an autobiography. Even outside this particular scenario, most autobiographies are either, like Augustine's, conversion narratives of how the person came to accept this or that philosophical position, or, like Rousseau's, manifestation narratives—narratives of how the person's unique soul came to be.

That *Infants* was such an unconventional autobiography explains the muffled reception of this book and of its successor volumes. Yet it is not without self-consciousness. Powell describes a moment of self-discovery when he was about five or six: "The truth came flooding in with the dust-infested sunlight. The revelation of self-identity was inescapable. There could be no doubt about it. I was me" (*Infants,* 8). This concise and convincing account of self-consciousness allows there to be such a thing as personal identity, for there to be a constructive, perceiving self—something for which not all ideologies or philosophical viewpoints allow, indeed sometimes specifically associated with certain brands of humanism or psychological optimism) without at all compelling the reader to subscribe to an over-arching narrative that can or will potentially cover the experiences of the reader as well. Powell relates experiences that are simply his own and allows the reader to have ones simply their own as well; they do not have to concert or mature. This combination of insight and distance is maintained throughout the first volume. Powell, for instance, expresses vividly his hatred of his preparatory school, his relative happiness, yet without particular nostalgic or celebratory overtones, at Eton, and his discontent at Oxford. The Oxford passages of *Infants* are among the most surprising, as people who know Powell principally as a friend of Evelyn Waugh or Graham Greene identify him largely with a sensibility formed by that of Oxford in the 1920s. It is a sensibility from which Powell seems determined to distance himself; aware of the power of myth making, as seen in Beals's conjectures in *Fisher,* Powell early on wants to inoculate the reader against the overcredulity seen in previous journalistic accounts of this milieu.

Powell describes his relationship with C. M. (Maurice) Bowra, an Oxford academic who might be taken to be congruent with Sillery of *Dance* but who Powell insisted was not such a model. His insistence is convincing for three reasons. First, Bowra, born in 1898, was much younger than Sillery, whose sensibility, like that of St. John Clarke, was essentially that of late Victorian or Edwardian progressivism adapted to suit more extreme times. Second, Bowra's prestige lay much more in his scholarship than did Sillery's; Bowra was an internationally respected classical scholar, an early advocate of twentieth-century Russian poetry, and somebody who, though not a systematic thinker, made major contributions to the academic record (Sillery is not represented as anything like this and is not recorded as writing any substantial books of scholarship). And third, Bowra clearly had a romanticism about Oxford that Sillery, much more the operator, did not; he used it as a power base and not much more. It is this latter trait of Bowra's that aggravated Powell as an undergraduate. Powell describes his time at Oxford, though in many ways productive, as filled with "deep melancholy" (*Infants*, 153) and made the mistake of confiding this to his mentor. Coolness and distance resulted, leading Powell to conclude, in one of the many nuggets of practical wisdom contained in the memoirs, that "it is better to keep deeply felt views about oneself to oneself" (*Infants*, 152). With respect to Bowra, Powell concluded that "it was better to escape early from Bowra's imposed judgments. There was a touch of something inhibiting. It was preferable to know Bowra for a time, then get away; returning in due course to appreciate the many things he had to offer" (148). Powell records his break with Bowra even though for the most part Powell is circumspect about relationships with people he no longer likes; witness the difference between how his friendships with Evelyn Waugh and Henry Green are portrayed in the memoirs and in the *Journals*.

Because the school and university scenes of *Dance* reverberate so vividly for readers, the equivalent scenes in *Infants* are inevitably lackluster by comparison and only fully appreciable on subsequent readings, although some details—Lord Curzon's sudden arrival at his stepson's rooms, for example—are funnier than their equivalents in *Dance* (in this case, Commander Foxe's visit to Oxford to check up on Stringham; note the lesser public importance of the fictional character, a near-constant when any connections between real and fictional people are traceable). On the other hand, the prep-school and foreign travel scenes, unparalleled in *Dance* and, in the case of the latter, only lightly sampled in *Venusberg,* are colorful and eminently readable. Powell got to do a lot when he was a young man, and this exposure contributed to the broad range of his fiction. But as the line from *Hamlet* that gives the book's title indicates, "The canker galls the infants of the spring," and many of the privileged youth depicted in this volume were not to have the fulfilled, mature lives that the standard autobiographical paradigms suggest are inevitable.

Messengers of Day (1978)

Those who have written about Powell's memoirs have faced a dilemma. The trajectory of his life is visible in *Dance* and, in any event, is not prioritized in the memoirs. Simply listing the personages profiled therein would only fortify the impression that they are a kind of narrative *Who's Who.* Perhaps the solution is a *close reading* of specific passages that can give a sense of both the texture of the memoirs and the subtleties of the approaches Powell deploys in them.

The scene of *Messengers,* for instance, is London; indeed, it is the only one of the four books to take place mainly in London. Powell, after leaving Oxford, decides to move to a specific neighborhood, Shepherd's Market, on account of reading Michael Arlen's *The Green Hat,* a "novel of youth" of that era (its genre not far different from *Afternoon Men,* though its writing style far more elaborate). Years later—in fact, out of the time frame of *Messengers* itself, these flash-forwards being a constant in the memoirs—he encounters Arlen:

(By an odd chance I found myself giving luncheon to Arlen tête-a-tête thirty years later, and was able to reveal what had prompted my first London garçonnière. Small, slight, neat, infinitely sure of himself, yet somehow set apart from other people, he twice repeated at the table a personal definition: "I, Dikran Kouyoumdjian, an Armenian." Dikran is the equivalent of Tigranes, the name of several kings of Armenia in classical times. Arlen talked entertainingly of books and sexual relationships, saying among other things that, unlike most men he knew, he did not believe in sleeping with friends' wives.) (*Messengers*, 2)

Powell always notes other people's level of self-satisfaction. Indeed, he is something of a theoretician of self-satisfaction; it is one of his great themes in human, or even animal (the Field Marshal's dog in *Military Philosophers*), character traits. The modifier "infinitely" is one of Powell's favorites; it is slightly hyperbolic, as what is really meant is emphatically, beyond normal measure, its goal being to make the reader notice this trait, not just assimilate it to a banal, already constituted perception of what other people are likely to be like. The French word *garçonnière*, not really idiomatic in English even as a borrowed phrase, is chosen not out of pretension but out of a need for economy, a sense of le mot juste even if the lexicon has to be slightly stretched to include it, and to cover up the preposterousness of the situation, not only Powell choosing where to live out of enthusiasm for a novel not of the first rank but of explaining to its considerably older author how this novel fit into the young Powell's incipient personal mythology. The name Michael Arlen does not automatically identify Armenian descent (even though *The Green Hat,* despite its English setting, has a certain vaguely Levantine, "perfumed garden" air to it), and for it to be related in the anecdote that Arlen was, in fact, Armenian might be informative on behalf of the memoirist, but recording the idiosyncrasy of Arlen actually pronouncing so empathically his Armenian name certainly goes the extra mile, as does the detail of his repeating this delphic utterance *twice.* Even saying, "I, Dikran Kouyoumdjian, an Armenian" once is funny, let alone twice, but what also is conveyed here is the comedy of Arlen having adopted a plausibly non-Armenian identity then reaching back so theatrically to proclaim, not entirely without deliberate humor, his Armenian self. The Tigranes reference is erudite and classicizing (extending even to the northeastern margins of the classical world), but once it is made, it is both crisp and vague, performed with a kind of urbane offhandedness that makes the reader feel they have always known this fact, even if, empirically, they have not. There is no turgid encyclopedic detail about the various Tigraneses in Armenian history, no burdening the reader with too much information. For a writer who puts so much in, Powell leaves as much out—he has so much to say, but the imperatives of discipline, concision, and understatement rein in any discourse that might otherwise tend toward the expansive or embroidered. The mention of "books and sexual relationships," as if the two topics were adjacent categories that might without difficulty be substituted for each other in any context in life, is characteristic, as is the deliberate mixing of temporal registers, as the phrase "sexual relationships," as Philip Larkin might well have appreciated, is of twentieth-century vintage, whereas the idea of "books" in the sense that Powell means it, not just reading books but the book trade, the professional life of an author, was certainly of Victorian or earlier origin. The phrase about sleeping with friends' wives is interesting, as Powell, the relating narrator, makes no judgment on Arlen's main proposition, hidden away from his overstatement, that most men do sleep with their friends' wives; both Arlen's opinion and the entire framework on which it is based are allowed to speak for themselves, with no endorsement, no opinion, nothing but a kind of imperturbable though cheerily casual serenity that hands on the information to the readers to make of it what they will.

During the time Powell wrote his memoirs, several of the key people referred to in them were still alive. This is already beginning to change in the early *Journals*—the difference between having friends in their sixties and seventies and then in their eighties and nineties—and is one of the reasons, generic differences aside, for the greater candor in the *Journals*. This earlier opacity has an impact on *Messengers* most of all the volumes, especially relating to acquaintances not to play a large role in later life. But what Powell is not opaque about is his literary awareness and his tastes in reading. The chapter "Set Books," in which Powell simply goes through the books that have influenced him and were necessary to the consolidation of his literary identity, is the takeoff point for the memoirs, much as *Lady Molly's* is the takeoff point of *Dance,* and the 27 January 1986 entry is the takeoff point for the *Journals.* This is not to say that there are not excellent passages before these points, indeed, as many before as after, but that after the takeoff point the reader fully understands the design and the rationale of the overall conception. Witness these words on Balzac, a writer who, to General Liddament's horror, was to so influence not only Jenkins but also *Dance:* "There can be no doubt that the dedicated Balzacian must accept a torrent of vulgarity, but, in matters of situation and behaviour, a great deal of improbability too. Never mind. Balzac's improbabilities do not prevent many do his least likely climaxes from being the best ones.

Besides—something never to be forgotten—with all novelists one must put up with something" (*Messengers*, 116).

The last sentence, as an aphorism, may end up being one of Powell's most memorable sayings, and its import—that no given novelist, no matter how enthusiastic the reader's response, should be regarded as the greatest thing since sliced bread—is salutary. But the context in which it is embedded is also worth notice. The interpolation of "never mind," as if, in the middle of a literary disquisition about a long-dead novelist in a formal memoir by another novelist we are suddenly in the midst of casual conversation between two people who know each other, is disarming in its informality. It is also, in its leavening of abstract discourse by an acknowledgment of the audience, similar to the "so far so good" and "all that is clear enough" in Widmerpool's otherwise totally obverse Old Boy speech. This informality particularly matters, given that Powell is, in essence, laying down rules of reading. He is not "a totalitarian" (letter to John Monagan, 14 March 1969). His rules of reading are in the first place for himself, not for others, and if then, only fortuitously.

Powell's concentration on reading the books of other people, rather than recording personal drama that might have informed works of his own, reminds us again what a counterintuitive autobiographer is, although more allegedly introspective biographies, even the *Confessions* of St. Augustine, are also in large part records of the author's reading, in Augustine's case, of the Bible (something scholars of Augustine as autobiographer only recently began to note). Powell's emphasis on reading is a needed deflation of our overromantic expectations of life stories. In general, we expect too much slam-bang action or tortured self-consciousness in autobiography, whereas most of life, especially for an intellectual, is encountering other people, books, ideas, events, and coming to terms with their significance. In spending so much time on the books he has read, Powell does as much as possible to avoid the generic constraints of autobiography, which can come to determine the content of the autobiographical narrative as much as events in the underlying life. This enables Powell to be at once accurate in his own recollections and yet not adhere to any overarching psychological paradigm of "self" as part of that recollective process. What Martin Seymour-Smith says about Powell's fiction could well be said of his memoirs: "The process of life, for once, unfolds before us as it is; without even the feelings Powell himself possesses."[7] Powell is almost an anti-autobiographer, much like certain late modernist fiction writers saw themselves as antinovelists. As Jeremy Treglown puts it, Powell "reverses the cardinal modern Western assumption that the inner life is all-important."[8] But this is to overstate things. Powell does not go all the way; whether from within or without traditional biographical structures, there is some sense of life's total shape, some belief that it has a meaning and a purpose. Powell does not share the prejudices of Wyndham Lewis (surely the comparison Treglown's remarks are meant to evoke) that time and introspection are ipso facto chimerical. In fact, Powell, though influenced by aspects of Lewis's savage comedy, did not make Lewis's (pro-Nazi) political errors because he did not follow the older writer in his antihumanist, antitemporal philosophical errors. Powell had a "warmth" and an "intellectual magnanimity" (*Messengers*, 153) of the sort he found lacking in Lewis, full of "unsatisfactory characteristics" (*Journals*, 27 May 1986). The introspection of Joyce is indeed negatively contrasted with the "brutal, luminous" (112) style of Lewis in *Messengers*. But it is

Joyce who is reread by Powell in the more informal and personal *Journals.*

Powell himself seems uneasy about the lack of traditional narrative design in his memoirs. Witness the final sentences of *Messengers:* "Scrutinizing the work of novelists past and present, one ponders this matter. Have novelists simply got a certain amount in them, which, if not cut off by early death, is in due course exhausted? Or does some manner of existence stimulate or dry up these powers? Do certain ways of life build up reserves? If so, what are these ways of life; how should they be practised? Is there no rule?" (200). There is a plaintiveness here, and a sense of the writer throwing up his hands, unable to discern a plan in life or a prescribed model of the always tetchy relation of life to work, half wanting one, doubting that anyone else knows where to find it—maybe challenging the reader to suggest solutions. The sense of there being a reserve of experience in life, and of writing having a kind of hydraulic relationship to this experience, is not the only model of the relationship of life to writing Powell will use, but it is an interesting one, especially in its suggestion that, as in the extraction of oil, or for that matter water, from the earth, the means by which this extraction is done are crucial. Both in fiction and memoirs, Powell meditates cogently on such processes.

Faces in My Time (1980)

All of the titles of the individual memoir books come from Shakespeare. In fact, it is from the late 1970s, when the memoirs are written, that the importance of Shakespeare in Powell's writing begins to manifest itself, as is seen in the *Journals* and the Shakespearean jokes toward the end of (the not entirely chronological) *Writer's Notebook*. Shakespeare, somewhat surprisingly, is not all that much in evidence in *Dance*, either overtly or covertly, although the Welsh war scenes in *Valley of Bones* recall the Henriad plays. What is interesting about Powell's titular use of the Shakespeare quotes in the memoirs is that the quotes, in their full context, always seem to make the opposite point from what a casual reader, applying the title to the book, might think. This seems deliberate, though whether the effect is to tease Shakespeare or Powell's reader it is hard to say. We have already seen how "the canker galls the infants of the spring," even though the last five words alone conjure an image of idyllic pastoral. "Messengers of day" comes from a conversation between three of the minor participants, Decius Brutus, Casca, and Cinna in the conspiracy to assassinate Julius Caesar in Shakespeare's play of that name. The phrase is "yon grey lines that fret the clouds are messengers of day," referring to the earliest hint of dawn, which Cinna descries. A reader enthralled to convenient autobiographical patterns might judge that Powell, in writing about his young maturity in London, sees it as the beginning of the dawn, a time of unparalleled youthful hope and bliss. But in the actual play, the day does not quite dawn at that point, and when it eventually does dawn, it proves to be the day of the questionable assassination of the nation's leader, for which all those who participate in it will eventually be killed. Somewhat of an unpromising portent, one might think. *Faces in My Time* seems a very genteel title of "garnered" reminiscences. But consider the quote in its Shakespearean context in *King Lear,* when the imprisoned Kent says, "I have seen better faces in my time than lie before me at this instant." The phrase "faces in my time" is not positive. So the titles, whether they wrench phrases from Shakespeare's original meaning or direct readers to the ironies and qualifications inherent in their use, are not straightforward; they are not like the title of Sillery's book, *Garnered at Sunset.* They mean something, substantively; they are engaged in verbal play.

That being said, much of *Faces* is indeed devoted to serial portraits of encountered individuals.[9] Powell's portraits of people show exactly the things people would later see as mattering. In their pithiness, they tally well with later received opinion, although they do not agree with the received opinion of the time in which they were written. They do not distort or filter through a prejudiced personal agenda. A comparison to John Aubrey is inevitable, as future generations may look back on Powell's memoirs as not only uncommonly well written but also preserving just what information is needed to understand both people who are currently seen as prominent and those who one day may emerge as important—for example, the great-grandfather of someone significant in a later time. Reading the memoirs confirms the sense that an ideal encyclopedia is one written by a single person, as one person can provide a unified sensibility and his or her prejudices, if present, will soon become revealed with the accumulation of entries. *Faces* is the volume of the memoirs in which Powell comes closest to presenting an encyclopedia of British social life.

The individual chapter titles of the memoirs serve as crystallizations of the account's overall meaning. As always, subunits are organizationally crucial for Powell, and how he handles the masonry of their relationship to the overall unit helps add to the book's structural integrity and creative tension. Each book is like a trilogy of *Dance*, titled chapters are like individual novels, numbered subsections are like the subdivisions in *Dance*—all on a smaller scale. The mathematics of this are not exact but suggestive. The chapter titles in *Faces—Ô saisons, ô châteaux!* "Great Ormond Street," "North Palm Drive," "Chester Gate," "Cambridge Waters," "Kierkegaard in White-hall," "Departmental Exchanges," "Demob Outfits," "What's the Drill?" and "Upper Grub Street"—are a characteristic mix of the straightforwardly descriptive and the deliberately arch. Chapters 2, 3, and 4 refer, simply, to the places Powell lived at the time under discussion; others are quotations or idioms applied to relevant life situations. With "Kierkegaard in White-hall," we see Powell having to, for the second time, find an adequate title to describe his experiences in military intelligence, *The Military Philosophers* already having been used. The point here is that not all the chapter titles are the same sort; as in *Dance,* there is a diversity of titles, which enables the books to sample many different moods or at least plausibly mirrors that process. "Upper Grub Street," the title alluding to George Gissing's novel *New Grub Street,* is one of the most paradigmatic of all of the chapter titles. A plausible alternate title for *Books Do Furnish a Room,* it demonstrates how Powell does not artificially exalt the literary world and his place in it. He manages the rare and admirable combination of being idealistic but not romantic about literature. This hard-nosed quality also may suggests that his lack of interest in flamboyant self-reference has its origin in the absence of narcissistic illusions about the literary way of life.

Of all of the many portraits in *Faces,* two stand out—one of a very well known man, the other of an obscure one. This of F. Scott Fitzgerald in Hollywood:

> He was smallish, neat, solidly built, wearing a light grey suit, lightcoloured tie, all his tones essentially light. Photographs —seen for the most part years later—do not do justice to him.

Possibly he was one of those persons who at once become self-conscious when photographed. Even snapshots tend to give him an air of swagger, a kind of cockiness, which, anyway at that moment, he did not at all possess. On the contrary, one was at once aware of an odd sort of unassuming dignity. There was no hint at all of the cantankerous temper that undoubtedly lurked beneath the surface. His air could be though a trifle sad, not, as sometimes described at this period, in the least broken-down. When, years later, I came to know Kingsley Amis, his appearance recalled Fitzgerald's to me, a likeness photographs of both confirm. (*Faces*, 64)

The emphasis on how individual personality is displayed in reaction to photography is reminiscent to the discussion of Henchman's craft in *The Fisher King*. Powell is trying to disentangle F. Scott Fitzgerald from not only accreted literary-historical stereotypes but also misleading impressions conveyed by actual photographs of him. The reference to "dignity" recalls the mention of Pringle's false nose in *Afternoon Men*, which ornament lent him "an unaccustomed dignity"—as if Powell, rather than looking to puncture the balloon of the dignified, is trying to find dignity in a cavalcade of souls most of whom are already punctured—indeed, far more than Fitzgerald is at the moment of contact. Powell throughout his career is trying to correct false impressions, stereotypes, and popular images (this may well be a principal task of all imaginative writing), but here he feels the truth is occluded by both other people's memories of Fitzgerald and his image in photographs. The writer's less fixed, but more emotionally responsive, point of view has to work at its maximum to redeem Fitzgerald for a more equable vantage point. It is interesting, though, that for all his yearning to display Fitzgerald as unselfconscious, Powell's record of his talking about America sees Fitzgerald as more or less a typical American, which he could be no more than could his greatest creation, Gatsby. This image of Fitzgerald as representative American man mystically counterbalances the casual, light portrait of him in personal conversation, as if fulfilling the Fitzgeraldian axiom that even if you begin with an individual, you end up with a type. Of course, Powell would be the first to concede that he is not recording the objectively true Scott Fitzgerald; he is assimilating Fitzgerald, as observed, to the scrupulous consciousness of Anthony Powell and then trying to get him right, both sides of the equation here being absolutely necessary. Powell spoke often about the alchemy required to transmute a real person into a fictional character, that it was not just a matter of straightforward translation. Here is somewhat of an instance of the alchemy of making a real person into a character in a *memoir*—and succeeding.

Then there is the far less conspicuous case of Major E. C. Bradfield, who worked alongside Powell as liaison officer to the Norwegian government-in-exile during the war, one of the minor "military philosophers":

Bradfield's history was as out of the way as his personality. Ostensibly the son (youngest child by several years in a comparatively large family) of a Norfolk farmer and his wife, he seemed from his earliest days to have been under the wing of a Danish margarine tycoon named Horniman, who had formed the habit of making an annual visit to East Anglia for the fox-hunting season. Finally Mr Horniman (always referred to as "my guardian") more or less adopted Bradfield as his son. Speculation was irresistible as to whether a blood relationship did not indeed exist between them, an ambiguity by no means diminished by Bradfield's own features. In fact Dru—familiar with clerical aspects of Danish life from Kierkegaard studies, and producing book illustrations to prove his point—used to say: "All Bradders needs to make him look a typical 19th century Danish pastor is a black gown and ruff round his neck." (*Faces*, 151)

The beckoning, inexplicable fascination of "a Danish magazine tycoon named Horniman" (not, for instance, "Horniman, a Danish margarine tycoon," which would have an entirely different effect) lies in its at once introducing the reader to a personage never before encountered and assuming that the reader, as does the writer, already knows how to imagine or construct such a figure within existing terms of reference. There is also a slight irony in the enunciation of "Horniman," not that Powell wishes us to think him especially mordant with regards to this name, but because of the tinge of irony present whenever Powell makes reference to *any* proper name—an irony that is not sneering but emanates from a nuanced sense of prudent skepticism. This skepticism, though, is not so distant as not to constitute a kind of *connaissance,* a knowing worldliness, navigating, without anxiety, many different social levels and situations. Powell colludes with his readers to conjure a sensibility so at ease in English social formations that it can easily stretch itself to include Danish ones, much like a reference book on the United States can, without effort, include aspects of Canada as well. Bradfield's "history" (not "Bradfield's life," which would connote a more subjective *and judgmental* approach than Powell is wont to take) is allowed its own sphere, one with which others may come into contact, but is essentially not interpenetrable. Note also that Bradfield being the natural son of Horniman is neither confirmed or refuted; the possibility is raised, so decorously that it does not come close to slander or even gossip, and then is allowed to radiate out into a general discussion of national type, in which Powell clearly believes (without at all believing in any kind of national *essence,* which is quite different). The Horniman reference testifies to the sheer locality and diversity of experience and to a sense that the complexity of life in Europe is equal to that of Britain.

The relative compatibility in tone between the portraits of Fitzgerald and Bradfield demonstrate that the war is not as much of a quantum divergence as it is in *Dance.* There is not nearly so much of a disruption in mood, nor does the cast of characters—at least, the general tenor of the cast of characters, if not the specific people—so appreciably changed. There is always the danger, in situations like that of *Dance* and the memoirs, in which there is clearly some substantive though not mechanical relationship between life and art, of the nonfiction work lifting the curtain too high, letting the reader see too much of what had been kept in "reserve," to use Powell's own phrase from *Messengers* (200) in the fictional sequence. But it is interesting to realize that the memoirs have their secrets as well. The rival editor of John Aubrey, for instance, who Powell is too circumspect to name in *Faces,* is Oliver Lawson Dick; the fact that this is, tacitly, revealed in the *Journals* (16 October 1991) is an indicator of the difference in intimacy level between the two works—and that the memoirs do not simply supply the unvarnished truth, if autobiography as a genre can in fact do this any more than can imaginative fiction.

A portrait in *Faces* that has a special status is that of T. S. Eliot. Eliot is a figure highly comparable to Powell in that he shares a love of cats, a fascination with the seventeenth century, and an affection for both England and America, for tradition and the new world. Powell's comment, with respect to Eliot's religious drama *Murder in the Cathedral,* "As it happens, I am more pro–Henry II than Becket" (*Journals,* 29 April 1986), is revealing. Powell would put the monarchy before the church, Eliot the church before the monarchy, although both men are, to different degrees, sympathetic to both institutions.

Also, Powell was much more a man of the latter half of the twentieth century, as opposed to Eliot, who personified the 1900–50 period. Eliot was seventeen years older than Powell (really, not that much—the same gap as existed between Powell and Kingsley Amis, who are often seen as sharing a sensibility), but that this is not merely a chronological difference can be seen in the way Evelyn Waugh, two years older than Powell, was so much a man of the century's first half, Powell, who published probably seven-eighths of his work after 1950, a man of its second half. (See Powell's comments, *Journals,* 20 March 1991, on how Waugh began to see himself as an old man "in his late forties.") Yet Eliot's age and his generational differences do not rule out some affinity between them. Powell's portrait of Eliot, of all the other literary personalities portrayed in the memoirs, exudes a faint yet palpable sense of kinship. Powell is not a writer self-consciously indebted to immediate predecessors, or even any writers he knew personally. As the Liddament scene in *Soldier's Art* reveals, his precedents are largely dead and on the Continent (bearing in mind that, as said above, Shakespeare seems to influence Powell more in his nonfiction than in his fiction). But Eliot is certainly treated very respectfully. Powell also does not overstate his closeness to Eliot, taking care, in fact, to represent it in the most casual, understated, and self-deprecatingly dismissive way. This small grace note is but a symptom of the keen decorum that attends Powell's style throughout the memoirs. If in his fiction Powell showed himself to be a writer of genius, in his nonfiction he reveals himself as a person of conscience and principle.

The Strangers All Are Gone (1982)

The fourth volume of Powell's memoirs has the structural role as the final trilogy of *Dance,* more foregrounded by the need not to worry how the plot turns out: the way a sensibility, nurtured in one era, perceives a very different era in which it is yet still participating and flourishing. As Powell grows older, outliving most of his generation, his point of view, in terms of the circumstances that shaped it, becomes a rarity, so that by virtue partially of his age, partially of his always independent temperament, he can provide a kind of minority report on what by now is a world dominated by people a generation or two younger.

The memoir's title comes from *Romeo and Juliet,* although Powell is seen as a comic not tragic writer, all his Shakespeare-derived titles come from the tragedies. In the context of the book, the title might be assumed to refer to the vanishing of most of Powell's old friends, much as Jenkins's had vanished after the war. (The reader notices that, proportionately, more of Jenkins's friends seem to have been lost in the war than Powell's, so Powell's later life seems slightly more "peopled" and "furnished" than Jenkins's.) But in the original play, the quote, spoken by the Nurse, refers to the young Juliet's temporary relief from the burdens of courtship and marriage, Juliet herself being so inexperienced as to be "a stranger in the world." This reversal of engrafted expectation, this image of youth where we might look for age, finds confirmation in the book, which like the later volumes of *Journals,* is, for all the greater age of the person being written about, the most exuberant of all four volumes of the memoirs.

There is relatively little discussion of Powell's own novels within the memoirs—there is in fact more of this in the *Journals* —even though this presumably is one of the reasons somebody picking up the books would be interested. This is in contrast to the standard variety of literary memoir, which is completely pre-occupied with the writer's youth and ends when the fledgling writer is first published, as if that publication is a crowning moment that is both the annunciation and the end of self. Pow-ell, on the other hand, simply has life go on; the perceiving self continues after the cathartic triumph. He announces his fiction as he publishes it—and it is true that the ends of the second and third volumes of the memoirs to correlate with cruxes in the unfolding of his novel-writing career: the felt limitations of his early mode at the end of *Faces,* the conception of the overall canvas of *Dance* at the end of *Faces.* But Powell as memoirist is only an occasional resource for the deeper understanding, or at least the explicit deeper understanding, of Powell as novelist.

Strangers is notable for Powell's descriptions of his travels to two very different parts of the world—Asia and the United States. The Asian trip once again makes the point that this author is not Eurocentric, a point that should not have to be made were it not for the assumption that a classicist and con-servative must uniquely value, or overrate, the European, or that to be non-Eurocentric means to adopt the sort of leftist, "pro–Third World" agenda that was abhorrent to Powell. (See also Powell's comments on African sculpture at *Journals,* 19 October 1988, and the knowledge of different African peoples displayed at *Faces*, 54.) Powell's descriptions of Asia are not in the customary British tradition of travel writing: they are less jocular and free-wheeling, more spare and literary; there is an economy, a leaving-out, that is against the grain of travel writing with its sense of panoply and bizarrerie.

Powell's perspective in *Strangers* does not seal off the past. It opens up the future. Mention is made in the section of Powell's (abortive, as he was never let off the airplane) trip to Cambodia that Prince Sihanouk, at the time of writing (1982), exiled from his country and then of no present relevance to its foreseeable future, could serve as a "potential force to grapple with the tribulations of his native country" (*Strangers*, 140)—as indeed he did, at least as nominal king. More subtly, in his description of his visit to Amherst, a prestigious college in Massachusetts, Powell comments that the students' prose style made clear a "long American abandonment of Latin" (102). But he allows that "this survey of mine was all twenty years ago" and might have changed. Where another writer would have indulged in an English put-down of American effacement of the past, or a sentimental adherence to a metanarrative of decline, Powell leaves the door open (and indeed, Latin became very much a hot commodity in this sort of elite school during the next two decades). This is perhaps a cheap way of reading, as chronological succession—as Powell once put it, knowing how the story turns out— is the one decisive advantage the reader has over the text. But this retrospective fact checking points out one of the differences between the last volume of a nonfictional series and that of a fictional one: the former is much more open-ended, less subject to the manacles of conclusiveness. In *Strangers*, though, Powell makes a particular effort to not give up history for done, remaining always awake, always alert, always vigilant, heeding

Stringham's reminder that "improvement is possible, that roles can be reversed" (*Soldier's Art*, 185).

A late trip to Bulgaria for a writer's congress in 1977, at first reluctantly but then enthusiastically undertaken, is among the most entertaining chapters, especially this exchange:

> "The Bulgarians are sometimes called the English of the Balkans"
>
> "The English are undoubtedly the Bulgarians of north-western Europe." (*Strangers* 185)

The very inexactness of the latter regional designation shows how ludicrous the scale of the comparison, and the humor is both in the anxiety of the Bulgarians to be seen as comparable to the English and the ironic if also generous "undoubtedly"; there is even a mild deflation of the pretensions of "northwestern Europe." Of course, underlying this is that Bulgaria and England are in some ways comparable historically, especially in the demographic overlay of indigenous and invader peoples. What was the motive for Powell's presence in Bulgaria? Why, at seventy-one, when he was beginning to eschew foreign trips, did Powell go? What did the Communist Bulgarian government possibly think it could get out of Powell's presence, when the writer had been historically anti-Communist and had denounced Soviet satellites in Eastern Europe in several of his novels? What did Powell do in Bulgaria that could possibly have been of use to it? The account in *Strangers* raises all these questions. The one motive that is absolutely explicable, though, is Powell's own: he did it out of curiosity. Never something he would have sought voluntarily, when the opportunity came to him, he was only too glad to take it up. The Bulgarian trip at the conclusion of Powell's memoirs supplies the final chord to the subdominant Eastern European motif that had begun with Count Scherbateff and Count Bobel in Powell's second novel nearly half a century earlier.[10]

On the domestic front, there are some surprises. Chapter 4, "Fit for Eros," relates how Powell was listed on the roll for the defense in the obscenity trial over D. H. Lawrence's *Lady Chatterley's Lover.* Powell did this not because he particularly liked the novel, admired Lawrence as a writer, or was an apostle of sexual license, but merely because he valued freedom of imaginative expression and was not stuffy or censorious about sex. The general air of acceptance of the modern world, of not confusing what will always be wrong with the world with problems endemic to a particular era, emanates from many of this volume's anecdotes. Despite stereotypes of Powell's conservatism, he is liberal on some issues: for example, his acceptance of the homosexual content of Shakespeare's sonnets 1–126, when in that era, most establishment scholars were seeing them as ratifications of preexisting *topoi* written to formula in order to please a patron.

The reader of this book who has not read *Strangers* might wonder why Powell is speaking of Shakespeare at all. The route to this is circuitous. Powell goes back to Asia, in a way, for the two summary reflections of the memoirs. The first is more indirect, as it was when Powell was in Tokyo in 1964 for the four hundredth anniversary celebration of Shakespeare's birth. He was asked "What he thought of Shakespeare," his Japanese interlocutor not realizing that that question, or the way it was asked, was far too capacious for anyone to answer, that Shakespeare, for a reader of English, is a world of its own, not just a simple "author" as another writer would be. Powell's answer, given confessedly in place of "general conclusions" (*Strangers,* 196), is in some ways rather expected (as in the defense of Shakespeare under criticism from seventeenth-century French classicists, although we should remember that it is *Powell* whose classicism is always seen, mistakenly, as restrictive fuddy-duddiness by critics), in other ways bracing and original, as in the discussion of the Sonnets and of *Taming of the Shrew,* both of which see the texts as filled with motility and variance, not static totems to be revered and ignored. The other return to Asia occurs when Powell related a scene witnessed on one of two expeditions to the Indian subcontinent he and Lady Violet took under the leadership of Sir Mortimer Wheeler, the great archaeologist known for excavating the cities of the ancient Indus Valley civilization. At the temple of Durga in Benares, Powell takes note of the monkeys living near the temple, which mark its distinctive feature. He describes a monkey that seems to be in the act of contemplating a newspaper that happens, for whatever reason, to be lying on the floor: "Then, suddenly—as if all at once uncontrollably exasperated with the world as it is today—he jumped up, cast the paper from him, leapt from where he was sitting. Bounding upward he made a steep ascent, flying from buttress to buttress, projecting point, to projecting point, higher and higher, always gaining altitude, until he had reached the topmost edge where a secluded niche could be found in which to rest, meditate, regain lost composure" (*Strangers,* 193).

By deputizing the glimpsed monkey to be dyspeptic on his behalf, Powell shies away from a dyspeptic, Dutch-uncle finale. In spite of the annoyances that exasperate man and simian alike, we are urged to "remain calm." The Monkey Temple description is a combination of outrage and cold intelligence without *hauteur.* It avoids the extremes of "the world is going to hell in a handcart" or "a new day is dawning." There is no sense of conclusive revelation; though we might expect it after twelve volumes of fiction, four of memoirs, we get no sense of the meaning of life. If in the early stages of any autobiography the danger is excessive self-consciousness and an exaggeration of themes of development, in the later stages of the generic autobiography, the peril is an excessive prescriptiveness, a dogmatic laying down of truths, from which Powell forebears. Powell certainly does not follow Trelawney in attributing value to windy pronouncements such as "The Essence of the All Is the Godhead of the True" or "The Vision of Visions Heals the Blindness of Sight," which might, in other contexts, suffice not only as occult slogans but as concluding statements of autobiography. In Powell's memoirs, there is no paradigmatic maturity or cathartic personal revelation in which the reader is, compulsorily or voluntarily, enrolled. Equally, there is no insistence on development as the only trajectory or graphic metaphor with regard to a person's life. The book's final, inexpressibly haunting image of Michelangelo fashioning a snowman is a grainy parable of what, in art and life, endures, what prevails, what lasts. Does the impact of a work, or a life, occur all at once, or when distilled through time, long after the passing of its origin and milieu? This question, also posed elsewhere in Powell's late work (*Wheel*, the *Journals*) sounds the tentative, inquisitive note on which Powell closes his account of a life that may, in the opinion of the person who lived it and of others, have been well lived but was not imposed on others as a universal pattern.

CHAPTER 6

Such Ideas as One Has
Understanding Powell's *Journals*

Powell's *Journals* stand with other memorable British diaries of the twentieth century, such as those by Chips Channon, Frances Partridge, and, above all, James Lees-Milne. But a fully adequate comparison can only be to Virginia Woolf, the only imaginative writer of similar strength and daring to write as good a journal. Despite Powell's acute differences with Woolf on many points, their journals have two salient traits in common: a supreme responsiveness, whether to art, nature, or the passing show of life, and an acute and largely disinterested knack for social observation. Like Woolf's diaries, Powell's journals give the reader a sense of the sources of his fiction—but also like Woolf, a sense of aspects of the author not revealed in his imaginative work. Both Woolf's and Powell's diaries provide a perspective upon history, a sense of how individuals and ideologies reinvent themselves, a sage skepticism. There are differences in the two writers' diaries. Woolf kept her journals in the midst of her greatest imaginative work, whereas Powell's were kept only at the conclusion of his writing career and take off only after he had finished any novel writing. As he puts it, in perhaps the most dramatic remark made in the *Journals*' entire course (31 December 1987), "Such ideas as one has will go into this *Journal*." Whereas Woolf's essays and diaries can stand on their own with respect to each other, Powell's diaries have a more symbiotic relationship with the rest of his nonfiction.

Powell's other nonfiction is catalyzed and opened up by the *Journals.* The memoirs can be seen as an extended list of dramatis personae for the *Journals,* or as an elaborate list of defined terms that are then deployed more dynamically by the *Journals.* The *Journals,* in turn, gloss the memoirs, expand on them, not just in time but in meaning. The two sets of works operate very much in tandem, the memoirs providing the base, the *Journals* the superstructure. The manuscripts of the memoirs now deposited at the Eton College Library show how extensively and systematically Powell redrafted them, apparently though a systematic series of three drafts in which not only was the prose more precisely sculpted but instances of personal opinion, particularly rough or hostile assessments of people, were progressively screened out. This process of redrafting, in generic terms not available in the *Journals,* makes, in itself, a difference between the two forms even when they are dealing with the same characters. Someone could presumably read the memoirs first on a particular person in Powell's life, say Henry Green, then go to the *Journals,* and then decipher what is in the memoirs in a new light, as if an emotional cryptological key had suddenly been revealed. The *Journals* are denied their full reverberation if they are not allowed to work in tandem with the memoirs. Similarly, the critical "equities" in *Verdicts* and *Review* gain scope from being seen against the backdrop of the live reading that Powell conducts in the journals and the subtle differences (e.g., between his comments on Truman Capote at *Journals,* 17 January 1987, and his review of John Malcolm Brinnin's book on Capote in *Verdicts*).

The *Journals,* though, are not just a sequel to the memoirs. They are a sequel to *Dance.* They have the same addictive quality, the same sense of rereadability, even though the cast of character is not the same, in either composition or size. Some admirers of *Dance* do not like the *Journals*. Some of them are disconcerted by Powell moving in such exalted social circles. What this really means is that Powell has convincingly presented Nicholas Jenkins as everyman, so we tend to disregard the more exalted aspects of his social surroundings, or conversely, that Jenkins's perception of his own ambience is how Powell truly sees the world, without the impediments of outward titles and stations that we inevitably see in the *Journals*.[1] There are times when Powell, or at least the Powell persona-as-diarist, evinces opinions more typical of other characters in *Dance* than Jenkins: Stringham, Moreland, Trapnel, and sometimes even Uncle Giles. But we have to remember that Powell, even though instanced, or epitomized, in the books as "Jenkins," in fact created all the characters. Similarly, there are incidents, attitudes, or even names in the *Journals* that, if presented in fiction, would have been thought deliberately parodic, but here they are part of lived reality. This shows that in *Dance,* Powell was not simply transcribing his own life and attitudes. There is in the fiction, we now see, a distancing, a reformulation of intrinsically personal attitudes, a distribution of characteristics that produces a sharply different mix than in the *Journals,* as much as the same presiding sensibility can be seen at play in both genres.

The journal entries are, on average, half a page to a page long, though some are as long as seven or eight typed pages. They are usually made once every two or three days; rarely does a week pass without an entry. Fortuitously, since the division was presumably made for reasons of conventional book length, not content, each books of *Journals* falls into a slightly different emphasis. *Journals, 1982–1986* (often known as "the beige volume" by Powellians) deals with years when Powell was still writing fiction and still went frequently to London. This book casts the greatest social net, and Powell often seems to be attending a party filled with prominent personages once a week. *Journals, 1987–1989* ("the blue volume") is the most intellectual of the three, centered around Powell's many rereadings and reconsiderations of an astounding range of books and ideas. *Journals, 1990–1992* ("the red volume"), written when Powell's physical mobility began to be restricted, is the most personal (and, inexplicably, the most rereadable). In it he gives his most unvarnished opinions of key figures in his life such as Henry Green, Evelyn Waugh, and Malcolm Muggeridge. After his illness in the fall of 1990, Powell becomes more detached from the outside world. Reports of external events seem more and more like sepulchral, incanted intrusions, no longer vitally linked to daily life.[2] But the diarist's intellectual acuity remains intense. The *Journals* in a way become *more* interesting when Powell is physically restricted. He becomes more reliant on his mind alone and becomes deeper and more confidential in his musings. The last six or seven years of entries are of an impressively sustained excellence.

Only the first volume of the *Journals* was extensively reviewed, and this of course only in Britain. The reviews were generally very positive, but the few negative ones, which probably prevented the *Journals* from being immediately published in the United States as well (as all of Powell's previous fiction *and* nonfiction since 1951 had been), focused on what was seen as the elite social atmosphere recorded in them. This was the life, the reader was told, of a privileged man hobnobbing with an aristocratic in-crowd. This assertion of some sort of moral wrong in knowing rich and powerful people is fascinating, particularly since most of the journalists who made it must, by dint of their vocation if nothing else, known many more rich and powerful people, and surely a greater proportion of youthful and currently influential ones, than did Powell. The prestige level of Powell's friends and acquaintances are no more than the kind of drift that would characterize, say, a retired athlete from a working-class background who had achieved celebrity through his skills on the playing field and thus was acquainted with, in his retirement years, a higher social stratum than he had in his youth. Probably the added discomfort on the part of the critics was due to the mention of titled aristocrats in the *Journals*. These mentions, not abundant (Powell's dentist, Howard Sussman, is mentioned much more, and with more affection), are also not panegyric. Comments on HRH the duke of Kent (18 May 1982) and the marquess of Bath (30 June 1992) cannot be accused of fawning. Powell remarks skeptically on the limits of "aristocratic sweetness and light" (13 November 1990). Other comments on aristocratic figures, such as the comment that Percy Seymour, eighteenth duke of Somerset, was "good value for a Duke" (*Journals*, 13 March 1982), are judgments the independent validation of which is impossible for most readers, British or American. But presumably Powell had a basis for his judgment. If this is what he thinks, should he not write it down if his judgment impels him to do so, even if none of his judgments on individual title holders are as inferentially scathing as that of John Aubrey on the first earl of Pembroke?[3] Is he expected to censor his own opinion to remain within some permissible confine beyond which literature, in the eyes of its maintainers, must not stray, rightward or leftward, upward or downward? The reason we read writers, of whatever race, class, or background, is because we want to know what they think. If we reject what a writer thinks, it should be because we, individual reader by individual reader, reject it, not because the writer's thought is inhibited by a monitoring consensus. The kind of patrolling that would say otherwise is likely to censor not the privileged but the underprivileged; it should be curtailed. Powell's original comment, incidentally, implies that many dukes are *not* good value. But subtleties like this, which should be observed on behalf of any writer no matter what his or her stance, are all too little granted to Powell.

In any event, only the first volume of *Journals* is at all social in emphasis. The second and third are more intellectual and personal, and because of the sort of reviews the first book received, the second and third books are underappreciated. This is much like people thinking all of *Dance* is about sneering at boys who wear the wrong overcoat at an elite school because such a figure is mentioned in the first volume. What the *Journals* are about is the rich mental life of a knowledgeable and perceptive elderly man; they incarnate T. S. Eliot's exhortation in "East Coker" that "old men ought to be explorers."[4] There is no resting on laurels, no squatting on a previously achieved perch. When the eighty-six-year-old Powell reads the Koran for the first time (11 May 1992) or tries once again to make sense of the intricacy of Henry James's most difficult novel (25 October 1992), the effect is astoundingly moving, somewhat like the last poems of a Thomas Hardy or a Wallace Stevens, though with much less high seriousness. One could count the amount of well-known imaginative writers in the English-speaking world who had read the Koran in 1992 on two hands. That one of them was the octogenarian Powell is a subject for endless wonderment. The persistent curiosity, the sheer intelligence, that is present throughout all of Powell's work is there, undiminished, in old age. If anything, the years have sharpened them, given them a longer perspective, a keener sense of the sweep of time.

It is unusual for a writer to begin a journal so late in life. Part of the interest in the *Journals* is that they were begun so late; therefore, whatever the age of the author, they have a generic freshness, as in perhaps a minor and unmetaphysical but still substantial way, the person who writes memoirs and the person who writes journals will be different personae in the different genres. There is a slightly heteronymic sense to this generic interplay, which is not often recognized in writing of nonfiction although perhaps overemphasized in speaking of fiction, for example, the distinction between Jenkins and Powell in *Dance*. Powell had in his twenties considered writing a diary but did not feel he had the "particular sense of personal motivations" (*Messengers,* 108) required to do so. He also mentions that keeping a diary and writing a novel at the same time are apt to interfere with each other, as the diary will intercept the potential germs of fiction and prevent them from manifesting themselves, rich and changed, on the printed page. With Powell winding down his novel-writing career in the 1980s, this second impediment is removed, even though he is writing *Wheel* and *Fisher* concurrently with the first four years of *Journals.* The sense of personal motivation, which Powell had at seventy-six but lacked earlier, is less isolable. If one had to guess, one might venture that the motivation has to do with Powell's own literary reputation, combined with the story of his generation (the subject of the 27 January 1986 entry in the *Journals,* the longest, most revealing, and arguably most significant entry in all three volumes) and the various challenges and temptations it faced.

The *Journals* are not innocuous—not just in their honest appraisals of people, ideas, and reputations, but in the high and inevitably, to some, astringent standards Powell sets for his own observations. It would be a mistake to assume the *Journals* are filled with brief, anecdotal jottings. There are several epic entries, like the 27 January 1986 entry on upwardly mobile aesthetes, the 10 January 1989 reassessment of *Dance,* and the 14 December 1990 meditation on the death of Malcolm Muggeridge. There is also the visit to Buckingham Palace, or, as General Conyers might refer to it, "Buck House," for the bestowal of his Companion of Honour award, a journal entry that has a special status of its own, and is, if not a shedding of daylight upon magic, certainly one of the instances where Powell matchlessly takes the reader inside a situation most readers will never go, giving a sense of what it is like to be there on the inside, all the while maintaining a sense of decorum and rectitude.[5] There has been little reference to the monarchy in *Dance,* other than the court service of Conyers and of Frederica Budd, and so here again the *Journals* are able to glimpse a dimension of society that was not given much scope in the sequence.

This is also true of Powell's comments on party politics, especially the figure of Margaret Thatcher. Some readers of the *Journals* were clearly surprised by Powell's Toryism, even though this was evident in *Dance* to any reader with even a general knowledge of politics. The political schemes of the negatively portrayed leftist characters in *Dance* are viewed with contempt. The reader of the *Journals* waits to see how Powell himself will act when confronted with the burden of approval from the power holders, as he is invited to two dinners with the prime minister and other prominent intellectuals. What is impressive is the extent to which Powell is able to forcefully express his own political views but leave the reader in no doubt that any single individual's political opinions are not to be taken as authoritative. There is a coruscating mixture of clear and unstinting admiration for Thatcher as a person and the principles for which she stood, balanced with a clear skepticism toward the conclusive moral effectiveness of any party-political stance, even the right one. Powell was never the sort of Great Writer whose mission in life was to promote the Great Doctrine. Lady Violet Powell, in her introduction to the first volume of the *Journals,* captures this mix with precision when she says of the prime minister's dinners, "Afterwards, the London Library provides never failing solace." (One of the most winning features of the *Journals* is when the author admits he is exhausted or tired by a social occasion, not manifesting an eager-beaverish, plodding, propagandistic refusal to admit that the exertions of life, whether happy or sad, take their toll.) The genealogical researches Powell conducted at the London Library, in their quirky, unmoored puttering, are as independent of ideology, polemics, and power as anything possibly can be. The dinners with the prime minister are not for Powell a culminating personal triumph as they might be for some others, as is revealed by a passage at the end of this entry (27–28 March 1985), written after Powell had gone to London to see not only Margaret Thatcher but also his friends the authors John and Hilary Spurling and the painter Adrian Daintrey (in some respects the model for Barnby, who, characteristically, dies far earlier in fiction than in life):

> All the same, I felt a bit upset on the way to Paddington. Forty-eight hours spent in London seemed to have provided an allegorical vision of life: the young Spurlings (one feels in a sense "deep in the earth, forever young," like Tannhauser and the Queen of Love), their new house in a pioneering district

for intellectuals, abstract pictures, latest literary talk; then Downing Street, the world of power, up to a point Learning and Letters (so far as a few writers, reinforced by academics and Life Peers could be held to represent those)—The Charterhouse, memories of an artist's career, bohemian goings-on, the beau monde, love, lust, decay, death. One was reminded of that strange 18th century dyptich that used to hang in Gerald Reitlinger's house, Woodgate (where Adrian so often stayed, tho' he always abused The Squire, up hill and down dale, particularly when they shared a house in Bramerton Street, Chelsea) which symbolized the Human Lot. This also amusingly illustrated by how the 18th century regarded the 17th century:

My father and my mother that go stooping to your grave,
Pray tell me in this world what good I may expect to have?
My Son, the good you may expect is all forlorn,
Men do not gather grapes from off a thorn.

The import of this, to reduce it to the crudest possible level, is that a journey to the seat of political power, even to meet a much and appropriately admired politician, has its limits when such an event is displayed against the full canvas of humanity. Just as no era perceives its predecessor correctly, no current eras can merely be summed up by who holds political power in it. Very little amounts to anything in concrete terms, even if the journey, and the people encountered within it, are more than worth the while. There are always the old and the young, the ambitious and the decaying, and these constants of life, with the same mixture of exactitude and myth as the signs of the Zodiac, provide a harmonious and reassuring, if hardly dithyrambic, backbeat against which the thuds of politics, good or bad, are not omnipotent.

As with Jenkins in *Dance* and with Powell's autobiographical persona in his memoirs, there is little sense of change or development in the *Journals;* even the inevitable deterioration in Powell's health, other than in a few pages at the end of 1990, rarely makes an obtrusive impact. But the tone of the *Journals* does shift slightly at the beginning of 1986, when Powell is no longer writing *The Fisher King* and the *Journals* became the primary imaginative vehicle for Powell. The first demonstration of this shift occurs in the 27 January 1986 entry, in which Powell meditates on the interaction between literary achievement and social climbing in the writers of his generation. He is motivated to do this by reading a biography of the minor painter Rex Whistler, written by Whistler's brother Laurence. Reflections on an entire generation are occasioned by reflecting on Whistler, whom Powell only briefly encountered in person:

> One has impression of an intense narcissism . . . perfect knowledge of which side his bread was buttered, superhuman free-loading, all brought to his highest pitch, almost more than a touch of male bitchery, yet on the whole a nice nature. I can now see why, at that particular moment of my life, I found him utterly intolerable. I don't think I exactly got him wrong, and later would myself probably have been less censorious. All this caused reflections on other contemporaries who, from unpromising background, took the beau monde by storm; similarities, differences, parallel with Rex Whistler.
>
> Of course everyone has their own personal criteria as to definitions of social success or failure, for that matter what

constitutes being "smart"; beau monde wide term, which to some small extent one might be said to live in, or have lived in, oneself, at least relatively smart occasions from time to time. What I mean in these special instances examined here, is perhaps those who saw regularly, over a given period of some length. persons of a smart world, relatively speaking, with whom they had no particular tastes in common; just saw each other because they were "smart," anyway smartish. To underline fallibility of such judgments, it should be added that someone staying with Gerry Wellington (seventh Duke) was unwise enough to refer to a woman they both knew as "smart." Gerry drew in his breath slightly. "A nice woman, certainly. But smart? I don't recollect ever having seen her at the Sutherlands, or the Ancasters."

One just notes this to underline that there are no more than a few outstanding examples of individuals known to myself, holding cards comparable with Whistler's, ending by passing fair amount of their time with people who may not have been smart in Gerry Wellington's eyes (in which presumably high birth had to be one concomitant), but might have been held so by less exacting standards. Nothing absolute is intended.

There is almost an element of sociological study here, of an academic exercise deliberately and disinterestedly undertaken. The fact that these writers, artists, and photographers felt that they needed to leverage their talent in order to gain some sort of literal social position is at once contemptible, pathetic, and tragic; Powell looks on, appalled and chagrined, but his sympathy is also with the aspirers, as their belief in themselves and their own principles is obviously so slight and that is to be pitied. In

addition, as subtle indications in the first and sixth books of
Dance aver, the entire concentration on the arts as a field of
effort owed a lot to the trauma of the First World War and the
subsequent disillusionment with more military and athletic exertions.[6] An easy moralism is as much out of the question as a
laissez-faire acceptance of dishonorable and scheming conduct.
There is also the question of how artists, in a society where art
does in and of itself not make one a lot of money, should maintain themselves financially. These sorts of dilemmas of artistic
upward mobility are particularly interesting in that they do not
really occupy much of *Dance;* in fact, the character most associated with them is St. John Clarke, from very much the former
generation. Perhaps if Mark Members had been a more significant character in *Dance,* this sort of material would have been
more stressed; but he is not, and it is not. In *Dance,* Jenkins does
not talk much about his relationships with his contemporaries
as writers, aside from thinly referenced figures such as Members, whose identity as writer in any event comes into the definition of his character only peripherally. Powell's description of
Cyril Connolly is an apt example. Connolly,

> devoted to mystique of smartness, at same time never
> achieved it himself, in spite of bringing off fantastic benefac-
> tions of various sorts (financial, etc), stretching from, say
> Maurice Bowra to Harry Goldsmid. That (getting money out
> of people) is something rather different, an art of its own.
> Connolly's inability to put up with sustained smart life
> largely owing to his own cantankerousness, even his intelli-
> gence, was to some extent a fact (on the whole doing him
> credit) that he could not mask such characteristics in himself,
> notwithstanding fantastic powers of ingratiation, if he de-
> sired to exercise them.

Connolly's lack of a kind of lulling smoothness is to his intellectual credit (indeed, among Powell's contemporaries, Connolly emerges from the *Journals* as one whom Powell most respects).[7] Powell is not so carried away by the vastness of the opportunities open to his generation that he is unaware of the ethical temptations, and aesthetic lapses, of taking advantage of such opportunities. These studies of the interaction of art and social "success" is an exercise in rigorous aesthetic judgment, especially as, though he does not at all anatomize his own case, Powell is also measuring himself. It would have been all too easy, Powell implies, for him to succumb, Zouch-like, to the lure of being the artist among the social grandees, and residing in that position, not in the practice of art. Powell (again, very implicitly, as this is nowhere said overtly in the passage) kept away from this by dedication, by applying himself to his work and to the nuts and bolts of reviewing and reading the books of others, and by a sense of vigilant standoffishness, which pervades all his writing, in particular this journal entry. It is a kind of watchfulness that distances the writer from what he is describing, not out of coolness or remoteness, but out of a desire to serve as a representative of the reader. It does not accept, as a perquisite, any badge of adherence to a given situation (whether it be participation in social revolution, conversion to religious dogma, or fawning over a titled aristocrat) that would catapult the reader into a situation in which their moral freedom would be compromised. At the end of the 27 January 1986 entry, Powell mentions that the pattern of the individuals he had just laid out was clear to him, though he was uncertain whether it would be clear to "the reader." This solicitation of the reader is remarkable. Up to this point in the *Journals*—there have been nearly four years' worth of entries already—we have had no sense of whom the journals are being written for, or whether they are being written for eventual publication at all. Here, we see Powell had a reader in mind, on top of that a reader not necessarily acquainted with the predicament of his generation or the social forms of twentieth-century England. The reader here is someone far in the future, reading Powell as a novelist, not as a social historian or society writer, and trying to know what to make of his work. The sense of futurity or posterity in the *Journals,* though rarely mentioned this explicitly, is strong. Powell is concerned about his reputation not for the short term, but for the long term, well beyond his own lifetime. The fact that most of the other people mentioned in the *Journals,* at least on the present-day level, are one or two generations younger than Powell also heightened the sense of futurity. When Powell, in speaking to the artist Henry Mee, who must have been fifty or sixty years his junior, hears of the 1980s computer game Daleks (27 November 1989) and dutifully takes this down, we have the sense of a writer projecting himself forward into the future, a couple of generations beyond his own time—all the while stretching back into the past, so that when he says of his father's friend Colonel F. R. Packe that "he was 'Equerry to Princess Beatrice'" (13 July 1992), anyone reading this, necessarily in 1997 or after, will have to jog their mind to realize that the intended referent is not the current Princess Beatrice, already alive at the time the entry was made as she was born in 1988, but the one born in 1857.[8]

It can also be said that the *Journals* are "about" reading. Reading, in fact, has the place in them that the observation of nature, politics, or manners has in other journals. Powell's *Journals* are a rare specimen of the joy of reading and rereading. They are a work by someone for whom reading is a way of life and reading well is second nature. Powell may seem hard on other writers, including many unquestioned greats. But he is approaching the books as a fellow creative writer, saying not "How should this book be written?" but "How might I have written this book"? This does not mean that he is a particularly subjective reader; very few of the collected reviews refer to Powell's own work or to his status as a writer (in other words, an untutored reader picking up the *Daily Telegraph* on any given Thursday and not knowing otherwise who Anthony Powell was would not have gotten the impression that the reviewer was a "great writer" from the review itself), and he writes of modern literature with an impartiality more typical of the academic than of the practicing writer doubling as a literary journalist. The entire idea of creative writing is that a creative writer will perceive experience (including his or her reading of other writers) in a nonstandard way. To expect a ratification of consensus from Powell is unrealistic not only with respect to his own peculiar tastes and temperament but also with respect to any writer of serious imaginative aspiration. It would have suppressed his own feelings; if he had, say, been nicer about E. M. Forster, he would not have been telling the truth, and certainly Powell's adverse critics, who if anything tend to prize emotional authenticity more highly, at least in sloganeering terms, than did Powell, would not have wanted him to suppress the truth. If he had done so, it would have robbed us of the unpredictability and buoyantly opinionated verve of Powell's reflective entries, which reach something of a peak in 1988, where, for many pages on end, there is nothing but intellectual exhilaration, as Powell ranges over an incredibly wide ground with inspired rigor.

One of the major differences between *Dance* and the *Journals* is that *Dance*, subject to the need for narrative schematization, and written largely in the 1960s and the 1970s, when the

Left was at its height of cultural influence, does (although not unfairly) tend to concentrate on the menace from the Left. The odd thing is that when Powell, in the 1980s, becomes more even-handed in his criticism, his left-wing castigators—for example, Christopher Hitchens, who sees the *Journals* as conveying the attitudes of a "disaffected country squire"—do not notice it.[9] This utterly ignores Powell's critiques of Waugh (10 March 1991) and Muggeridge (14 November 1990) as being, to the extent that the limited rubrics of "right" and "left" have any real meaning, too right-wing. Powell criticizes Muggeridge as manifesting "humbug" and Waugh as displaying "religious mania." In one of the latest entries in the *Journals,* 2 November 1992, he chastises the poet Philip Larkin for racist and anti-working-class statements that, unlike other commentators, he will not dismiss as products of a curmudgeonly persona. And there is this remarkable entry for 15 May 1984:

> I returned home in morning feeling shade exhausted. Some weeks ago something called the Ingersoll Foundation, Rockwell, Illinois, wrote to say I was under consideration for the Foundation's T. S. Eliot Award for Creative Writing ($15,000), which, if bestowed, involved going to Chicago to receive the Award, and making a speech to members of the Foundation. It was added that, in special circumstances, this could be undertaken by a surrogate. Various points at once arose. In the first place I really cannot face the journey to Chicago these days. Formerly a few drinks would have got one through, nowadays I am too old for that, quite apart from fact that it would disrupt work with jet-lag for weeks on return. In addition, I am not clear what this evidently Right Wing organization stands for (defined in their explanatory

pamphlets as "Judaeo-Christian Standards" and the "Ten Commandments"), which, even if broadly speaking sympathetic to a "traditional Tory," I certainly should not be prepared to make a speech recommending, tho' perhaps implicit (rather than explicit) in my books. Also one certainly wants to avoid anything of fascist flavour. I outlined the above in letter of reply.

Actually, the Ingersoll Foundation, though conservative, is a legitimate organization and publishes an interesting journal, *Chronicles,* to which Powell contributed an article (the lecture given on his behalf in lieu of his actually going to pick up the award, which he eventually accepted with enthusiasm). But Powell's initial, vigilant skepticism demands attention. It shows that, for him, there were enemies to the Right. The Right was not to be given carte blanche. This means something beyond mere politics, because so many people who write about literature, especially literary journalists, assume that the purpose, or at least the message, of literature is to give one or another political position carte blanche, to, in a way, transparently represent one sort of politics and exclude another. It is key to the process of understanding Anthony Powell to realize that his approach is not only too skeptical, but too serene, too self-contained, and too idiosyncratic for this.

Powell does not just interpret the outside world in the *Journals.* He redirects the way we see his own work. It is not overdoing it to say that, without the *Journals,* the interpretation of Powell in the twenty-first century would have been very different. Indeed, the *Journals* helped this interpretation occur at all, not only in keeping his name alive and in the reviews sections (at least the British ones) but also in providing new rationales, above those already existent, to read his work. Powell's own perspective—more referential, more social, more bound up with a variety of traditions and categories—is radically different from any other critiques of his work, most of which, aside from mere journalism, adhered to formalist paradigms. This is not to say that an author has any special interpretive control over his work. A writer is no more an authoritative commentator on his own work than a general is an authoritative historian of a war in which he has been in command. An author has no especial authority over his or her work once it is published. Once the product has been sent forth, it is the reader's as much as the author's, something Powell recognized many times; as a former publisher, he always retained a publisher's consciousness of the many different stages involved in the production and consumption of a work of literature, avoiding an egoistic or heroic concentration on "the author." Nonetheless, Powell's comments on his own work in the *Journals* in a way served to refound the entire tradition of Powell criticism, even after so many articles and books had been written. Even if the comments on *Dance* in the *Journals* were not written by "Anthony Powell" they still would have totally reoriented our sense of the work.

The other writer to which Powell devoted a considerable amount of time, William Shakespeare, will not have the way he is read so drastically affected by the comments in the *Journals*. But the constant presence of Shakespeare therein is an intriguing one. Powell's Shakespeare comments seem to be lightweight at first, especially when compared to academic Shakespeare criticism. But when read in conjunction with the plays, they are astonishingly perceptive, pithily arriving at insights unachieved by more voluminous commentators. Just one example—one mocked by the reviewer of *Journals, 1987–1989,* in the *Times*

Literary Supplement—is "Had Mariana inherited the moated grange" (27 March 1987), an inquiry about the forlorn once-betrothed of Angelo in *Measure for Measure*. It certainly violates the "how many children had Lady Macbeth" dictum, but the reviewer meant to suggest that Powell was too preoccupied with social status, and in a case in which Shakespeare, admitted by all to have been preoccupied with social status at times in his work, seemingly is not. Among well-known Shakespeare critics, Powell's perspective bears a resemblance to that classical violator of the aforementioned Lady Macbeth dictum, A. C. Bradley, especially in the notes at the end of Bradley's book *Shakespearean Tragedy*. A typical Powell comment on Shakespeare can be seen in this passage (24–28 October 1986):

> I reread *Antony & Cleopatra*, one of my favourites. I had forgotten how long the play continues after Antony's death. It is a good moment when Cleopatra attempts to swindle Octavian in assessment of her property. After she is caught out, Octavian (cf. the Unjust Steward) agrees she was right to try and preserve something for herself (construction much used in 7th century, now objected to by pedants ignorant of past phraseology, which avoids repeated preposition). Rereading *Macbeth*. Typical piece of donnish rubbish that Shakespeare did not write the Witches passages, when they were probably the bits of the play he enjoyed writing most ("Paddock calls, etc"), tho' of course un-Shakespearian in the sense that "To be or not to be" might be called Shakespearian. One would agree Hecate may be an interpolation.

Powell's comments on Shakespeare do not necessarily imply that he is putting himself on the same level as the man from

Stratford; he is giving us Shakespeare as an individual who, whatever his nonpareil talents, makes the same choices in his writing that any writer has to make. There is an ease with the material, a confidence in the commentator's own relation to it, that permits him to rove widely and speculatively, but do so concisely and economically, not requiring long passages of exposition. He seizes upon the key points, transmits them to the reader as soon as possible, and then proceeds to another matter. This ability to spot just what most people are later to find interesting, a trait already noted with respect to the memoirs, is if anything even more salient in the *Journals*. The people mentioned in the *Journals* have, in many cases, become more prominent since the time Powell wrote about them. Tina Brown (10 September 1983) went on to her various transatlantic editorial positions, Andrew Motion (14 April 1983) became poet laureate, and Jay Parini (22 May 1985) became a prominent man of letters. This is not to mention Hilary Spurling becoming an acclaimed biographer and V. S. Naipaul winning the Nobel Prize (happily, contrary to Powell's suspicion [*Journals*, 30 December 1989], that he never would). This is unlike other writers' diaries (Edmund Wilson's name springs to mind), in which the pictured personnel seem to have become less prominent and interesting with time. This is not just a tribute to Powell's social acuity but to his powers of observation, the same powers that made him such a fine social historian in his fiction and such an astute observer of literary history in his criticism.

This entire spectacle of reputations shifting is of course as relevant to the diarist himself as to any of his subjects, and this is tacitly acknowledged, if only rarely mentioned on the surface, by the *Journals*. Powell was anxious for his work to gain more visibility, particularly in terms of a television adaptation (which he lived to see finally done, in 1997, although Powell's intuition that the adaptation would have had more impact in the 1980s is probably correct). But is there such a thing as too much visibility? Is the retrieval of an author's reputation always a positive development for that author? An article by the British journalist Geoffrey Wheatcroft (who is mentioned at *Journals,* 26 July 1991) in the September 2002 edition of *Harper's* raises this issue. Wheatcroft opines that "it may now be Kipling's turn to eclipse Yeats."[10] Powell would agree with Wheatcroft's judgment 100 percent. One can infer by his near-total silence on Yeats that he disapproved of the Irish poet (especially, we may assume, in his Irish nationalist politics, although the two writers shared interests in the occult). Powell certainly highly praised Kipling, calling him at one point the British writer with the greatest sense of responsibility and sacrifice since Shakespeare, and referring to him frequently in memoirs, journals, and criticism. (Powell's love for Kipling is only really visible in his *non-fiction;* had we read only the fiction, we would know Kipling only as a children's writer read—unperceptively—by a failed junior infantry officer.) But the bombast, the sense of accounts settled, the almost Orwellian aura of rewritten history in Wheatcroft's comment cannot have gone down well with somebody who distanced himself from those who interpreted books in a "particular committed way" (*Verdicts,* 130) and cherished understatement and self-effacement as much as did Powell. What Wheatcroft's remark conjures, of course, is an equivalent rehabilitation for Powell such as the one Wheatcroft mounts on behalf of Kipling. In place of Yeats, perhaps, as the old-style modernist to be discarded, we might suggest Woolf, or better yet Joyce. After all, we might think, haven't we had enough of Joyce? Is not his studied avant-gardism so "yesterday"? Is not it

time "now" for Powell to "eclipse" Joyce? No more Joyce! Up
with Powell! Sound the trumpets! But can one imagine Powell
enthusiastic about a process of rehabilitation so grandiose, so
overbearing? Would he have wanted the trumpets to sound?[11]

In Wheatcroft's defense, there is the sense of distinctions
being made overly black and white for an American audience all
too ready to accept such distinctions. There is no need, in an
introductory book on the work of Anthony Powell to take a
journalistic statement like Wheatcroft's with excessive seriousness. As a statement, it is on the order of Widmerpool's pro-
nouncement, before the Huntercombe ball in *Buyer's Market,*
that "the nationalists have got to Pekin," this supposition re-
porting changes of power or status in various parts of the world
will quantifiably change the times we live in over and above the
actual impact of the event. Powell's attitude toward all these
statements was that this too would pass, and this sane, healthy
reluctance, as mentioned in the Monkey Temple episode of
Strangers, to discharge "inward discontents, rage, contempt,
despair" (*Strangers,* 193), is pervasive in Powell's work. But
now Powell himself has left the scene, and we are faced with the
problem of a writer, severely and unfairly underrated in his own
time, for whom the most plausible scenario for heightened visibility is to be revalued just the way Wheatcroft is revaluing
Kipling.

So the entire scenario merits a second look. Just as Kipling
is to replace Yeats, so could Powell replace Joyce or Woolf or
E. M. Forster. One could dismiss these latter three writers as
avatars of a misbegotten meliorist modernism, as overrated by
an (counter-) establishment intent on heightening febrile innovation, and rewrite literary history, just like that. Despite his pronounced lack of respect for Woolf and Forster, Powell would

not want to see them shoved to the side for political reasons—the opening letter in his long correspondence with Congressman John Monagan was a demurral from how he was quoted on Forster in a newspaper interview, that even though he did not like Forster's work, he did not want to be "totalitarian" about such things (letter to the Hon. John Monagan, 14 March 1969). Even more, Powell would not want his work to replace Joyce, whose fiction, especially *Ulysses,* he admired and reread (his comments on Joyce at *Journals,* 20 June 1986: "extremely good . . . exceptional command of language . . . extremely funny"). Moreover, he particularly admired Joyce's lower-middle-class Irishness over his experimental technique, notably, as Powell was more of an experimentalist than he was a lower-middle-class Irishman. Even with respect to Joyce's language, Powell speaks, certainly not without praise, of Kipling's "passionate interest in words and language" (*Verdicts,* 131), which he compares to Joyce's. Kipling is seen as "one of the great revolutionaries" (131), a category in which Powell makes clear Joyce belongs as well. Powell thus cannot be used as a tool to roll back Joycean innovation. It is regrettable that Powell's reputation is caught between the Scylla of reviled, or even refined, obscurity and the Charybdis of a "revivalist" mentality (*Journals,* 14 November 1990).

Powell's novels hint that there are right and wrong ways to revive reputations. Mr. Deacon's rediscovery in *Hearing Secret Harmonies* seems cyclical and natural; its occurrence is part of the triumph of time, even of an spontaneous, or at least unpremeditated, healing process. Grigham's deliberately engineered revival of Winterwade in *Wheel,* however, is forced, an act of cultural aggression. Mr. Deacon may be no better a painter than Winterwade is a writer, but Deacon's revival is conducted in a

more humane and civilized manner. A Powell revival is undoubtedly on the agenda—but it should be like Deacon's, not Winterwade's, even though as an imaginative figure Powell is far superior
to either. Any potential Powell revivalists should take heed
of what Powell said about Kipling: "His books present at one
moment, one view of life; at the next, another" (*Verdicts*, 130).

Powell's reaction to the revealed failures of his own century
was not a strident or triumphalist one. Powell, for instance,
observes the fall of communism in 1989 and after (mattering
not just objectively but because it relates so much to the political content of *Dance*) with a sort of mute stoicism. He was
certainly aware of it, unlike his former friend Malcolm Muggeridge, for whom, sadly, "the breakup of Communism under
Mikhail Gorbachev came too late for him to grasp what was
happening."[12] Powell might, with justice, not be begrudged a
small or even a large chortle at how correct his political views
had turned out to be in worldly terms. But the only example
coming anything close to this is on the death of Roy Fuller. Powell mentions that Fuller, who held left-wing views at least for
some of his career, "must have been surprised by recent demol-
ishing of Lenin's statues" (28 September 1991). But clearly what
is most important here is his friendship for Fuller and respect for
his poetry and fiction, the latter of which he is at pains to speak
well of throughout the memoirs and *Journals*. Fuller's one-time
daffy politics are a tolerable eccentricity much like so many others—they are more in the line of Erridge's or Quiggin's politics
than of Widmerpool's, and there is a difference between how
these three *Dance* characters are seen by the narrative, even
though all were Marxists and, at least for a time, pro-Soviet.

As with his own characters going back to Vernon Passenger
in *From a View*, Powell is not triumphalist or vindictive *even*

when he is proven right. As much as it is desirable that Powell should be read and valued more in this new century, if he is valued only in Right-revivalist terms, it would be an aesthetic disaster, similar to what would have happened if twentieth-century critics had seen Charles Dickens and Thomas Hardy merely as surly left-wing agitators with a grudge against the maldistribution of wealth. It must once again be made clear that Powell was a man of the twentieth century who, however much he regretted some of its historical development, was happy living in that century. For his characters in *Dance,* the temptation of nostalgia was vintage cars, not neo-Victorian imperialist fervor. Unlike Valentine Beals in *Fisher,* Powell did not write historical novels, nor pageants of traditional, or even revisionary, Englishness, and he did not wallow in nostalgia. Powell spoke of Muggeridge, a man much more prone to Right revivalism, as "humbug" (14 December 1990), the same term Lady Donners used of Widmerpool in *Hearing Secret Harmonies.* There is another problem here, in that the moralism of Wheatcroft's comment, and hypothetical Right-revivalist comments elevating Powell over more canonical modernists, the sense that the sprightly, neo-imperial Kiplingites have it all over the dour, passé-modernist Yeatsians, is reminiscent of just the sensibility against which Powell particularly defined himself—that of the Bloomsbury group. The essential self-concept of this group was that they were always right, their opponents always wrong, and that this was the result of a superior personal or collective virtue. A similar combat to Wheatcroft's envisioned Yeatsian-Kiplingite shootout staged between, say, Powellians and Joyceans, may make a substantial amount of Powell's appreciative readers as reluctant to participate energetically in the conflict as was the loutish Private Sayce in a hundred times more worthwhile a struggle in *Valley of Bones.*

Faced with such threatened reductiveness, Powell might well repeat his advice from the bracing and valedictory Monkey Temple passage in *Strangers:* "Better to remain calm; try to remember that all epochs have had to suffer assaults on commonsense and common decency, art and letters, honour and wit, courage and order, good manners and free speech, privacy and scholarship; even if sworn enemies of these abstractions (often wearing the disguise of their friends) seem unduly numerous in contemporary society" (193–94). The "all epochs" signifies Powell's classicism, the "wearing the disguise of their friends' " his skepticism, qualities that always have an emollient effect on any statement, correct or incorrect, right or wrong, which might tend toward the polemical. Note though the assumption that "art and letters" are as ipso facto positive attributes as decency, honor, wit, and courage. As seen as early as Widmerpool's crucial *absence* from the Theocritus scene in *A Question of Upbringing,* in Powell's world, no one with any interest in the arts is totally irredeemable. This is a belief Powell professes with surprising straightforwardness and even innocence; he wears his heart on his sleeve here, as he more than occasionally does not while traversing other, more furrowed polemical routes.

These subtleties are important not only to the political perception of Powell but also to the twenty-first-century canonicity of all the *Brideshead* generation, or second-generation British modernists, or whatever we choose to call them—Powell, Waugh, Greene. One feels that, if the culture permits us to read these writers at all, we will have to read them as Right-revivalist, neo-Bloomsburian receptacles of rediscovered or revisioned political virtue—in a manner certainly moral or political but not aesthetic. A line from Powell's criticism, in fact, Powell quoting verbatim from A. N. Wilson's excellent biography of Tolstoy, comes to mind: "[Tolstoy's] moral aspirations—

as they occur in his fiction and in his life—are moving, while his moral presumption is so repulsive" (*Review,* 429). Moral presumption—a quality very different from morality, or, as Wilson puts it, "moral aspirations," of which Powell is in strong favor —and literature coexist uneasily at best. The discerning reader might well rather read no writer at all than the best possible writer in a morally presumptuous way. Understanding Anthony Powell, understanding his generation and his entire literary impact, requires a subtler, softer, more modulated perspective, far from any unearned moralistic assumptions.

This perspective on Powell needs no external provider. It can come from Powell himself—namely, the *Journals.* It is distressing that the *Journals* are not, as of 2004, commercially available in the United States, and that their in-print status in Great Britain does not seem perpetually assured. The *Journals* are endlessly entertaining, and because of Powell's unusual interest in people half or even a quarter of his age, they mention individuals still likely to be active well into the twenty-first century. But the *Journals* also possess a purely literary importance. Not only can they act as an adjunct and vade mecum to Powell's work far better than any secondary source, including this one, but they can give readers a full glimpse of how subtle, observant, and, for all his fierce convictions, unprejudiced a writer he was. We must have a greater appreciation of Powell as practitioner of prose, not just storyteller, of observer of the scene around him, not just creator of unforgettable characters.

Dance is obviously Powell's major achievement. But it is not his only one. Powell's comments on *Dance* in the 10 January 1989 entry gives the impression that he feels, despite his perception of his own success in the twelve-volume sequence, that any concession to novelistic contrivance is a compromise; in that way, *Afternoon Men* is his purest novel. But the *Journals* themselves have some of the unstructured randomness of Powell's first novel; they are replete with thickly strewn incident, although they are easier to read as their world is our own. The *Journals* are a surprising combination of pensée, aphorism, sketch, and familiar essay. The chronology of time, the forward movement of the dates, is virtually the only narrative stay against the spree of facts, references, observations going back and forward in time; the calendrical progress is like a girder staying the anarchic flux of actuality. Powell, in *Messengers,* speaks of his early works as possessing a lyricism that the more narratively coherent *Dance* inferentially lacked; the late *Journals* are infused with just this sort of lyricism, to the point of including dramatic and exact nature descriptions, such as of a place near his house: "it has grown up a lot since I was last round there, the woods looking marvellous in the wet autumn afternoon" (20 October 1992).

There is a kind of heedless, responsive, though intellectually disciplined, ecstasy in Powell's response to nature that extends to his response to books: "I also reread the Gerard Manley Hopkins Selection with pleasure. Hopkins in principle is not very much up my street, but I find him a marvellous poet, fascinating innovations of language. Jesuitism all but did in his poetry entirely. If he had kept clear of it (probably impossible of Roman Catholicism entirely) he would have written much more, become immense influence on the poets of the Nineties" (19 June 1988). Though Hopkins, as a Roman Catholic religious, a convert, and a Jesuit to boot, is indeed not much up Powell's street, Powell does not quarrel with the integrity of Hopkins's own religious beliefs, recognizing that, no matter what, this poet would have been drawn to the doctrines of

Roman Catholicism. Powell sees through any question of religious or philosophical differences and goes straight (the "find" is no accident, as reading is a kind of quest, a seeking, for Powell) to the heart of Hopkins's talent. The use of "marvelous," in most other hands a gratuitously superlative adjective, is genuine in Powell's, as the sense of wonder resonates with the clang of the reader's empirical contact with the poetry (note that the same word was used of the woods in the passage quoted earlier). This is an example of the pure joy of reading—motivated not by prestige, remuneration, or ideology, or even a self-congratulatory sense of aesthetic superiority, but totally for its own sake.

The *Journals* also reveal Powell's intense kinship with animals—the sheep grazing outside his house, the goat to whom Powell "talks," and of course his series of cats (Powell's Cornish Rex cat Trelawney is more deeply mourned than many of the human friends who pass on in the course of the *Journals*). Powell, like his character Blanche Tolland, "meets animals on their own terms" (*Harmonies*, 8). There is a solidarity with nature, with insensate phenomena, an attunement to silence, to what there is to be seen, away from the hubbub, the noise, the chitchat, the hum of the public world.[13] This exhibits a different sense of that phrase, "acceptance world": a knowing passivity, a trust in what is actually there. Retrospection—the ability to construct an account that imposes meaning on experience through memory—is both the blessing and curse of fiction. The *Journals* are different; they simmer with a vibrant immediacy; they present experience as such.

With scrupulous accuracy, Powell records developments concerning people he will probably never meet again and who are of no practical significance to him. If a reader will pursue, in other sources, any information mentioned in the *Journals,* she or he will find that Powell has not only gotten the information right, but has miraculously isolated the key point, the nub about a given individual as it has been revealed later in time. As the *Journals* proceed, this striving for accuracy—a striving not burdened by grasping after greater certainties—becomes a mission in itself. It is a happy selflessness, an ascetic enjoyment. In writing about his friend, the poet and historian Robert Conquest, Powell speaks of him as "one of the few—as one gets older one realizes how few they are—to take an interest in extraneous things (e.g. Roman Britain) for their own sake" (*Strangers,* 163). The outstanding denizens of Powell's world are the few—such as Lord Huntercombe chipping open Mrs. Foxe's cabinet—who take an interest in extraneous things. The *Journals* show again and again that Powell was one of them.

Notes

1. See George Lilley and Keith C. Marshall, ed., *Proceedings of the First Anthony Powell Conference* (London: Anthony Powell Society, 2001), 116.

2. Robert L. Selig, *Time and Anthony Powell: A Critical Study* (Rutherford, N.J.: Fairleigh Dickinson University Press, 1991), 13.

3. See Lilley and Marshall, ed. *Proceedings,* 24–25.

4. Lynette Felber, "The Fictional Narrator as Historian: Ironic Detachment and the Project of History in Anthony Powell's *A Dance to the Music of Time.*" *CLIO: A Journal of Literature, History, and the Philosophy of History* 22, no. 1 (fall 1992): 21–35.

5. Robert K. Morris, *The Novels of Anthony Powell* (Pittsburgh: University of Pittsburgh Press, 1968), 74.

6. See G. U. Ellis, *Twilight on Parnassus: A Survey of Post-War Fiction and Pre-War Criticism* (London: Joseph, 1939). The wars are different, the fiction resulting from the first but the criticism, in Ellis's view, foreboding the second, even though the time period is the same in each case.

7. Jay Parini, "Anthony Powell, 1905–2000," *Sewanee Review* 109, no. 3 (summer 2001): 437.

8. Ian Ousby, *The Cambridge Guide to Literature in English* (Cambridge: Cambridge University Press, 1993), 205.

9. See Lucy Apsley Hutchinson, *Memoirs of the Life of Colonel Hutchinson, with a Fragment of Autobiography/Lucy Hutchinson,* ed. N. H. Keeble (London: Dent; Rutland, Vt.: Charles E. Tuttle, 1995). The officer in question is named Joseph Widmerpoole. Widmerpool/Widmerpole is a well-established Nottinghamshire name and crops up in other contexts; for example, the wife of the Elizabethan explorer Sir Martin Frobisher was Elizabeth Widmerpole. Other names on *Dance* (e.g., Trapnel) also may well have seventeenth-centruy sources.

10. Edith Wharton, *A Backward Glance* (New York: Touchstone, 1998), 201.

11. See Felicien Marceau, *Balzac and His World,* trans. Derek Coltman (New York: Orion Press, 1966), 11.

12. For the story from Muggeridge's perspective and a substantial excerpt from the review, see Richard Ingrams, *Muggeridge: The Biography* (London: HarperCollins, 1995), 195, which also contains one of the most blunt assessments of Powell's alleged snobbery.

13. When Christopher Hitchens and Tariq Ali debated at Georgetown University in April 2002 on the response of the Left to the 2001 terrorist attacks (see Michael Berube, "Ali vs. Hitchens: Battle on the Left," *Chronicle of Higher Education,* 3 May 2002, B13), an interesting sidelight was that both these feuding leftists were acknowledged fans of Anthony Powell!

14. In her letter to John Monagan (9 July 1990), Lady Violet Powell imputed Waugh's behavior to a "mixture of malice and silliness."

15. For a typical assessment of the television series as out of step with the times (specifically the election of Tony Blair and the mourning for Princess Diana), see Mark Lawson, "Second Thoughts: Out of Step, Out of Time," *Guardian,* 16 October 1997, 10. These sorts of reviews, combined with the series' length in a sound-bite era, no doubt helped keep the television films off the air in the United States, though they were shown in such unlikely venues as Serbia in 2001.

16. For the impact of end-of-the-century lists, see Joanne Jacobs, "A Lot of Great Books—and One Clever Gimmick," *Denver Post,* 14 August 1998. The end-of-the-century lists also had more distant reverberations. A portrait of Powell, by the American painter Duncan Hannah, was used for the U.S. paperback cover of William Boyd's 2003 *Any Human Heart,* a novel purporting to be the diaries of Logan Mountstuart, a fictional member of Powell's literary generation, and indicates the growing comprehension of Powell as a literary figure. Also, Brian Evenson, in *Review of Contemporary*

Fiction, fall 2003, page 139, says, "Powell is worthy of a second look." This was the general sentiment fertilized by the end-of-the-century lists.

17. There was a previous Anthony Powell Society, headed by Nancy Cutbirth of Western Michigan University, and also involving the late William Stone of Indiana University, Northwest, mentioned in the *Journals* at 9 June 1987; Stone died on 8 February 2000. In the 1980s, this society briefly published an irregular newsletter, *Anthony Powell Communications.*

18. See Martin Seymour-Smith, *Funk and Wagnall's Guide to Modern World Literature* (New York: Funk and Wagnalls, 1973), ix.

19. An index of the way the obituaries propelled Powell to more canonical status is that, in the 1999 list of "Notable Writers of the Present" as provided by the *World Almanac* (Mahwah, N.J.: World Almanac Books, 1998), 344–45, Powell is not mentioned, but in the list provided by the 2001 edition of prominent writers of the past (Mahwah, N.J.: World Almanac Books, 2000), 341, he is included. I know at least two very well-read people who had not heard of Powell before reading the *New York Times* obituary of him.

20. Humphrey Carpenter evinces a similar concern about Evelyn Waugh's latter-day reputation when he says of Waugh at the conclusion of *The Brideshead Generation: Evelyn Waugh and His Friends* (London: Weidenfeld and Nicolson, 1989), "Whether a resurgence of political Conservatism on a popular scale, accompanied by a return to traditional values in the arts and in British social life, would seriously have pleased him must, however, be gravely open to doubt. All his professional life, he refused to go along with the majority. . . . It is hard to imagine him delighting . . . in the fact that the Century of the Common Man have evolved into the Century of Get Rich Quick." True for Waugh with respect to the 1980s, these admirably expressed sentiments of Carpenter's are doubly true for Powell in the twenty-first century.

Chapter 2

1. Neil Brennan, *Anthony Powell,* rev. ed. (1974; repr., Boston: Twayne, 1995), 42.

2. See Seymour-Smith, *Funk and Wagnall's Guide,* 288–89.

3. As Robert Polhemus says in *Erotic Faith* (Chicago: University of Chicago Press, 1990), the nineteenth-century novel is characterized by an erotic faith consisting of the "conjunction of lover's being . . . representative form . . . and the verbal collage of passions in bodies and texts" (312). In the predecessor book to *Erotic Faith,* the equally valuable *Comic Faith* (Chicago: University of Chicago Press, 1980), Polhemus speaks of the comic novel as consisting of "a process of hope and regeneration," a process that is absent in the undeniably comic *Afternoon Men.* For a general sense of how the modernist novel problematizes its nineteenth-century inheritance, see Robert Caserio, *The Novel in England, 1900–1950* (New York: Twayne, 1999).

4. Christopher Ames, *The Life of the Party: Festive Vision in Modern Fiction* (Athens: University of Georgia Press, 1991), 92.

5. John Gielgud, Playbill for Richard Burton's performance of *Hamlet,* Lunt-Fontanne Theater, New York, New York, 1964, p. 13, Stage Directions column.

6. Evelyn Waugh, *The Essays, Articles, and Reviews of Evelyn Waugh,* ed. Donat Gallagher (Boston: Little, Brown, 1983), 550.

7. John Bowen. "The Melancholy of Modernity: Anthony Powell's Early Fiction." In *Recharting the Thirties,* ed. Patrick Quinn, 102–23 (Selinsgrove, Pa.: Susquehanna University Press, 1997).

8. Morris, *Novels of Anthony Powell,* 74.

9. Some reviewers of Powell's posthumously published *Writer's Notebook* assumed that what is obviously an earlier version of this line, "I want to meet Chesterton, Belloc, writers who really count" (*Writer's Notebook,* 6) meant that Anthony Powell, as a biographical individual, wished to meet those authors instead of the ones he was meeting, and thus evinced more Anglo-Catholic proclivities than visible. But from *Afternoon Men* one sees this is a piece of

quoted dialogue, spoken by a character behind whom the narrative does not throw its full weight. This entire issue—of the worth and the import of what is being said being determined by who is saying it, and in what context—occurs continually in Powell's work. Quoted dialogue cannot be transparently read as verifiable opinion.

10. Harry Defries, *Conservative Party Attitudes towards Jews: 1901–1950* (London: Frank Cass, 2001) notes that those (by no means the majority) of the Conservative Party in this era who were anti-Semitic spotlighted the perceived bolshevism of world Jewry; Verelst, wealthy and clearly no revolutionary, would not qualify as such, nor is Verelst similar to the anti-Semitic portraits in the poetry of T. S. Eliot and Ezra Pound.

11. Max Jakobson, the renowned Finnish diplomat who narrowly lost the election for the United Nations secretary generalship, which lamentably elevated Kurt Waldheim (see Risto E. J. Penttilä, review of Jakobson, *Väkivallan vuodet*, *Foreign Policy* [spring 2000]: 178–80), mentions Powell's depiction of Finland/Estonia in *Venusberg* as an instance of the tendency in the 1920s of Western intellectuals to see the newly independent states as "artificial creations, not to be taken seriously" (Max Jakobson, *Finland in the New Europe*, with a foreword by George Kennan [Westport, Conn.: Praeger, 1998], 21), a response similar to that of many Western intellectuals of the 1990s to most of the newly free former Soviet republics.

12. Neil McEwan, *Anthony Powell* (London: Macmillan, 1991), 28.

13. James Tucker, *The Novels of Anthony Powell* (London: Macmillan, 1976), 29.

14. Hugh Massingberd, *Daydream Believer: Confessions of a Hero-Worshipper* (London: Macmillan, 2001), 182.

15. T. S. Eliot, *Four Quartets* (London: Faber and Faber, 1943), 39.

16. Morris, *Novels of Anthony Powell*, 93.

Chapter 3

1. Waugh, *Essays, Articles, and Reviews,* 548.

2. Herodotus, *The Histories,* trans. Aubrey de Selincourt, rev. A. R. Burn (Harmondsworth: Penguin, 1972), 273–75.

3. Morris, *Novels of Anthony Powell,* 248.

4. John Aubrey, *Brief Lives,* ed. John Buchanan-Brown (Harmondsworth: Penguin, 2000), 294.

5. Wharton, *Backward Glance,* 210.

6. Arthur C. Danto, *Narration and Knowledge* (New York: Columbia University Press, 1985), 362.

7. Thomas C. Wallace, conversation with author, Riverside, Conn., 8 June 2001.

8. Theocritus also crops up in the work of an Etonian contemporary of Powell—Cyril Connolly. William Empson, in a review of A. E. Housman published in *Poetry* magazine in 1937, mentions that Connolly, who had claimed that no classical poet wrote about the lower classes, did not yield when a correspondent mentioned Theocritus, who wrote about poor shepherds in Sicily, claiming that Theocritus "had no serious personal feelings about the lower classes" and that his doing so was in stark contrast to Housman's sentimentality about them. This may indicate that Theocritus, as a poet rather than just a motif, is more present in the Le Bas episode than at first seems the case, although the potential sentimentality precluded is, far from being about the lower classes, about the boys' privileged experience at school itself. See Empson, *Argufying* (Iowa City: University of Iowa Press, 1987), 419.

9. See Lilley and Marshall, *Proceedings,* 53–54.

10. See Matei Calinescu, *Rereading* (New Haven: Yale University Press, 1993), 5.

11. Steve Nimis, *Narrative Semiotics in the Epic Tradition* (Bloomington: Indiana University Press, 1987), 60.

12. In a valuable but little-known source, a response to a questionnaire on the role of classics and classical education in his work

in a 1964 symposium held by the American center-Right classical journal *Arion,* then in the first of its so far two incarnations, Powell admits to the indelible influence of Latin prose patterns on his own but states his knowledge of Greek as inadequate. Powell also speaks of the numerous bores to be found among the classical writers. These answers are not particularly revealing, but they are reassuringly humble in the midst of the pomposity of most (not all) of his fellow contributors. Powell confesses to not knowing very much ancient Greek, although he has a better knowledge of Latin. (Powell's comments on the "academic obscurantism" of operating in Latin rather than in English in the modern age is seen, with regard to the *seventeenth* century, in his remarks on Anthony à Wood's dealings with the notorious Dr. Fell in *Aubrey,* 156–57.) Particularly striking is Powell's response to the question, in the *Arion* symposium, of whether the idea of the *musée imaginaire,* of a polyglot world culture accessible by the mechanical reproduction of texts and images, was liberating or not. Powell replied that it was "liberating." This answer demonstrates that Powell, though a classicist, was not someone who used classicism to buttress an incurious or repressive old-fogeyism. See "Classics and the Man of Letters," *Arion: A Quarterly Journal of Classical Literature* 3, no. 4 (winter 1964): 68. The journal's Notes on Contributors referred to Powell as a "well-know" [*sic*] English writer.

13. See Hugh Massingberd, obituary of Anthony Powell, *Daily Telegraph,* 29 March 2000.

14. The language incidentally does *not* rule out Jenkins himself in a kind of *Roger Ackroyd* solution; and he is also a possible suspect for the "certain extraneous details" (160) that appeared a couple of days later.

15. As many have observed (and as the Roy Fuller parody illustrates), "Iron Aspidistra" is intended to parody the early poems of W. H. Auden; what is not often noted is that Members's later masterpiece, *H-Bomb Eclogue,* probably refers to the "Hiroshima" poems of Dame Edith Sitwell.

16. Hilary Spurling, *Handbook to Anthony Powell's "Dance to the Music of Time"* (London: Heinemann, 1977), reprinted as *Invitation to the Dance* (Boston: Little, Brown, 1977), 312–13. Incidentally, Powell gives the dates in *Journals* at 10 January 1989 as 1927–28.

17. See Jeffrey Perl, *The Tradition of Return* (Princeton, N.J.: Princeton University Press, 1984).

18. Morris, *Novels of Anthony Powell,* 147.

19. Christopher Hitchens, "Powell's Way," *New York Review of Books,* 28 May 1998. Reprinted in *Unacknowledged Legislation: Writers in the Public Sphere* (New York: Verso, 2001).

20. F. Scott Fitzgerald, *The Great Gatsby,* ed. Matthew Bruccoli (New York: Scribner's, 1995), 186. The mention of Flannigan-Fitzgerald in the first book may also be an allusion to Fitzgerald.

21. John Russell, *Anthony Powell, a Quintet, Sextet and War* (Bloomington: Indiana University Press, 1970), 233, says, on Jenkins's similarity to Carraway, that "the two are nearly identical in their way of observing life and in their slow approach to loyalty," although both Carraway and Jenkins seem to like or dislike people rather intuitively.

22. Bruccoli, in Fitzgerald, *Great Gatsby,* vii.

23. Widmerpool certainly achieves a power victory over his former rival in *Acceptance World,* one which in the bedroom wrestling scene involves an almost physical mastery. This sense of victory over Stringham is one eventually cemented in overtly sexual terms when Widmerpool marries Stringham's niece, Pamela Flitton. The television adaptation expresses them well when Widmerpool is putting Stringham to bed, his buffoonery concealing a half-conscious bid for sadistic hegemony. Similarly, Widmerpool inherits what money and possessions Stringham had, although one of the possessions, the Modigliani etching, is simply invisible to him in terms of its true worth; he can no more appreciate it than he could have guessed the author of the Theocritus poem read by Le Bas.

24. Isobel, however (*Kindly Ones,* 99), does seem to know of the relationship, and from the wording of her comment, not from

Jenkins as source. One would have to presume that she had ultimately heard from Umfraville, remembering the night at Foppa's, through Frederica.

25. Mary Louise Pratt, *Imperial Eyes: Travel Writing and Transculturation* (London: Routledge, 1992).

26. Spurling, *Handbook,* 127.

27. Isobel, indeed, senses Widmerpool's overt menace before Jenkins does (*Casanova's Chinese Restaurant,* 102).

28. Russell, *Anthony Powell,* 164.

29. Trelawney, rebaptized as a female academic, is clearly (over and above Shelley's associate of the same name) referred to in J. K. Rowling's *Harry Potter* books.

30. Julian Allason proposes, as model for Sir Magnus, William Maxwell Aitken, Lord Beaverbrook. Beaverbrook was longtime proprietor of the *Daily Express* and a key advisor to Winston Churchill. Unlike Donners, Beaverbrook, as with so many British press barons, was Canadian, and his politics seem a step to the right of those of Sir Magnus; that is, "Sillery" might not be so enthused by them. Sir Magnus, of course, was also not involved with journalism but with heavy industry and natural resources. But the identification seems, provisionally speaking, plausible. For a biography of Beaverbrook, see Anne Chisholm and Michael Davie, *Lord Beaverbrook: A Life* (New York: Knopf, 1993).

31. Hitchens, "Powell's Way," 198.

32. See the Canadian historian Martin Kitchen, *Europe between the Wars* (New York: Routledge, 1988), 296–302.

33. Gerhard Weinberg, *A World at Arms: A Global History of World War II* (Cambridge: Cambridge University Press, 1994), 27.

34. Winston Churchill, *The Gathering Storm* (New York: Houghton Mifflin, 1948), 302ff.

35. Morris is wrong when he sees Uncle Giles's death as occurring "a year after" the Hitler-Stalin pact; it in fact occurs the day before, on 23 August 1939, that signature day for the revelation of "the natural solidarity of all the revolutionary totalitarian systems." Oscar Halecki, *A History of Poland* (New York: Mckay, 1976), 308.

36. Morris, *Novels of Anthony Powell,* 227.

37. Tucker, *Novels of Anthony Powell,* 163.

38. Woolf, as quoted in Daniel Mark Fogel, *Covert Relations: James Joyce, Virginia Woolf, and Henry James* (Charlottesville: University Press of Virginia, 1990), 87. The Hergeshimer referred to in the quote is Joseph Hergesheimer (1880–1954).

39. Muggeridge, as quoted in Ingrams, *Muggeridge,* 194.

40. See Robert Browning, "Childe Roland to the Dark Tower Came," stanza 15, in *Robert Browning: The Poems,* vol. 1, ed. John Pettigrew (New Haven: Yale University Press, 1981), 588. A conversation with John Powell, 14 September 2002, drawing upon information recorded in manuscripts left by Lady Violet Powell, indicated that Anthony Powell found this quote while taking a selected Browning volume with him while on vacation in the early 1960s.

41. Hogbourne-Johnson is, incidentally, Hogbourne-Jones on the original Little, Brown dust jacket of the first U.S. edition of *The Soldier's Art.*

42. Hitchens, "Powell's Way," 190.

43. Selig, *Time and Anthony Powell,* 37.

44. John Milton, Sonnet 16, in *The Poems of John Milton,* ed. John Carey and Alastair Fowler (London: Longman, 1968), 330.

45. Steg, in Lilley and Marshall, *Proceedings,* 101.

46. See the less heightened draft of the passage at *Writer's Notebook,* 119 for a comparison.

47. Hitchens, "Powell's Way," 188.

48. Though the basis for a Wales-Poland context in *Dance* may be laid by the fact that the memoirs of the real-life General Wladyslaw Anders, mentioned several times in *Military Philosophers,* were in fact published in Montgomeryshire, Wales, in 1946.

49. Louis Robert Coatney, "The Katyn Massacre: An Assessment of Its Significance as a Public Issue in the United States and Great Britain, 1943–1990" (Master's thesis, Western Illinois University, 1993), gives a good account of the canonicity of Katyn during the years Powell was writing.

50. On Jedwabne, see Abraham Brumberg, "Poles and Jews,' *Foreign Affairs* 81, no. 5 (September/October 2002): 174–87.

51. Hitchens, "Powell's Way," 200.

52. The first, and bravest, major work in English about Katyn is J. K. Zawodny, *Death in the Forest* (South Bend, Ind.: University of Notre Dame Press, 1962). To the extent that this book was read, though, it was read by Polish Americans and committed right-wingers, not by a broad audience. Vladimir Abarinov, *The Murderers of Katyn* (New York: Hippocrene Books, 1993), is a valuable, repentant perspective from the Russian point of view.

53. Robert Conquest, *Reflections on a Ravaged Century* (New York: Norton, 2000), 131. Perhaps the source of Conquest's wording is to be found at *Messengers* (90), where the Burgess-Maclean anecdote Conquest references is recorded, in which Powell speaks of his friend Adrian Daintrey as "the least political of men." Although Powell is not this statement's antithesis, he can certainly in no way be governed by it.

54. Powell's legendarily prompt responses to letters he received even from total unknowns may be seen as "responding to constituents" with a skill that certainly showed Powell was not without political talents, even though Powell's responsiveness emanated simply from good cheer and native enthusiasm.

55. Selig, *Time and Anthony Powell*, 38.

56. Russell, *Anthony Powell*, 183.

57. Powell regretted that Spurling did not include Q (Ops) Colonel; he added that his "real name" was Wansborough-Jones. Letter to Margaret Boe Birns, 29 January 1980.

58. D. J. Taylor, *After the War: The Novel and English Society since 1945* (London: Chatto and Windus, 1993), 23.

59. Northrop Frye, *Anatomy of Criticism: Four Essays* (Princeton, N.J.: Princeton University Press, 1957), 37.

60. Ibid., 38.

61. Its source may be a line of the Regency wit Sydney Smith: "No furniture so charming as books." Robin Hyman, *The Quotation Dictionary* (New York: Macmillan, 1962), 303.

62. Paul Gaston, "'This Question of Discipline': An Interview with Anthony Powell," *Virginia Quarterly Review* 61, no. 4 (autumn 1985): 642.

63. John Gould, in Lilley and Marshall, *Proceedings,* 119.

64. Michael Barber, "The Art of Fiction LXVIII," *Paris Review* 20, no. 73 (spring 1978): 61.

65. Hitchens, "Powell's Way," 188.

66. Spurling, *Handbook,* 100. Powell, in a letter to a Mr. Jenkins, 7 October 1966, describes "Jenkins," as a name, as "combining an essential Welshness at one end of the scale, with no necessarily Welsh commitment at the other."

67. Gould, in Lilley and Marshall, *Proceedings,* 125.

68. See John Rupert Martin, *Baroque* (New York: Harper and Row, 1977), 34.

69. See Sir Kingsley Amis, *Memoirs* (London: Hutchinson, 1991), 153.

70. Waugh, *Essays, Articles, and Reviews,* 550.

71. Gould, in Lilley and Marshall, *Proceedings,* 126.

72. Massingberd, *Daydream Believer,* 201.

73. On Tiepolo's era, Harold S. Stone discerns a "lack of interest in eighteenth-century Italy" as "the Italian Renaissance was a tough act to follow." See Stone, "The Achievement of Franco Venturi," *American Scholar* 64 (summer 1995): 408–14.

74. McEwan, *Anthony Powell,* 70. Arthur Mizener commented more aptly on Tokenhouse, noting that he is "sustained by the very ideological commitment that makes him so bad a painter, heroic without knowing it, blinded by vanity to his own hopeless badness." Mizener to Anthony Powell, 3 October 1973, courtesy of Jonathan Kooperstein.

75. Spurling mistakenly says *Edward* Arlington Robinson (*Handbook,* 249).

76. Hon. John Monagan, conversation with author, Washington, D.C., 28 March 2002.

77. Michael Henle, APlist, http://www.anthonypowell.org.uk, 6 January 1999.

78. Derek Leebaert, *The Fifty-Year Wound* (Boston: Little, Brown, 2002), 195.

79. See Hitchens, "Powell's Way," 190.

80. *Writer's Notebook* (84) says, "Extreme skepticism is the only possible terms" on which religion can be accepted, although, as with many of the entries in the notebook, one is not totally sure that this is not a piece of dialogue intended to be dramatically attributed to a character.

81. See Massingberd, *Daydream Believer,* 203.

82. See McEwan, *Anthony Powell,* 72.

83. Ingrams, *Muggeridge,* 194.

84. Would that make Étienne Delavacquerie the poet John Fuller?

85. Kislinger, http://www.anthonypowell.org.uk, 8 May 1999.

86. Tucker, *Novels of Anthony Powell,* 188.

87. See Empson, *Argufying,* 85.

88. Gould, in Lilley and Marshall, *Proceedings,* 181.

89. See Franco Russoli, *Modigliani* (New York: Abrams, 1959).

90. Edwin Bock, conversation with author, Riverside, Conn., 20 July 2002.

Chapter 4

1. Also see Powell to Margaret Boe Birns, 13 December 1984, where he speaks with surprise at the American reception of *Wheel* being so much more positive than the British reviews.

2. Ibid.

3. Detective fiction seems to have particularly attracted this sort of obloquy. See Nicholas Birns with Margaret Boe Birns, "Agatha Christie: Modern and Modernist," in *The Cunning Craft: Original Essays on Detective Fiction and Contemporary Literary Theory,* ed.

Ronald G. Walker and June M. Frazer, 120–34 (Macomb, Ill.: Western Illinois University, 1990).

4. On the contemporary British academic novel, see Ian Carter, *Ancient Cultures of Conceit: British University Fiction in the Post War Years* (London: Routledge, 1990).

5. Jonathan Kooperstein, conversation with author, New York, 20 July 2002.

6. Very few nonhistorical novels have been written about historical novelists; one that leaps to mind is the Portuguese writer Eça de Queiroz's *Illustrious House of Ramires*.

7. See Joanna Motion, "O, How the Powell Becomes It," *Scripsi* 4, no. 3 (1987): 177–82.

8. That this ending was composed as a set piece can be seen from *Writer's Notebook,* 159.

9. Kingsley Amis, *The Amis Collection, Selected Non-Fiction 1954–1990,* ed. John McDermott (London: Hutchinson, 1990), 62.

10. McEwan, *Anthony Powell,* 118.

11. The Lilley bibliography has no publication or sales details for the American edition of *Fisher,* but (Thomas C. Wallace, conversation, 8 June 2001; conversation with author, New York, 21 December 2001) they were, though respectable, not large.

Chapter 5

1. Powell to Margaret Boe Birns, 13 December 1984.

2. Selig, *Time and Anthony Powell,* 144.

3. Richard Freadman, *Threads of Life: Autobiography of the Will* (New York: Cambridge University Press, 2001), 24.

4. Ibid., 262. Interestingly, Dostoevsky, one of Powell's literary benchmarks, "rarely mentions Rousseau in his literary works and other writings, and whenever he does refer to the philosopher, it is in a negative light." Hilary Fink, "Rousseauian Visions in Dostoevskij's 'Dream of a Ridiculous Man,'" American Association of Teachers of Slavic and East European Languages conference, New Orleans, 28 December 2001.

5. Laurie Adams Frost, *Reminiscent Scrutinies: Memory in Anthony Powell's "A Dance to the Music of Time"* (Troy, N.Y.: Whitston, 1990), 51.

6. Freadman, *Threads of Life,* 241.

7. Seymour-Smith, *Funk and Wagnall's Guide,* 289.

8. Jeremy Treglown, "Class Act," *New Yorker,* 18 December 1995, 108.

9. Brennan, *Anthony Powell,* 150.

10. Gore Vidal, *Palimpsest* (New York: Knopf, 1995), 298.

Chapter 6

1. Hugh Massingberd, in "A Hero of Our Club: Anthony Powell at the Travellers, 1930–2000," *Anthony Powell Society Newsletter* 8 (autumn 2002): 2, says that "clubs do not feature a great deal in *Dance.* That is to say gentlemen's clubs. There are plenty of more louche and raffish establishments featured." That gentlemen's clubs play a (relatively) more prominent role in the *Journals* is more a comment on how universal Powell has made the situations in *Dance* than a comment on the comparative exclusivity of some of the venues mentioned in the *Journals.*

2. The outside world is less a presence in the later journals, although Powell duly notes the Gulf War, the coup against Gorbachev, and the election of Bill Clinton. This incidentally is a comment not about Powell as biographical individual but about the *Journals.* For instance, Powell, in his letter to John Monagan of 10 August 1992, predicts that, as far as the U.S. election goes, Bush will "manage it by the skin of his teeth," a sentiment unaverred in the *Journals.* (Powell was right, but eight years later—and regarding a different Bush.) Also, in his letter to Monagan of 19 February 1991, Powell denounces Saddam Hussein by name; from the *Journals* it is clear only that he wished the allied effort in the Persian Gulf well. This suggests that the more inward stance of the *Journals* may on occasion be an effect of genre than a reflection of the person Anthony Powell was at the time.

3. See Aubrey, *Brief Lives and Other Selected Writings*, ed. with an introduction and notes by Anthony Powell (London: Cresset Press, 1949), 31; the observation about the Earl's behavior to the nuns during and then after the reign of Mary I is especially tart.

4. See T. S. Eliot, *Four Quartets*, 32.

5. At the end of the first volume (31 December 1986), Powell mentions a letter to him from the Cambridge/Bloomsbury figure George (Dadie) Rylands in which he mentions "references in leaders . . . to the announcement of the CH in Honours," but Powell's CH award was not given until the following year. Then, in the introduction to *Journals, 1990–1992,* Lady Violet Powell refers to the CH being bestowed in 1987. The confusion here can be cleared up when it is realized that Rylands received the CH in 1987. It was Rylands's award to which Powell is referring in the 1986 year-end entry, and Powell's own award was announced a year later and bestowed, as is recorded in the *Journals,* in February 1988.

6. See Michael C. Meredith, in Lilley and Marshall, *Proceedings,* 21.

7. On the general course of Powell's relationship with Connolly, see Jeremy Lewis, *Cyril Connolly: A Life* (London: Jonathan Cape, 1997), esp. 101–3, 564–65. Peter Quennell's early schoolboy success as a poet matches that of Members, so Connolly is often ascribed as enjoying the Quiggin "slot."

8. The potential need for annotation here leads to the issue of the errata in *Journals, 1990–1992* (probably transcription errors): The biographer of Conrad (21 June 1991) is Zdzislaw Nadjer, not Nadja; the translator of the Koran (11 May 1992) is M. J. Dawood, not Dashwood (who presumably would have done a more Jane Austen–esque job). James Weaver, who wrote Powell a fan letter, mentioned at 10 February 1992, was not a current member of the United States House of Representatives in 1992; perhaps he was James Weaver (D-Oregon, 1975–87), noted for his opposition to lumber interests, or, otherwise, a member of the lower house of a state legislature. The American critic who interviewed Powell on 20

February 1990 was Octavio Roca, not Rocca, and he did so not for the *Washington Post* (for which Charles Trueheart had just interviewed Powell; see 26 September 1989) but for the *Washington Times*. (Congressman John Monagan made this correction on his copy of Powell's letter to him of 22 February 1990 concerning the interview; see Powell-Monagan correspondence in Georgetown University Library.) Also, a different, witty, if less exact, person seems to have indexed and edited the third volume; see the listings in the index for Southwood and Moisey, and then look up what Powell says about them. There are extensive footnotes for the first volume (there are far fewer in the second, none in the third). A conversation with John Powell on 14 September 2002 indicated that Anthony Powell was responsible for editing the first volume, Lady Violet the second and third.

9. Hitchens, "Powell's Way," 190.

10. Geoffrey Wheatcroft, "A White Man's Burden: Rudyard Kipling's Pathos and Prescience," *Harper's* 305, no. 1828 (September 2002): 84.

11. Adam Holm speaks helpfully (with respect to Thomas Mann, alluded to at *Temporary Kings,* 7) of the "virtue and skepticism" of non-authoritarian conservatism; see Holm, "Danish Radical Conservatism," *Totalitarian Movements and Political Religions* 2, no. 3 (2001): 21.

12. Ingrams, *Muggeridge,* 244.

13. See Margaret Boe Birns, "Anthony Powell's Secret Harmonies: Music in a Jungian Key," *Literary Review* 25, no. 1 (fall 1981): 91, for delineations of an equivalent mood in the fiction.

Bibliography

Works by Anthony Powell

Fiction

Afternoon Men. London: Duckworth, 1931. Paperback reprint, London: Mandarin, 1992. First U.S. printing, New York: Henry Holt, 1932.

Venusberg. London: Duckworth, 1932. Paperback reprint, London: Mandarin, 1992. Published with *Agents and Patients* as *Two Novels by Anthony Powell*. New York: Little, Brown, 1961. Reprint, Los Angeles: Green Integer, 2003.

From a View to a Death. London: Duckworth, 1933. Paperback reprint, London: Mandarin, 1992. First U.S. edition, *Mr. Zouch, Superman*. New York: Vanguard, 1934.

Agents and Patients. London: Duckworth, 1936. Paperback reprint, London: Mandarin, 1992. Published with *Venusberg* as *Two Novels by Anthony Powell*. New York: Little, Brown, 1961.

What's Become of Waring. London: Cassell, 1939. Paperback reprint, London: Mandarin, 1992. U.S. edition, Boston: Little, Brown, 1963.

A Question of Upbringing. London: Heinemann, 1951. New York: Scribner's, 1951.

A Buyer's Market. London: Heinemann, 1952. First published in the United States with *A Question of Upbringing* and *Acceptance World* as *The Music of Time*. Boston: Little, Brown, 1955.

The Acceptance World. London: Heinemann, 1955. New York: Farrar, Straus and Cudahy, 1955.

At Lady Molly's. London: Heinemann, 1957; Boston: Little, Brown, 1957.

Casanova's Chinese Restaurant. London: Heinemann, 1960. Boston: Little, Brown, 1960.

The Kindly Ones. London: Heinemann, 1962. Boston: Little, Brown, 1962.

The Valley of Bones. London: Heinemann, 1964. Boston: Little, Brown, 1964.

The Soldier's Art. London: Heinemann, 1966. Boston: Little, Brown, 1966.

The Military Philosophers. London: Heinemann, 1968. Boston: Little, Brown, 1969.

Books Do Furnish a Room. London: Heinemann, 1971. Boston: Little, Brown, 1971.

Temporary Kings. London: Heinemann, 1973. Boston: Little, Brown, 1973.

Hearing Secret Harmonies. London: Heinemann, 1975. Boston: Little, Brown, 1975.

O, How the Wheel Becomes It! London: Heinemann, 1983. New York: Holt, 1984. Reprint, Los Angeles: Sun and Moon Classics, 1999. Reprint, Los Angeles: Green Integer, 2002.

The Fisher King. London: Heinemann, 1986. New York: Norton, 1986.

A Dance to the Music of Time. Chicago: University of Chicago Press, 1995. Four volumes.

Drama

Two Plays: "The Garden God" and "The Rest I'll Whistle." London: Heinemann, 1971.

Poetry

Caledonia. With a musical contribution by Constant Lambert and illustrations by Edward Burra. Privately printed, 1934. Reprinted (with very selective excision, by Powell, of obscure allusions and possibly some passages contributed by Constant Lambert) in *Oxford Book of Light Verse*. Edited by Kingsley Amis. London: Oxford University Press, 1978.

Note: "Iron Aspidistra" by "Mark Members" is not by Powell but is a parody-pastiche by Powell's friend Roy Fuller.

Satire

A *Reference for Mellors*. Originally published in *New Savoy* 1 (1946). Reprint, London: Morehouse and Sorenson, 1994.

Nonfiction

John Aubrey and His Friends. London: Heinemann, 1948. First U.S. printing. New York: Scribner's, 1949. Rev. ed., New York: Barnes and Noble, 1963.

Infants of the Spring. London: Heinemann, 1976. New York: Holt, Rinehart, and Winston, 1977.

Messengers of Day. London: Heinemann, 1978. New York: Holt, Rinehart, and Winston, 1979.

Faces in My Time. London: Heinemann, 1980. New York: Holt, Rinehart, and Winston, 1981.

The Strangers All Are Gone. London: Heinemann, 1982. New York: Holt, Rinehart, and Winston, 1983.

To Keep the Ball Rolling. London: Heineman, 1984. Chicago: University of Chicago Press, 2001. A four-volume abridged version (abridged by Powell himself) with an introduction by Ferdinand Mount (a slightly amended reprint of his *New York Times Book Review* essay of 30 April 2000).

Miscellaneous Verdicts. London: Heinemann, 1990. Chicago: University of Chicago Press, 1992.

Under Review. London: Heinemann, 1992. Chicago: University of Chicago Press, 1994.

Journals, 1982–1986. London: Heinemann, 1995.

Journals, 1987–1989. London: Heinemann, 1996.

Journals, 1990–1992. London: Heinemann, 1997.

A Writer's Notebook. London: Heinemann, 2001.

Edited and Introduced Volumes

Barnard Letters, 1778–1824. Edited by Anthony Powell. London, Duckworth, 1928.

Aubrey, John. *Brief Lives and Other Selected Writings*. Edited with an introduction and notes by Anthony Powell. London: Cresset Press, 1949.

Brooke, Jocelyn. *The Orchid Trilogy.* Introduction by Anthony Powell. London: Secker and Warburg, 1981.

Bede, Cuthbert. *The Adventures of Mr. Verdant Green.* Introduction by Anthony Powell. Oxford: Oxford University Press, 1982.

Partial List of Uncollected Articles Late in Powell's Career

"Literature and the Real Person." *Chronicles of Culture*, January 1985, 18–22.

"Painters and Sitters." *Modern Painters* 3, no. 1 (May 1990): 44–47.

"How to Curry Favour." *Spectator* 279 (8 November 1997): 38–40.

"Book of the Century: *The Great Gatsby.*" *Daily Telegraph*, 9 March 1998.

Obituary comment on Lady Pansy Lamb. *Daily Telegraph*, 22 February 1999.

Miscellaneous

The Album of Anthony Powell's "A Dance to the Music of Time." Edited by Lady Violet Powell, with a preface by Anthony Powell and introduction by John Bayley. London: Thames and Hudson, 1987.

Adaptations

A Dance to the Music of Time. Channel 4 (U.K.), October 1997. Written for the screen by Hugh Whitemore, directed by Alvin Rakoff. Available internationally from Video Collection International, http://www.vci.co.uk. Radio adaptation of *Dance* on BBC Radio 4, adapted by Frederick Bradnum, 1972 to 1982. The adaptation was rebroadcast on BBC Radio 7 in late spring 2003.

A Dance to the Music of Time. Audiocassette read by David Case. Books on Tape. Unabridged. 6 vols., 2 books per volume, totaling 65 cassettes. 1996. There are also versions read by Simon Callow (London: Hopper Headline, 1997) and Simon Russell Beale, (London: Cover to Cover, 1997).

Critical Works on Powell

Selected Books

Bader, Rudolf. *Anthony Powell's "Music of Time" as a Cyclic Novel of Generations.* Berne: Francke Verlag, 1980. The interaction between generations is a major theme of *Dance,* and Bader's book was a substantial first step in its consideration.

Barber, Michael, *Anthony Powell: A Portrait.* London: Duckworth, forthcoming 2004. Promises to be the first full-length biographical work on Powell.

Bergonzi, Bernard. *Anthony Powell.* Rev. ed. Edited by Ian Scott-Kilvert. London: Longman for the British Council, 1971. Bergonzi, always a respectful reader of any given writer, does not see each individual novel of *Dance* as self-contained in any viable way but praises the sequence as a "vast intricate collection" of "brief and cryptic anecdotes," which winsomely captures an aspect of Powell's approach, even if this is not all there is. Bergonzi also goes into the technical intricacies of Powell's prose style. Bergonzi was the first critic to use John Aubrey as a tool for understanding Powell's work, a technique approved of by Powell in a 1962 letter to Bergonzi on deposit in the Powell manuscript collection at Eton.

———. *The Situation of the Novel.* Pittsburgh: University of Pittsburgh Press, 1970. Able and balanced discussion of Powell (113–28) in the context of his literary contemporaries and situation by one of the leading academic critics of twentieth-century British literature.

Brennan, Neil. *Anthony Powell.* 1974. Reprint, Boston: Twayne, 1995. A valuable survey, containing an extensive biographical introduction, including possible identification of character models for *Dance* characters; although some guesses are astute (V. S. Naipaul, partially, for Delavacquerie) and were later confirmed by the *Journals,* most have been superseded by the list compiled by Keith Marshall and Julian Allason on the Anthony Powell Society web site, http://www.anthonypowell.org.uk, and some of Brennan's conjectures were simply misfires. Powell's very dismissive remarks on Brennan's work (see *Journals,* 29 October 1991) do not, though, impede its usefulness to the reader of Powell on several points. The revised edition is particularly good on *Wheel* and *Fisher.*

Burgess, Anthony. *The Novel Now: A Student's Guide to Contemporary Fiction.* London: Faber and Faber, 1967. Brief discussion of Powell by a fellow novelist is the first treatment to address the "formalized" nature of the dialogue in *Dance.*

Carpenter, Humphrey. *The Brideshead Generation: Evelyn Waugh and His Friends.* London: Weidenfeld and Nicolson, 1989. A capacious and informative account that provides a good overview of Oxford and its aftermath as experienced by Powell's generation. Despite its title, it is largely on Waugh, as Michael North's *Henry Green and the Writing of His Generation* (Charlottesville: University Press of Virginia, 1984) is almost entirely on Green. Noel Annan's *Our Age* (New York: Random House, 1990), although covering many other areas of twentieth-century British life, is more of a composite portrait. Carpenter's book is extremely well written and has a very valuable list of dramatis personae at the end that will be of service to any students of this literary generation.

Conrad, Peter. *The History of English Literature: One Indivisible, Unending Book.* Philadelphia: University of Pennsylvania Press, 1985. Conrad's few pages on Powell are valuable in that they place him within the overall skein of English literary history, from which he is so often excluded by the standard academic accounts.

Davin, D. M. *Snow upon Fire: A Dance to the Music of Time.* Swansea: University College of Swansea, 1977. This printed version of the 1976 W. D. Thomas Memorial Lecture address by Dan Davin, the expatriate New Zealand poet and Roman

Catholic intellectual, praises Powell's accomplishment but ultimately sees it as skeptical and lacking any definitive sense of the meaning of life. This pamphlet has had an extraordinary influence disproportionate to its very limited availability.

Ellis, G. U. *Twilight on Parnassus: A Survey of Post-War Fiction and Pre-War Criticism.* London: Joseph, 1939. The first serious literary response to Powell's work, notable in its prescient anticipation of Powell's talent even before he had embarked upon the works for which he is best known.

Felber, Lynette. *Gender and Genre in Novels Without End: The British Roman-Fleuve.* Gainesville: University Press of Florida, 1995. Considering Powell along with Dorothy Richardson and Anthony Trollope (a choice that would make General Liddament smile), Felber argues that the *roman fleuve,* or river-novel, subverts the traditional contours of the novel genre by its inchoate sprawl, the way it privileges middles over beginnings and ends. Important in suggesting that one of the reasons Powell is not more popular is not the sheer length of his major work but because it is somehow generically uncanonical.

Frost, Laurie Adams. *Reminiscent Scrutinies: Memory in Anthony Powell's "A Dance to the Music of Time."* Troy, N.Y.: Whitston, 1990. Paying particular attention to philosophical issues in Powell's work, this published version of a 1988 Rice University dissertation is a refined, decorous, and highly intelligent piece of criticism. Frost is good on Widmerpool's comic *and* monstrous aspects. Strongly recommended.

Gorra, Michael. *The English Novel at Mid-Century.* Basingstoke: Macmillan, 1990. Competent work by a well-known critic who has written proficiently on both English and postcolonial literature. Gorra's treatment of Powell as being of the same literary era as Greene, Waugh, and Green is correct in terms of dates of birth and generational identity. But Gorra neglects the fact that, unlike Greene and Waugh, Powell did unquestionably his best work after the Second World War, whereas Waugh and Greene had, arguably, done the work for which they are most remembered before the war; thus Powell's writing belongs to a distinctly later bracket. Also, Gorra is too dismissive of the two post-*Dance* novels. Nonetheless a skillful treatment of Powell, if tinctured by what can only be called the author's reverential stance toward Waugh.

Green, Martin. *Children of the Sun.* New York: Basic Books, 1976. Ostensibly about the early careers of Brian Howard and Harold Acton, this book in fact chronicles the entire generation of British aesthetes who matured within an upper-class ambience in the 1920s. Green is mildly unsympathetic toward Powell, and he is thesis-minded to the point of ignoring contrasting evidence, but he provides an incisive and entertaining treatment, and in fact is more insightful than several more encomiastic works. Green's and Carpenter's are the two books about Powell's literary generation as such (Michael North's *Henry Green and the Writing of His Generation* [Charlottesville: University Press of Virginia, 1984], almost exclusively concerning Henry Green), and neither are perfect; Green is too despairing, Carpenter too celebratory. But both Green and Carpenter are writers of substance, not slapdash literary journalists, and both will reward and broaden readers' senses of the past.

Joyau, Isabella. *Investigating Powell's "A Dance to the Music of Time."* New York: St. Martin's Press, 1994. A sympathetic and intelligent survey, it pays more attention to individual characters than other treatments and is especially good on Moreland. Also see review by Peter Kislinger in articles section below.

Lilley, George. *Anthony Powell: A Bibliography.* Winchester: St. Paul's Bibliographies, 1994. Very few bibliographies of writers are as good, or as pleasurable to read, as this one. Not only is it comprehensive (for primary works up to 1992; for secondary works up until 1984) but it is sensibly arranged and compiled with a deep feeling for and understanding of its subject. Contains a valuable list of the vast majority of Powell's publications in newspapers and periodicals, vital for an appreciation of the full range of his work. Also has fascinating particular details such as exact publication dates, variant editions, and sales figures for individual books.

Lilley, George, and Keith C. Marshall, ed. *Proceedings of the First Anthony Powell Conference.* London: Anthony Powell Society, 2001. The first foretaste of Powell studies in the twenty-first century, ranging from background on Powell's (and Jenkins's) Eton years (Michael Meredith and Michael Barber) to genealogy in Powell's life and work (Hugh Massingberd), remarks on translating *Dance* into Dutch (Auke Leistra), and intriguing speculations on the "future" in *Dance,* that is, the gap, measured forward, between the setting of the narration and the actual time of the writing (John Gould) and the unobtrusive but pivotal wife of the narrator (Cathleen Ann Steg). Open discussions after the talks were tape-recorded and also included, which is an especially nice feature. The book also contains the full text of Roy Fuller's parody, "Iron Aspidistra."

Massingberd, Hugh. *Daydream Believer: Confessions of a Hero-Worshipper.* London: Macmillan, 2001. One of Powell's good friends and strongest supporters recounts the genesis and progress of his Powell enthusiasm; interesting also is Massingberd's choice of *From a View to a Death* as his favorite of Powell's prewar novels.

McEwan, Neil. *Anthony Powell.* London: Macmillan, 1991. A compressed but perceptive survey, quick and confident in its judgments. Refreshingly, it departs from a strictly chronological narrative in explicating *Dance,* approaching the sequence in terms of theme and motif rather than a direct progression from first to last book. Commended by Powell himself, this is the best book to go to for a quick overview. McEwan also wrote on Powell in *The Survival of the Novel: British Fiction in the Later Twentieth Century* (Totowa, N.J.: Barnes and Noble, 1981) and intelligently anthologized him in *The Twentieth Century, 1900–Present* (Basingstoke: Macmillan, 1989).

Mizener, Arthur. *The Sense of Life in the Modern Novel*. Boston: Houghton Mifflin, 1964. The acclaimed first biographer of F. Scott Fitzgerald and longtime professor at Cornell University was a good friend of Powell's. Though atypical in seeing James Gould Cozzens as being in the same league as Powell, Mizener is so far the only critic to lay stress on Powell's individualism, a gesture quintessentially American, even though Mizener casts it as quintessentially British! Mizener is particularly good on the character of Uncle Giles.

Morris, Robert K. *The Novels of Anthony Powell*. Pittsburgh: University of Pittsburgh Press, 1968. This book's legendary misinterpretation of the sexual encounter between Nick and Gypsy in *A Buyer's Market* (an understandable one) should not at all impede its usefulness to latter-day Powellians. Morris's ease with the plot and characters anchors his grappling with the sequence's overall pattern, all the more notable considering that he was writing after only eight of twelve novels had been published and thus, as W. D. Quesenbery pointed out in *Contemporary Literature* (1969), was analyzing a fragment. Morris's inductive, rather than deductive, treatment of *Dance* serves the reader well. Author of the first book-length work solely on Powell, Morris was a pioneer and set the contours of discussion for the many critical assays that have followed.

Neill, S. Diana. *A Short History of the English Novel*. New York: Collier, 1964. Neill's book devoted several pages to Powell at an early point and situates him well in the tradition of the English novel going back to the eighteenth century, an achievement all the more notable for Neill's own cultural views (quasi-Leavisite) clearly being very different from Powell's.

Powell, Lady Violet. *The Departure Platform*. London: Heinemann, 1998. Sheds valuable, inimitable, and entertaining background on the period in which Anthony Powell was writing the early volumes of *Dance*. Sheds particular light on *The Acceptance World* and *At Lady Molly's*.

Russell, John. *Anthony Powell, a Quintet, Sextet and War.* Bloomington: Indiana University Press, 1970. Despite the disadvantages of writing when the *Dance* sequence was only three-quarters complete, a very reliable survey. It is insightful on the way the war novels are different from the rest of the sequence, an insight rewarding when the sequence was only three-quarters complete but as or more productive afterward.

Selig, Robert L. *Time and Anthony Powell: A Critical Study.* Rutherford, N.J.: Fairleigh Dickinson University Press, 1991. Selig uses rigorous narratological theory, especially that of Gérard Genette, but the book is very readable and understands the importance of shifts of time and narrative indirection in Powell. Selig performs both narrative analysis and plot summary in the same stream of exposition, which serves the reader well. Contains an excellent bibliography.

Seymour-Smith, Martin. *Macmillan Guide to Modern World Literature.* London: Macmillan, 1985. This is the second edition of Seymour-Smith's monumental and entertaining encyclopedia. Seymour-Smith is discerning about Powell in both editions but in the second elevates him to a higher, Nobel Prize–worthy stature. His work is particularly good on the character of Nicholas Jenkins—how Jenkins's fundamental decency at once empowers and paralyzes him.

Spurling, Hilary. *Handbook to Anthony Powell's "A Dance to the Music of Time."* London: Heinemann, 1977. Reprinted as *Invitation to the Dance* (Boston: Little, Brown, 1977). The indispensable book on *Dance,* not only for its thorough and witty indexing of the characters and references in the novel but also for its meticulous chronology and for Spurling's outstanding introductory essay, "The Heresy of Naturalism: Some Notes on Structure." Even the most factual of the entries possesses or yields interpretive insight as well. Sadly out of print; its reissuance is a high priority.

Swinden, Patrick. *The English Novel of History and Society, 1940–80: Richard Hughes, Henry Green, Anthony Powell, Angus*

Wilson, Kingsley Amis, V. S. Naipaul. London: Macmillan, 1984. Swinden's measured treatment of Powell is especially useful in that it follows an equally judicious discussion of Henry Green, a rare negotiation between two writers, whatever their generational affinity, who tend to have distinct constituencies. Swinden, in a crypto-Leavisite way, cavils at what he sees as the upper-class, metropolitan emphasis of Powell's work. He also overestimates the extent to which the United States, in contrast to Britain, is free of class bias, treating the anti-Powellian remarks of Edmund Wilson in a way that violates Barbara Goring's generally wise injunction not to be "sentimental." But Swinden's analysis is fundamentally fair. It is unfortunate that Swinden's work is not more cited in Powell scholarship, as he is a good critic whose work should be respected.

Taylor, D. J. *After the War: The Novel and English Society since 1945.* London: Chatto and Windus, 1993. Taylor's book is different from the other surveys that include Powell not only in being better written but also in putting the work into the context of its period; especially good on the Victory Service in *Military Philosophers*.

Tucker, James. *The Novels of Anthony Powell.* London: Macmillan, 1976. This is the best book on Powell to include all twelve *Dance* novels. Written by an Englishman who is also the celebrated detective writer "Bill James," it is particularly valuable for its insights into novelistic technique and the English class system, which plays such a role in the backdrop of Powell's oeuvre.

Selected Articles and Book Chapters

Baker, Robert. "Anthony Powell." *Contemporary Literature* 20, no. 2 (spring 1979): 251–59. An assessment of the wave of critical books on Powell that appeared around and after the close of *Dance*. Baker speaks eloquently of the "sanity and decency" of Powell's vision.

Barber, Michael. "The Art of Fiction LXVIII." *Paris Review* 20, no. 73 (spring 1978): 44–86. One of the best full-length interviews of

Powell. Conducted at the close of the *Dance* sequence, the interview canvasses the role of coincidence in the books and the relation between Powell's characters and real-life figures in his life.

Bayley, John. Introduction to *Album of Anthony Powell's "Dance to the Music of Time."* Edited by Lady Violet Powell, with a preface by Anthony Powell. London: Thames and Hudson, 1987. Bayley's introduction is one of the most intelligent and scrupulous general discussions of *Dance*.

Bényei, Tamás. "Memory and Melancholy: Remembering (in) Anthony Powell." *Hungarian Journal of English and American Studies* 5, no. 2 (1999): 163–94. A poised and sophisticated account of time and narrative perspective in *Dance*.

Birns, Margaret Boe. "Anthony Powell's Secret Harmonies: Music in a Jungian Key." *Literary Review* 25, no. 1 (fall 1981): 80–92. The most thorough definition of "coincidence" in the sequence, one which reverberates on both empirical and occult levels. Also, until Hitchens, the only commentary to fully comprehend the enmeshment of the coincidences in the novels with the political events of the two world wars.

Bowen, John. "The Melancholy of Modernity: Anthony Powell's Early Fiction." In *Recharting the Thirties*, edited by Patrick Quinn, 102–23. Selinsgrove, Pa.: Susquehanna University Press, 1997. The most thorough and reflective consideration of Powell's early work available; particularly helpful in seeing the works in the context of literary modernism. Bowen is reportedly doing more work on Powell that will no doubt contribute greatly to the field.

Colt, Rosemary M. "Anthony Powell's Archetypal Characters." In *Writers of the Old School*, edited by Rosemary M. Colt and Janice Rosseu, 55–71. London: Macmillan, 1992. A useful article that shows that Powell's fictional personages draw upon a reservoir of assumed types without being reducible to stock roles or Theophrastan characters.

Facknitz, Mark A. R. "Self-Effacement as Revelation: Narration and Art in Anthony Powell's *Dance to the Music of Time*." *Journal of*

Modern Literature 15, no. 4 (spring 1989): 519–29. Concentrates, as one might expect, on Nicholas Jenkins as narrator, stating that "Jenkins can be known largely by what he chooses to hide behind." It is satisfying in its comprehension that this posture reveals as much as it conceals. A particularly complex and rewarding essay.

Felber, Lynette. "The Fictional Narrator as Historian: Ironic Detachment and the Project of History in Anthony Powell's *A Dance to the Music of Time.*" *CLIO: A Journal of Literature, History, and the Philosophy of History* 22, no. 1 (fall 1992): 21–35. The best discussion so far of Powell as both social and narrative historian. Gives *Dance* its proper due as a project that, while certifiably fictive, takes on some of the storytelling and truth-telling tasks of prose history.

Gaston, Paul. "'This Question of Discipline': An Interview with Anthony Powell." *Virginia Quarterly Review* 61, no. 4 (autumn 1985): 638–54. One of the most candid interviews. It focuses on *Dance,* especially the concept of an extended novel stretching across years both in setting and composition, but also discusses the memoirs and *Wheel.*

Gutierrez, Donald. "The Doubleness of Anthony Powell: Point of View in *A Dance to the Music of Time.*" *University of Dayton Review* 14, no. 2 (spring 1980). Gutierrez, author of one of the first dissertations on Powell (Gutierrez, Donald K. "A Critical Study on Anthony Powell's *A Dance to the Music of Time.*" [Ph.D. diss., UCLA, 1969], 15–27.), provides one of the principal statements of the position that the narrative is excessively anti-Widmerpool—a provocative if flawed analysis—otherwise, he concentrates on narrative technique.

Harrington, Henry. "Anthony Powell, Nicolas Poussin, and the Structure of Time." *Contemporary Literature* 24, no. 4 (winter 1983): 431–48. Harrington's skillful essay makes sense of the twelve-book structure of *Dance* more than any other attempt; the astrologically inclined, as well as those particularly interested in the visual arts, will be especially intrigued. Harrington gives an as-yet-unsurpassed reading of the final few scenes of *Harmonies* and the sequence as a whole.

Hillier, Bevis. "Irritable Powell Syndrome." *Spectator*, 17 May 1997, 37–39. An admiring and informative, but hardly rhapsodic, discussion of the *Journals*.

Hitchens, Christopher. "Powell's Way." *New York Review of Books*, 28 May 1998. Reprinted in *Unacknowledged Legislation: Writers in the Public Sphere*. New York: Verso, 2001. The well-known controversialist writes one of the few articles that fully engage Powell's registering of twentieth-century European and world history. Only Hitchens, for instance, could have spotted the detail about Miss Walpole-Wilson working on behalf of the Bosnian Muslims and immediately seen its 1990s relevance. Hitchens also presents potential political criticism of Powell's world view at its most compelling. Like many British readers of his generation, Hitchens likes the last two novels of *Dance* less than the first ten. Hitchens, here and in his subsequent review of the reissued *To Keep the Ball Rolling* in the *Atlantic* (June 2001), could not be more laudatory about Powell, and these articles enormously increased Powell's visibility in the United States.

Jones, Richard. "Anthony Powell's *Music*: Swan Song of the Metropolitan Romance." *Virginia Quarterly Review* 52 (1976): 353–69. Jones, a Welshman, sees *Dance* as possibly a parable of the decline of the British upper class; the phrase "metropolitan romance" connotes a sense of social exclusivity. The last few novels of *Dance* are criticized, particularly for their treatment of the cold war. Jones generously assesses Jenkins's broad interests as narrator and discusses Powell's debt to the nineteenth-century novel and to Proust.

Karl, Frederick. "Sisyphus Descending: Mythical Patterns in the Novels of Anthony Powell." *Mosaic: A Journal for the Interdisciplinary Study of Literature* 4, no. 3 (1971): 13–22. Karl, an American critic who has written well on a wide array of authors, is one of the first to see *Dance* as having levels beyond the merely social.

Kermode, Frank. "Isherwood and Powell." In *Puzzles and Epiphanies*. London: Routledge, 1962, 126–30. One of the few prominent academic literary critics to discuss Powell at any length, Kermode seems to prefer the prewar novels to *Dance*, partaking of a strand of opinion that, though inevitably in the minority, should have had more of a presence in the subsequent criticism. Although written early in the progress of the sequence (the immediate occasion was the publication of *Casanova's Chinese Restaurant*), Kermode's analysis is deft and responsive to the works.

Kislinger, Peter. "Über Isabelle Joyau, *Investigating Powell's 'A Dance to the Music of Time.'*" *Sprachkunst: Beiträge zur Literaturwissenschaft* 27, no. 2 (1996): 374–82. This review of Joyau's book by the leading Powell scholar in continental Europe provides the occasion for an unusually sophisticated discussion of Powell's novelistic technique. Translated into English in number 4 of the *Anthony Powell Society Newsletter.*

Kitson, Arabella. "Astrology and English Literature." *Contemporary Review,* October 1996, 200–201. One of the rare forays into serious discussion of the occult in Powell's work, though Harrington's article goes deeper.

Massingberd, Hugh. Obituary of Anthony Powell. *Daily Telegraph,* 29 March 2000. Online at http://www.telegraph.co.uk. The best place to get the basic facts on Powell, as well as a sense of his overall character and importance.

McCooey, David. "Secret Harmony." *Australian's Review of Books* 3, no. 3 (April 1998): 20–21. An Australian critic emphasizes the complexity and allusiveness of the narrative. Also touches on the *Journals* and television films. Valuable in being written from an Australian perspective, giving a needed variation in the Anglo-American volley of discourse on Powell.

McSweeney, Kerry. "The Silver-Grey Discourse of *The Music of Time.*" *English Studies in Canada* 18, no. 1 (March 1992): 43–58. A skilled, practical critic based in Canada provides one of the most interesting critical articles on Powell to date. Although McSweeney admires *Dance* as a significant fictional achievement

of the postwar era, he chides it for being insufficiently self-reflexive, concluding that this lack of self-reflexivity prevents the
sequence from achieving true greatness. Though, as Powell might
opine, this rather misses the point. McSweeney's case is well presented, with specific examples of self-reflexive passages in *Dance*
whose potential could have been carried further, and is definitely
worth a read by anyone familiar with the idea of the self-reflexive novel and interested to see where *Dance* fits in. One quibble:
McSweeney seems to define self-reflexivity as "referring to
the writing process in a novel" (for instance. Trapnel's rumina-
tions on naturalism are self-reflexive to McSweeney), whereas
one might alternately define self-reflexivity as "consciousness of
the fact that the particular novel being read by the reader is in fact
a composed artifact." Examples of where Powell might display
this sort of self-reflexivity are contained in this book's discussion
of *Books*.

Monagan, Hon. John. "A Visit with Anthony Powell: Time's Musician." *American Scholar* 65, no. 3 (summer 1996): 433–40. One
of Powell's closest American friends, a former congressman from
Connecticut, recounts a number of visits to Powell at the
Chantry. Monagan is eloquent in detailing Powell's "unique and
lasting contribution to letters and to humanity." This is one of the
best available portraits of Powell as man and writer. Monagan is
currently working in London on another retrospective mono-
graph on Powell, which was published as "The Master and the
Congressman" by the Anthony Powell Society in April 2003.

Moore, John Rees. "Anthony Powell's England: A Dance to the
Music of Time." *Hollins Critic* 8, no. 4 (1971): 1–16. A concise
general survey by a skillful American critic, this is one of the first
American journal articles to focus on Powell's style. It is also one
of the best attempts to grasp the boundaries and scope of Jenkins's narrative stance.

Motion, Joanna. "O, How the Powell Becomes It." *Scripsi* 4, no. 3
(1987): 177–82. The best piece on *Fisher;* it surveys the novel's
ambitions and sees them as being less grand than those of *Dance*

but still considerable. Taichi Koyama, "Katari no jikan, jikan no katari: Anthony Powell no The Fisher King." *Eigo Seinen/Rising Generation* 146, no. 9 (December 2000): 558–62, concentrates more on theoretical issues relating to Henchman's voyeurism.

Mount, Ferdinand. "The Last of All His Kind." *New York Times Book Review,* 30 April 2000. Later reprinted with slight revisions in the University of Chicago reprint of *To Keep the Ball Rolling,* 2001. An obituary tribute by a British novelist and intellectual who was Powell's nephew by marriage and knew him very well. Especially good in refuting the myth of Powell's snobbery.

Parini, Jay. "Anthony Powell, 1905–2000." *Sewanee Review* 109, no. 3 (summer 2001): 437–38. Appreciative and discerning obituary, which sees Powell's work as encompassing the totality of the twentieth century, its calamities and its survivals.

Piper, William Bowman. "The Accommodation of the Present in Novels by Murdoch and Powell." *Studies in the Novel* 11 (1979): 178–93. Skilled comparison of Powell with one of his most distinguished contemporaries. Piper appreciates the openness to experience of Jenkins's narrative voice.

Potter, John. "Cult and Occult in Powell's *A Dance to the Music of Time.*" Kobe Yamate Women's Junior College, *Annual Report* (Japan) 34 (December 1991): 47–62. This article (also available on the Anthony Powell Society web site, http://www.anthony-powell.org.uk), is a sustained and entertaining treatment of a theme often referred to in passing by most essays on Powell.

Pritchard, William H. "Anthony Powell's Gift." *Hudson Review* 37, no. 3 (fall 1984): 363–70. One of Powell's most sympathetic and dedicated American readers, a superb practical critic and man of letters, gives a glimpse of Powell's matchless comic talent. Pritchard also reviewed the University of Chicago reissue of *Dance* in the *New Republic* 215 (19–26 August 1996), a piece that, importantly, emphasizes the extent to which Powell is *not* nostalgic.

Quesenbery, W. D., Jr. "Anthony Powell: The Anatomy of Decay." *Critique: Studies in Contemporary Fiction* 7 (1964): 5–26. A

penetrating if slightly appalled gaze into Powell's world. Quesenbery's pessimistic sense of *Dance* (similar to that of D. M. Davin)
seems unshared by a more skeptical author. Quesenbery, who
taught at Augusta College in Georgia, provides a valuable early
piece, in fact one of the best written before 1970 and one of the
best by an American ever.

Riley, John J. "Gentlemen at Arms: The Generative Process of Evelyn Waugh and Anthony Powell before World War II." *Modern
Fiction Studies* (1976): 165–81. A pioneering essay on the prewar
books that is both enabled and limited by the comparison with
Waugh. Riley provides a glimpse of the dissertation on the two
authors Riley completed in 1973 at Tufts University.

Ruoff, Gene W. "Social Mobility and the Artist in *Manhattan Trans-
fer* and the *Music of Time*." *Wisconsin Studies in Contemporary
Literature* (1964): 64–76. This early study, by a critic who later
went on to be a prominent romanticist, is valuable for understanding the theme of social class (especially in the second trilogy)
and the extent to which *Dance* is "naturalist."

Schwartz, Lynne Sharon. "Listening to Powell." *Salmagundi* 126–27
(spring-summer 2000): 140–55. A novelist of a different generation and background from Powell provides a substantial appreciation in the form of a personal essay based on listening to *Dance*
as Books on Tape as read by David Case. Schwartz is especially
good on her mistaken assumptions of how names are spelled
(e.g., thinking "Erdleigh" is "Erdly" or "Umfraville" is "Umpher-
ville," which also brings up larger interpretive differences
between media.) Schwartz is, in general, reflexively categorical
about Powell's social stance. But even there her points are constructive.

Teachout, Terry. "The 'Politics' of Anthony Powell." *New Criterion*
10, no. 9 (May 1992): 24–32. Teachout uses "politics" in the
sense of sagely knowing one's limits in the political world. Little
stress is given to Powell's actual politics, although Widmerpool's
leftism is mentioned. Although this is valuable in, correctly, not
casting Powell as a kind of right-wing polemicist, it does, to a

degree, curtail the field of reference. Teachout is also dismissive of much of the latter half of *Dance*. Nonetheless, this is a discerning tribute by a talented critic.

Treglown, Jeremy. "Class Act." *New Yorker,* 18 December 1995, 106–13. A tribute to Powell by the former editor of the *Times Literary Supplement* and eventual biographer of Henry Green on the occasion of Powell's upcoming ninetieth birthday based on a 1995 meeting at the Chantry. Treglown's article contains several interesting nuggets, and its publication in the leading American high-cultural magazine foreshadowed the recent rise in Powell's reputation in the United States. Treglown's utterance, to the eighty-nine-year-old Powell, of the observation that "the self-reflexive novel is as old as the Arabian Nights" is perhaps not what would be said by most readers of *Dance* on such an occasion, although it does provide an enjoyably surreal element to the piece. Treglown is laudatory and perceptive about Powell's work, although he does make it seem as if Powell's work inhabits only one side of classic-romantic, objective-subjective dichotomies, for example, adducing not only John Aubrey but also Alexander Pope as a precursor. Treglown also provides a glimpse of the then-upcoming television films and, after only the first, most social volume of them had appeared, is negative about the *Journals*. An American conservative, or at least anti-communist, riposte to Treglown is Arnold Beichman, "Anthony Powell, Anti-Communist," *Weekly Standard* 1, no. 22 (19 February 1996): 38–41.

Wallraff, Barbara. "Life's Choreographer." *Atlantic Monthly,* January 1996, 77–82. Characteristic of the generally very laudatory essays that appeared when the University of Chicago reissued *Dance* in four attractively designed paperback editions in 1995. It is perceptive on the way the narrative acquires richness through "sheer accumulation," as well as how its portrait of the 1970s gains relevance as time passes, and is particularly valuable in being written by an American (most articles on

Powell in general-interest American magazines have been by British writers). Also see the Pritchard articles mentioned above.

Wilcox, Thomas W. "Anthony Powell and the Illusion of Possibility." *Contemporary Literature* 17, no. 2 (spring 1976): 223–39. Examines the way that, in Powell's work, specificity and anecdote not only coexist with but reinforce its fictive structure. One of the most thoughtful of the academic essays on Powell of this period.

Wilson, Keith. "Pattern and Process: The Narrative Strategies of Anthony Powell's *Dance to the Music of Time*." *English Studies in Canada* 11, no. 2 (June 1985): 214–22. This direct and trenchantly written treatment by a Canadian critic is especially good in its analysis of the relationship between Jenkins as narrator and protagonist, surrounding its subject in far less narrato-logical density than usual. Wilson is also gratifyingly adept at selecting key scenes to analyze, for instance, his examples from *Lady Molly's* and the "Widmerpool as DAAG" scene in *Valley of Bones*.

Wiseman, T. P. "The Centaur's Hoof: Anthony Powell and the Ancient World." *Classical and Modern Literature* 2, no. 1 (fall 1981): 7–23. One of the few direct considerations of the extent of Powell's classicism. Also rare in considering a specific theme or source in Powell's work, and not just attempting a synthetic overview. This essay, written by a prominent British classical scholar, was particularly commended by Powell himself. Wiseman's later comment on the *Journals* and historiographic convenience, "Thucydides and *logographoi*: A Modern Parallel?"—one of the few speculative responses to the *Journals* so far—was published in the British online classical journal *Histos* in 1997 at http://www.dur.ac.uk/Classics/histos/1997/wiseman.html.

Wolfe, Alan. "When the Music of Time Stops." *Chronicle of Higher Education* 46, no. 33 (21 April 2000). An interesting tribute by a prominent "public intellectual."

Zigerell, James. "Anthony Powell's *Music of Time*: Chronicle of a Declining Establishment." *Twentieth-Century Literature* 12, no.

2 (October 1966): 138–46. Zigerell does not see the mythic and metaphorical levels of *Dance* and, therefore, in its era, his article is inferior to the Karl article cited above. It includes what must be, after that of Malcolm Muggeridge, the second most dyspeptic commentary on *Valley of Bones*.

Recommended Dissertations

These as-yet-unpublished dissertations have made substantial contributions to the body of critical work on Powell.

Colletta, Lisa. "The Triumph of Narcissism: Dark Humor and Social Satire in the Modern British Novel (Virginia Woolf, Ivy Compton-Burnett, Evelyn Waugh, Anthony Powell)." Ph.D. diss., Claremont Graduate University, 1999. Discusses the inherently social nature of humor in British modernist fiction —its use as a tool to dispel ideological constructs. One of the most critically up-to-date excurses on Powell.

Colt, Rosemary Mizener. "The Ghost Railway: Anthony Powell's *A Dance to the Music of Time* and the 1930s." Ph.D. diss., Brown University, 1984. This dissertation by the daughter of Arthur Mizener does not just focus on the second trilogy, as might be expected, but ranges across Powell's career. Emphasizes historical connections. It is perhaps a bit too insistent on the classical reserve of Jenkins's moral stance, as opposed to his narrative tone.

Edmonds, Joanne Haldeman. "Memories of Things Real and Imagined: Narratives of Youth and Middle Age in Anthony Powell's *A Dance to the Music of Time*." Ph.D. diss., Ball State University, 1993. Beginning where Bader's generational study left off, this dissertation is useful in focusing on specific themes, not just narratological generalizations.

Kislinger, Peter. "Some Truths Seem Sometimes Falsehoods, Some Falsehoods Almost Truths: Erzähltechnik, romaninhärente Poetik und intertextuelles Erzählen als 'konstruktiv-ironische' Demonstration der Wahrheit des Romans in Anthony Powell's *A*

Dance to the Music of Time." Ph.D. diss., University of Vienna, 1993. (In German, though an English abstract is attached.) Kislinger examines the operations of such deconstructive rhetorical figures as aporia and mise-en-abyme in Powell's work but is not dogmatic, as he also takes seriously occult and zodiacal influences as related to the thought of Schopenhauer and Jung, as well as parallels between Powell's work and such modernist perceptive schemes as cubism. Despite its very high level of abstraction, this study is sympathetic to Powell's work and enlightening in explicating it.

Laws, Monica. "For Everything There Is a Season: The Spiral History in Anthony Powell's *A Dance to the Music of Time.*" Ph.D. diss., St. Louis University, 1989. Sees Jenkins's maturation as counterbalancing social decline; an important corrective to the historical pessimism often imputed to *Dance* by critics.

Meixner, Susan Turnquist. "Partisan Politics and the Sequence Novels of Anthony Powell, C. P. Snow, and Evelyn Waugh." Ph.D. diss., University of Kansas, 1979. One of the few considerations of "actual" politics with respect to Powell and his world; it deserves wider dissemination. Meixner diagnoses Powell as a Liberal, which is wrong in party-political terms, despite his apparent friendliness with one-time Liberal Party figure Jo Grimond (*Journals,* 9 November 1982), but arguably correct in spirit.

Other Resources

The Anthony Powell Society

The Anthony Powell Society, founded shortly after the writer's death in 2000, is headquartered in London but possesses an inter-national membership and focus. It publishes a quarterly print newsletter and maintains an extensive web site, http://www.anthonypowell.org.uk, which contains the latest news about society events and conferences as well as the most exhaustive and scrupulous list of character models for *Dance* (compiled by Julian Allason and Keith Marshall), plot summaries for all the *Dance* novels, a cast list and photo stills from the television films, and a comprehensive bibliography of books by and about Powell. There is also an Internet mailing list on Powell; information about joining it is available on the society web site, which also includes archives of the extensive and intellectually acute discussions. Membership in the society is available by writing the Honorary Secretary, Anthony Powell Society, 76 Ennismore Avenue, Greenford, Middlesex, UB6 0JW, U.K.

Powell Collection at Georgetown University

Largely consisting of Powell's correspondence with former congressman John Monagan, the collection at the Lauinger Library at Georgetown University (in Washington, D.C.), also has letters from Powell to London bookseller Handasyde Buchanan as well as other material relating to Powell's life and work. The Special Collections Room at Georgetown also contains material relating to Evelyn Waugh, Christopher Sykes, Graham Greene, and other contemporaries of Powell's as well as a rare copy of the August 1970 issue of *Summary,* a literary magazine edited by Andrew Mylett, including, on pages 34–128, provocative comments on Powell's work by a wide variety of distinguished intellectuals. (Powell characterized this as a "curious little symposium"; *Journals,* 4 September 1984.)

Powell Collection at Eton

Following the success of the initial Anthony Powell Society conference there in April 2001, the Powell family donated the original manuscripts of all the author's novels (excepting *Venusberg,* which is not extant) to the Eton College Library (Berkshire, England). The collection is under the curatorship of College Librarian Michael C. Meredith and is available for scholarly consultation. As the manuscripts reveal how systematically Powell redrafted his works, the collection at Eton is of great value to students of Powell. The library also holds an extensive collection of Powell's contemporaries and other information and items relating to Powell's schoolboy milieu.

Index

Page numbers in bold type indicate extended discussion. Primary works listed are all by Powell unless otherwise indicated.